Making Higher Education Christian

The History and Mission of Evangelical Colleges in America

Edited by

Joel A. Carpenter

and

Kenneth W. Shipps

CHRISTIAN
UNIVERSITY
PRESS

A subsidiary of the
Christian College Consortium
and
William B. Eerdmans Publishing Company
Grand Rapids, Michigan

To the evangelical academy

Available from Wm. B. Eerdmans Publishing Company
255 Jefferson Ave. SE, Grand Rapids, Michigan 49503

Library of Congress Cataloging-in-Publication Data

Making higher education Christian.
1. Church colleges—United States—History.
I. Carpenter, Joel A.   II. Shipps, Kenneth W.
LC621.M35 1987   377′.8′0973   87-20121

ISBN 0-8028-0253-2

Contents

III. ADVANCING THE MISSION

Contributors

Thomas A. Askew is professor and chair of history at Gordon College, Wenham, Massachusetts. His most recent book, with Peter W. Spellman, is The Churches and the American Experience *(Grand Rapids: Baker, 1984).*

Virginia Lieson Brereton, after spending a year in research and writing as a Radcliffe Scholar, now teaches history at a school for girls near Boston. She is the author of several articles on women, religion, and education.

Joel A. Carpenter is the administrator of the Institute for the Study of American Evangelicals, associate professor of history at Wheaton College in Illinois, and the editor of a forthcoming series, American Fundamentalism, 1880–1950, *to be published by Garland.*

William A. Dyrness is principal of New College, Berkeley, California, and the author of Christian Apologetics in a World Community *(Downers Grove, Ill.: InterVarsity, 1983).*

Douglas Frank teaches in the Oregon Extension program of Houghton College, Houghton, New York, and is the author of Less Than Conquerors: How Evangelicals Entered the Twentieth Century *(Grand Rapids: Eerdmans, 1986).*

Nathan O. Hatch is associate dean of the College of Arts and Letters at the University of Notre Dame and co-director of the Institute for the Study of American Evangelicals. Among other publications to his credit, he has most recently co-edited, with Harry S. Stout, Jonathan Edwards and the American Experience *(New York: Oxford University Press, forthcoming).*

George M. Marsden is professor of the history of Christianity in America at Duke University Divinity School. The latest of his several books on evangelicalism and fundamentalism is Reforming Fundamentalism: Fuller Seminary and the New Evangelicalism *(Grand Rapids: Eerdmans, 1987).*

Warren Bryan Martin is scholar in residence and senior program officer at the Carnegie Foundation for the Advancement of Teaching. His book A College of Character *(San Francisco: Jossey Bass, 1982) won the Frederick M. Ness Award in 1984 as the best book on liberal education.*

Richard J. Mouw, professor of Christian philosophy and ethics at Fuller Theological Seminary, is the author of When the Kings Come Marching In: Isaiah and the New Jerusalem *(Grand Rapids: Eerdmans, 1983).*

Alvaro L. Nieves, who has worked as a senior research scientist at Battelle Pacific Northwest Laboratories in Richland, Washington, is now associate professor of sociology at Wheaton College. His monographs range from academic sociology to energy technology.

Mark A. Noll is professor of history at Wheaton College in Illinois and co-director of the Institute for the Study of American Evangelicals. His latest book is Between Faith and Criticism: Evangelicals, Scholarship, and the Bible in America *(New York: Harper and Row, 1986).*

William C. Ringenberg, professor and chair of history at Taylor University, is the author of The Christian College: A History of Protestant Higher Education in America *(Grand Rapids: Eerdmans, Christian University Press, 1984).*

Leland Ryken is professor of English at Wheaton College in Illinois. His most recent book is Worldly Saints: The Puritans As They Really Were *(Grand Rapids: Zondervan, 1986).*

Ruth A. Schmidt, president of Agnes Scott College, has authored two books on Spanish literature, served as provost of Wheaton College, Norton, Massachusetts, and is currently chairing the Women's College Coalition.

Kenneth W. Shipps, vice president for academic affairs and dean of the faculty at Phillips University and author of several historical monographs, is the architect of several major grants and programs in faculty and curriculum development for the Christian College Consortium and the Christian College Coalition.

Timothy L. Smith is professor of history and education at The Johns Hopkins University. He has written many works on American religion, ethnicity, and education, notably Revivalism and Social

Reform in Mid-Nineteenth Century America *(rev. ed.; Baltimore: Johns Hopkins University Press, 1980) and* Uncommon Schools: Christian Colleges and Social Idealism in Midwestern America, 1820–1950 *(Indianapolis: Indiana Historical Society, 1978).*

John Van Engen, associate professor of history and director of the Medieval Institute of the University of Notre Dame, is the author of Rupert of Deutz *(Berkeley and Los Angeles: University of California Press, 1983) and of* The Brothers and Sisters of the Modern Devotion *(forthcoming).*

Mary Stewart Van Leeuwen is now professor of interdisciplinary studies at Calvin College after serving for many years at York University in Toronto. Her latest book is The Person in Psychology: A Contemporary Christian Appraisal *(Grand Rapids: Eerdmans, 1985).*

David K. Winter is president of Westmont College. He currently serves as chair of the Association of Independent Colleges and Universities and in the past has held this office in the Christian College Consortium and in the Christian College Coalition.

Nicholas Wolterstorff is professor of philosophy at Calvin College and the Free University in Amsterdam. He has written, among other works, Educating for Responsible Action *(Grand Rapids: Eerdmans, 1980) and* Until Justice and Peace Embrace *(Grand Rapids: Eerdmans, 1983).*

Acknowledgments

Most of the essays in this book were first presented as papers at a conference held under the title "The Task of Evangelical Higher Education" at the Billy Graham Center in Wheaton, Illinois, in May 1985. This meeting, which was planned and hosted by the Institute for the Study of American Evangelicals, benefited from the cosponsorship of the Christian College Coalition and the Christian College Consortium and also from a generous grant from the Lilly Endowment. Yet this book does more than just report conference proceedings; we hope and believe that it presents a coherent evaluation of the history and mission of evangelical colleges. The "Task" conference has made this possible by providing the opportunity for the authors to assemble and test their ideas amid constructive discussion. For the success of the conference we offer our thanks to the many participants. In addition, Carl Lundquist of the Christian College Consortium and John Dellenback and Karen Longman of the Christian College Coalition have earned a special word of gratitude. They gave us valuable encouragement, cooperation, and advice at each stage of the project.

Three of the chapters in this volume are revised versions of works published elsewhere. Mark A. Noll's essay "The Revolution, the Enlightenment, and Christian Higher Education in the Early Republic" is drawn substantially from his essay "Christian Colleges, Christian Worldviews, and an Invitation to Research," which served as the introduction to William C. Ringenberg's book *The Christian College: A History of Protestant Higher Education in America* (Grand Rapids: Eerdmans, Christian University Press, 1984). Ringenberg's essay "The Old-Time College, 1800–1865" borrows parts of the second chapter of the same book. And Noll's second essay included here, "The University Arrives in America," closely follows his article "Christian Thinking and the Rise of the American University" in the *Christian Scholar's Review* (9 [1979]: 3-16).

Words can scarcely give enough credit to Brenda Buchweitz, secretary of the Institute for the Study of American Evangelicals, whose skilled management and word-processing mastery eased this book through its many stages. Larry Snyder and Ron Frank, graduate assistants at the Institute, also deserve thanks for their help in many capacities.

Evangelical scholars and educators, despite their disagreements, show a degree of camaraderie and interdisciplinary sharing rarely witnessed elsewhere in academic life. We are indebted to this community in too many ways to mention. The least we can do is dedicate this book to them.

Preface

Protestant evangelicals comprise one of the largest and most vigorous religious groupings in the United States today. This has been one of recent history's surprises, for evangelicals have certainly not always held such a prominent position. This development has prompted cultural analysts to scrap predictions of irreversible secularization and to begin a reconsideration of religious endurance and change. So far, they have focused on the more visible and volatile aspects of the evangelical resurgence such as politicized fundamentalism and religious broadcasting. But very little attention has been paid to some of evangelicalism's quieter but perhaps more powerful institutions: its colleges.

This book is designed to be a guide to the history and character of evangelical liberal arts colleges, which have shared in the renaissance of the varied traditions and movements that make up evangelicalism. These hundred or so "uncommon schools," as Timothy L. Smith calls them, have prospered and matured over the past few decades, but until recently they were almost invisible to the larger academic establishment.

Compared to other institutions of higher education in the United States, evangelical colleges are young and quite modestly scaled. While some, such as Taylor University and Geneva College, were founded before the Civil War, most are products of twentieth-century evangelical movements, and not a few have achieved full collegiate status only in the past three or four decades. Only a handful offer graduate programs or have enrollments of more than three thousand. Only twenty rank among the top two hundred four-year colleges in the number of graduates who eventually earn doctorates. Clearly, evangelical colleges are more student-cultivating institutions than research centers.

These colleges have a unique strength, however, in their commitment to engender a distinctly Christian worldview in their students and communities. This stands out in contrast to trends elsewhere, as a variety of critics have accused contemporary higher education of failing at the most critical of its cultural tasks, the transmission of a coherent set of values. Evangelical scholars, after several generations of second-class academic citizenship, are thus growing more confident now that their thoughts about seeking, imparting, and living the truth may be of interest to the larger world of higher learning.

These educators have earned their hearing. Twenty-five years ago, when a group of evangelical leaders dreamed of establishing an evangelical research university, they found that Protestant orthodoxy simply did not have the critical mass of accomplished scholars to sustain such a project. The situation is quite different today. Evangelical scholars abound in every discipline, teaching and researching in major universities as well as in graduate seminaries and small colleges. Through their academic societies, journals, and books, they comprise an extended evangelical university, a scholarly community of discourse. It is no longer accurate, then, to characterize evangelical colleges as having been "untouched by the academic revolution," as David Riesman once did.

One of the by-products of the academic revolution that evangelical scholars do not share, however, is its prevailing set of positivistic, utilitarian, and reductionistic assumptions, which support what Theodore Roszak called the "myth of objective consciousness." This myth has been under critical fire for two decades now. One of the results has been that in nearly every discipline, scholars recognize that pretheoretical commitments and philosophical assumptions about the nature of reality inescapably shape their thought and research. Evangelical scholars have recognized this and are asserting—alongside others whose scholarship had been marginalized for allegedly lacking objectivity—that they too are entitled to a hearing in academic forums. Together with Jews and other Christians, evangelicals see new opportunities for scholarship based on theistic presuppositions, and they are taking advantage of them to put forth fresh contributions in research and teaching. The essays that comprise this volume, then, arise from this growing evangelical prominence. We hope that they may help evangelical scholars and educators recall their roots, assess their shortcomings and achievements, refine their vision, and take on the new challenges their colleges and constituents face.

Timothy L. Smith's introductory survey of the contemporary evangelical college movement reveals its surprising diversity, its recent accomplishments, and its commitment to the common good of humanity, both here and abroad. It provides a perceptive introduction both for those who know very little of these colleges and also for the busy insiders who scarcely look beyond their immediate work.

Smith sets the stage for Part I of this book, which examines the educational and religious roots of American evangelicals: the struggle, since the Middle Ages, to develop a Christian foundation and purpose for higher learning. The authors in this section show how this synoptic vision has been transmitted and transformed through the Reformation, the Puritan movement, and the nineteenth-century heyday of evangelical influence. As Mark Noll's chapter on the evangelical response to the modern academic revolution points out, this vision endured, despite being scarred, narrowed, and virtually extinguished. These essays mediate between the authors' expertise and the broader interests of their readers. While avoiding the temptation to draw easy and simple lessons from the past, the contributors offer insights for the task of evangelical higher education today.

Part II examines the specifically Christian and evangelical vision for higher learning, using the vantage points of history, theology, social science theory, educational philosophy, and ethics. The scholars who write in this section insist that there must be renewal in the theoretical foundations, sense of purpose, and strategies of learning and living of evangelical colleges. Each draws upon the insight that Christian thinking and acting is inescapably incarnated in its cultural milieu. Perspectives vary, however. Nathan Hatch argues that the selective cultural attachments of evangelicals have strengthened the movement's popular appeal while weakening its commitment to scholarship. Mary Stewart Van Leeuwen, however, turns to the contemporary scholarly warfare over the character of knowledge and pleads for mutual forebearance among Christian scholars in their debates over the degree to which cognition and research are culturally determined. Nonetheless, each author in this section calls for a more effective pursuit, through education, of a Christian cultural witness.

Part III looks closely at some of the issues confronting evangelical colleges at the end of the twentieth century. The authors here focus on problems in the contemporary cultural climate: the need for effective and humane organizations and leaders, growing strains in college-government relations, the spiritually and intellectually deadening consumerist ethos, the need to assess the role of women in the shaping of civilization and how to reflect that in college curricula, narrowing educational opportunities for minorities, and the evangelical hesitation to foster advanced scholarship. A typically evangelical tension between renouncing the world and responding positively to cultural trends pervades this section. Douglas Frank, for example, condemns the appropriation by evangelical colleges of the corporate world's values and techniques, while Warren Bryan Martin finds some helpful insights in recent literature on management. Moreover, the authors of these essays do not hesitate to offer practical prescriptions. They are convinced that pursuing the unfinished business of making higher education Christian must involve work on such broad issues as those covered herein. Meaningful curricular and pedagogical reform will come only from a forthright encounter with such problems.

Some explanations are in order about the cast of this book. Its first concern is the "evangelical academy," that religious community of educators serving movements of Protestant orthodoxy and revivalism. Added to these are the many Christian scholars serving in nonevangelical institutions. The book's main focus within this community, however, is on the study of the arts and sciences (though see Virginia Lieson Brereton's essay on Bible colleges). No slight is intended to the several score of graduate seminaries and hundreds of undergraduate Bible colleges that emphasize divinity studies and education for professional religious vocations. Indeed, the liberal arts colleges have been enriched by their association with these sister schools, for the intellectual renaissance of evangelicalism began in theological and biblical studies. Yet colleges of arts and sciences have been central to a second stage of this renaissance, which has witnessed the quickening of evangelical scholarship in every realm of thought. This latter development constitutes much of the occasion for this book, so the liberal arts colleges are the proper focus.

We also invite educators and scholars who are not evangelicals to listen in, as it were, to the authors of these chapters. Their discussion can afford outside observers a realistic assessment of the current state of evangelical higher education. Few documents give more valuable evidence of a movement's sense of identity and mission than its internal discourse about achievements, shortcomings, and goals.

Finally, the tone the authors use to convey their thoughts varies somewhat. We have allowed two sympathetic observers who work outside the evangelical college movement, Timothy L. Smith and Warren Bryan Martin, to be far more complimentary and encouraging than any insiders could afford to be. Some of the essays are detached and analytical, and not a few pointedly expose problems. Others, most dramatically Douglas Frank's, earnestly contend with readers' hearts as well as their minds. But we hope that readers will see throughout that evangelical educational thought, despite its common basic convictions, is by no means monochromatic or dull, but richly diverse and full of vision and hope.

Introduction:
Christian Colleges and
American Culture

Timothy L. Smith

Evangelical liberal arts colleges fill a large but relatively unknown place in American higher education. Commentators on American culture may be somewhat familiar with two or three of these several hundred institutions but regard them as exceptions to some supposed general rule.[1] Even the leaders of these colleges are often not fully aware how numerous and diverse are the schools that their local example represents. My purpose in this essay, then, is to illuminate the scope and special character of these colleges and to introduce the essays that comprise the remainder of this book by estimating the collective contribution they make to American life.

Some of these institutions became better known in 1971 when they formed the Christian College Consortium in order to help them raise funds, develop cooperative programs, and refine evangelical educational philosophy.[2] Wheaton, Westmont, and Gordon colleges, in Illinois, southern California, and Massachusetts respectively, all have fundamentalist roots but are not denominational. Neither are Asbury College in Kentucky and Taylor University in Indiana though both have tended to be largely Methodist. Houghton, a college of first rank in western New York, Malone in Ohio, George Fox in Oregon, Seattle Pacific on Puget Sound, and Greenville in southern Illinois represent the Wesleyan, Evangelical Friends, and Free Methodist communions. All five are heirs of the Methodist way but draw a majority of their students from other traditions. Bethel College in St. Paul is Swedish Baptist (now called the Baptist General Conference). Trinity, just north of Chicago, is maintained by Evangelical Free congregations, of mostly Scandinavian background. Rapidly expanding Messiah, near Harrisburg, Pennsylvania, is supported by a tiny and quite Wesleyanized Mennonite communion, the Brethren in Christ.

Around seventy institutions are, like these Consortium schools, members of the Christian College Coalition, formed in 1976.[3] The Coalition includes the oldest evangelical college in America, Milligan, in eastern Tennessee, one of two liberal arts schools sponsored by the moderate middle wing of Alexander Campbell's Disciples movement. Calvin College in Grand Rapids, Michigan, the most distinguished member, with four thousand students, is sponsored by the conservative wing of the Dutch Reformed tradition in America, the Christian Reformed Church. Two other colleges named Bethel—at North Newton, Kansas, and Mishawaka, Indiana—serve various branches of Mennonites, as do Eastern Mennonite in Virginia, Goshen in northern Indiana, and Tabor in Kansas.

Azusa Pacific University, just west of Pasadena, and John Brown University, in Arkansas, are interdenominational as is The Master's College near Los Angeles and The King's College in the lower Hudson valley. Nearby is Nyack, a child of the Christian and Missionary Alliance. This once interdenominational movement, which also sponsors Simpson in San Franciso, long intermingled Wesleyan and fundamentalist doctrines; but it has now become an independent communion, notable for its extensive overseas missions.

The Assemblies of God, America's largest Pentecostal denomination, maintains Evangel College, located in the foothills of the Ozarks in southwest Missouri, and Southern California College, at Costa Mesa. Other Pentecostal schools are Lee College in Tennessee and Oral Roberts University in Oklahoma, whose 4,500 students make it the largest school in the Coalition.

Other Wesleyan institutions in the Coalition include eight sponsored by the Church of the Nazarene; among them is Northwest Nazarene at Nampa, Idaho, one of the finest undergraduate schools in the nation.[4] Added to these are perhaps others coming out of the Wesleyan tradition, such as Roberts Wesleyan in New York and Spring Arbor in Michigan, sister Free Methodist enterprises to Greenville College and Seattle Pacific University. Central Wesleyan in South Carolina, Marion in Indiana, and Bartlesville Wesleyan in Oklahoma are supported, like Houghton in New York State, by the Wesleyan Church. Friends University in Wichita, although not a Coalition member, has, like George Fox and Malone, grafted onto Evangelical Quaker convictions many Wesleyan ones. The Wesleyan and non-Pentecostal communion called the Church of God sponsors Anderson College in Indiana and Warner Southern and Warner Pacific, in Florida and Oregon respectively.

Schools identified with the Reformed tradition are Dordt and Northwestern, both in Iowa, and Trinity Christian at Palos Heights, Illinois, serving, principally, evangelical congregations of Reformed background, as does Calvin. Of kindred convictions, though not in the Coalition, are Hope, also in Michigan, and Central, in Iowa.

The Coalition's eight Baptist colleges include Bethel of St. Paul; the American Baptists' Eastern, near Philadelphia, Judson in Illinois, and Sioux Falls in South Dakota; and the Southern Baptists' Grand Canyon in Arizona, Dallas Baptist, Palm Beach Atlantic, and Mississippi colleges. Several member colleges represent one or another party of conservative Presbyterians: Belhaven in Mississippi, King and Covenant colleges in Tennessee, Geneva in Pennsylvania, Sterling in Kansas, and Whitworth in Washington State. All these schools are deeply committed to both evangelical faith and academic excellence. Their faculties generally distance themselves from the right-wing ideology recently championed by such independent fundamentalist schools as Bob Jones University in South Carolina and Jerry Falwell's Liberty University in Virginia. But the Coalition welcomes other fundamentalist schools like Biola University (formerly the Bible Institute of Los Angeles), Northwestern in Roseville, Minnesota, and Grace in Winona Lake, Indiana.

Although the members of the Christian College Coalition comprise a cross-section of the multifaceted evangelical community in America, scores of similar schools, some of which are identified above, do not yet belong. The Coalition has not enlisted more than a tithe of the liberal arts colleges sustained by the Southern Baptists or Pentecostals, and up to now it has enrolled none of the Seventh-Day Adventist institutions (among which are Andrews University in Berrien Springs, Michigan, and Loma Linda University in southern California). Of those schools sponsored by the Church of Christ, the most conservative wing of Alexander Campbell's Disciples movement, only one belongs: Northwest Christian in Oregon. Remaining outside are Pepperdine University in California, Abilene Christian University in Texas, Harding Wallace in Arkansas, and David Lipscomb in Tennessee.

Evangelical colleges are surrounded by several hundred Bible colleges that, though not offering majors in the liberal arts, have similar social, religious, and educational objectives. Among these are such fine institutions as the long-famous Moody Bible Institute, Fort Wayne Bible College, William Tyndale College near Detroit, and the Philadelphia College of the Bible, all spawned in the early stages of the fundamentalist movement. Also included are perhaps two dozen Bible colleges sponsored by the Christian Churches and an equal number that call themselves Pentecostal. In addition, perhaps a dozen Roman Catholic liberal arts colleges and universities are developing relationships with the Protestant institutions, partly as a result of the various renewal movements going on in Catholicism.

Even more significant is the intellectual support coming from a group of truly remarkable graduate theological schools. Among these are seven of the ten largest seminaries in the nation: Southwestern Baptist, Southern Baptist, Fuller, Asbury, Gordon-Conwell, Dallas, and Trinity Evangelical. Many others enroll fewer than five hundred students but are nonetheless larger than most American divinity schools. These include Bethel (Baptist General Conference), Westminster (conservative Presbyterian), Denver and Western (Conservative Baptist), Andrews (Seventh-Day Adventist), Eastern Baptist, Northern Baptist, North American Baptist, and five that are Wesleyan (Western Evangelical, Nazarene, John Wesley, Anderson, and Evangelical), and three that are Pentecostal.

Here, then, is an array of academic institutions that are making a formidable, but by no means monolithic, impact upon American culture. They train volunteers for literally scores of foreign missionary enterprises, including those sponsored by the evangelical denominations themselves and such independent boards as OMS International (formerly the Oriental Mission Society), World Gospel Mission, Wycliffe Translators, and SIM International (formerly Sudan Interior Mission). They are the mainstays of such socially oriented ventures as World Vision and Food for the Hungry. Most of them belong to one or another of the national organizations that unite churches and colleges with similar traditions—for example, the Christian Holiness Association, which serves the Wesleyans; the New Call to Peacemaking, which draws together Brethren, Mennonites, and Evangelical Friends; the Southern Baptist Convention; or the National Association of Evangelicals.

Paradoxically, perhaps, from the point of view of some outside observers, these liberal arts colleges are almost as estranged from right-wing religious publicists and politicians as religious and political liberals profess to be. They find stridency on conservative political positions a threat to both evangelical culture and democratic ideals. The unpublicized influence of faculty members of these various institutions upon the emerging political attitudes and ideals of their tens of thousands of students is a chief explanation of why such organizations as Evangelicals for Social Action, World Vision, and Young Life, as well as many of the smaller evangelical denominations themselves, oppose the right-wing militancy of the so-called "moral majority."

Virtually all the evangelical colleges are in good financial health. Only Barrington, in Providence, Rhode Island, has recently closed its doors, having officially united with Gordon, north of Boston. Most of the rest are holding their own and some are actually growing in enrollment, a trend that stands out sharply during the years when the national average slumps. And few of the institutions are any less intensely devoted to religious faith than they were twenty years ago. The evangelical surge that has appeared throughout American religion has strengthened all of them. It has, among other things, relieved them of the sense of inferiority and isolation that shallow and cynical critics once fostered.[5]

What is the relationship of this evangelical collegiate world to that of the great universities that dominate academic culture, not only in Canada and the United States, but across both the Atlantic and Pacific oceans? It is not simply one of antagonism, despite the occasional reports of conflict in the press. Most of the faculty members in evangelical colleges were trained in such universities, under the same outstanding professors who trained the generation of scholars now rising to prominence in the secular academic world. Since evangelical institutions were growing steadily during the 1960s and 1970s, they employed many able university graduates who had managed to earn their Ph.D. degrees while keeping their religious commitments central. The average age of their faculties, therefore, is at the lower end of the scale for American higher education. Moreover, all these schools have strived to achieve and maintain full accreditation, not only through membership in their regional collegiate associations (which virtually all enjoy) but also through state certification of teaching, nursing, and social-work majors. Many have begun to develop graduate programs in these fields, and a few have founded schools of engineering, business, law, or medicine.

These factors, added to the continuing personal ties between evangelical scholars and their former professors and colleagues teaching at frontline secular universities, have impelled the faculty members of

Christian colleges to keep up with their fields and to distinguish themselves as teachers. They have usually organized their courses and selected their textbooks as though the larger world of scholarship was looking over their shoulders. And they have secured admission and financial aid for their brightest students at the best institutions in the land, especially those where they themselves were trained. They have usually escaped the intense striving to produce scholarly publications that characterizes younger faculty members in secular universities; but a growing number are nonetheless publishing in their fields. They regularly attend important scholarly meetings in their professions, and sometimes, because of the interest that their own former professors take in their work, become participants in research programs at the major universities. Recently the Christian College Coalition has commissioned a number of these scholars to produce a series of supplemental textbooks to provide Christian perspectives on the major academic disciplines.

The sense of self-respect that prevails on evangelical campuses rests, then, not simply upon the conviction that Christian thought and morality are "best" for every culture, but upon the presence of faculty members who have made their mark as teachers and often as research scholars. This self-respect is greatly enhanced by the intention of so many undergraduates from such colleges to go on to graduate school and by the interest of nearby universities in tapping this pool of able and serious students.[6] Many an evangelical institution has won accreditation after a few of its alumni did brilliant work in the graduate schools of nearby universities.

Yet all of this is done while evangelical faculty members lead an energetic religious life both on and off their campuses, and while they maintain deep commitments to the vision of a Bible-centered culture. They are usually loyal to one or another congregation, and write for or speak to Christian groups of many sorts. Their dedication to both evangelical faith and academic excellence has prompted the historians among them, for example, to join Christian historians in nonevangelical institutions in a society called the Conference on Faith and History. The Conference publishes a fine scholarly journal, *Fides et Historia,* and schedules sessions at annual meetings of the American Historical Association. The pattern is similar among members of other disciplines, such as literature, philosophy, sociology, and biology. For all these reasons, evangelical college teachers have found it natural and desirable to maintain close ties with the nonevangelical university world.

One sign of the important role these colleges play in the evangelical movement is that they stand so firmly for an internationalist approach to culture and politics. This runs counter to the strident superpatriotism that some media evangelists and Christian journalists promote. The several thousand evangelicals who went to Pasadena in May 1984 for the conference on "The Churches and Peacemaking in a Nuclear Age" made this international concern clear. We need to consider the sources of this concern in order to understand its depth.

Nearly every one of these institutions has sustained a close relationship to the foreign missions endeavor. The older ones participated eagerly in the late nineteenth-century Student Volunteer Movement, which represented a surge of interest in missions that eventually divided over the rival claims of biblically based evangelism and modernist accommodation to other religious cultures.

Nyack College grew out of a Bible school in New York City which was founded to train men and women for home and foreign missions. Northwest Nazarene was linked for fifty years with a hospital and clinic which contributed substantially to the expansion of Nazarene medical missions in India, Swaziland, and China. Asbury College and Seminary has been for nearly seventy-five years the prime supporter of the Oriental Missionary Society (now OMS International).

These missions-rooted global ties promote international commitments on evangelical campuses. Students in Wheaton's Human Needs and Global Resources (HNGR) program serve on Christian development projects around the globe, from Kenya to Nepal to Honduras; and Goshen students must each spend a trimester as an intern in a developing nation. Both Loma Linda and Andrews universities have supported the immense expansion of Seventh-Day Adventist medical and evangelistic missions to Europe, Africa, and the Caribbean, and they willingly recruit students from overseas. As a result, Andrews enrolls a larger proportion of foreign students than any other college or university in America. These students often speak to one another in their own language, wear their native garb, and awaken in their American fellow students all kinds of interest in the folk customs as well as the high culture of their homelands. Missions-related ties have also nourished the annual Multicultural Lectureship program at Calvin and have prompted a profound commitment there to a global vision of justice and reconciliation. A recent scholar in residence was Allan Boesak, a black

Reformed leader of the antiapartheid movement in South Africa. And very recently the Christian College Coalition has opened a Latin American Studies program in Costa Rica to allow students to live, serve, and learn among fellow evangelicals in the Third World.

Similar stories could be told of literally dozens of schools. From the point of view of these colleges, the widely touted demise of the foreign missions movement in the twentieth century simply has not taken place. There are now far more missionaries from the United States serving in overseas posts than at any time in the nineteenth or early twentieth centuries, supposedly the heyday of the foreign missions movement. Although the old-line Protestant denominations have trimmed their budgets, curbed their staffs, and given up many of their foreign missionary enterprises, the vigorous evangelical movements—both under denominational and nondenominational auspices—have multiplied budgets, facilities, and services. They have also relied heavily upon evangelical liberal arts colleges to provide their missionaries and to train them in such fields as anthropology and rural economics, so as to enable them to serve effectively both the physical and the spiritual needs of developing peoples.[7]

The internationalism of evangelical colleges often springs also from strong ties to Europe through their sponsoring denominations, particularly those denominations whose early members were largely of immigrant extraction. It has simply been impossible for Calvin College, for example, to ignore the religious and political events taking place in the Netherlands. Ethnic and denominational ties to the Netherlands have resulted in a breadth of cultural perspective that has helped make Calvin one of the finest four-year colleges in the nation. Likewise, Bethel, Trinity, and North Park colleges (at St. Paul, Deerfield, Illinois, and Chicago), are monuments to the ethnic feelings that long bound Swedish Baptist, Mission Covenant, and Scandinavian Free Church congregations to their spiritual kin in northern Europe. Similar ties between Missouri Synod Lutheran, Moravian, Quaker, Brethren, and Mennonite schools and their European kinsfolk are not simply a part of their historic background but deeply affect their present academic enterprises. Evangelicalism is not a peculiarly American phenomenon at all; it has been continuously involved with kindred movements around the globe.

Preoccupation with internationalism has stemmed also from certain special causes. All of the colleges whose roots lay in fundamentalism, especially Wheaton and Gordon, have a long history of association with the Keswick and Inter-Varsity evangelical movements among British Anglicans. Moreover, the dispensational premillennialism of fundamentalism is rooted in the widespread impact of John Nelson Darby's Brethren movement upon Great Britain and the Commonwealth. This doctrine, which signaled a reaction against the optimism of most nineteenth-century evangelicals, has deeply influenced most American Bible schools and many of the evangelical colleges. It disdained the nations of this world and looked for the early return of Jesus Christ to bring them all to judgment. Disdained all but Israel, that is. Christian Zionism, as chronicled in the historical work of David Rausch,[8] has been a major force in American foreign policy and remains so to this day, in no small part because of fundamentalists' pro-Zionist interpretations of biblical prophecy. Hence the readiness of Jewish Zionists to maintain a degree of friendship with fundamentalists.

Evangelicals who believed all or some of these premillennial doctrines, however, also have shared the flowering of concern for peace and for the world's suffering poor that swept across America in the last two decades. One of the most notable charitable organizations among evangelicals has been World Vision, based in Monrovia, California. With an annual budget running beyond $200 million, it has sponsored a large array of overseas efforts, usually carried on by indigenous agents, to bring relief and development assistance to impoverished people. And it has taught congregations as well as college student bodies in America the importance of integrating evangelistic missions with both emergency aid and agricultural and economic reforms. During the last twenty years, despite the anti–social gospel rhetoric of some college administrators, many students simply began to pray for, think about, and give to this and other such agencies. Many of those who became interested in the problem of poverty in the far corners of the world eventually enrolled in the Peace Corps during the 1960s, and many more supported President Jimmy Carter's human rights campaign at the end of the 1970s.

Meanwhile, many evangelical college faculty members taught their students to discriminate between international leaders who took seriously the commands of Moses and Jesus to care for the poor and politicians who made a fetish out of blaming the needy themselves for their condition. The result, nourished by such organizations as Evangelicals for Social Action, Theological Students Fellowship, and the New Call to Peacemaking, and by periodicals such as *Sojourners*

magazine, has been the growth of a social conscience that sees strident
nationalism as one of humanity's most dangerous temptations.

A by-product of this internationalism has been a growing opposition to racism and a mounting interest in urban missions in the United
States, Britain, and Canada. Many evangelical colleges have established some kind of urban social center dedicated to interracial evangelism and social justice. And dozens of them have sent students to the
American Studies program sponsored by the Christian College Coalition in Washington, D.C. The aim of this program is to teach students
the pitfalls and the promise of pursuing peace and justice as office-
holders and civil servants in the federal government, but the students
study social problems in Washington as well. The leaders of the
program hope thus to revive the late nineteenth-century conviction that
the Christian approach to both home and foreign service should be essentially internationalist.

At the same time, the commitment of evangelical higher education
to the Hebrew and Christian ideal of *shalom* for American culture has
grown strong once again, despite the confusion of that issue by the current raucous debate over whether the United States is—or should be—
a Christian nation. Historically, most evangelicals have not believed
America was Christian; hence their earnest efforts to convert its citizens
and reform its life. By Abraham Lincoln's time, however, their success
in making Christian colleges symbols of American culture, particularly in the Ohio and Mississippi valleys, was notable. Scores of such colleges, sponsored by many denominations, thought of themselves as engines of Christian civilization. They hailed the coming of a culture that
was both evangelical and democratic and believed that this culture and
faith were destined to encircle the globe.

Indeed, the notion that such colleges were bearers of civilization
was a prominent feature of America's expansion from the Alleghenies
to the shores of the Pacific. Town boosters founded such schools in the
early days of every new frontier, often mixing economic with cultural
goals, personal ambition with social hope. A band of Yale graduates
founded Illinois College at Alton in 1828, not because they dreamed of
a wilderness retreat but because they thought Alton was destined to become a great metropolis! Dozens of such schools were sustained in their
earliest years by a frontier land speculation that rested on expectations
that settlers would rapidly fill up the surrounding territory. Clothing and
sometimes hiding this actual economic foundation was the rhetoric of

the college founders who preached the dependence of American culture upon Christian schools.[9]

This same idea prevailed in the founding of colleges for blacks in the South after the Civil War. Fisk University, in Nashville, Shaw University, in Raleigh, Atlanta University, Bishop College, in Dallas, and Coppin, named for a black Methodist minister in Baltimore, were among the scores of schools for blacks that depended upon mission funds and aimed at enlarging both religious and social opportunities for black people. A combination of humanitarianism, Christian idealism, and, ironically, faith in the superiority of Anglo-American culture was thus responsible for the education of the first generation of black leaders in America.

In similar fashion, religious colleges serving recent immigrants to the United States aimed not only at their Americanization but also at the cultural uplift of those whose forebears overseas had been peasants. City dwellers did not easily move to the new land in America, for reasons that are still somewhat obscure; but impoverishment and occasional agricultural crises, along with growing railroad access to European seaports, combined to encourage hard-pressed peasants to migrate. Once here, the leaders of each immigrant group saw the importance of securing education for their people, so the Protestant penchant for founding colleges captured their imagination. North Park College, a small Swedish Covenant institution on the north side of Chicago, is a monument to the dreams of a generation of immigrant pastors, heirs of a revival among the peasants of their homeland. So are St. Olaf, Augustana, Augsburg, Calvin, the several Concordias, Tabor, and three of the nation's four Bethels.

Critics have often complained that American Christian colleges keep students isolated from the principal currents of cultural life. What in fact they have done throughout our history, whether among old-line Protestants in the Midwest, blacks in the South, or immigrants in the North, is quite the opposite. They have harnessed group identity and traditions of mutual aid to help common people, and sometimes very poor people, push their children far beyond their parents' social position into a multitude of professions, including teaching, medicine, law, and the ministry.[10]

But, one may ask, was there not a more exclusively denominational pattern evident, in which some of these colleges were but the instruments of religious groups whose purpose was not nearly so much to educate as to indoctrinate? Certainly all students of American history can point to occasional examples of such schools, and to the unhappy consequences. Among them are the otherwise admirable institutions sponsored by the Seventh-Day Adventists; the colleges of the Churches of Christ (among which Pepperdine University is in this respect only less aggressive than David Lipscomb or Abilene Christian); two sponsored by the General Association of Regular Baptists, a stridently fundamentalistic group; several Southern Baptist institutions; and perhaps all eight of the Nazarene schools. The last group, my own, reminds me of what one writer said of the Jews in New York City. "We Jews," he is reported to have said, "are not sectarian; we simply find our own inner life so interesting!"

Some colleges that have been earnestly nondenominational but in fact exclusively fundamentalist have been, however, the most obvious advocates of cultural isolation. Traces of resentment of this isolation appear in several of the essays included here whose authors are graduates of such institutions. But indoctrination is not the sole preserve of evangelical Protestants. Certain radically secular, earnestly Catholic, black nationalist, and Jewish colleges have been accused, more or less correctly, of nurturing the same preoccupations with group identity. They are in that sense like the institutions of Protestant denominations that believe they have a precious uniqueness to protect.

Exclusiveness often flows unintentionally from cultural uniqueness. Some institutions cater to religious denominations with recent immigrant backgrounds, as we have seen. Faculty members at Dordt, for example, do not have to struggle to make the college an instrument of Dutch evangelical indoctrination: its recruitment of both students and faculty naturally appeals strongly to the Christian Reformed population of the upper Midwest. Though displaying no overt discrimination, the cultural atmosphere of the college, like that of its sister institutions, Calvin and Trinity Christian in Chicago, is thoroughly saturated with Dutch evangelicalism. The same pattern is true of the several Mennonite colleges I have mentioned and of Huntington College, a United Brethren institution that caters to the conservative and still-independent branch of that German-American denomination, most of whose congregations joined the United Methodist Church in 1968.

Part of the charge that such colleges nurture sectarianism comes from institutions that have abandoned their nineteenth-century denominational roots and exchanged their sectarianism for secular conformity. Several great urban universities with Methodist roots are examples of this, including the University of Southern California, the

University of Denver, Vanderbilt, Southern Methodist University, Northwestern, and Boston Univerity. But so are some of the schools supported by state associations of the Southern Baptist Convention, from Furman to Baylor to Wake Forest. They have not so much freed themselves from Baptist culture as they have witnessed that culture's growing domination of the society around them. Many Southerners cannot tell the difference between being a Baptist, a Christian, and an American. Most evangelical academics, however, believe that such distinctions are still valuable, for assertive particularity can undergird cultural pluralism and religious freedom.

Furthermore, even within sectarian exclusiveness there is great complexity. The Nazarenes, for example, become concerned when enrollment of students from Nazarene families in the denomination's colleges drops below 75 percent (though Point Loma College in San Diego has long since passed that demarcation line). Sister institutions in the Wesleyan, Free Methodist, or Brethren in Christ branches of the Wesleyan movement, however (such institutions as Houghton, Seattle Pacific, Greenville, and especially Messiah), pay little attention to this problem, thinking their task is to educate young people from the entire evangelical community. The result is that the Nazarenes become year by year more like an ethnic community while such tiny and once-ethnic denominations as the Brethren in Christ seem open to all the world.

The effects of exclusivity upon the maintenance of faith and commitment at these colleges has received little careful attention.[11] I join other more casual observers in perceiving little difference in the outcome. Certainly all these institutions enroll students from many denominations and from none; and despite the fact that evangelical colleges usually require a statement of Christian faith from prospective faculty members, all in fact employ and retain instructors who belong to different denominations. Simple academic considerations do not explain this willingness to bend. The existence of large evangelical communities within every great American tradition of Protestant faith and, increasingly, within the Roman Catholic and Eastern Orthodox communions makes it easy for presidents and deans not bound tightly by denominational rules to welcome diversity among both faculty and students. This explains the similarity of religious goals of such nondenominational institutions as Westmont and Gordon and those of such intensely denominational ones as Abilene Christian and Trevecca Nazarene.

Looking back across the last fifty years, then, one may conclude that nearly all of these colleges identified themselves with what they deemed the best aspects of American life, and they find common identity today in their determination to serve our troubled culture as sources of moral and intellectual consistency. All of them, certainly, move with the cultural tides. Some of them, however, have drifted into an intense patriotism that insists upon the ideological unity of Christianity and American culture. Yet all, by intent as well as by accident, have contributed to American intellectual life—they have caused the tides to move with them as well. Their brightest graduates have gone on to distinguished careers in the professions, politics, business, entertainment, science, and the arts. Every great American university employs numerous faculty members who came from the evangelical communities that sponsored these colleges. Some of them attended and graduated from these schools before going on to advanced university work. The prevalence and prominence of evangelical scholars in secular institutions has escaped observation by critics and publicists outside the evangelical tradition. By contrast, we are well aware of how much Jews have affected higher education in America, partly because most Jewish scholars did their undergraduate work in public or non-Jewish private institutions. That we know so little about the contributions of evangelicals in American universities is an intellectual scandal.

To read the essays that follow in this book, then, is to open the door on a world that nonevangelical scholars and publicists have only recently begun to take seriously. Nearly all the essays were written by administrators or faculty members from one or another of these institutions and hence illustrate the depth of scholarship there and the clarity of their understanding of themselves. True enough, the writers are for the most part addressing their own colleagues, so they occasionally lighten up a bit on academic analysis and concentrate upon issues that are pressing in the evangelical community. For most readers, that will seem all to the good. Nearly every essay offers a thoughtful view not available anywhere else.

NOTES

1. See, for example, Richard N. Ostling, "All That and Billy Graham Too: At Wheaton College, a Rare Blend of Brainpower and Piety," *Time,* 22 September 1980, 83; see also "America's Best Colleges," *U.S. News and World Report,* 25 November 1985, 46-49.

2. See "Evangelical Colleges Plan Consortium," *Christianity Today* 9 (April 1971): 44-45. The best overview of the goals of evangelical higher education is Arthur F. Holmes, *The Idea of a Christian College,* rev. ed. (Grand Rapids: Eerdmans, 1987).

3. The Coalition's *Guide to Christian Colleges,* rev. ed. (Grand Rapids: Eerdmans, 1984), gives a profile of each of these institutions.

4. The eight Nazarene colleges are Northwest, Bethany (Bethany, Okla.), Eastern (Quincy, Mass.), Mid-America (Olathe, Kans.), Mount Vernon (Mount Vernon, Ohio), Olivet (Kankakee, Ill.), Point Loma (San Diego), and Trevecca (Nashville).

5. Sharon Johnson, "The Harvard of the Bible Belt," *Change* 6 (March 1974): 17-20, exemplifies such critical condescension. More recent critics probe beyond the stereotype; see Kenneth Briggs, "Evangelical Colleges Reborn," *New York Times Magazine,* 14 December 1980, 140-54, and David Riesman, "The Evangelical Colleges: Untouched by the Academic Revolution," *Change* 13 (January/February 1981): 13-20.

6. Eight Coalition colleges—Wheaton, Calvin, Mississippi, Goshen, Houghton, Geneva, Asbury, and Greenville—ranked, along with another dozen schools of similar religious convictions, among the top 200 private, primarily undergraduate, institutions (out of 867 total) in the number of their graduates who later earned Ph.D.'s. The highest ranking of these twenty Christian colleges were Wheaton (12th), Calvin (27th), and Hope (36th). These figures are from the Office of Institutional Research, *Baccalaureate Sources of Ph.D.s: Rankings According to Institution of Origin* (Lancaster, Pa.: Franklin and Marshall College, 1982). This study covered the period 1920-1980, which of course favored older schools and may have masked more recent achievements. For example, in a study also done at Franklin and Marshall in 1975, which reported on only the Ph.D.'s awarded between 1968 and 1973, Wheaton moved to fifth nationwide, and Calvin moved into the top twenty-five.

7. Ostling, "The New Missionary," *Time,* 27 December 1982, 50-52, reports the tremendous growth and the Christian internationalism that the contemporary missions movement expresses. See also Lamin Sanneh, "Christian Mission in the Pluralist Milieu: The African Experience," *International Review of Mission* 54 (April 1985): 199-211.

8. Rausch, *Zionism within Early American Fundamentalism, 1878-1918: A Convergence of Two Traditions* (New York: Edwin Mellen, 1979).

9. My *Uncommon Schools: Christian Colleges and Social Idealism in Midwestern America, 1820-1950* (Indianapolis: Indiana Historical Society, 1978) supports this and the preceding paragraph.

10. For this paragraph and the two immediately preceding, see my "Immigrant Social Aspirations and American Education, 1880-1950," *American Quarterly* 21 (1969): 523-43; and my "Native Blacks and Foreign Whites: Varying Responses to Educational Opportunity in America, 1880-1950," *Perspectives in American History* 6 (1972): 309-36.

11. See James Davison Hunter's study of this question, *Evangelicalism: The Coming Generation* (Chicago: University of Chicago Press, 1987), which is based on his comprehensive survey of students and faculty of institutions of the Christian College Consortium.

I
Assessing the Heritage

Christianity and the University: The Medieval and Reformation Legacies

John Van Engen

Any discussion of Christianity and higher education in America takes as its subject institutionalized forms of higher education inherited ultimately from the medieval university. Medieval historians grow accustomed after a while to having their period of history brushed over with a few sweeping strokes, to having generations and even centuries of society and culture lumped together in a sentence or two. Unfortunately, this paper will require even more than the ordinary amount of lumping, for my charge is to summarize the first five hundred years in the history of the European university—from their earliest formation around the year 1150 until the foundation of the first college in the New World around 1650—and to consider the impact of Christian commitment upon that history.[1] I begin with certain basic definitions and realities, quite different from our own, that held to varying degrees throughout the period historians have taken to calling "Old Europe."

Consider first the very state or status of Christianity during this half millennium of European history. Christian faith and practice was not then—as in large measure it is today—a matter of individual commitment in a pluralistic society. Christianity permeated and shaped the entire cultural environment of medieval and Reformation Europe. The church was powerful, rich, and ubiquitous; her law covered many aspects of human life now judged "civil," including universities; and her teachings shaped the religious culture of all Europe. Indeed, except for a handful of Jews, who generally had no access to universities, every person in Europe was a baptized Christian. Even during the Renaissance, with its enthusiastic return to antique culture and its growing skepticism, the Christian religion remained altogether fundamental in society. Nor was this altered by the division of Christendom after 1517: universities still functioned in cultural settings in which the Christian tradition predominated, but now it was a particular tradition—Catholic, Lutheran, or Reformed.

The situation in Old Europe, then, was exactly the reverse of that generally prevailing today. While we take higher education as a given and occasionally ask how we might better bring Christianity to bear upon its institutions, our forebears in Old Europe accepted Christendom as a given and occasionally asked what institutionalized higher education might have to offer it. We reflect on ways to Christianize within higher education, they on ways to educate within Christendom.

Consider next the state or status of education. Christianity is a "book religion" and so necessarily concerned in some measure with questions of literacy. In the period of the Late Roman Empire the church fathers took Roman education largely for granted and reacted vigorously when Julian the Apostate cleverly attempted to deny them access to higher education or when their own people opted for a kind of "holy ignorance." Augustine in particular drafted a most influential defense of *Christian Learning* (this the proper translation of a title often wrongly rendered *On Christian Doctrine*) in which he demonstrated that pagan knowledge and education could contribute significantly to the understanding and preaching of Scripture.[2] But his vision of Christian learning, for him essentially an apologetic move, became in the early middle ages, largely by default, nearly the whole educational program. The collapse of the western Roman Empire left only churchmen to maintain literacy, and they did so mainly to ensure that there would always be those who could read Scripture, conduct worship, and administer the church.[3]

This early medieval development had manifold consequences that affected the interrelationship of education and the Christian church down to the end of Old Europe. Literacy became very nearly the exclusive preserve of the church. Learning was identified with clerics (indeed, the word *clerk,* which derives from *cleric,* meant simply a Latin scholar), and "illiteracy" and "idiocy" were simply common terms used to refer to the universal state of unlettered laypersons.[4] Moreover, in the midst of so many barbarian peoples with hundreds of different Romance, Germanic, Celtic, and Slavic dialects, Latin became the normative language for both church and learning, remaining so into the later seventeenth century and beyond (even, I might add, for our Protestant forebears, who wrote many things in the vernacular for the people but at least as much in Latin for their colleagues). Scripture largely replaced the pagan classics as the norm for literacy: boys learned their letters from the Psalms, clerics sang and preached from texts appointed for the divine office, and scholars quoted and echoed the Vulgate Scriptures continuously, much as later writers would quote and draw inspiration from the King James and Luther Bibles. From the church's point of view, then, education was what we would call "vocational"; its goal was the preparation of a select number of churchmen for pastoral and administrative responsibilites. Down to about 1150 virtually all education took place in ecclesiastical settings, chiefly cathedrals and monasteries, where young boys were prepared for their life's work.[5]

Yet even after the church had emerged as the guardian of education, there was—ironically or happily, as you prefer—an additional factor that had immeasurable importance for education in Old Europe. Medieval and Reformation learning remained fundamentally literary, and the tools and models for good Latin lay ultimately beyond Scripture in pagan antiquity. Pagan authors consequently never entirely disappeared from sight. Indeed, from time to time, in periods historians call "renaissances," clerics enthusiastically set out to recover those ancient texts and their "propaedeutic" arts (grammar, rhetoric, dialectic, arithmetic, geometry, astronomy, and music).[6] Already during the Carolingian renaissance of the ninth century, clerics manifestly thrilled to the sheer intellectual stimulation of this body of thought and literature, though their work on it always remained subordinate in principle to the study and understanding of Scripture.[7] The renaissance of the twelfth century went still farther. Its "humanistic" authors, including monks like Peter Damian and Bernard of Clairvaux and clerics like John of Salisbury, wrote superb Latin; its educators translated and absorbed whole new reaches of ancient thought, particularly in philosophy, science, and medicine; its lawyers recovered Roman law; and its poets rejoiced in Ovid, Juvenal, Horace, and others.[8] In the fifteenth century, finally, the Renaissance in Italy initiated a systematic recovery and imitation of ancient culture from a linguistic and philological base enriched now with the study of Greek.[9]

So much then for the ambivalent heritage of education in Old Europe—at once singularly religious and churchly and yet unavoidably reliant on ancient pagan texts. In the midst of the renaissance of the twelfth century, with its unparalleled socioeconomic boom and urban expansion, clerics like Peter Abelard began slowly and daringly distancing themselves from cathedrals and monasteries in order to pursue learning and teaching on their own. In the eventual association and independent organization into guilds of these wandering scholars, at

Bologna, Montpellier, Paris, and elsewhere, lies the origin of the European university.[10] (The term *university* was not at first unique to institutions of higher education; it originally referred to any collectivity or guild gathered to protect and represent its corporate interests—in this instance a guild of masters and students.)

These scholarly guilds organized to protect their interests on two fronts. In an age when sovereignty was weak and violence, especially against foreigners, common, masters and students as a group sought separate juridical status to protect themselves from drunken townsmen, gouging landlords, and brutal police forces. For most medieval universities this juridical document, issued by king, prince, or prelate, established publicly their independent status. Frederick I, Barbarossa, for example, granted the students at Bologna certain immunities in 1158 as did King Philip I, Augustus, to students in Paris in the year 1200. This privilege also regulated, as similar documents did for other guilds, matters of organization, policy, dress, burial, and so on—even such particulars as their right to work on holy days (holidays).[11] Guilds of masters soon emerged as a privileged and independent force in Christendom, set alongside kingdom and church as the third pillar of Christian society *(regnum, sacerdotium, studium)*.[12] Beginning in 1224, with Emperor Frederick II's foundation of a university at Naples, and then especially after 1350, every proud and powerful prince wanted to form a new university on his own territory, as Frederick of Saxony did in Wittenberg. By 1650 there were nearly a hundred universities in Europe, three-fourths of them established prior to the Reformation. In the late medieval and Reformation periods princes and patrons intervened rather freely, but in Old Europe universities retained a uniquely privileged position.

Guilds of masters, not surprisingly, wanted their own way in scholarly matters as well. This provoked a struggle against diocesan officials charged with overseeing instruction and granting the "license" or, in our terms, the diploma. In this instance, it was not the kings but the popes who intervened on behalf of masters and against local church officials, mainly to guarantee a steady supply of qualified and learned men for the church. By agreement reached very early in Paris the chancellor of Notre Dame was compelled to license any person approved by the masters, without discrimination or fee. And thereafter until the Reformation all universities, whether founded by prince or prelate, were chartered by popes with the right to confer a *licentia docendi* (license to teach) upon their graduates, enabling them to secure work in teaching positions and in other capacities.

Endowed with a privileged standing over against both civil and ecclesiastical authorities, guilds of masters organized themselves internally into four different faculties or disciplines—the arts, law (civil or canon), medicine, and theology—though very few *studia generalia,* or "general centers of higher studies," boasted all four. Throughout the middle ages Paris remained the center of theological studies, but it had no faculty of civil law. Bologna was the center of legal studies, though without a faculty of theology. Montpellier and Salerno led all others in medical studies, but their faculties of law and theology were weak or nonexistent. Down into the fifteenth century, then, a half dozen universities set the course of higher education for all Christendom. After the Reformation the Wittenberg theological faculty set the tone for much of Lutheranism, as did the Genevan Academy, Heidelberg, Leiden, or Cambridge for most Calvinists.

In the universities of Old Europe teaching itself centered upon the mastery of a fixed set of texts. Masters commented in their lectures upon these prescribed texts, and students were responsible for learning the text, the "ordinary gloss" upon it, and probably the master's "disputation" of problems inherent in it. Advanced students became bachelors or teaching assistants and themselves led beginning students through a "cursory" reading of the text. Thought in medieval universities thus developed by way of commenting upon (or glossing) and disputing about a certain body of texts. Hundreds of those lectures and disputations still exist today in student accounts *(reportationes),* and a few in the notes of the masters themselves. Some of Luther's earliest lecture notes still exist, for instance, and working through them has become a major industry among Reformation historians seeking the origins of his ideas on justification by faith.

With this background in mind, we may examine Christianity's relationship to the universities of Old Europe from two directions: from the viewpoint of Christian teachings within universities and then from the perspective of the universities' impact upon Christendom.

By far the largest faculty in most universities (generally comprising well over three-fourths of all masters and students), and the one prerequisite in principle to all others, was the faculty of arts. The arts faculty arose from a study of the seven disciplines inherited from antiquity—the trivium, which consisted of grammar, rhetoric, and logic, and the quadrivium, which consisted of arithmetic, music, geometry, and astronomy. In practice, however, the arts faculty came to emphasize a thorough mastery of Aristotle's teaching on logic, on metaphysics or first philosophy, and on natural philosophy (his works on *Physics*, the *Soul*, the *Celestial Orbs*, and so on). In addition, an arts student might also receive some introduction to Euclid on geometry, Ptolomy on astronomy, or Boethius on arithmetic and music, but the quadrivium generally received far less attention than the trivium. In certain instances works of ancient authors were eventually summarized and supplied with Christian examples: a grammar by Alexander of Ville-Dieu drew from the Latin grammarian Priscian, and a textbook on logic by Peter of Spain (later Pope John XXI) drew substantially from Aristotle's works on logic.[13]

In all this the most striking feature is certainly logic's domination among the introductory arts. Augustine had already taught that human beings bear the image of God especially in their rationality, and the university scholars of Christian Europe concentrated upon deductive logic as the God-given instrument for truth seeking and upon natural philosophy and metaphysics as the best guides to the principles inherent in creation. The papacy resisted at first, proscribing in 1210, 1215, and 1231 all books on natural philosophy, most of which were by Aristotle, though with Neoplatonic overlays by way of Arabic translators and commentators. But in 1255 the books became a set part of the medieval curriculum, and in the 1260s and 1270s their teachings provoked the first major crisis between churchmen and university men. An intensive reading of these texts naturally produced inspired and even radical Aristotelians, who argued from their texts for the primacy of reason, the eternity of the world, and the oneness of intellect in all human souls. It was Albert the Great and Thomas Aquinas, more than any others, who undertook in brilliant commentaries to get at what, in their view, Aristotle had "really said"; then they worked mightily to demonstrate a general compatibility between Aristotelian philosophy and Christian theology.[14]

The bishop of Paris was not convinced, however, and in 1277 condemned 219 propositions of the university scholars, some of them taken from Thomas' work. Succeeding scholars in the fourteenth century attempted to put far greater philosophical distance between the God of Scripture, upon whose absolute power and will all creation hung, and the God of being, approachable and even knowable through Aristotelian logic and metaphysics.[15] Yet the general enterprise Thomas represented came to be taken largely for granted, and the notion that a philosophical foundation was necessary for learning about the divine—what is rather imprecisely called "scholasticism"—has marked Catholic and some Protestant movements down to recent times. In the fifteenth century the Thomistic approach and metaphysic came to be called the "old way" *(via antiqua)* and the nominalist or "terminist" approach, sometimes linked to Ockham, the "new way" *(via moderna)*. Luther was trained in, though he later repudiated, the *via moderna*, while many of those who remained Catholic relied on the *via antiqua*. In many arts faculties the two fought so fiercely that a university had to opt for one or the other.

There is little evidence that any of these "artists" thought of themselves as leaving Christianity behind, either as a personal commitment or as a cultural tradition. But they certainly revered Aristotle as "the master of those who know," as Dante put it, and after years of teaching and absorbing his texts were prepared to assert positions that, as they put it, seemed true, "speaking philosophically."[16] Indeed, within the minds of individual masters or students, and even generally within the arts faculty, this "philosophical" outlook may at times have assumed a kind of autonomy over against and yet within the prevailing Christian tradition. The artists' situation was not unlike that of their colleagues in medicine and civil law, where the prescribed texts contained views of the human body and of the body politic that hardly squared with the church's; yet for generations, sometimes under a measure of suspicion, baptized Christians worked hard at teaching in those faculties. Especially after the condemnations of 1277, masters of theology encouraged and even instructed the more lowly artists to leave the "big questions" to them. The result, ironically, was a greater concentration still upon logic within the arts faculty, which is partially responsible for the new nominalist teachings on terms and language so much admired today, and also upon natural philosophy, which produced physical teachings in which some see the seeds of modern science.[17]

Beginning in Italy around 1350 and spreading into northern Europe after 1450, a new kind of intellectual emerged, initially dubbed a "poet" or "orator." Especially in the early days their writings vigorously and relentlessly attacked the empty and useless disputations of the schoolmen. And yet the main word and concept bequeathed to us from their movement—*humanism*—originated in Italian universities from the slang expression for a student or teacher of the humanities (from the expression *studia humanitatis* comes the word *umanista*). These humanists preferred the study of ancient poetry, rhetoric, and literature to logic, the study of history to school traditions in Aristotelian ethics and politics, and the study of moral philosophy to metaphysics. At the root of their educational reform lay a passionate enthusiasm for the recovery and imitation of ancient literary texts read directly in their original languages, lost treasures from a golden age obscured by an intervening middle or dark age.

This cultural movement generated a series of issues with serious consequences for the universities. The first was precisely the relationship of the new intellectual movement to the existing schools. Most of the early Italian humanists flourished outside university faculties and depended upon the patronage of princes or cities for their livelihood. Many were laymen, and some gathered in informal "academies." Admission to arts faculties, or, rather, the addition of masters or chairs in humanities to arts faculties, came slowly in many places.[18] North of the Alps, however, humanist positions opened up more readily, usually at the insistence of the prince who founded or oversaw the university, presumably to keep his school in the forefront of intellectual fashion. In Germany, the universities at Erfurt and then Wittenberg led the way, and by the third decade of the sixteenth century most others had followed. Earlier texts and methods never entirely disappeared, but many faculties now insisted on better translations of Aristotle and read him apart from the received commentaries of the schoolmen (such as Thomas' commentary on the *Physics*). In any case, by the latter part of the sixteenth century universities everywhere had accepted a much broader conception of the arts.

Once this new movement had made its way into the university faculties, it raised a second issue: it effectively added yet another body of pagan texts, now to be read with a heightened sensitivity to their original language and meaning, and made them the prerequisite for every educated person in Christendom. Once again enthusiasts went beyond the pale—Platonists toward a vague mysticism, Stoics toward a vague determinism or skepticism, civic humanists toward an intense political realism, and litterati toward a vague aestheticism. Like those in Paris who claimed to "speak philosophically" with Aristotle, there were humanists caught up in "speaking Latin" like Cicero or "speaking Greek" like Socrates. More specific results of this return to ancient sources include Erasmus's pioneering edition of a Greek New Testament, complete with critical notes, which threatened to undo centuries of commentary and learning built up around the Latin Vulgate text, and a fresh reading of Roman law (called the "French way"), which challenged three centuries of scholastic commentary elaborated at Bologna (the "Italian way").

Once again Christians had to sort through and incorporate the new learning. "Christian humanism," as it is called, was best represented by Erasmus, though some recent scholars (among them Charles Trinkaus) have found Calvin an equally good representative.[19] The real fruition of Christian humanism, however, despite the contributions of Erasmus and the views of some modern liberal scholars, probably came mostly in the Catholic and Protestant reform movements.

The third influence of humanism on the universities was its replacement of logic with rhetoric as the central instrument and measure of human learning: disputations gave way to orations, syllogisms to grammar, and Aristotle to Cicero and Quintilian. Masters and students cast aside complicated arguments and focused instead upon the qualities of complex literary texts. To move the will seemed more important than to convince the mind. Historians have traditionally linked this shift in emphasis to the political culture of the new cities and courts, which is doubtless true to an extent; but certainly a strong religious commitment also underlay the shift. The image of God in man, these thinkers believed, was grounded more in the will than in reason: to act virtuously was more important than to know right doctrine. Reform in the arts faculties meant dispensing with all the useless disputations of the philosophers and providing a much fuller foundation in the humanities.

Reformation of the church built directly and immediately upon reform of the arts faculties in the universities. It was the reformers, both Catholic and Protestant, in the main who definitively installed the new humanist program in the universities of modern Europe. Already in his "Theses against the Scholastics" of September 1517 and then more vigorously in 1520, Luther protested, "What else are the universities . . . than as the book of Maccabees says, 'Places for training youth in Greek glory,' in which loose living prevails, the Holy Scriptures and the Christian faith are little taught, and the blind, heathen master Aristotle rules alone, even more than Christ? In this regard my advice would be that Aristotle's [philosophical works] be altogether discarded. . . ."[20]

Zwingli and Calvin received humanist educations; Melanchthon came to Wittenberg to teach Greek and implement educational reform; and Cardinals Pole and Jiménez rooted their Catholic reforms in humanist programs. But the church reformers, while presupposing a humanist curriculum, shifted the emphasis in the languages studied, the works studied, and the use to which each would be put.[21] For them education in the arts meant first of all expertise in the three languages necessary for a better understanding of Scripture—Greek, Latin, and Hebrew. The addition of Hebrew, already a humanist move, had created a terrific row in Cologne in 1517 in the famous Reuchlin affair; but eventually for the growing numbers of Protestants and later and more slowly for Catholics as well it became fundamental. Furthermore, while the pagan classics remained central as a foundation for learning, reading the church fathers in their own languages and as whole pieces became ever more important to the reformers. Erasmus published new editions of Jerome and many others; and Calvin in particular acquired an astonishing knowledge of both the Greek and Latin Fathers. Finally, studies in the arts were put to a new purpose. Rhetoric remained central, but not just as a display of learning or a tool of persuasion; now it was to be a tool for articulating and communicating the word of God. Its end was to move people's hearts to faith and scholars' minds to Christian wisdom and understanding. For this task, the reformers were equipped in very great measure by their humanist educations in early sixteenth-century universities.

Of the three remaining and so-called higher faculties (recall that the four faculties were the arts, law both civil and canon, medicine, and theology), all much smaller in size than the arts, let us set aside medicine and civil law and examine canon law and theology. The faculty of canon or church law was by far the largest and most influential of these other faculties. This may strike Protestants as unusual, but through most of the period of Old Europe the church maintained the most sophisticated institution in society, one from which secular monarchs took lessons in law and administration. Because of this, there was an almost limitless demand for teachers and practitioners of church law.[22] The prescribed teaching texts in this case supplied sanctions for the courtroom as well as for the classroom. Gratian's *Concord of Discordant Canons* gathered roughly four thousand snippets from church councils, church fathers, and papal letters; the *Decretals* of 1234 embraced an equally large body of papal law issued mostly between 1140 and 1230 (and remained the official lawbook of the Catholic church until 1917). So close was the connection between church rule and university teaching that from 1208 on popes regularly sent collections of their rulings to the canon law faculty in Bologna. These texts were solemnly authorized to serve both as binding lawbooks and as the prescribed textbooks for students. Canonists used them both ways but in their teaching explicated the texts in a great variety of ways, so that historians now distinguish many different schools of thought among medieval canon lawyers.

Even as the church permeated every aspect of life, so these masters of canon law elaborated an enormous body of teaching on ecclesial structures, political notions like office and representation, social practices like marriage, burial, and inheritance, and economic issues like usury and taxation. The masters sought to spell out legally the obligations inherent in Christian profession and membership in the Christian community. Church law governed the clergy (up to 10 percent of the population) together with all their possessions (as much as 25 percent of the whole), but it also reached into the lives of individual Christians, particularly through the sacraments and the system of penances and indulgences. There can be little doubt that by the end of the middle ages average and not-so-average Christians thought of their religious commitment overwhelmingly in terms of legal structures and obligations, and it was the canonists who were to teach and administer all of this.

This no doubt helps to explain the great fury Luther and most other reformers directed against canon law, repudiating it even more totally and vehemently than they did Aristotle. Most of the issues Luther criticized in his "Open Address to the German Nation," calling upon noble laymen to take them into their own hands, had fallen for generations under the canonists' jurisdiction. In general, however, the reformers dismissed much too blithely the wealth of learning these masters of canon law had deployed on the problems of office, property, marriage, and all the rest, always in terms of defining a Christian's obligations. Indeed, once the Protestants developed state churches of their own, forms of canon law reemerged, though never, it must be said, with the same prestige and prominence accorded it by medieval and Catholic people. All the same, in my own Dutch Reformed tradition the most prominent seventeenth-century figure among the orthodox was Gisbertus Voetius, who produced a thousand-page work on ecclesiastical polity.

It may seem odd that a discussion of Christianity and the early universities would leave the theology faculty to last; but the fact is that while theology enjoyed enormous prestige as the queen of the sciences its faculty remained very small and its graduates rarely got good jobs outside the university. After the middle of the thirteenth century, its masters came overwhelmingly from among the mendicant orders, that is, from professed religious, and its subject matter often seemed dauntingly speculative and abstract. And yet the contribution of medieval theological faculties to Western Christendom is beyond measure.

The organization of such a faculty at Paris between 1150 and 1200 brought Christianity's sacred dogmas under the purview of an academic discipline called theology (literally, "God-talk"), a word first made current by Peter Abelard in the 1120s. A good century later Thomas' introductory *Summa Theologiae* ("sum of theology") opened with an argument that theology represents a distinct science in the Aristotelian sense of the term—a body of coherent knowledge based on demonstrable propositions, drawn in this instance from revelation. Consider, by way of comparison, the situation in the East. Sacred dogma in the Orthodox church rested on an immutable tradition, and this deposit was entrusted exclusively to the hierarchy, mostly monastic; it was never to be profaned by contact with secular learning. Thomas, Luther, Calvin, and all the others, by contrast, drew upon the best learning at their command, whether Aristotelian or humanist, to study, defend, understand, develop, and even correct the dogmas of the church.

Theological faculties had, broadly considered, two lasting effects upon medieval and Reformation Christian thought. First, holy Scripture was made an academic textbook. While this did not deny the Bible's authority or inspiration, it certainly broadened its use and interpretation beyond the sole contexts of church and worship. Medieval and Reformation masters of theology were first of all teachers of Scripture. Medieval masters concentrated much of their attention on the Psalms and the Pauline epistles as being the most fruitful for doctrine. They made an effort to get at the historical and literal meaning of the text, sometimes using Jewish help; yet it was only in the wake of the humanists that the text was read in its original languages. Masters taught Scripture in the classroom by means of authoritative commentaries built up around it and organized into the "ordinary gloss," which guided their approach to the text and pointed up the doctrines they should find in it. But however oriented toward tradition and the creeds of the church, these masters of theology nonetheless turned Christianity's sacred book into a textbook, just as the lawyers had done with the community's sacred laws. Luther, it is good to remember, vastly altered his life and convictions, but he never gave up his position, before or after the Reformation, as a master of theology teaching Scripture at Wittenberg. In fact, he stood upon it as conferring the right to challenge popes and councils in their reading of Scripture, a point not original with him but raised at least as far back as the Council of Basel (1431–1449).

The masters recognized, secondly, a need to systematize the teachings of Scripture and the church. Around 1160 they adopted a handbook by Peter Lombard containing excerpts from the Fathers organized around such central themes as God, creation, redemption, the sacraments, and so on. Bachelors and masters worked through this material as the authoritative introduction to Christian doctrine. The inherited authorities were not always harmonious, however, so they applied the logical and philosophical skills learned in the arts faculty to produce a consistent and reasoned treatment of Christian doctrine. The result was what we now call systematic theology. This philosophical investigation and articulation of theological teachings acquired a momentum all its own, which even the leaders of the Reformation could not stop. Melanchthon's *Commonplaces,* Calvin's *Institutes,* and any number of other works in later years ended up filling the same function, as Protestant theology also became enveloped in the scholastic mode. These "systems" were by no means all alike, and the medieval church, intentionally or not, allowed a great variety of schools to flourish and to challenge one another.[23] Charges of heresy often arose as much from competition as from fear for the well-being of Christendom. But what these university masters accomplished can hardly be gainsaid, however sadly out of favor they may be these days: after them, educated Christians always expected to have and to know a "theology," a systematic presentation of the teachings of their faith.

Guilds of masters in Old Europe, in sum, established learning as an independent enterprise endowed with its own legal recognition and protection, scholarly standards, and prescribed curricula. But they did so within the confines of Christendom—they were granted the privilege to do so precisely in order that they might serve the cause and institutions of Christianity. The heart of the university's service was its learning, applied in turn to the basics of human knowledge, to the church's law, institutions, and practices, and even to church dogmas. The issue then to which we must turn now, and with which we will conclude, is that of the larger impact university learning had upon Christendom— how did the universities influence and alter the society and culture of the faithful as a whole?

The guilds brought literacy and learning to a society that both sought and resisted it. Early medieval society—sometimes called the dark ages—barely survived endemic warfare, subsistence-level standards of living, and the near total collapse of literacy. In Old Europe after 1200, by contrast, dozens and later hundreds of graduates took up ecclesiastical and secular positions each year, in which, as lawyers and administrators, they sought to transform raw power into rational administration. Many even attained authority themselves, civil lawyers as advisors to kings and leaders of communes, canon lawyers as prelates and popes. Laymen increasingly swelled the ranks, first in Italy and then—especially after the Reformation—in the north. Such men advanced their careers solely by their learning, eventually forming a new class, what the Germans call a *Bildungsstand*—roughly, a class that owes its position to learning rather than blood or some other consideration.[24] (In English the title "master" eventually became a more general form of address—"mister.") Graduates, after all, received a privilege, a right, a "license." Already by the thirteenth century masters were compared to knights, and inevitably this new privileged elite clashed with the noble elite who for generations had led European Christendom by right of blood and sword. In medieval vernacular literature a number of risqué poems disputed whether the cleric or the knight, brains or brawn, made for the better lover. This rivalry never got totally resolved in Old Europe. But the number and influence of university men grew steadily.

Learning (*scientia,* also the word for Aristotelian "science") was not just a matter of improved administration or successful careers, though. It was a gift of God—in medieval schemes one of the seven gifts of the Holy Spirit—and therefore, like piety or mercy, a good in itself. In the thirteenth century the mendicant orders made learning at universities a key part of their religious and contemplative life. Even Calvinists, with their activist proclivities, professed that the highest end of humanity was "to know God and to enjoy him forever," and they were among the quickest to found academies wherever they went. Learning gained recognition as a God-given good, and thus displays of learning were applauded and encouraged. Twice a year masters of theology took questions on whatever subject a student was bold or interested enough to raise. During Advent of 1269, for instance, Thomas Aquinas received and answered questions on subjects as varied as the composition of angelic being and the extent of the obedience a child owed his parents.[25] In short, masters questioned and reflected on every conceivable aspect of life in Old European Christendom. No longer could either church or state (*sacerdotium* or *regnum*) even imagine carrying on any more without learning *(studium),* now the third pillar of Christian society.

Allow me to conclude by discussing three specific types of people who embodied the new emphasis on learning and whose learning in turn reached out to affect the life of Christendom at large. The expertise of the medieval canon lawyer, the first of these types, ranged beyond law to areas we would now assign to political science, sociology, and economics. We must note two important points about their influence on Christendom, one practical and one theoretical. First, from the medieval foundation of the university down to within living memory, canon lawyers—not theologians—have governed the Catholic church. It was they who elbowed out noblemen to become popes, bishops, and local administrators; and indeed by the late middle ages noblemen often sent their sons off to study canon law if they intended them for high positions in the church. Second, the law these men learned and applied—the binding pronouncements of popes, councils, and Fathers—carried a divine sanction in their eyes (Protestants particularly need to be reminded of this). In principle, then, canon lawyers undertook the ultimate integration of faith, learning, and practice: the daily application of divine norms to the right ordering of a Christian society. In practice, canon lawyers during the high middle ages were doubtless the most influential university graduates in the church.

The second type is the Renaissance gentleman. Humanists at first acquired the very same positions that the scholars in the faculty of the arts had held before them: as teachers, clerks, advisors, and possibly lawyers. It is interesting to note that the papal court in Rome was one of the first to import humanists with their facility in Latin to carry out its administrative responsibilities and to build the magnificent library now in the Vatican. In time humanists also pursuaded the noble and patrician leaders of society that chivalry, the hunt, and swordplay were not enough to make them true gentlemen; they also needed a little Latin and Greek. Until recently historians have tended to emphasize the secular and aesthetic sides of the nobles' learning—the ancient history and poetry they were supposed to read and enjoy. But there was also a deeply religious side. Many, maybe even most, of these nobles were very intrigued with questions on the human condition, moral wellbeing, and the pursuit of God outside the monastery. They read the church fathers as well as the ancient moralists, and many of them eventually took an active part in the Reformation movement, on one side or the other.

The last type is the Protestant pastor. During the middle ages there were no seminaries with pastoral training. Though by the end of the period perhaps as many as one-fourth of all priests had attended university at some point, most training in the pastorate remained by apprenticeship. While masters of theology often took up pastoral matters in their works, their discussion generally remained at a speculative level. During the conciliar era theological masters played a crucial role in resolving the great schism, but their leadership in the church would not fully emerge until the Reformation. This was a doctrinal matter, and so masters of theology generally defined the issues and led the movements and countermovements.

In Protestant areas especially, with competition from popes and bishops gone or minimized, professors of theology emerged as the learned leaders of Reformed or Lutheran society. But princes and professors alike insisted that all ordinary pastors be competent to guide and instruct the people. This was defined, in humanist-Reformation manner, as competence in the languages of Scripture, in the dogmatic teachings of Scripture, and in the oratorical skills required to preach Scripture. Such university-trained pastors, almost to within living memory, provided the leadership in local Christian communities, their qualification for leadership resting as much or more on their learning as on their ordination (as was the case with their medieval counterparts).

This was the medieval and Reformation legacy of the universities to Christendom. Scholars, lawyers, gentlemen, and pastors carried out their tasks in the community with a commitment both to Christianity and to learning. Through most of the period from 1150 to 1650 their commitment to Christianity, though sometimes troubled or contentious, was never seriously questioned. The position of learning, on the other hand, underwent much more upheaval; the commitment to learning in European society was newer and thus constantly being reshaped and expanded. From the perspective of the modern world, where learning has generally waxed and Christianity waned, the early boundary disputes and rifts between them seem terribly important. But this, while interesting and sometimes even indicative, can be very misleading. From the vantage point of medieval and Reformation Christendom, by contrast, what seemed most important was the mutual benefit acquired when university learning was engaged to enrich, edify, and reform Christendom.

NOTES

1. I will restrict my footnotes to basic studies that include more detailed references. On medieval and Reformation universities, see Hastings Rashdall, *The Universities of Europe in the Middle Ages*, 3 vols., rev. ed., ed. F. M. Powicke and A. B. Emden (Oxford: Clarendon, 1936); Jacques Verger, *Les universités au moyen âge* (Paris: Presses Universitaires de France, 1973); Adam B. Cobban, *The Medieval Universities: Their Development and Organization* (London: Methuen, 1975); Peter Classen, *Studium und Gesellschaft im Mittelalter* (Stuttgart: MGH Schriften 29, 1983); James M. Kittelson and Pamela J. Transue, eds., *Rebirth, Reform and Resilience: Universities in Transition, 1300–1700* (Columbus: Ohio State University Press, 1984); this last work has a good bibliography on 324-57.

2. The Latin title of Augustine's work is *De doctrina christiana*. The most common English translation is that by D. W. Robertson, Jr., *On Christian Doctrine* (New York: Liberal Arts, 1958); and the best general interpretation is in Henri Ireneé Marrou, *Saint Augustin et la fin de la culture antique* (Paris: E. de Boccard, 1938).

3. See Pierre Riché, *Education and Culture in the Barbarian West: Sixth Through Eighth Centuries*, trans. J. J. Contreni (Columbia: University of South Carolina Press, 1978).

4. See H. Grundmann, *"Litteratus-illitteratus:* Der Wandel einer Bildungsnorm vom Altertum zum Mittelalter," in his *Ausgewählte Aufsätze* (Stuttgart: MGH Schriften 25, 1978), 3: 1-66.

5. The best overview of this period now is P. Riché, *Les écoles et l'enseignement dans l'occident chrétien de la fin du Vᵉ siècle au milieu du XIᵉ siècle* (Paris: Aubier Montaigne, 1979).

6. Definitions of "renaissance" vary enormously, but most make some reference to a rebirth of classical traditions. See E. Panofsky, *Renaissance and Renascences in Western Arts* (New York: Harper and Row, 1972); R. R. Bolgar, *The Classical Heritage and its Beneficiaries from the Carolingian Age to the End of the Renaissance* (Cambridge: Cambridge University Press, 1954)—note, however, that the discussion here of the medieval period is now dated; Warren Treadgold, ed., *Renaissances before the Renaissance: Cultural Revivals of Late Antiquity and the Middle Ages* (Stanford: Stanford University Press, 1984); and G. B. Ladner, "Terms and Ideas of Renewal," in *Renaissance and Renewal in the Twelfth Century*, ed. Robert L. Benson and Giles Constable (Cambridge: Harvard University Press, 1983), 1-33.

7. See M. L. Laistner, *Thought and Letters in Western Europe, A.D. 500–900*, 2d ed. (Ithaca: Cornell University Press, 1966); Riché, *Les écoles et l'enseignement dans l'occident chrétien*, 47-118; J. Contreni, "The Carolingian Renaissance," in *Renaissances before the Renaissance*, ed. Treadgold, 59-74, with literature and sources.

8. See Charles Homer Haskins, *The Renaissance of the Twelfth Century* (Cambridge: Harvard University Press, 1927); Benson and Constable, *Renaissance and Renewal in the Twelfth Century*, which includes essays with extensive bibliographies; and S. Ferruolo, "The Twelfth-Century Renaissance," in *Renaissances before the Renaissance*, ed. Treadgold, 114-43.

9. See in this context all the works of Paul Oskar Kristeller, especially *Renaissance Thought: The Classic, Scholastic and Humanistic Strains* (New York: Harper and Row, 1961), and *Renaissance Thought and its Sources* (New York: Columbia University Press, 1979); see as well the essays of Charles Trinkaus in *The Scope of Renaissance Humanism* (Ann Arbor: University of Michigan Press, 1983).

10. Compare Haskins, *The Rise of the Universities* (New York: H. Holt, 1923);

H. Grundmann, "Vom Ursprung der Universität im Mittelalter," in *Ausgewählte Aufsätze*, 3: 292-342; and P. Classen, "Die Ältesten Universitätsreformen und Universitätsgründungen des Mittelalters," in *Studium und Gesellschaft im Mittelalter*, 170-96.

11. Pearl Kibre, *Scholarly Privileges in the Middle Ages* (Cambridge: Harvard University Press, 1962); Gaines Post, "Parisian Masters as a Corporation, 1200–1246," in his *Studies in Medieval Legal Thought: Public Law and the State* (Princeton: Princeton University Press, 1964), 27-60; and Jacques Le Goff, "How Did the Medieval University Conceive of Itself?" and "The Universities and the Public Authorities in the Middle Ages and the Renaissance," both chapters in his *Time, Work, and Culture in the Middle Ages* (Chicago: University of Chicago Press, 1980), 122-49.

12. H. Grundmann, "*Sacerdotium, Regnum, Studium:* Zur Wertung der Wissenschaft im Mittelalter," in *Ausgewählte Aufsätze*, 3: 275-91.

13. On the curriculum of the arts college, see the general introduction by A. Kenney and B. Dod in the *Cambridge History of Later Medieval Philosophy: From the Rediscovery of Aristotle to the Disintegration of Scholasticism, 1100–1600*, ed. Norman Kretzman, et al. (Cambridge: Cambridge University Press, 1982), 9-79; Rashdall, *The Universities of Europe in the Middle Ages*, 1: 439ff.; *Arts liberaux et philosophie au moyen âge* (Actes du quatrième congrès international de philosophie médiévale, Montreal and Paris, 1964); and J. M. Fletcher, "The Faculty of Arts," and P. Osmond Lewry, "Grammar, Logic, and Rhetoric 1220–1320," both in *The History of the University of Oxford*, ed J. I. Catto (Oxford: Oxford University Press, 1984), vol. 1, *The Early Oxford Schools*, 369-434.

14. The best general introduction to this problem of compatibility is by Fernand van Steenberghen, *Thomas Aquinas and Radical Aristotelianism* (Washington, D.C.: Catholic University Press, 1980); see also his *La Philosophie aux XIII*^e *siècle* (Louvain: Publications Universitaires; Paris: Beatrice-Nauwelaerts, 1966).

15. For an introduction to later medieval philosophy and theology, see the works of Heiko A. Oberman, especially his *Harvest of Medieval Theology: Gabriel Biel and Late Medieval Nominalism*, 3d ed. (Durham, N.C.: Labyrinth, 1983); and his *Masters of the Reformation: Rival Roads to a New Ideology* (New York: Cambridge University Press, 1981); see also the essays of William J. Courtenay collected now in *Covenant and Causality in Medieval Thought: Studies in Philosophy, Theology and Economic Practice* (London: Variorum Reprints, 1984).

16. See van Steenberghen, *Thomas Aquinas and Radical Aristotelianism;* and Mary Martin McLaughlin, *Intellectual Freedom and its Limits in the University of Paris in the Thirteenth and Fourteenth Centuries* (New York: Ayer, 1977).

17. Excellent introductions to all aspects of the teaching of both logic and natural philosophy can now be found in the *Cambridge History of Later Medieval Philosophy.*

18. See James H. Overfield, *Humanism and Scholasticism in Late Medieval Germany* (Princeton: Princeton University Press, 1984); see also the outstanding essays in *Itinerarium Italicum: The Profile of the Italian Renaissance in the Mirror of Its European Transformation: Dedicated to Paul Oskar Kristeller on the Occasion of His 70th Birthday* (Leiden: Brill, 1975).

19. Charles Trinkaus, *In Our Image and Likeness*, 2 vols. (Chicago and London: University of Chicago Press, 1970); and his essay "The Religious Thought of the Italian Humanist," in *The Scope of Renaissance Humanism*, 237-62.

20. Martin Luther, in his "Open Letter to the Christian Nobility of the German Nation," in *Three Treatises* (Philadelphia: Fortress, 1960), 93.

21. See Stephen Ozment, "Humanism, Scholasticism, and the Intellectual Origins of the Reformation," in *Continuity and Discontinuity in Church History: Essays*

Presented to George Huntston Williams, ed. F. Church and T. George (Leiden: Brill, 1979), 133-49; G. Lytle, "Universities as Religious Authorities in the Later Middle Ages and Reformation," in *Reform and Authority in the Medieval and Reformation Church,* ed. Guy F. Lytle (Washington, D.C.: Catholic University Press, 1981), 69-97.

22. The best introduction to the place and influence of canon law in the universities is by Gabriel Le Bras, *Prolégomènes,* vol. 1 of *Histoire du droit et des institutions de l'Église en Occident* (Paris: Sirey, 1955).

23. Besides general histories of theology, see Oberman, "Fourteenth-Century Religious Thought: A Premature Profile," *Speculum* 53 (1978): 80-93; also his *Harvest of Medieval Theology* and his *Masters of the Reformation;* see also Courtenay, *Covenant and Causality in Medieval Thought;* and J. I. Catto, *History of the University of Oxford,* 471-518.

24. This viewpoint is best stated now by Classen, *Studium und Gesellschaft im Mittelalter;* but see also J. W. Baldwin, "Masters at Paris from 1179 to 1215: A Social Perspective," in *Renaissance and Renewal in the Twelfth Century,* ed. Benson and Constable, 138-72.

25. Thomas Aquinas, *Quodlibetal Questions 1 and 2,* trans. Sandra Edwards (Toronto: Pontifical Institute of Medieval Studies, 1983).

Reformation and Puritan Ideals of Education

Leland Ryken

In his essay "Modern Education and the Classics," T. S. Eliot expressed a principle that has always been the hallmark of Christian education: "We must derive our theory of education from our philosophy of life. The problem turns out to be a religious problem."[1] While agreeing with the broad outlines of this foundational principle, various Christian traditions have nevertheless interpreted and applied it in specific contexts and have as a result generated distinct educational ideals.

I propose here to examine the ideals of the Protestant Reformation, especially as it was expressed in English Puritanism, for no Christian tradition has been more influential in the development of evangelical Protestant education than these movements. Reformation and Puritan ideals of education have served as both model and inspiration to Christian higher education in our century; they have molded a tradition that Christian education today must continue to draw upon as it adapts to changing cultural conditions. I would like, then, to sketch here the character of Reformational educational ideals in the belief that they contain some timeless and viable insights.

I

It is misleading to think of the Reformation movement in narrowly theological terms, for it embraced much more than changing religious ideals and conceptions. One of the greatest contributions of the Reformation was in the realm of education; in fact, education was probably the leading means by which Protestantism became entrenched in the countries where it eventually triumphed.

The Reformers' interest in education began with Luther. As early as 1523 he helped draft plans for a public fund to support education in

38

the city of Leisnig;[2] a year later he circulated his "Letter to the Mayors and Aldermen of all the Cities of Germany" urging education for all children;[3] and six years later he sent a "Sermon on the Duty of Sending Children to School" to all pastors for reading to their congregations. Next to theology and the church, education was Luther's lifelong preoccupation, and a new educational system in Germany became the foundation for the new Lutheran church.

Calvin was just as preoccupied with education as Luther was, and in 1538 he published a plan for a system of elementary education in Geneva.[4] In the years that followed, he was instrumental in organizing colleges or secondary schools in Geneva (where the Academy opened in 1559) and neighboring villages.[5] Students (including John Knox, the future leader of the Reformation in Scotland) flocked to these colleges from all over Europe, and both schools and students became leading forces in the spread of Calvin's influence.[6]

This interest in education spread from continental Protestantism to the English branch of the Protestant Reformation, especially to the Puritans, a trend that is revealed by the doubling of the number of grammar schools in England while the Puritans were in the ascendancy.[7] Between 1640 and 1660, Puritan authorities took an active role in regulating the nation's schools and establishing new ones, and the Propagation Act of 1641 produced sixty free schools in Wales (all of which disappeared, however, after the Restoration, the return of the monarchy under Charles II in 1660).[8]

John Knox, one of the prototypes for Puritan leaders, likewise lent impetus to education. He admonished the Great Council of Scotland that "your Honours be most careful for the virtuous education and godly upbringing of the youth of this realm."[9] Oliver Cromwell founded or refounded scores of elementary schools, sent commissioners throughout the nation to ascertain educational needs, and was personally responsible for establishing a college at Durham.[10] Contrary to a popular stereotype of the Puritans as uneducated, modern historians of education credit them with great educational accomplishments. J. W. Ashley Smith has concluded that "in several respects the Commonwealth was a period when university studies reached a peak," and Richard Greaves believes that in contrast to other groups, "with the exception of the Presbyterians, Puritans evidenced more interest in educational questions than issues of ecclesiastical polity."[11]

Zeal for education was equally evident in Puritan New England. No other English-speaking colonizers established a college as soon after their arrival as the Puritans did: in 1636, just six years after the establishment of the Massachusetts Bay colony, the General Court voted four hundred pounds "toward a school or college."[12] The account of this founding of Harvard College in *New England's First Fruits* (1643) is well known: "After God had carried us safe to New England and we had builded our houses, provided necessaries for our livelihood, reared convenient places for God's worship, and settled the civil government, one of the next things we longed for and looked for was to advance learning and perpetuate it to posterity."[13] Founding schools eventually became as much a hallmark of Puritanism in New England as it had been in England. A 1647 law of Massachusetts—followed by a similar law in Connecticut three years later—ordered the establishment of schools. Government rules soon ordered their use as well: the New Haven Code of 1655 ordered all parents and masters to provide also the means for educating their children and apprentices.[14]

In sum, one of the foremost activities of the first two centuries of Protestantism was a thoroughgoing involvement in education. The first educational lesson that we might learn from the Reformation, then, is that there can be (at least there has been) no long-term flourishing of the church apart from a concern to educate each generation. Moreover, although we associate Reformation education with the movement's great leaders like Luther and Calvin, Protestant support for education tended to be populist. Harvard College provides a case in point. It was kept alive during its early years in part by farmers who contributed wheat to support its teachers and students.[15]

II

What kind of education did Reformation and Puritan zeal produce? It produced an educational theory governed by goals. Unlike our day, which Albert Einstein characterized as having perfect means and confused goals, the early years of Protestant education were marked by inchoate means and well-defined goals. The Reformers knew what education was *for*, their ultimate goal being moral and religious growth in the life of every student. For John Knox, for example, the goals of education were "the virtuous education and godly upbringing of the youth of this realm" and "the advancement of Christ's glory."[16] The statutes of Emmanuel College, the most Puritan of the Cambridge University colleges, offered "three things which above all we desire all the Fellows of this college to attend to, to wit, the worship of God, the increase of the faith, and probity of morals."[17] American Puritans voiced the same goals. The immediate occasion of the founding of Harvard College was the determination not "to leave an illiterate ministry to the churches, when our present ministers shall lie in the dust."[18] Common sentiments of the day were expressed in the words of one Thomas Shepard to his son on the latter's entrance into Harvard: "Remember the end of your life, which is coming back again to God, and fellowship with God."[19] These thoughts are reflected also in a rule observed at the college that "every student be plainly instructed and earnestly pressed to consider well [that] the main end of his life and studies is to know God and Jesus Christ which is eternal life, John 17:3, and therefore to lay Christ in the bottom, as the only foundation of all sound knowledge and learning."[20] The 1642 charter of Harvard College consequently empowered the administration to make such rules as would further the college's members "in piety, morality, and learning."[21] In addition, the motto "In Christi Gloriam" appeared on the college seal of 1650.[22]

A religious conception of education is equally evident in the most famous educational act ever passed in America. In "Ye Old Deluder Act," which established free public education in Massachusetts in 1647, the General Court of Massachusetts asserted as the reason for establishing reading schools that it is "one chief project of ye old deluder, Satan, to keep men from the knowledge of the Scriptures."[23] In short, education—at least knowledge of the Scriptures, which would be furthered by the schools—can help to stave off the old deluder.

Protestant aversion to the notion of secular education devoid of a religious purpose received its greatest expression in Milton's famous words in "Of Education": "The end then of learning is to repair the ruins of our first parents by regaining to know God aright, and out of that knowledge to love him, to imitate him, to be like him."[24] Milton here defines education in terms of what it is designed to accomplish, and what it is designed to accomplish is more than intellectual. Even the terminology in which Milton couches the goal of education is tinged with theological concepts of redemption and sanctification.

This short look at the Reformation legacy reveals the belief in a Christian basis and goal for education. How then was this put into practice—what educational structures and practices did the moral and religious goals of Reformation education produce? There are two apparent emphases in this tradition's view of education: it emphasized on the one hand a certain curriculum and on the other a set of rules for college living—both of them designed to direct education to a Christian goal.

At the curricular level, the religious goal meant that the Bible and theological study were the most important ingredients in a student's study. Luther was again the first to sound the keynote: "Above all, the foremost reading for everybody, both in the universities and in the schools, should be Holy Scripture. . . . I would advise no one to send his child where the Holy Scriptures are not supreme."[25] The curriculum at Calvin's Geneva Academy suggests what this emphasis was like in practice. Of twenty-seven weekly lectures, three were in theology and three in ethics.[26] On Saturday afternoons, theology students heard ministers expound Scripture, and once a month they wrote and defended propositions in theology.[27]

The Puritans agreed with this emphasis on the Bible and theology. The statutes of Emmanuel College at Cambridge stated, "It is an ancient institution in the church . . . that schools and colleges be founded for the education of young men in all piety and good learning and especially in Holy Writ and theology, that being thus instructed they may thereafter teach true and pure religion."[28] The rule at Harvard was very similar: "Every one shall so exercise himself in reading the Scriptures twice a day that he shall be ready to give such an account of his proficiency therein . . . as his tutor shall require. . . ."[29] Students at Harvard "read lectures" in ethics twice a week, had "practice in the Bible" one afternoon each week, and "divinity catecheticall" once a week.[30] Concomitant to the emphasis on Bible knowledge was the preoccupation with language study. The Reformers and Puritans alike assumed that a leading goal of education was the mastery of Hebrew and Greek so a student could read the Bible in its original languages—a preoccupation that reveals the Renaissance roots of the Reformation.

The Bible and theology were central to the curriculum of the Reformers and Puritans, but that study was not isolated from other pursuits. The goal in fact was to measure all human knowledge—not just Christian knowledge—by the standard of Christian truth. Although Milton's proposed curriculum in "Of Education" contained an abundance of classical writers and texts, writers like Plato and Plutarch were subjected finally to "the determinate sentence of David or Solomon, or the evangels and apostilic scriptures."[31] Thomas Hall wrote that "we must . . . bring human learning home to divinity to be pruned and pared with spiritual wisdom."[32] A stipulation at Rivington School in Lancashire, England, one of many grammar schools founded by Puritans, was that the instruction must be in accord with "that which is contained in the holy Bible."[33]

Supplementing and supporting this curricular emphasis on the ethical and religious aims of education was a host of rules and practices that governed college living. The picture is largely the same, whether we look at the Geneva Academy or Emmanuel College or Harvard College. The themes are, moreover, immediately recognizable to anyone familiar with evangelical Protestant colleges in our own century.

Early Protestant colleges were concerned, for example, that students read their Bibles and hear the preaching of the Word outside of formal course work. At Emmanuel, students attended "public prayers" every day.[34] In Calvin's Academy, students "on some days" sang psalms from eleven to noon, on Wednesday mornings heard "a religious sermon," and spent "all Sunday in hearing religious worship and in meditating on sermons."[35] At Harvard, students were required to be in their tutor's chamber at seven in the morning and five in the evening for "opening the Scripture and prayer."[36]

Equally prominent was a certain moral earnestness that showed itself in rules of conduct for students. At the Geneva Academy, students were forbidden to dance, play cards or dice, go to taverns, take part in masquerades, or sing "indecent" songs.[37] Among the "vicious manners forbidden to every Fellow" at Emmanuel were frequenting "public taverns, houses of ill fame, or any improper place," engaging in "drinking parties and carousals," venturing "at all outside the precincts of the College after nine o'clock," and playing at "knucklebones, dice, or cards, even for recreation."[38] The rule at Harvard was more succinct: "None shall under any pretence whatsoever frequent the company and society of such men as live an unfit, and dissolute life."[39] If one wishes to get a "feel" for what it was actually like to be a conscientious student under these rules, see Samuel Ward's diary of his student days at Christ's College, Cambridge—one of the best sources there is.[40]

The Reformation and Puritan ideal was first of all a religious education. Its goal was the education of the whole person, morally and spiritually as well as intellectually. Both the curriculum and the campus climate were governed by a religious purpose aimed at the glory of God and the Christian nurture of the student, by a tone of moral earnestness, and by an antisecular bias that refused to separate education from religious concerns.

III

That the Reformers and Puritans advocated education oriented toward religious and moral goals is a familiar story. Not so familiar, but equally integral to their educational practices, was an emphasis on the liberal arts. While the aim of education was religious and moral, its content was humanistic. Protestants formed schools in order to ensure an educated clergy and a laity that could read the Bible, but they did not found what today we would call Bible schools, or even seminaries. Instead, they established institutions that we today would recognize as Christian liberal arts colleges.

The Reformation goal was the integration of faith and learning because the Reformers, and those who followed in their paths, believed that neither theology nor human knowledge was by itself sufficient for life in this world. Calvin did not wholly reject human knowledge when he wrote that "knowledge of all the sciences is so much smoke apart from the heavenly science of Christ."[41] Indeed, when he was planning a practical system of education he wrote, "Although we yield the first place to the Word of God, we do not reject good training.... The Word of God indeed is the foundation of all learning, but the liberal arts are aids to the full knowledge of the Word and are not to be despised."[42] Or, as Luther's colleague Philip Melanchthon put it, "Some teach absolutely nothing out of the Sacred Scriptures; some teach the children absolutely nothing but the Sacred Scriptures; both of which are not to be tolerated."[43]

What did the Reformers and Puritans mean by a liberal education, and why did they favor it? They defined their program partly in terms of its goal and partly in terms of its content. The goal was a person well grounded in all human disciplines and therefore able to perform competently in any area of life. Luther sounded the keynote in his letter "To the Councilmen of all Cities in Germany That They Establish and Maintain Christian Schools": "If I had children and could manage it, I would have them study not only languages and history, but also singing and music together with the whole of mathematics.... The ancient Greeks trained their children in these disciplines; ... they grew up to be people of wonderous ability, subsequently fit for everything."[44] "Fit for everything"—this has always been the goal of a liberal education, and it is what adherents of the Reformation wanted because they saw the usefulness of it. For example, the English Puritan preacher Robert Cleaver theorized that regardless of one's profession, "the more skill and knowledge he hath in the liberal sciences, so much the sooner shall he learn his occupation and the more ready . . . shall he be about the same."[45]

The most famous Puritan statement of the ideal appears in Milton's "Of Education," where he balances his definition of Christian education with this description of a liberal education: "I call therefore a complete and generous education that fits a man to perform justly, skilfully, and magnanimously, all the offices, both private and public, of peace and war."[46] At the heart of Milton's definition is the idea that an adequate education is that which is comprehensive, just as the Reformers and Puritans proposed. Such an education frees one to perform skilfully in every area of life; it is not a narrow vocational training.

Although the Puritans stressed the need to establish colleges to ensure a learned ministry, they did not believe that a knowledge of the Bible and theology alone was adequate to the task. Thus while the immediate occasion for the founding of Harvard College was the desire to perpetuate an educated ministry for the churches, Cotton Mather praised Harvard president Charles Chauncy not only for "how constantly he expounded the Scriptures to them in the college hall" but also "how learnedly he . . . conveyed all the liberal arts unto those that sat at his feet."[47] Chauncy himself said that "as far as it concerns a minister to preach all profitable and Scripture truths, the knowledge of arts and sciences is useful and expedient to him to hold them forth to his hearers."[48]

Even today, ministers in the Reformed or Puritan tradition are expected to have a college education in addition to their seminary training, in contrast to what prevails in some other evangelical traditions. This emphasis can be traced back to the Reformation. The British Puritan Richard Bernard asked, "What art or science is there which a divine shall not stand in need of? . . . Grammar, rhetoric, logic, physics, mathematics, metaphysics, ethics, politics, economics, history, and military discipline" are all useful.[49] William Shurtleff said in a sermon that "the knowledge not only of the learned languages but of the whole circle of arts and sciences may be of use to a Gospel minister."[50] And Matthew Swallow praised his pastor, John Cotton, for excelling "in the knowledge of the arts and tongues, and in all kind of learning divine and human."[51]

Along with the usefulness of the liberal arts, there was the delight that they bring to an educated person. In his sermon "On Keeping Children in School," Luther spoke of "the pure pleasure a man gets from having studied, even though he never holds an office of any kind, how at home by himself he can read all kinds of things, talk and associate with educated people."[52] Richard Holdsworth, a master at Emmanuel College, drew up a list of readings specifically for people who came to college purely for enrichment, "not with intention to make scholarship their profession, but only to get such learning as may serve for delight and ornament and such as the want whereof would speak a defect in breeding rather than scholarship."[53] Oliver Cromwell, in his own way a devotee of culture, wrote regarding his son, "I would have Richard mind and understand Business, read a little History, study the Mathematics and Cosmography: these are good, with subordination to the things of God."[54]

The question remains whether this theoretical commitment to the broad spectrum of human knowledge actually found its way into the curriculum. In fact, it did. Of twenty-seven weekly lectures in the Geneva Academy five were in Greek orators and poets, three in physics and mathematics, and five in dialectic and rhetoric (remember, as noted above, that there were only three lectures in theology and three in ethics each week). Texts included works by Vergil, Cicero, Ovid, Livy, Homer, Aristotle, Plato, and Plutarch.[55] The bylaws also prescribed that three "public professors" at the college be named in the areas of "Hebrew, Greek, and the liberal arts."[56]

The curriculum at Harvard was similarly humanistic in the Renaissance sense of comprehensiveness and classical emphasis. Ministerial students not only learned to read the Bible in its original languages and to expound theology; they also studied mathematics, astronomy, logic, rhetoric, philosophy, poetry, ethics, and history.[57] J. W. Ashley Smith concludes that "there was no distinction between a liberal and a theological education, and its two sources were first, Calvinism, and second, Aristotle."[58] Samuel E. Morison similarly concludes that "Puritanism in New England preserved far more of the humanist tradition than did non-puritanism in the other English colonies."[59] And finally Perry Miller notes that "perhaps we have laid bare the innermost essence of the Puritan mind when we find that its highest philosophical reach was a systematic delineation of the liberal arts."[60]

Part of the reason the Reformers and the Puritans generally saw the value of studying pagan classical writers was their acceptance of the doctrine of common grace, according to which God's grace is bestowed upon and expressed through all people, not just Christians. Luther asserted that "the fine liberal arts, invented and brought to light by learned and outstanding people—even though those people were heathen—are serviceable and useful to people for this life. Moreover, they are creations and noble, precious gifts. . . . [God] has used them and still uses them according to his good pleasure, for the praise, honor, and glory of his holy name."[61] Increase Mather claimed as well that "some among the heathen have been notable moralists, such as Cato, Seneca, Aristides, etc.," and he urged students at Harvard to "find a friend in Plato, a friend in Socrates and . . . in Aristotle."[62] And Charles Chauncy asked in a commencement sermon, "Who can deny but that there are found many excellent and divine moral truths in Plato, Aristotle, Plutarch, Seneca, etc.?"[63]

We must remember in this regard that the Reformation and the Renaissance went hand in hand for more than a century in northern Europe. The two movements had much in common, including a repudiation of the medieval church, a desire to return to a more distant past, and a preoccupation with ancient written texts as the key to the recovery of truth. That is why C. S. Lewis can write that "there was no necessary enmity between Puritans and humanists. They were often the same people, and nearly always the same sort of people: the young men in the Movement, the impatient progressives demanding a 'clean sweep.'"[64]

The correspondence between Puritans and humanists becomes clear when we look at the following excerpts from a college curriculum: "Easy Latin sentences learnt orally, and repeated as practice in conversation . . . the eclogues of Vergil read . . . Latin syntax continued. Cicero's *Letters* begun; composition exercises are based on these. . . . Cicero, *Letters, De Amicitia, De Senectute,* these treatises to be turned into Greek. The *Aeneid,* Caesar, and Isocrates read. . . . Homer and Vergil also analysed for rhetorical purposes." Is this curriculum based on humanistic ideals or on Reformation goals? In fact the description comes from the course of study at Calvin's Geneva Academy.[65] Milton's discussion in "Of Education" reveals the same inclination. It should not surprise us that C. H. Conley's detailed study reveals that the first translators of classical texts into English were radical Protestants or Puritans.[66] This humanistic bias was equally evident in the curricula of the dissenting academies that represented the last chapter in the history of Reformation educational ideals.[67]

As Christian humanists, the Reformers endorsed the study of both the arts and the sciences. In regard to the former, there was a strong conviction that theology and biblical studies would thrive only if the study of literature and the humanities flourished. The strongest statement comes from Luther: "I am persuaded that without knowledge of literature pure theology cannot at all endure, just as heretofore, when letters have declined and lain prostrate, theology, too, has wretchedly fallen and lain prostrate; nay, I see that there has never been a great revelation of the Word of God unless He has first prepared the way by the rise and prosperity of languages and letters."[68] Increase Mather may have had Luther's statement in mind when he told the legislature that "some have well and truly observed that the interest of religion and good literature hath risen and fallen together."[69]

Reformation Protestants also gave impetus to the study and advancement of the sciences. Indeed, the question of whether they were actually responsible for the rise of modern science has become an enormously learned debate.[70] What is indisputable is that they helped produce the climate in which modern science arose and flourished and also that they accepted the sciences into their course of study. The students at Calvin's academy had three lectures each week in physics and mathematics;[71] and those at Harvard studied physics, astronomy, botany, and natural science.[72]

This, then, was the educational ideal of Reformation Protestantism: a comprehensive study of human knowledge in all its branches within a context of biblical revelation. The seven liberal arts were "a circle of seven sections of which the center is God."[73] The result was what today we would call Christian liberal arts education—the pursuit of the integration of all human knowledge with the Christian faith, and the formation of people qualified to function competently in all areas of life.

The shape of Reformation and Puritan education as I have described it was firmly rooted in a coherent theology that I can only summarize here. It began with a conviction that all truth comes from God and has been revealed by God in two books—the Bible and nature. In the areas the Bible directly addresses, it is authoritative; and human knowledge in those areas is subordinate to the words of Scripture. Yet human knowledge is not everywhere secondary and derivative. Buttressing the study of art and science is the doctrine of common grace, which asserts that God has endowed all people, believers and unbelievers alike, with a capacity for truth, goodness, and beauty.

The Reformers and Puritans regarded piety and learning as complementary parts of a whole. The phrases they used in talking about schools and education reveal their profound rejection of any antagonism between knowledge and faith: "seed plots of piety and the liberal arts"; "piety, morality, and learning"; "knowledge and godliness"; "progress in learning and godliness"; "that fit persons of approved piety and learning may . . . employ themselves in the education of children in piety and good literature."[74] They all draw the two together.

IV

Of what importance is the Reformation and Puritan tradition today? First, the Protestant tradition that I have outlined gives contemporary Protestant education a place to stand. When considered in terms of the total educational scene today, after a century of academic secularization, professionalization, and fragmentation, Christian liberal arts education is a tiny trickle. Yet history shows that its heritage is the original mainstream of Western education. While in the contemporary context Christian liberal arts education can hardly avoid seeming like an anomaly, from the perspective of the entire history of Western education secular and vocational education is the true and recent aberration.

Second, a scrutiny of the educational ideas of the Reformers and Puritans helps define what constitutes the Protestant tradition in education. In some conservative Protestant circles today, "secular humanism" has become the popular whipping boy. The leading voices of the conservative movement make disparaging comments about knowledge that comes from non-Christian sources. Biblical and theological studies increasingly squeeze other subjects out of the curriculum. There is presently a very real danger that this movement will come to be seen— in the popular conception at least—as the mainstream Protestant tradition of education. Members of the movement itself already seem to think that they stand within the traditional Protestant mainstream.

A look at the Reformation's educational ideals reveals something far different, however. The Reformers and Puritans did not disparage human knowledge and culture. Rather, they were champions of the idea that it was good to know the best of Western thought and culture, regardless of whether it came from Christian or pagan sources. These leaders were not content to know only the Bible and Christian theology but sought to infuse a Christian perspective into all of life and thought. Hallmarks of the Reformation tradition were education of the whole person for all of life, the interaction of the Christian faith with all human knowledge, and an embracing of all that is true, good, and beautiful in human culture.

Third, the Reformation tradition suggests that the modern attempt to drive a wedge between liberal arts education and social responsibility is a fallacy. When we look at the curricula of Protestant schools of the Reformation era, we are inclined to regard them as distanced or divorced from everyday life. They relied on a study of ancient languages and rhetoric more than anything else. What could possibly be farther removed from the reform of society than that? That may be how it seems; yet let us allow the record of the Reformers and Puritans to speak for itself. They did, in fact, turn their world upside down. In their view, a classical, liberal education was a preparation for social responsibility. Milton conceived of his heavily classical curriculum as a means of equipping people to perform "all the offices, both private and public, of peace and war,"[75] and his own education enabled him both to write poetry and to become one of the most influential public figures of his day.

For the Reformers and Puritans, the aim of education was social responsibility; indeed, they saw it as the chief tool for reforming society and the church. John Knox exhorted parents to educate their children "to the profit of the church and to the commonwealth."[76] In North America, the Roxbury Act of 1645 established education "as a means of the fitting of instruments for public service in church and commonwealth."[77]

With a Reformational model, then, we should avoid panic when faced with the contemporary assault on liberal education for its alleged impracticality. A scholar will always have resources that a technician lacks. Preachers who are widely read and broadly educated will preach more interesting and applicable sermons than those who know only the Bible and theology.

A fourth legacy of Reformed and Puritan education that remains a valid guide for us today is its insistence on wholeness in education. History shows how difficult it is to maintain a balance between intellectual education of the mind and spiritual and moral education. The two are always engaged in a tug of war on Christian campuses. Students and teachers who get caught up in the intellectual quest seem prone to find little time for spiritual nurture, while those who are morally and spiritually earnest easily neglect the pursuit of intellectual excellence. Limitations of time are sufficient in themselves to cause one to veer to one side of the dichotomy or the other. The schools of the Reformation era, however, afford a therapeutic glimpse of a balanced educational experience. In these colleges, Milton's two famous definitions of education come together: to become like God and to prepare oneself to do well all that a person might be called to do.

Finally, contemporary Christian educators should explore Reformation ideals in education to get a focus on the educational practices that are inherent in their religious premises. Too much has intervened between the Reformation and contemporary Christian education to discern the precise lines of historical influence, or to attempt a simple repristination of our academic life. Yet there is a "deep structure" that characterizes Christian education in any era. Reformed and Puritan colleges can help us to see more clearly the educational program that should follow when we assent to the authority of the Bible, acknowledge God as creator of the world and the source of all truth, seek to serve God and humanity, and form a biblical view of the person.

In sum, the educational ideals of the Reformation can spare us from several dead-ends in Christian education today. In a day when education has increasingly conformed to the specialization of modern society, the Reformed tradition offers a picture of comprehensive education. To a pluralistic world in which teachers despair of finding common ground with their classes, the Reformed tradition holds out the possibility of knowledge grounded in a shared theology and a shared acceptance of the authority of the Bible. At a time when education has become purely intellectual and its aim is defined in narrowly vocational and self-serving terms, the Reformed tradition stands for education that is moral and spiritual as well as intellectual, and designed to serve God and society.

NOTES

1. T. S. Eliot, *Essays Ancient and Modern* (New York: Harcourt, Brace and Company, 1932, 1936), 169.

2. Joan Simon, *Education and Society in Tudor England* (Cambridge: Cambridge University Press, 1967), 131.

3. Another important document is Luther's "Letter to the Christian Nobility of the German Nation Respecting the Reformation of the Christian Estate" (1520).

4. Ellwood P. Cubberly, *A Brief History of Education* (Boston: Houghton Mifflin, 1922), 175.

5. Cubberly, *Brief History of Education*, 175; J. B. Babington, *The Reformation* (1901; reprint, Port Washington, N.Y.: Kennikat Press, 1971), 172-73.

6. For more on Calvin's Academy, see W. Stanford Reid, "Calvin and the Founding of the Academy at Geneva," *Westminster Theological Journal* 18 (1955): 1-33.

7. M. M. Knappen, *Tudor Puritanism* (Chicago: University of Chicago Press, 1939), 469. Foster Watson likewise concludes that "the English Grammar Schools gained much of their vitality and inspiration from . . . Puritanism"; Watson, *The English Grammar Schools to 1660: Their Curriculum and Practice* (Cambridge: Cambridge University Press, 1908), 538-39.

8. Margaret James, *Social Problems and Policy During the Puritan Revolution, 1640–1660* (1930; reprint, New York: Barnes and Noble, 1966), 314-26.

9. John Knox, "Book of Discipline," in *Puritanism in Tudor England*, ed. H. C. Porter (Columbia: University of South Carolina Press, 1971), 19.

10. Richard L. Greaves, *The Puritan Revolution and Educational Thought* (New Brunswick, N.J.: Rutgers University Press, 1969), 15; Maurice Ashley, *Oliver Cromwell and the Puritan Revolution* (London: English Universities Press, 1958), 142.

11. J. W. Ashley Smith, *The Birth of Modern Education: The Contribution of the Dissenting Academies 1660–1800* (London: Independent Press, 1954), 12; Greaves, *The Puritan Revolution*, 329.

12. *New England's First Fruits*, in *The Puritans*, ed. Perry Miller and Thomas H. Johnson (New York: Harper Torchbooks, 1963), 2: 700.

13. Ibid.

14. Cubberly, *Brief History of Education*, 195-96.

15. Miller and Johnson, introduction to *The Puritans*, 1: 14.

16. Knox, in Porter, *Puritanism in Tudor England*, 198.

17. Porter, *Puritanism in Tudor England*, 185.

18. *New England's First Fruits*, in Miller and Johnson, *The Puritans*, 2: 701.

19. Thomas Shepard, letter to a son, in Miller and Johnson, *The Puritans*, 2: 715.

20. *New England's First Fruits*, in Miller and Johnson, *The Puritans*, 2: 702.

21. See Kenneth B. Murdock, *Increase Mather: The Foremost American Puritan* (Cambridge: Harvard University Press, 1925), 45.

22. See Samuel E. Morison, *Three Centuries of Harvard, 1636–1936* (Cambridge: Harvard University Press, 1936), 24.

23. Massachusetts Laws of 1648, as quoted in Edmund Morgan, *The Puritan Family* (1944; reprint, New York: Harper and Row, 1966), 88.

24. Milton, "Of Education," in *Complete Prose Works* (New Haven: Yale University Press, 1959), 2: 366-67.

25. Luther, "To the Councilmen of all Cities in Germany That They Establish and Maintain Christian Schools," in *Luther's Works* (Philadelphia: Muhlenberg, 1962), 45: 369-70.

26. See "Bylaws of the Academy of Geneva," in Frederick Eby, *Early Protestant Educators* (1931; reprint, New York: AMS, 1971), 253.

27. See ibid., 267.

28. Porter, *Puritanism in Tudor England*, 182.

29. *New England's First Fruits*, in Miller and Johnson, *The Puritans*, 2: 702.

30. See Ellwood P. Cubberly, *Readings in the History of Education* (Boston: Houghton Mifflin, 1920), 293-94.

31. Milton, "Of Education," in *Complete Prose Works*, 2: 397.

32. Thomas Hall, "Vindiciae Literarum," as quoted in Greaves, *The Puritan Revolution*, 122.

33. "Victoria County History of Lancashire," as quoted in Derek Wilson, *The People and the Book: The Revolutionary Impact of the English Bible 1380–1611* (London: Barrie and Jenkins, 1976), 136.

34. Porter, *Puritanism in Tudor England*, 185.

35. Eby, *Early Protestant Educators*, 258-59.

36. Cubberly, *Readings in the History of Education*, 292.

37. See Georgia Harkness, *John Calvin: The Man and His Ethics* (Nashville: Abingdon, 1958), 53.

38. Porter, *Puritanism in Tudor England*, 187-88.

39. Cubberly, *Readings in the History of Education*, 292.

40. Samuel Ward's diary is printed in *Two Elizabethan Puritan Diaries*, ed. M. M. Knappen (1933; reprint, Gloucester, Mass.: Peter Smith, 1966). This diary is a record of self-accusation for personal failings and is unwittingly among the funniest of all Puritan documents.

41. Calvin, commentary on 1 Cor. 1:20, in *The First Epistle of Paul the Apostle to the Corinthians*, trans. John W. Fraser (Grand Rapids: Eerdmans, 1960), 38.

42. Calvin, quoted in Earle E. Cairns, "The Puritan Philosophy of Education," *Bibliotheca Sacra* 104 (1947): 327.

43. Melanchthon, quoted by Carl S. Meyer, "Philip Melanchthon," in *A History of Religious Educators*, ed. Elmer L. Towns (Grand Rapids: Baker, 1975), 152.

44. Luther, letter "To the Councilmen," in *Luther's Works*, 45: 369-70.

45. Robert Cleaver, in "A Godly Form of Household Government," quoted in Knappen, *Tudor Puritanism*, 468.

46. Milton, "Of Education," in *Complete Prose Works*, 2: 377-79.

47. Cotton Mather, in *Magnalia Christi Americana*, quoted by Samuel E. Morison, *Harvard College in the Seventeenth Century* (Cambridge: Harvard University Press, 1936), 1: 324. Elsewhere Mather voiced his dream to "fill the country with a liberal education"; see his *Serviceable Man*, quoted in Perry Miller, *Nature's Nation* (Cambridge: Harvard University Press, 1967), 48.

48. Charles Chauncy, quoted in Perry Miller, *The New England Mind: The Seventeenth Century* (1939; reprint, Cambridge: Harvard University Press, 1954), 85.

49. Richard Bernard, *The Faithful Shepherd*, quoted in William Haller, *The Rise of Puritanism* (New York: Columbia University Press, 1938), 138.

50. William Shurtleff, "The Labour that Attends the Gospel Ministry," quoted in Morison, *Harvard College in the Seventeenth Century*, 1: 166. Thomas G. Wright claims that Cotton Mather's writings show his acquaintance with over three hundred authors, including Aristotle, Cato, Livy, Homer, Ovid, Plutarch, Vergil, and Tacitus; see his *Literary Culture in Early New England, 1620–1730* (1920; reprint, New York: Russell and Russell, 1966), 244-53.

51. Matthew Swallow, quoted in Miller, *The New England Mind: The Seventeenth*

Century, 311. Cotton Mather praised John Cotton for the same qualities, calling him "a most universal scholar, and living system of the liberal arts and a walking library"; see Mather, *Magnalia Christi Americana,* quoted in W. Fraser Mitchell, *English Pulpit Oratory from Andrewes to Tillotson* (London: SPCK, 1932), 102.

52. Luther, "On Keeping Children in School," in *Luther's Works,* 46: 243.

53. Richard Holdsworth, quoted in Mark H. Curtis, *Oxford and Cambridge in Transition, 1558–1642* (Oxford: Oxford University Press, 1959), 131.

54. Oliver Cromwell, quoted in F. H. Hayward, *The Unknown Cromwell* (London: George Allen and Unwin, 1934), 351.

55. Eby, *Early Protestant Educators,* 253; Reid, "Calvin and the Founding of the Academy at Geneva," 13, 16.

56. Eby, *Early Protestant Educators,* 265.

57. Miller and Johnson, *The Puritans,* 2: 698-704.

58. Smith, *Birth of Modern Education,* 71.

59. Samuel E. Morison, *The Intellectual Life of Colonial New England* (New York: Washington Square, 1956), 17.

60. Miller, *The New England Mind: The Seventeenth Century,* 161.

61. Luther's comment, from an inscription in a book of classical poetry, is cited in Ewald M. Plass, ed., *What Luther Says: An Anthology* (St. Louis: Concordia, 1959), 1: 450. Calvin makes the same point in both the *Institutes of the Christian Religion* (II.ii.15-16) and his commentaries. In his comments on Genesis 4:20, Calvin affirms as God-given "the liberal arts and sciences," even though they "have descended to us from the heathen"; see his *Commentary on the First Book of Moses,* trans. John King (Grand Rapids: Eerdmans, 1948), 218.

62. Increase Mather, "Woe to Drunkards," in Miller and Johnson, *The Puritans,* 1: 22; and idem, "A Presidential Address," in Miller and Johnson, *The Puritans,* 2: 721.

63. Chauncy, in Miller and Johnson, *The Puritans,* 2: 706.

64. C. S. Lewis, *Studies in Medieval and Renaissance Literature* (Cambridge: Cambridge University Press, 1966), 122. The art historian Eric Mercer similarly concludes, "Where they had so much in common it is not always possible to draw a distinction between the reflection of Renaissance and of Reformation ideas. . . . At first . . . the two worked in harmony and many of the most Renaissance-conscious men of the mid-century were the most extreme Protestants." Mercer, *English Art, 1553–1625* (Oxford: Oxford University Press, 1962), 6-7.

65. Cubberly, *Readings in the History of Education,* 273. Quirinus Breen states that Calvin's thought on the matter of humanistic education can be expressed in the words, "Even though you would be a preacher, be first a humanist." Breen, *John Calvin: A Study in French Humanism* (Grand Rapids: Eerdmans, 1931), 154-55. Curtis, in *Oxford and Cambridge in Transition,* documents the extent to which Puritan education also consisted of classical texts.

66. Conley speaks of the "inherent harmony between Protestantism and classicism." *The First English Translators of the Classics* (New Haven: Yale University Press, 1927), 76. Knappen claims that "in the schools where Puritan influence was strongest, Cicero and Ovid, Demosthenes and Homer continued to dominate the course of study." *Tudor Puritanism,* 473.

67. The curriculum of the dissenting schools has been surveyed in these studies: Curtis, *Oxford and Cambridge in Transition;* H. McLachlan, *English Education under the Test Acts, Being the History of the Non-Conformist Academies, 1662–1820* (Manchester: Manchester University Press, 1931); J. W. Ashley Smith, *The Birth of Modern Education;* and Irene Parker, *Dissenting Academies in England* (Cambridge:

Cambridge University Press, 1914). In addition, Roland M. Frye, *Perspective on Man: Literature and the Christian Tradition* (Philadelphia: Westminster, 1961), 178-79, claims that the dissenting academies were pioneers in the academic study of English literature.

68. Luther, in *Luther's Correspondence, 1521–1530*, trans. Preserved Smith and Charles M. Jacobs (Philadelphia: Lutheran Publication Society, 1918), 2: 176.

69. Increase Mather, "Discourse Concerning the Danger of Apostacy," in Miller and Johnson, *The Puritans*, 1: 21.

70. The strongest case for Puritan influence on modern science is Robert K. Merton's book *Science, Technology, and Society in Seventeenth Century England* (New York: Howard Fertig, 1970). See also Christopher Hill, *Intellectual Origins of the English Revolution* (Oxford: Oxford University Press, 1965); and John Dillenberger, *Protestant Thought and Natural Science* (Garden City, N.Y.: Doubleday, 1960). For some key essays and full bibliographic data on the ongoing debate, the best source is Charles Webster, ed., *The Intellectual Revolution of the Seventeenth Century* (London: Routledge and Kegan Paul, 1974).

71. Eby, *Early Protestant Educators*, 253.

72. *New England's First Fruits*, in Miller and Johnson, *The Puritans*, 2: 703-4.

73. The quote is from a Harvard thesis of 1607, cited in Miller, *The New England Mind: The Seventeenth Century*, 160.

74. I have taken the quoted phrases, seriatim, from John Milton, "An Apology against a Pamphlet," in *Complete Prose Works*, 1: 923; the 1642 Charter of Harvard College; the 1650 Charter of Harvard College; *New England's First Fruits;* and the Parliamentary Propagation Act of 1641.

75. Milton, "Of Education," in *Complete Prose Works*, 2: 379.

76. Knox, quoted in Porter, *Puritanism in Tudor England*, 199.

77. Quoted by Cairns, "The Puritan Philosophy of Education," 331.

The Revolution, the Enlightenment, and Christian Higher Education in the Early Republic

Mark A. Noll

The 1807 summer semester at Princeton College began on May 8 with an unusual ceremony. The school was reassembling under a cloud, for a student insurrection had closed the college at the end of the winter semester in early April. During that semester twelve of Princeton's two hundred students had been disciplined by the faculty for offenses ranging from drunkenness and disorder to assaults upon residents of the village and insults directed at the faculty. Two fires were set in the college basement, and miscreants burned the outhouse to the ground. Then, in late March, 160 students signed a petition to overturn a faculty decision suspending three of their fellows. When the professors rejected the petition as evidence of an illegal conspiracy, tumult and violence ensued. The students took over the college, and the authorities shut the school down. But before they did they suspended over half the student body.

Now the new semester was at hand. One hundred ten students had returned, including some of the suspended scholars who were petitioning for readmission. Princeton's board of trustees directed its most distinguished member, Elias Boudinot, to prepare a formal admonition. Boudinot, president of the United States Congress in 1783, director of the United States Mint from 1795 to 1805, a friend of George Washington, and a respected lay leader in the Presbyterian Church, was a man to command attention.

As he addressed the Princeton scholars, he concluded that the disturbances of the winter semester were the result of anti-Christian ideas being spread abroad in the world at large. Principal villains in Boudinot's mind were William Godwin, the English radical who scoffed at political tradition and conventional morality, David Hume, Scotland's skeptical epistemologist, and Tom Paine, who had turned from writing propaganda for American independence to promoting

Deism. The "loathsome deformity" characterizing the ideas of these men entailed no less than the subversion of "the Ideas and Experience of Ages." Students, Boudinot thought, "will naturally enquire what effect these boasted Systems have produced upon social order, either in States or subordinate communities; and how far they have added to the stock of human happiness." Since these figures taught ideas that sapped "all the foundations of Society," leveled "all the props of morality," and extinguished "every Sentiment which raises [Humans] above the Brute," Boudinot felt sure his hearers would join him in embracing "that blessed *System of Life and Immortality,* which has been brought to light by the divine Messenger from Heaven, and which it has always been . . . the principal Aim of this Institution, to impress upon your minds and establish in your hearts." Princeton existed, as Boudinot trusted the students themselves would exist, "to render this blessed System effectually instrumental to your eternal Interests." And so, with students at least reasonably reconciled to their tasks, a new semester began.[1]

Several questions about this incident remain for the modern observer. Why did Boudinot perceive Godwin, Hume, and Paine as the inciters of Princeton's riot? How could a proper collegiate education counter the threats posed by them? And why did he picture Christianity and infidelity as "systems" locked in mortal combat? Answers to these questions are somewhat involved, but they make it possible to place the history of Christian higher education in America between the Revolution and the Civil War within the appropriate external contexts, social as well as religious, political as well as intellectual.

The Revolutionary Generation

From the end of the French and Indian War in 1763 to well beyond the turn of the century, America's cultural values were in flux.[2] Within the space of a half-century, Americans threw over the rule of the world's most powerful nation. They also dallied with several forms of the European Enlightenment before coming to embrace a conservative expression of that great movement, embarked on a love affair with the idea of liberty which had both bracing and unsettling consequences, and reestablished Christian thinking and the churches on new foundations. It is hardly surprising that in this rapid realignment of values, the nature of instruction at the country's colleges, and the colleges themselves, also changed dramatically.

Intellectual change had much to do with the consuming passion of the American Revolution. Edmund S. Morgan has summarized perceptively the long-term intellectual results of that era: "In 1740 America's leading intellectuals were clergymen and thought about theology; in 1790 they were statesmen and thought about politics. . . . One may properly consider the American Revolution . . . to mean the substitution of political for clerical leadership and of politics for religion as the most challenging area of human thought and endeavor."[3] This intellectual revolution had immediate implications for the new nation's colleges. Most obviously, with the excitement of politics in the Revolutionary age, the number of graduates choosing the ministry declined rapidly in favor of careers in law, business, and public service. American colleges have never trained as high a proportion of ministers since the colonial period as they did then. Princeton's experience was not atypical when it saw the proportion of its graduates entering the ministry decline from 47 percent during the period 1748–1775 to 13 percent for the period 1776–1806.[4]

The changes underway in the new United States, however, involved much more than a mere shift in the vocational preference of college graduates. In simplest terms, the entire Revolutionary generation represented the abandonment of tradition, history, and hierarchy in favor of innovation, the future, and egalitarianism. It was a time when the heady wine of liberty communicated an intoxicating message to almost every sphere of American life.[5]

The ideology that lay behind the War for Independence certainly played an important part in the change of expectations and plans. Stress on the corruption of the Old World, insistence upon "natural rights" in the face of Parliament's "tyranny," and a vision of history as a never-ending struggle between forces of oppression and freedom shaped perceptions not only in politics but in every sphere of American life. Thus upstart religious bodies broke from the settled traditions of established denominations; the older denominations themselves were forced to reconstitute on new, particularly American, principles; formerly respected professions like the law came under attack as unjustly privileged sanctums; and politicians began to make much of "the people."[6] In general, the forces which led both to Tocqueville's *Democracy* and to Andrew Jackson's "age of the common man" were set in motion.

Perhaps even more important than the specific ideology of the Revolution were the general intellectual guidelines that many

Americans embraced at this time. In order to justify resistance to Great Britain, in order to challenge the heavy hand of encrusted tradition, and in order to strike out confidently on behalf of liberty, Americans turned enthusiastically to a conservative stream of the European Enlightenment.

In talking about this subject it is useful to distinguish between different ways in which Americans perceived the Enlightenment in Europe. The historian Henry May has provided four convenient categories for this purpose.[7] What May calls the *moderate* Enlightenment, first, is exemplified by the work of the Englishmen Isaac Newton and John Locke.[8] It was characterized by explanations of natural and human phenomena cast in comprehensive mechanistic and mathematical terms. Its practitioners gloried in the advances achieved by the empirical pursuit of natural law, but they did not see these advances as irreligious or as an assault upon traditional moral principles.

Exemplars of a *skeptical* Enlightenment, on the other hand, did contend that the advances of the eighteenth century superceded more than just the natural science of the past.[9] In France, Voltaire caustically contrasted the gaudy trophies of unfettered inquiry with the dreary strictures of *l'infame,* traditions of the established church and state. Rousseau cast aside the encumbrance of traditional morality in order to exalt the sacred intuitions of the beautiful soul. And in Great Britain the much less sensational David Hume wrote philosophical treatises that seemed to question all the commonplaces of the knowing process itself.

Toward the end of the eighteenth century the Enlightenment temper produced figures whose thought was more *revolutionary* than skeptical.[10] These were the figures that so troubled Elias Boudinot. The attacks of peripatetic Tom Paine upon monarchy and orthodoxy, the affronts to traditional morality of William Godwin, and the anarchy unleashed by the French revolution all seemed to assault the very foundations of the Christian West.

In contrast to these first three styles of Enlightenment—moderate, skeptical, and revolutionary—the fourth has received much less attention. It is what Henry May calls the *didactic* Enlightenment, centered in the universities of Scotland.[11] Here philosophers and moralists like Thomas Reid and Dugald Stewart wrestled with radical implications of the continental Enlightenment and sought to bring them under control. Yet these individuals too held certain commitments in common with representatives of the other varieties of the Enlightenment. With other figures of the European Enlightenment, these men also displayed a greater interest in secular than in sacred matters, a preference for natural explanations over supernatural ones, and a general inclination to slight reasoned deduction and revelation as paths to truth in favor of observation and experimentation.[12]

When we think of the Enlightenment, we commonly consider only those groups that May has called skeptical and revolutionary, but to do so leaves the false impression that the new United States remained outside the orbit of Enlightened thought. It is true that American intellectual opinion turned passionately against radical extensions of eighteenth-century European ideas.[13] Yet Americans were nonetheless very receptive to Enlightened voices from Great Britain such as Newton, Locke, and Reid. While rejecting the Deism, agnosticism, and moral revolution of the Enlightenment, American intellectuals were still very much taken with its commitment to science, its love affair with the individual, and its Lockean commitment to empiricism as *the* road to truth.[14] And these commitments were as thoroughly modern, as thoroughly a part of the Enlightenment, as the more radical sentiments of Voltaire and Hume.

It is from these moderate figures that Boudinot drew support for a Christian "system" opposing the thought of the Enlightenment's skeptics and radicals. They made it possible to mount a tradition-free, scientific defense of natural law, social liberty, and the innate powers of human intellect and morality. The didactic Enlightenment had been vital for America's politicians in the Revolutionary era because it provided a means to hold in check the centrifugal forces of liberty without having to fall back onto the hierarchical authoritarianism of Europe. It was similarly important for America's Christians. The didactic Enlightenment enabled them to agree with the wider American culture in rejecting the corruption of the past while yet maintaining the truthfulness of historic Christianity. As might be expected, such a broad intellectual movement also had great impact on American colleges.

The didactic Enlightenment made its most notable advances in the colleges during and immediately following the War for Independence. Christian leaders like John Witherspoon (1723–1794), president of Princeton, and Timothy Dwight (1752–1817), president of Yale, faced two pressing needs, one theoretical, the other practical. The theoretical task was nothing less than to defend the knowability and reality of the external world in response to a threat epitomized by the speculative philosophy of David Hume. How could Americans maintain liberty, justice, and order if a philosophical sophistry was unleashed that made such concepts meaningless? The practical need was to save Christian social morality from the threats of infidelity, French anarchy, and the wanton antinomianism released by the Revolution itself.[15] Committed as they were to the freedom the War for Independence had gained, leaders like Witherspoon and Dwight nonetheless looked for ways to restrain the instability evidenced by rioters in western Massachusetts under Daniel Shays, by Masonic-like conspirators under the banner of the Bavarian Illuminati, and by the suspect humanism of political theorists like Thomas Jefferson.

These two needs, furthermore, cried to be addressed with *scientific* responses, for the great influence of Newton and Locke had already made its mark in America. It was an Englishman, Alexander Pope, who wrote, "Nature and Nature's laws lay hid in Night. / God said, Let Newton be! and all was Light," but his sentiment spoke for the New World as well.[16] In addition, Americans possessed an exaggerated fondness for Francis Bacon and the methods of empirical and inductive science he promoted.[17] They also had great admiration for John Locke, whose defense of English liberty in 1688 and his charting of "Human Understanding" had made his entire point of view extraordinarily influential in America.[18] By the Revolutionary period, in other words, the American idea of a good "explanation" was that which could rest on a Baconian appeal to "the facts," which could reduce complex phenomena to Newtonian-like laws, and which, following John Locke, could base knowledge on the orderly classification of sense experience.[19]

The problems confronting conservative Christian leaders in the new United States—like the Congregationalist Dwight and the Presbyterian Witherspoon—can be restated as follows. First, the theoretical, epistemological problem: How do we know that our ideas, which are formed by our sense experience, correspond to the reality of the external world? To suggest that no external reality exists beyond the minds of God and humans, as Bishop George Berkeley had done, or to affirm with David Hume that we can never know if our ideas match what is "out there," was a solution too upsetting for American intellectuals. Second was the practical, ethical problem: How do we know that our moral convictions have authority if our ideas come only from our senses? That is, given the Lockean belief that all our ideas—including our idea of what is right and wrong—come through sense experience, is it possible to defend time-honored Christian social principles? How do we know that God rewards good and evil appropriately, that citizens should be loyal to church and state, that political equality does not necessarily mean social equality? In the troubling days of the Confederation period, and on into the still-perilous years under the Constitution, these questions seemed to strike at the very hope for an orderly, moral, and godly United States. In terms of the four kinds of Enlightenment sketched above, many Christians in the new United States felt threatened by the agnosticism, or even atheism, of the skeptical Enlightenment. They also felt threatened by the social radicalism of the revolutionary Enlightenment.

In the two-pronged effort to overcome crises in the Revolutionary period and to exploit its enthusiasms, educated American Christians allied their own faith with the mentality of the didactic Enlightenment. In so doing they seemed to accept the underlying conviction of all who took part in the European Enlightenment that the fundamental reality was matter in motion and that fundamental truth depended upon human apprehension. The acceptance of these beliefs had momentous consequences for Christian higher education in America, both in the years immediately following the Revolution and in the century that followed.

President Witherspoon of Princeton, more than any other person, was responsible for bringing Christian higher education into line with the new cultural convictions of American society.[20] In providing solutions to the difficulties of the Revolutionary era, he also laid out the basic structure of the "moral philosophy" or "mental science" course, which tied together the college curriculum through the time of the Civil War and which influences evangelical colleges to this day. Witherspoon, a Scot, who became president of the College of New Jersey in 1768, brought to America the philosophical perspective known as Scottish Common Sense Realism. This point of view, in opposition to Hume, began by *assuming* that the world we perceive really exists. It began by *assuming* that the normal perceptions common to humanity correspond to the way things really are. Hence the epistemological dilemmas posed by skeptics of the Enlightenment were solved through an appeal to the universal, or common, sense of humankind.

In the hands of Witherspoon and other Christian educators, Scottish Common Sense Realism did even more—it went on to solve social and moral problems. If intuition can assure us of the reality of the natural world, then surely it can teach us morality as well. What, in fact, do we find out about morality when we look at the common moral sensations of humanity and when we consciously reflect upon our own "moral sense"?[21] According to these thinkers, we find that the principles of traditional morality are just as real as the existence of the external world. Scottish Realists held that when by intuition we look into our own consciences, we discover the idea of a supreme judge who rewards good and evil. To the Scottish Realists, the very idea that God rewards good and evil reflects the reality of a just God as certainly as our perceptions of the physical world reflect the reality of that world. Intuition is thus not a phantasmagoria of the imagination but a scientific device capable of solving epistemological and ethical problems. Consequently, intuition or common sense became for the Common Sense Realists just as valuable for knowing the truths of epistemology as sense observation was for learning about the material world.[22]

In the creative hands of the Scottish philosophers and their American followers, this line of reasoning represented a tour de force. By scientific intuition—the systematic study of what humans hold in common—we can know with certainty that the world exists and that traditional morality is valid. What the Scottish philosophers and the American educators had done was to restate Christian morality in a scientific form without having to appeal to the special revelation of Scripture or to the authoritative traditions of the church. In fact, Scottish Realism seemed to provide the only means in the Age of Reason for retaining a belief in scriptural authority and the usefulness of the church, since it could demonstrate their reality on the basis of commonsense perceptions of the physical world and the transmissions of the internal moral sense. Through these means, the Scottish philosophy reestablished the validity of natural science and also reconfirmed traditional morality and demonstrated the continuing truthfulness of historic Christianity. Its great triumph was the salvation of the reality of the physical world and the reality of the eighteenth-century Enlightenment. The great question, however, became whether Christian higher education, having become so attached to the spirit of one age, would be able to adjust to the next.

Having put to rest theoretical problems about knowledge and morality, Witherspoon and like-minded Scottish Realists set about inculcating these principles into the nation's rising generation of leaders. In the colleges of the late eighteenth and early nineteenth centuries, educators like Witherspoon and Dwight did their best to defend the respectability of traditional morality.[23] They also did their best to impart a sense of duty to the graduates of Princeton, Yale, and other colleges. If the moral law was as scientific as the laws of nature, and if the moral law demanded Christian morality and good citizenship, then every effort could be lent to produce graduates inflamed with energetic zeal for God and country. When we remember the great influence exerted in politics by Witherspoon students like James Madison, or in society as a whole by Dwight students like the revivalist and social reformer Lyman Beecher, we begin to see how important the intellectual ideals of the college leaders actually were.[24]

As long as the United States remained overwhelmingly Protestant, Scottish Common Sense Realism remained the dominant perspective in American colleges, for it provided scientific support for traditional Protestant truths and for traditional Christian morality. As long as American popular culture remained under Protestant influence, no one would question the analogy that Common Sense philosophy drew between the mind and the universe, and no one would question the way in which "science" (then the unquestioned authority) had been used to defend the traditional morality whose moorings had been shaken in the Revolutionary period.

Almost unnoticed in the tumult of the times, a great change had taken place in Christian thinking and in the goals of Christian higher education. Puritans had grounded their thinking in special revelation and had worked to turn special revelation into a framework for all of learning. The educators of the new United States, however, grounded their thinking in the Enlightenment and worked to give special revelation a place within that framework. Or, to put matters another way, where Puritan education had proceeded from a Christian perspective, which sought to dominate the shape, purposes, and structure of learning, leaders in America's Christian colleges after the Revolution allowed truths of the didactic Enlightenment to lay out the shape, purposes, and structure of knowledge, within which they were delighted to find a place for Christianity.

The triumph of Christian higher education in the Revolutionary era was its survival at a time when everything from the past had become suspect, when Americans were dispensing with one after another of the traditions that had been passed down to them. The dilemma of Christian higher education after the Revolutionary era was the compatibility of the principles on which it was grounded with its goals, for it no longer rested on self-consciously Christian thinking as much as on Christian exploitation of Enlightenment thought. Yet in the first century of the new United States, the triumph was everywhere more evident than the dilemma. Indeed, that period may be called with justice the great age of Christian higher education in the history of the country.

A Christian-Cultural Synthesis

The intellectual taming of the Enlightenment was far from the only important development in the early republic, however. Just as significant for Christian higher education was the great series of revivals that began in the 1790s and continued in various forms for at least the next three-quarters of a century. In the years between the presidencies of Thomas Jefferson (1801–1809) and Abraham Lincoln (1861–1865), Christian values and the values of American public life joined in a powerful cultural synthesis. The ideology of liberty provided a powerful impetus for constructing a new nation, and the Revolution brought the United States into existence. Similarly, the movements of revival, often referred to as the Second Great Awakening, witnessed the conversion of many people, and its twin engines of evangelism and reform also offered means to reconstruct society.[25] When these two influences came together—as they did so clearly for the great revivalists like Charles G. Finney, the great reformers like abolitionist Theodore Dwight Weld, the great organizers like Lyman Beecher, the great educators like Noah Webster, and the great politicians like Lincoln— the result was a singularly powerful set of cultural values that decisively shaped the character of America's Christian higher education.

American society from the 1790s to the Civil War presents the picture of a self-confident, moral, and even Christian vision sweeping on to ever-greater triumphs.[26] All the major public events of this period can be understood in terms of the Christian-cultural synthesis—the revivals themselves and the momentous currents of reform that they inspired, the westward expansion, the symbolic rise of the common man in the person of Andrew Jackson, and finally the Civil War.[27] The major characteristics of the period were likewise products of the synthesis, the stuff of which had taken shape in the domestication of the Enlightenment. The synthesis was scientific, and so worthy of respect. It was moral, and so worthy of dutiful implementation. It was Christian, and so worthy of impassioned commitment. The spark that impelled the synthesis and recruited literally millions to its banner, however, was the great revival of the 1790s and early 1800s. This revival, in the words of a recent historian, was an "organizing process" that "helped to give meaning and direction to people suffering in various degrees from the social strains of a nation on the move into new political, economic, and geographical areas."[28]

In virtually every respect, American life before the Civil War reflected the impact of Enlightenment Christian moralism, which was constructed after the Revolution and set in motion by the Second Great Awakening. Socially, the country was experiencing a rapid and tumultuous growth that left foreign visitors like Alexis de Tocqueville in stunned, if also impressed, amazement.[29] The country was streaming westward, it was hastening through the first stages of industrial organization, and it was doing all these things without the benefit of settled European traditions. There was everywhere a sense that somehow God had given America and the Americans a unique opportunity to subdue an entire continent for liberty, for morality, for material abundance, and—not least—for Christ. It was, simply, America's Manifest Destiny.[30]

Politically, the distrust of Thomas Jefferson's democratic principles had long since faded away. True, the idealism of Jeffersonianism was giving way to a more down-to-earth Jacksonianism. Yet in the transition little of Jefferson's great faith in the individual was lost. The spoils system of Jackson's administration, his war against the aristocratic Bank of the United States, and his push for universal male suffrage all gave Americans the further confidence that their land was witnessing the flowering of democracy, the political system most compatible with Christianity.

The Christian faith in America was revivalistic, voluntaristic, benevolent, apocalyptic, and perfectionistic. Scoffers then and since might label the Calvinists of antebellum Princeton Seminary neoscholastics; they might call the Wesleyan perfectionists neomonastics; and they might pass off the new Christian sects as neofanatics. Nevertheless, the church saw tens of thousands converted through organized revival; men and women of the church directed powerful campaigns against a multitude of social evils, and many were inspired by the conviction that the stirrings of renewal in America were birth pangs of the millennium.[31]

Theologically, America was becoming less Calvinistic, more humanistic and legalistic. The message of religious leaders like Charles G. Finney was that humankind is able to know the truth and to do the truth that it discovered.[32] American theology in this age tended to be optimistic about evangelism, about ending evil in society, and about the return of the Lord. Theology was also not as important as it once had been, however, for the great need of the age was not speculation but action.

Philosophically, the emphasis was on function. The college course in moral philosophy was designed to produce good citizens.[33] America's moral philosophers cast a wary eye toward Europe and its idealistic speculations but remained committed to the science of Scottish Realism and to the provision of a scientific defense for the dominant American morality.

Three central beliefs governed the Christian-cultural synthesis. Antebellum America believed in America itself, it believed in individual freedom, and it believed in what could be called Protestant Newtonianism. The belief in America can be seen most clearly from the Northern perspective during the years immediately before the Civil War. For many in both North and South, this struggle brought together reform, millennialism, and the sense of America's unique destiny under God. For Northerners the preservation of the Union meant no less than breathing life into Manifest Destiny, overcoming slavery (the greatest evil remaining in America), and perhaps even foreshadowing the millennium. "Stand up, stand up for Jesus, the strife will not be long," wrote George Duffield in 1858, one eye looking askance at the Dred Scott decision of the previous year, which had treated slaves like property, the other cocked for the final kingdom of Christ. The words of the New School Presbyterians at their General Assembly of 1861 stood for many others: "Rebellion against such a government as ours . . . can find no parallel, except in the first two great rebellions, that which assailed the throne of heaven directly [Satan's revolt], and that which peopled our world with miserable apostates [Adam and Eve's]. . . . We here, in deep humiliation for our sins and the sins of the nation, and in heartfelt devotion, lay ourselves, with all that we are and have, on the altar of God and our country."[34] For their part, Southerners often looked at Yankees as lawless aggressors destroying the precious Christian heritage of the United States.

Christian America believed not only in itself as a nation but also in the individual freedom of its citizens. This second belief was propagated by much that was vital in America's young history: the stirring words of the Declaration of Independence, the convictions of Jefferson and Jackson, the philosophical individualism of John Locke and the Scottish Realists, the accelerating influence of the Methodists, and even the newer theories of some Calvinists.[35] In its extreme form the belief in individual freedom resulted in visions of human perfection— some coming from the Unitarian departure from Calvinism, others from the more advanced forms of Methodism. In its more usual forms, American individualism foresaw great social benefits arising from individuals organized against social evils—slavery, drunkenness, dueling, prostitution, Sunday mail, the theater, and frivolous amusements. America's infatuation with the individual was certainly not confined to Christian circles, but Christians no less than non-Christians gave their wholehearted commitment to the individual as the hope of the future.

Finally, the third belief the educated elite of nineteenth-century America committed themselves to was a worldview in which first principles were God-ordained laws and the human capacity to work with such laws. Apart from a few vastly overpublicized Transcendentalists,[36] most Americans who thought at all before the Civil War thought in terms of a Protestant Newtonianism. Americans were Protestant in their convictions about Scripture, their commitment to an American understanding of the priesthood of believers, and their primitivistic allegiance to first-century Christianity. They were Newtonian, and hence of the Enlightenment, in their commitment to simplicity in ideas and in a corresponding distaste for intellectual ambiguity. They reflected this Newtonianism even more in their commitment to a concept of static law. In their view, for example, it was as axiomatic as the law of gravity that national prosperity was a sign of God's blessing or that the exercise of correct stimuli in a revival would bring the desired results.[37] Protestant Newtonianism, then, was no more than the conviction that externally fixed laws governed the "facts" of national life and morality as surely as they did the "facts" of nature.

This then was the American Christian-cultural synthesis before the Civil War. It emerged when the content of a great revival was poured through the forms of a domesticated Enlightenment. It helps us understand how philosophies of life like Jacksonianism, Manifest Destiny, and voluntaristic reform could flourish. It enables us to make sense of social, political, and religious convictions in the nineteenth century. And it provides the proper context for understanding the education in America's Christian colleges.

Early American Colleges

Intellectual life in America's colleges before 1870 bears little resemblance to what we know today, as the following essay by William Ringenberg will make clear.[38] The curriculum of the old college consisted of a little mathematics; a great deal of praise for empirical science with, however, only meager opportunities to carry out actual experiments; much drill in the classics; and an exposure to systematic arguments for morality, civic virtue, and the existence of God. Modern languages and literature had no place in the curriculum, and history as a discipline was just beginning to be recognized. Instruction proceeded by recitation. The professor, acting more as scorekeeper than teacher, called upon the students to translate, parse, recapitulate, or summarize. Close discipline, extending well beyond the classroom, was the rule. Not surprisingly, the tedium of the classroom, the rigor of extracurricular discipline, and the natural feistiness of late adolescence led to student unrest. One of the less destructive ways in which students protested their lot was to disrupt the morning devotional by herding a compliant cow into the chapel. Yet student unrest often led to violence as well, including once or twice the murder of professors who had fallen from favor.

Some of the students' exuberance may have reflected their unconscious awareness of higher education's comparative lack of importance. Throughout the nineteenth century, a bachelor's degree in the liberal arts remained more an ornament of the upper middle class than a doorway to intellectual growth or economic success. It was not necessary to study the liberal arts before taking up a career in medicine or law, and only some of the country's new seminaries required ministerial candidates to stand a regular four-year undergraduate curriculum. In addition, the country's best engineers came not from the colleges but from the military academy at West Point.

Nor were college faculty members the country's intellectual elite. The faculty at the nation's oldest and most prestigious college, Harvard, was not even the dominent intellectual force in Boston. Henry Adams, reflecting on the Harvard faculty in the years surrounding the Civil War, wrote that "no one took Harvard College seriously." One of the reasons may have been the college's casual regard for scholarship, an attitude seen, for example, when the same Henry Adams was in 1870 appointed professor of medieval history, a subject about which he professed himself "utterly and grossly ignorant."[39]

By 1870 it was clear that the old college was barely keeping pace with the intellectual needs of the country. In that year the nation's colleges enrolled only about fifty-two thousand out of a general population of forty million (the equivalent proportion today would be only three hundred thousand students from our population of 240 million). Furthermore, the rate of growth in the number of college students was falling behind the rate of growth in the country as a whole. For all its weaknesses, however, the old-style American college had one important advantage: with very rare exceptions, it was founded and operated as an avowedly Christian institution. In the great westward expansion of the country before the Civil War, Protestant denominations exceeded one another in founding educational institutions to answer the Protestant need for a literate laity and a learned clergy, as well as the democratic American need for informed citizens.[40]

These institutions led a precarious existence, but at least they knew why they existed. The founders of colleges, and the parents who sent their sons to them, saw them as places of "intellectual stability and order in a fluid society."[41] Edward Everett, president of Harvard, could speak in 1846 of the three purposes for colleges: to convey knowledge, to train the mind, and to prepare good citizens. He went on to say that of these the third was far and away most important.[42] Colleges before the Civil War offered one of the ways for exuberant American society to retain a measure of order and cohesion. Moreover, at the vast majority of colleges, where evangelical conviction was stronger than at Harvard, Christian beliefs significantly influenced the ideals of order, cohesion, and citizenship.

The capstone of the college experience in those days was a yearlong course, often taught by the college president, in "moral philosophy" or "mental science." It was a course with vast horizons, much as Witherspoon had set it out, including everything having to do with human beings and their social relations (the subjects studied under this rubric would later become the separate disciplines of psychology, philosophy, religion, political science, sociology, anthropology, economics, and jurisprudence). The course almost always included an investigation of epistemology in general and of philosophical proofs for Christianity in particular. Its overall purpose was to provide final Christian integration for the college career and final exhortations concerning the kind of citizenship good Christians should practice.

From a modern Christian perspective, the instruction in moral philosophy had much to commend it. It represented an effort to treat all bits of knowledge as parts of a comprehensive whole, and to do so within a Christian framework—in modern jargon, a course seeking to integrate faith and learning. Moral philosophy provided college seniors with a respectable defense of God's existence and the moral law, and it offered comprehensive exhortations to live morally in society, to support religion, to put public good above selfish interests, and to work for the coming of God's kingdom in America.

Moral philosophy was useful in holding back atheistic skepticism, promoting democratic republicanism, and encouraging social morality. It nonetheless had several deficiencies, which, in the last third of the nineteenth century, occasioned the greatest crisis in the history of Christian higher education in America. My second essay in this collection, "The University Arrives in America, 1870–1930," will show how these flaws in moral philosophy contributed to its collapse in the face of the "academic revolution," when a series of major changes transformed the character of both public values and collegiate instruction.

Two final comments are appropriate in an effort to summarize the experience of Christian higher education in the early republic. The first of these has to do with the intellectual orientation of the colleges, which was strongly shaped by American versions of Scottish Common Sense philosophy like that communicated to the Princeton students by Elias Boudinot in 1807. The benefits of this long and fruitful relationship must not be gainsaid; yet it is possible to ask whether a commitment to a philosophical perspective—and a relatively recent one at that—should have so completely, yet unpretentiously, dominated the Christian thinking of three generations. The results of this domination were at times clear. When the challenge of Darwin appeared, for example, many Americans were constitutionally unable to distinguish an attack upon Lockean (or Newtonian) Common Sense philosophy from an attack upon the true essence of the biblical faith. In the confusion, all too many Christians perceived the new science as an assault upon the foundations of the faith. If we cannot do science our way, they seemed to say, we will not do science at all. And so, to borrow a phrase, the American Christians who were faithful in marriage to the moderate Enlightenment of their age found themselves intellectual widows in the next. Much the same may be said for Christian reactions to America's postbellum social crises.

A second comment is more positive, however. In spite of weaknesses in American intellectual culture before the Civil War, it is impossible to deny the vitality of Christian life throughout the period. The missionary movements of the nineteenth century, the crusades against slavery and other social evils, the vigorous revivalism of the period, as indeed its higher education, can all be faulted for one reason or another. Yet all advanced the Redeemer's plan in real ways.

And so in asking for a final evaluation of Christian higher education in the early republic we are left with two questions. Was the nineteenth century, with its revival, missions, and moral reform, in fact what Kenneth Scott Latourette has called "The Great Century"?[43] Or was it, with its uncritical Scottish Realism and its utilitarian moralism, the nadir of Protestant intellectual life since the Reformation? Our own common sense would urge us to decide one way or another. But perhaps Christian students, bound as all are to the forms of their culture even as they labor with their minds for the kingdom of Christ, might say yes to both questions.[44]

NOTES

1. A complete transcript of Boudinot's speech is presented in Mark A. Noll, "The Response of Elias Boudinot to the Student Rebellion of 1807: Visions of Honor, Order, and Morality," *The Princeton University Library Chronicle* 43 (Autumn 1981): 1-22; the quotations here are from 20-21.

2. Two sure guides to the ideological issues of the period are Bernard Bailyn, *The Ideological Origins of the American Revolution* (Cambridge: Harvard University Press, 1967); and Gordon S. Wood, *The Creation of the American Republic, 1776–1787* (Chapel Hill: University of North Carolina Press, 1969). I have addressed a few of the more general issues of the Revolutionary period, as they affected believers, in "Christian and Humanistic Values in Eighteenth-Century America," *Christian Scholar's Review* 6 (1976): 114-26.

3. Edmund S. Morgan, "The American Revolution Considered as an Intellectual Movement," in *Paths of American Thought*, ed. Arthur M. Schlesinger, Jr., and Morton White (Boston: Houghton Mifflin, 1963), 11.

4. These figures are from *Princeton University General Catalogue 1746–1906* (Princeton: Princeton University Press, 1908). A similar decline (at about the same time) in the number of Yale students entering the ministry has been noted by Steven J. Novak, *The Rights of Youth: American Colleges and Student Revolt, 1798–1815* (Cambridge: Harvard University Press, 1977), 136.

5. For indications of the extent of the influence of the idea of liberty, see Nathan O. Hatch, "The Christian Movement and the Demand for a Theology of the People," *Journal of American History* 67 (December 1980): 545-67; Gordon S. Wood, "Evangelical America and Early Mormonism," *New York History* 61 (October 1980): 359-86; David Hackett Fischer, *Growing Old in America*, rev. ed. (New York: Oxford University Press, 1978), especially the chapter "Transition: The Revolution in Age Relations, 1770–1820"; and Jay Fliegelman, *Prodigals and Pilgrims: The American Revolution against Patriarchal Authority, 1750–1800* (Cambridge: Cambridge University Press, 1982).

6. See, as examples of a large body of literature, Stephen A. Marini, *Radical Sects of Revolutionary New England* (Cambridge: Harvard University Press, 1982); and Frederick V. Mills, *Bishops by Ballot* (New York: Oxford University Press, 1978).

7. Henry F. May, *The Enlightenment in America* (New York: Oxford University Press, 1976). This is an excellent study which may be usefully supplemented by Donald H. Meyer, *The Democratic Enlightenment* (New York: Putnam, 1976); and, for international comparison, Roy Porter and Mikuláš Teich, eds., *The Enlightenment in National Context* (Cambridge: Cambridge University Press, 1981).

8. Margaret C. Jacob, *The Newtonians and The English Revolution, 1689–1720* (Ithaca: Cornell University Press, 1976), provides a sensitive treatment of the religious implications of Newton's work.

9. For a general picture, see Franklin L. Baumer, *Religion and the Rise of Skepticism* (New York: Harcourt, Brace and World, 1960), 1-127.

10. A good survey is found in Franklin L. Baumer, *Modern European Thought: Continuity and Change in Ideas, 1600–1950* (New York: Macmillan, 1977), 218-36.

11. See Gladys Bryson, *Man and Society: The Scottish Inquiry of the Eighteenth Century* (Princeton: Princeton University Press, 1945); and Amand Chitnis, *The Scottish Enlightenment* (Totowa, N.J.: Rowman and Littlefield, 1976).

12. For a general definition of the Enlightenment in these terms see May, *The Enlightenment in America*, xiv; and Meyer, *The Democratic Enlightenment*, ix-xix.

13. For an overview, see Perry Miller, *The Life of the Mind in America from the Revolution to the Civil War* (New York: Harcourt, Brace, and World, 1965).

14. For superb documentation, see Theodore Dwight Bozeman, *Protestants in an Age of Science: The Baconian Ideal and Antebellum American Religious Thought* (Chapel Hill: University of North Carolina Press, 1977); E. Brooks Holifield, *The Gentlemen Theologians: American Theology in Southern Culture 1795–1860* (Durham, N.C.: Duke University Press, 1978); and Herbert Hovenkamp, *Science and Religion in America 1800–1860* (Philadelphia: University of Pennsylvania Press, 1978). S. A. Grave, *The Scottish Philosophy of Common Sense* (Oxford: Clarendon, 1960), is a good introduction to the Scottish philosophers.

15. The sense of crisis is communicated well by David Hackett Fischer, *The Revolution of American Conservatism: The Federalist Party in the Era of Jeffersonian Democracy* (New York: Harper and Row, 1969); and Nathan O. Hatch, *The Sacred Cause of Liberty: Republican Thought and the Millennium in Revolutionary New England* (New Haven: Yale University Press, 1977), 97-175.

16. Alexander Pope, "Epitaph Intended for Sir Isaac Newton."

17. The finest discussion of American "Baconianism" is Bozeman's *Protestants in an Age of Science.*

18. For careful qualifications on the role of Locke, specifically for Revolutionary political theory, see Bernard Bailyn, *Ideological Origins of the American Revolution,* 27-28 and passim.

19. Basil Willey cogently discusses changes of "explanation" in the introductory section of *The Seventeenth-Century Background* (London: Chatto and Windus, 1949).

20. For authoritative biographical and intellectual accounts, see Varnum Lansing Collins, *President Witherspoon,* 2 vols. (Princeton: Princeton University Press, 1925); and Douglas Sloan, *The Scottish Enlightenment and the American College Ideal* (New York: Teachers College Press, 1971), chap. 4: "The Scottish Enlightenment Comes to Princeton: John Witherspoon." I have explored Witherspoon's direct connections with the Revolution in Mark A. Noll, Nathan O. Hatch, and George M. Marsden, *The Search for Christian America* (Westchester, Ill.: Crossway, 1983), 86-95.

21. Witherspoon follows the Scottish moral philosopher Francis Hutcheson on these matters. For a brief introduction to Hutcheson and a sample of his work, see Jane Rendall, *The Origins of the Scottish Enlightenment* (New York: St. Martins, 1978), 74-75. For Witherspoon's reliance on Hutcheson, see Jack Scott, ed., *An Annotated Edition of Lectures on Moral Philosophy* (Newark, Del.: Delaware University Press, 1982), 26-28, 35-37, and 42-43.

22. Norman Fiering provides a superb depiction of the development of ethics on the basis of intuition in *Moral Philosophy at Seventeenth-Century Harvard* and *Jonathan Edwards's Moral Thought and Its British Context* (both, Chapel Hill: University of North Carolina Press, 1981).

23. See D. H. Meyer, *The Instructed Conscience: The Shaping of the American National Ethic* (Philadelphia: University of Pennsylvania Press, 1972), for the best general study.

24. See James H. Smylie, "Madison and Witherspoon: Theological Roots of American Political Thought," *Princeton University Library Chronicle* 22 (Spring 1961): 118-32; and Stuart C. Henry, *Unvanquished Puritan: A Portrait of Lyman Beecher* (Grand Rapids: Eerdmans, 1973).

25. For excellent studies of revival movements see Timothy L. Smith, *Revivalism and Social Reform: American Protestantism on the Eve of the Civil War* (Nashville: Abingdon, 1957); Timothy L. Smith, "Righteousness and Hope: Christian Holiness and

the Millennial Vision in America, 1800–1900," *American Quarterly* 31 (Spring 1979): 22-45; and Donald Mathews, "The Second Great Awakening as an Organizing Process, 1780–1830," *American Quarterly* 21 (Spring 1969): 23-43, reprinted in *Religion in American History: Interpretive Essays*, ed. John F. Wilson and John M. Mulder (Englewood Cliffs, N.J.: Prentice-Hall, 1978), 199-217.

26. See Sydney Ahlstrom, *A Religious History of the American People* (New Haven: Yale University Press, 1972), 385-490.

27. See, for further details, Lewis O. Saum, *The Popular Mind of Pre–Civil War America* (Westport, Conn.: Greenwood, 1980); Edward Pessen, *Jacksonian America: Society, Personality, and Politics* (Homewood, Ill.: Dorsey, 1978); and James Moorhead, *American Apocalypse: Yankee Protestants in the Civil War 1860–1869* (New Haven: Yale University Press, 1978).

28. Mathews, "The Second Great Awakening," 203.

29. Alexis de Tocqueville, *Democracy in America*, first published 1835–1840 and often thereafter.

30. For background to this sense of a divinely granted opportunity see Ernest Lee Tuveson, *Redeemer Nation: The Idea of America's Millennial Role* (Chicago: University of Chicago Press, 1968).

31. For an excellent recent treatment, see Smith, "Righteousness and Hope."

32. Charles G. Finney, *Lectures on Revivals of Religion*, ed. William G. Mc-Loughlin (1834; Cambridge: Harvard University Press, 1960).

33. Meyer, *The Instructed Conscience*, deals at length with collegiate instruction.

34. New School *Minutes*, 1861, pp. 23-25, quoted in George M. Marsden, *The Evangelical Mind and the New School Presbyterian Experience* (New Haven: Yale University Press, 1970), 205; the general summary in this paragraph follows the interpretation in Marsden's fine study, 230-49.

35. See Nathan O. Hatch, "*Sola Scriptura* and *Novus Ordo Seclorum*," in *The Bible in America: Essays in Cultural History*, ed. Nathan O. Hatch and Mark A. Noll (New York: Oxford University Press, 1982), 59-78.

36. On the irrelevance of the Transcendentalists to most Americans, see Saum, *The Popular Mind*, xxi-xxii and passim.

37. See the section on Finney in the chapter discussing revivalism in John D. Woodbridge, Mark A. Noll, and Nathan O. Hatch, *The Gospel in America: Themes in the Story of America's Evangelicals* (Grand Rapids: Zondervan, 1979), 145-46.

38. For extensive documentation see Ringenberg, *The Christian College*, chap. 2.

39. Henry Adams, quoted in Robert A. McCaughey, "The Transformation of American Academic Life: Harvard University 1821–1892," *Perspectives in American History* 8 (1974): 263, 279.

40. For a recent sympathetic study of these old-style American colleges see Timothy L. Smith, *Uncommon Schools: Christian Colleges and Social Idealism in Midwestern America, 1829–1950* (Indianapolis: Indiana Historical Society, 1978).

41. Meyer, quoting Stow Persons, in *The Instructed Conscience*, 5.

42. Meyer, *The Instructed Conscience*, 65-66.

43. *The Great Century* is the general title Latourette gave to vols. 4-6 of his *History of the Expansion of Christianity* (New York: Harper and Brothers, 1937–1945). Together, these volumes deal with Christianity throughout the world in the nineteenth century.

44. This essay includes revised and annotated portions of my "Christian Colleges, Christian Worldviews, and an Invitation to Research," which served as the introduction

to William Ringenberg's book *The Christian College: A History of Protestant Higher Education in America* (Grand Rapids: Eerdmans, Christian University Press, 1984).

The Old-Time College, 1800–1865

William C. Ringenberg

Almost without exception, to be a college in America before the Civil War was to be a Christian college. Scholars do not dispute the validity of this statement, but they do disagree among themselves on whether the colleges of the antebellum period served the country well. During the 1950s and 1960s, the most influential educational historians expressed mostly critical comments about the antebellum colleges. A summary of their judgments would run something like this: The first half of the nineteenth century represents the low point in the history of American higher education, for this period witnessed the unfortunate proliferation of countless poor, weak colleges by competing Protestant denominations. These religious groups established institutions that were intellectually lacking and morbidly moralistic in their emphasis on evangelical piety and paternalistic discipline. Consequently, the students often rioted, the colleges became very unpopular with their larger constituencies, the enrollments declined, and many schools went out of existence. According to this argument, the salvation of higher education came with the reforms of the late nineteenth century, when many institutions gradually began to discard the anachronistic religious requirements and classical curriculum and to replace them with a broader range of relevant courses, more highly trained professors, and an intellectually open environment. The result was a popular and democratic system of higher education, which for the first time began to serve the real needs of the American public.[1]

Historians writing in the 1970s, by contrast, sharply challenged the validity of the above view. They argued that the older historians viewed the antebellum liberal arts college from their own perspective of the later secular university and that they based their too-easy conclusions on limited sources. And indeed, an increasing number of studies show that many of the previously accepted views were inaccurate.

This major revision of academic history presents the old-time college in a more favorable light. The pre–Civil War college was less dominated by narrow, sectarian purposes than by broad, Christian ones; the college served local needs as much as denominational ones; and the supposed proliferation of needless colleges was in fact a proliferation of "paper" institutions that never developed into legitimate colleges. Most colleges that survived long enough to develop a full four-year program and actually award degrees became permanent, viable institutions. In most respects these schools were very popular with their constituent groups and were important regional disseminators of American republican culture.[2]

I largely concur with the views of the revisionist scholars, and I agree with Mark Noll's assessment in the preceding essay that the antebellum college did much to sustain the nation's Enlightenment-Christian intellectual synthesis. This is not to suggest that there were no weaknesses in the old-time colleges, however. Indeed, institutional faults are more obvious than the intellectual flaws Noll has emphasized. These schools often suffered from a lack of commitment to providing adequate libraries and qualified instructors; from a constricted curriculum, dull teaching, and unimaginative religious exercises; and from minimal attention to the advancement of knowledge through research. Yet these limitations are less noteworthy than the positive contributions the antebellum higher education movement made. It produced the greatest boom in college growth in American history, the high tide of Christian influence in American higher education, and a flowering of student intellectual initiative in the literary society movement. This essay, then, as a complement to the preceding one by Mark Noll, will focus on the institutional history of the "old-time" colleges.

The Expansion of American Colleges

The American Revolution marked the end of the first chapter in the history of higher education in the new world. Until then, imperial control from England had served to limit the founding of colleges, especially in the South. Between the war and the end of the eighteenth century, however, the number of new permanent colleges to appear was approximately twice the nine of the colonial period, and by the time of the Civil War approximately 180 permanent institutions were in operation. Similarly, the college population in the period from 1800 to 1860 grew four times as fast as the overall population did.[3]

Several factors contributed to this great boom in college founding. One major stimulus was the religious zeal stemming from the Second

Great Awakening. Another was the growing tendency for local communities to want to have their own colleges. Finally, the growing spirit of democracy, which characterized American society during the administration of Andrew Jackson and beyond, resulted in a much higher percentage of middle-class and even lower-class students enrolling in college.

The Second Great Awakening (from approximately 1800 to 1835) transformed the American college from what may have been its lowest point spiritually into a thoroughly religious institution. A surprising number of college students in the late eighteenth century professed skepticism and even atheism while belittling orthodox Christian beliefs. At Dartmouth in 1798, only one member of the class of 1799 publicly professed the Christian faith; at Yale in 1796, only the senior class could claim more than one such professing believer. And the new Williams College in western Massachusetts (founded by the Congregationalists in 1793) identified as Christians only five of its ninety-three graduates in the 1790s.[4]

Then came the awakening that swept through all of the country and all of the major denominations and their colleges. The state of religion in the eastern colleges changed sufficiently that some referred to the revival as the "Protestant Counter-Revolution."[5] Stimulated by the Second Great Awakening, the eastern denominations sought to convert the West and accordingly sent home missionaries to the newly developing regions. In order to guarantee that the changes wrought by the missionaries would become permanent, denominational representatives together with local officials established colleges in the newly-opened regions of the expansion to train future ministers and to indoctrinate the aspiring leaders of society with the evangelical verities.

Thus colleges sprang up rapidly throughout the frontier regions between 1780 and 1860, with the greatest proliferation occurring after 1830. The traditional authority on college founding in this era identifies only 29 permanent colleges founded before 1830, while 133 began in the next thirty years. By the eve of the Civil War, the denominations with the most colleges were the Presbyterians with 49, the Methodists with 34, the Baptists with 25, and the Congregationalists with 21. The total college enrollment in 1860 was approximately 30,000.[6]

The Methodists and the Baptists, the two denominations that experienced the greatest increases in membership because of the awakening, became major factors in this rapid growth as they began to value higher education for their ministers and as their young people aspired to higher stations in life. Many of the new group of common-class young people now seeking higher education came from these denominations, both of which began to lose their fear of higher education after about 1830 and consequently began to establish colleges in each of the southern and midwestern states into which they were spreading. Consequently, in the generation after 1830, the Methodists founded such schools as Randolph-Macon (in Virginia), McKendree (Illinois), Wesleyan (Connecticut), Emory (Georgia), DePauw (Indiana), Emory and Henry (Virginia), Ohio Wesleyan, Centenary (Lousiana), Baldwin-Wallace (Ohio), Lawrence (Wisconsin), Taylor (Indiana), Albion (Michigan), Northwestern (Illinois), College of the Pacific (California), Wofford (South Carolina), Duke (North Carolina), Willamette (Oregon), Illinois Wesleyan, Cornell (Iowa), Hamline (Minnesota), Iowa Wesleyan, Birmingham-Southern (Alabama), Mt. Union (Ohio), and Baker (Kansas).[7] Also during the antebellum generation the Baptists organized Colby (Maine), George Washington (Washington, D.C.), Georgetown (Kentucky), Denison (Ohio), Shurtleff (Illinois), Franklin (Indiana), Mercer (Georgia), Samford (Alabama), Wake Forest (North Carolina), Richmond (Virginia), Hillsdale (Michigan), Mississippi, Furman (South Carolina), Rochester (New York), Carson-Newman (Tennessee), and Kalamazoo (Michigan).[8] Furthermore, from the same Baptist and Methodist sources, no doubt, came many students at the growing number of state universities, which operated almost without exception as Protestant institutions.

Often graduates of revival-fired colleges helped found and develop new institutions in the West. Especially significant in this respect were the alumni of Yale, Princeton, and Oberlin. Oberlin's students and faculty helped establish a number of institutions, including Adrian, Olivet, and Hillsdale in Michigan, Tabor and Iowa in Iowa, Drury in Missouri, Ripon in Wisconsin, and Carleton in Minnesota. Of the American college presidents in office before 1840, thirty-six had graduated from Yale, that "mother of colleges," and twenty-two from Princeton. Yale and Princeton exerted much greater influence than can be identified by direct connections, however, for it was their largely conservative religious and curricular patterns that set the tone for higher education in general during this period.[9]

As much as the Second Great Awakening influenced college founding in this era, many institutions came into existence because community leaders in the western expansion were anxious to help the churchmen found colleges. New communities competed for prestige, and colleges could be important drawing cards for settlers and businesses: a town with a college was more attractive socially and culturally than were its less sophisticated neighbors. Also important was the economic stimulus that a college could bring to a town, for the establishment of a successful school ensured the influx of a significant number of residents. More residents, of course, meant a greater volume of business for the town merchants. Enthusiastic preachers, working on their own initiative ahead of their denominations, frequently negotiated college start-ups with community leaders. For example, four frontier Methodist preachers in Michigan cooperated with a local business group known as "The Albion Company" to begin Albion College; and three pioneer farmers doubling as Free Will Baptist missionaries opened Hillsdale College after working to overcome the reluctance of their own denomination.[10]

The typical old-time college, then, operated more as a Christian community college than as a denominational institution, and rarely did it reflect narrowly sectarian interests. It gained wide local support both from the members of the affiliated denomination and from others. The town and surrounding area supplied a high percentage of the students, many of whom boarded in the community; and the college's public events made it a cultural center. Area citizens consequently responded favorably to fund drives; indeed, college agents did much of their fund raising within a fifty-mile radius of their schools.[11]

One of the reasons the colleges were popular in their communities was that they often provided the only secondary instruction in the area. In fact, the great majority of their students studied on the secondary, not the collegiate, level. At Oberlin, for example, whose enrollment surpassed thirteen hundred during the 1850s, only one-eighth of the students were enrolled in a regular college course, and only one-third were pursuing college work of any type. Similarly, only 10 percent of the Wheaton (Illinois) students in 1860 were studying at the college level, and when Colorado College opened shortly after the Civil War, only one-fourth of its enrollees were college-level scholars.[12] These Christian colleges devoted a major part of their attention to training secondary students—in part to meet local needs, in part to generate sufficient tuition revenues to subsidize instruction to a limited number of college students, and in part to assure a supply of students with adequate training and interest to enroll in their college programs.

The wide distribution of many new colleges meant that higher education was becoming increasingly accessible to the middle and lower classes. One should note, however, that like Jacksonian democracy, higher education in this period remained largely for white males, and that the curriculum did not yet reflect much of the growing middle class's interest in law, engineering, and business. Many students of modest means lived at home while studying, an especially significant trend in a day when room and board charges rather than tuition comprised the principal part of college expenses. The growing democratization of higher education was not limited to the West, though, for even New England after 1800 witnessed a sharp increase in the number of students from poor families. While some of these went to Harvard and Yale, they enrolled primarily at Brown, Dartmouth, and six new colleges: Williams, Middlebury (Vermont), Vermont, Bowdoin (Maine), Colby (Maine), and Amherst (Massachusetts).[13]

The overall increase in college enrollment since the colonial period occurred less from a sharp growth in individual colleges than from the growth of the number of institutions that served modest numbers of students. In the middle of the nineteenth century, Yale enrolled about 500 students, which made it a large school even by eastern standards. Beloit in Wisconsin, a typical school in the West, enrolled in 1860 only 60 college and 108 normal and preparatory students. Some institutions operated with even smaller student bodies, some as small as Franklin in Indiana, which in 1847 enrolled only 25 college and 25 preparatory students.[14]

A Christian Mission

The old-time college leaders sought to create an environment in which the Christian faith and Christian morality influenced every aspect of the collegiate experience. Founders often located their institutions in remote, rural places in an effort to protect the students from the snares of city life. James McBride, an Ohio legislator who was influential in the founding of Presbyterian-oriented Miami, argued for a rural location for the school by stating, "I had rather send my son to a seminary of learning provided there were able professors even though it should be immersed in the gloom of the deep woods than to send him to an urban setting like Cincinnati where he would be exposed to the temptations and vices which are always prevalent in large cities."[15]

College officials made certain that students properly observed the Sabbath. Most required that their students attend Sunday worship in one of the neighborhood churches, and some added a second service on campus later in the day. Some colleges held classes on Tuesday through Saturday, using Monday as the second weekend holiday and thus reducing the need to spend Sunday preparing for classes. Other institutions that did hold Monday classes found other ways to discourage study on the Sabbath. At Amherst, for example, professors arranged their assignments so that the students did not need to make specific preparation for Monday classes.[16]

Since the faculty members were often ministers and almost invariably dedicated Christians, they sought to promote the spiritual development as well as the intellectual growth of their students. Thus they watched for natural opportunities both inside and outside the classroom to lead unconverted students to receive Christ as Savior. Many parents even expected the college to serve as an evangelistic agent for their children. The parents of one Wofford student sent the faculty a letter expressing great appreciation for the recent conversion of their son, which they had planned and waited for: "We felt that if we could obtain the means of sending him to Wofford, God would convert him."[17]

The old-time colleges in fact played a larger role in evangelizing their students than contemporary Christian colleges do, because at that time the percentage of students at Protestant colleges who were professing Christians was much smaller than it is at evangelical colleges today. The explanation is simple. In a day when nearly every college was a Christian college, the non-Christian student who aspired to a higher education had little choice but to enroll in a religious institution. In turn, the colleges rarely imposed a religious test as a basis for admission.[18] Probably fewer than one-half of the antebellum students were professing Christians. One comprehensive study by the American Education Society in 1831 considered it very encouraging to note that following the Second Great Awakening, 683 of 3,582 students in fifty-nine colleges were "hopefully pious." An 1856 study by the Amherst College Society of Inquiry showed that little more than one-third of the students in eleven New England colleges claimed to be Christian. The highest percentages were at Wesleyan (75 percent) and Amherst and Middlebury (60 percent each), while the lowest percentage was at Harvard (10 percent).[19]

The most effective method for bringing a large number of unconverted students into the fold was the periodic revival. College after college reported almost annual sweeping revivals that not only converted many students but also led Christian youths to consider seriously careers as ministers and missionaries. Many students radically changed their manner of living in response to such revivals. During an awakening in the winter of 1814–1815 at Princeton, "in many a chamber where formerly mischievous youths plotted to burn an outhouse or to set off firecrackers in the lecture rooms, there was earnest prayer or anxious discussions over religious matters." Sometimes a revival upset the regular college routine, as at Randolph-Macon in 1852 where a student reported: "Lessons and text books are fast being supplanted by prayers and hymn books and Bible. Study seems today as if it were entirely a secondary matter." Sometimes such enthusiasm combined with the natural adolescent desire to seek temporary escape from the academic routine. In the midst of a revival at DePauw in 1842, a student burst into a classroom with an announcement to the scholars that "President Simpson preaches at the Campground at 1:00." The result was immediate confusion, and the students "without dismissal or leave gathered up their books and hastened away."[20]

Insightful revivalist leaders warned that emotional awakenings were not the ideal religious activity. Jonathan Blanchard, at different times president of Knox and Wheaton colleges (both in Illinois) preferred no revivals at all if the work of the church could be realized without them. "When they are successful," he said, "they tend to make us vain and conceited because we do so much. Then they beget disrelish for ordinary labors in the church and make them seem tedious, and they also exalt religious activity above the grace of God. If unsuccessful, they produce discouragement, faintness of heart, and fretfulness in the church."[21]

While evangelism was one aim of the old-time colleges, it was not their primary purpose. After all, churches could evangelize, but they could not provide the necessary education for aspiring ministers. Among clergymen and denominational officials, at least, the ministerial training function was cited regularly as the most important reason for founding a college. Yet contrary to popular opinion, very few colleges enrolled only—or even mostly—ministerial candidates. It is true, however, that colleges sometimes placed undue pressure on students to consider ministerial careers. One Denison student just after the Civil War stated that "it would be probably impossible to exaggerate the prominence given to the duty of devoting one's life to the ministry or missions." He especially remembered how "old Professor John Stevens speaking in chapel on the Day of Prayer for Colleges would cast his eyes solemnly over the assembly and remark 'Let those who must study law.'"[22]

The colleges eagerly welcomed (and pressed for) ministerial candidates, but they were also pleased to train students for a variety of other professions, especially law, medicine, and teaching. Usually no more than 25 percent of the graduates of a college were preparing for the ministry, but a great majority of them were planning to enter some profession. On the eve of the Civil War, approximately 16 percent of the students in eleven New England colleges were ministerial candidates. During the whole of the antebellum period, approximately 20 percent of the graduates of Randolph-Macon and between 20 and 25 percent of the graduates of the Michigan church colleges entered the ministry. By comparison, 80 percent of the graduates of Randolph-Macon and 90 percent of the graduates of Amherst prepared to enter one of the four major professions (law, medicine, teaching, and the ministry).[23]

A College Education

The 1864 Ripon College catalog stated: "Instruction will be conducted on Christian principles, and it will be the aim of the instructors to pervade it with a strong and healthful moral and religious influence." Most antebellum colleges shared this goal and regularly expected their instructors to apply biblical principles to their teaching and to interpret their disciplines in terms of a Christian philosophical framework. Indeed, the strategic center of the college curriculum was the senior year sequence in moral philosophy, as Mark Noll has made clear in the previous essay.[24] This intentionally religious focus of instruction during the rapid expansion of antebellum colleges was to make this period the high tide of Christian higher education in America. The curricular structure in which these commitments were couched, however, seemed rather out of step with the dynamic evangelicalism that fueled the schools.

The curriculum during the first half of the nineteenth century remained much the same as that of the late colonial period except that science instruction became increasingly important—particularly in the eastern colleges—and some institutions broadened the range of their course offerings. Latin and Greek served as the primary subjects for freshmen and sophomores and even continued into the junior year with major emphasis being given to such authors as Livy, Herodotus, Horace, Cicero, Euripides, and Homer. Mathematical studies, including algebra, geometry, trigonometry, and conic sections, served to "train the mind" and so were ranked next to the ancient languages in importance, especially in the curriculum of the lower division. During the junior and senior years, classical language and mathematical studies gave way to increased emphasis on science, philosophy, religion, social science, and, in some cases, literature.[25]

American educators in general, however, continued to believe that a classical curriculum provided the best intellectual framework for an educated person. Scholars studied the Latin and Greek classics because they contained eternal truths and values that every student should know. They translated them because the translation process was an excellent way of shaping the mind. Yet sometimes this emphasis upon mental discipline was so strong that it prevented the students from giving serious consideration to the ideas of the writers.

Perhaps the major change in curriculum in the first half of the nineteenth century was the expansion of science courses. After 1815 the northeastern colleges significantly improved their science programs, and by the early part of the century, instruction in natural science was a curricular staple, though it varied widely in quantity and quality. The schools in this region—which as late as 1830 still produced the majority of college graduates in the country—broadened their science curricula, purchased expensive laboratory equipment (or philosophical apparatus, as it was called), and hired well-trained and permanent professors to replace the transient tutors. Consequently, the number of science professors in America grew from twenty-five in 1800 to sixty in 1828 to over three hundred by 1850. Unfortunately, the status of science instruction did not improve nearly as rapidly in the South and West, where most schools offered no more than a smattering of introductory work taught by a single science instructor who often doubled as the mathematics professor.[26]

The approach of the scientists toward the Christian religion uniformly displayed what Theodore D. Bozeman has termed a "doxological" quality. Representative of nearly all were the views of Benjamin Silliman of Yale, Walter Minto of Princeton, and James Dwight Dana of Yale. Silliman, probably the leading scientist in the country, saw no difficulty in accepting both the findings of science and the record of Scripture, and viewed himself as "the honored interpreter of a portion of . . . [God's] works." Minto, a distinguished astronomer, believed deeply that

The study of natural philosophy leads us in a satisfactory manner to the knowledge of one almighty, all wise, and all good Being who created, preserves, and governs the universe. . . . Indeed I consider a student of [natural philosophy] . . . as engaged in a continued act of devotion. . . . This immense, beautiful, and varied universe is a book written by the finger of omnipotence and raises the admiration of every attentive beholder.

Dana told the American Association for the Advancement of Science in 1856 that "we but study the method in which boundless wisdom has chosen to act in creation," and then he observed that "almost all works on science in our language endeavor to uphold the Sacred Word." Not only were American scientists in this period often deeply religious; they also viewed their Christian beliefs as directly related to their scientific investigations, indeed, as providing the ultimate meaning to them.[27] Nothing could appear to be further from their mental horizons than the forthcoming revolution in science, which would crumble the foundations of Francis Bacon's inductive empiricism upon which both their science and their faith seemed to rest.

Only a few colleges officially introduced the teaching of written composition and literature before the Civil War, for many educators suspected that moral evil resulted from reading novels. Reflecting the concern of his college, one Oberlin student explained in verse what tends to happen when girls become addicted to novel reading:

The live, long day does Laura read,
In a cushioned easy chair,
In slip shod shoes and dirty gown,
And tangled, uncombed hair,
For o the meals I'm very sure
You ner' did see such feeding
For the beef is burnt and the veal is raw,
And all from novel reading.[28]

Despite this discouraging climate for modern literature, students could sometimes supplement their required courses by giving extra money and time to such pursuits. When the Yale tutors in the late eighteenth century wished to supplement the regular curriculum with English language and literature, the university approved only on the condition that the courses be taught to interested students outside the regular classroom schedule.[29]

Only rarely did a course in the English Bible appear in the official curriculum. President Alexander Campbell's Bethany College (of West

Virginia) was an exception; it opened in 1840 as the only literary college in America to maintain a Department of Sacred History and Biblical Literature as an integral part of the curriculum. Of like inclination was Geneva College, which from its start in 1848 offered a Bible curriculum as well as the prescribed classical curriculum. Biblical literature courses did not become common until the late nineteenth century, and then more because of the introduction of the system of elective courses than because of an administrative decision that Bible courses ought to be added to the curriculum of a Christian college.[30]

Study of the Bible nearly always appeared, though, as a vital part of the unofficial curriculum. In the early nineteenth century, Princeton students studied Bible lessons on Sunday after morning prayers and before breakfast. After morning church and dinner, they recited to the president on five chapters of the Bible. Oberlin in the 1860s required student participation in extracurricular Bible study courses that met one hour each week. During the typical four college years, an Oberlin student studied nearly the entire Scriptures. The Sunday requirements at Wake Forest included not only a Sunday morning worship service but also a Sunday evening Bible class for which all students prepared recitations. These nearly universal extracurricular Bible studies, when added to the regular senior-level religion courses and the frequent injection of biblical values into the entire curriculum, meant that students studied the Bible and the Christian faith roughly as much as students in the evangelical liberal arts colleges today do.[31]

With the increase in the number of middle-class students who brought to college their interest in agriculture and business, there gradually developed a demand for a less traditional curriculum. President Wayland of Brown led the movement for a program of study that would better meet the needs of the new type of student. He argued:

> That such a people should be satisfied with the teaching of Greek, Latin, and the elements of mathematics was plainly impossible. Lands were to be surveyed, roads to be constructed, ships to be built and navigated, soils of every kind under every variety of climate were to be cultivated, manufactures were to be established . . . all the means which science has provided to aid the progress of civilization must be employed if this youthful republic would place itself abreast of the empires of Europe.

In essence, Wayland was calling for the abandonment of the fixed, four-year course and the introduction of an elective system in which colleges would establish courses to meet newly developing societal needs and students would choose from a variety of offerings those which best met their intellectual needs and educational goals.[32]

The response of many American colleges before the Civil War was not to discard the old curriculum but rather to create an alternate "scientific" or "literary" degree program. This alternate curriculum either reduced or eventually replaced the classical studies and gave greater emphasis to modern languages, physical and biological sciences, history, literature, and the application of science to commerce. Students studying this curriculum earned a Bachelor of Science degree.[33] Before this alternative course of study caught on, however, students themselves created major intellectual supplements to the given course of study followed by most antebellum colleges—they founded associations called literary societies.

Student-Initiated Learning

Participation in a literary society was by far the most influential activity in American student life before the Civil War. The literary society movement began during the late colonial period, and while in some places it continued well into the twentieth century, it generally reached its peak during the first two generations of the nineteenth century. Nearly every college maintained at least two societies, which competed intensely against each other in a variety of activities. Each sought to recruit the most capable members of the freshman class, each sought to have a larger and better library collection than the other, each sought to outfit its society hall more lavishly than the other, and each sought to win the intersociety contests in oration, debate, and written composition.[34]

In each college the societies worked to enroll both the best and also the largest number of freshmen each fall with a vigor equal to that with which modern-day athletic coaches recruit athletes for their teams. Society scouts visited preparatory schools and delivered highly passionate speeches extolling the virtues of their societies while denouncing the opposition. Some of them even traveled to neighboring towns to board the trains bringing new students to the college so that they could beat the competition to the new prospects. At Wake Forest the Euzelian Society so desired to enlist the son of a China missionary that it promised to pay his tuition if he would join.[35]

It is amazing that students were willing to pay large sums of money, which in some cases equaled their tuition charges, to decorate their

lavish society halls and to build their societies' impressive library collections. At DePauw, for example, the students of one society spent over
eight thousand dollars just on portraits to hang in their hall.[36]

The societies often disciplined their members as rigorously—and
more effectively—than the colleges themselves did. The
Philomathesian Literary Society at Middlebury fined its members
twelve cents for absence from a society meeting and eight cents for tar-
diness. At Oberlin one society boasted in 1877 that not one member had
missed a society performance in eleven years. At Princeton the official
society censor carefully watched members' behavior. Any member who
neglected his work, wasted his time at a tavern, or displayed other than
exemplary behavior might be admonished or even suspended from the
society. On one occasion the society moderator himself received
punishment when he became irritated at the levity of a member whom
he was swearing into office and hit him over the head with a copy of
the organization's constitution.[37]

The most important society activities occurred at the regular meetings, where students competed in debates, oratory, and oral criticism.
This emphasis on developing articulate and persuasive speaking skills
served a functional purpose, as the great majority of students were
preparing for public careers in the ministry, politics, law, or teaching.
Often students exerted greater intellectual effort in preparing for
literary society activities than in studying for their regular classes. In
the days before the rise of athletics, the debate champion was the college hero. Winning the championship was an accomplishment even
more highly prized and honored than being the class valedictorian. The
most popular debate topics involved current events (e.g., "Have the
United States justly acquired Texas?"), but the students also enjoyed
debating historical issues (e.g., "Was the Reformation the Result of
Natural Causes or the Special . . . [Intervention] of Divine Agency?").
Philosophical and religious topics, on the other hand, received less attention from student debaters than they were given in the classroom.
Probably the single most popular debate topic during the decades
before 1860 was that of slavery.[38]

The highlight of the year for student orators occurred during commencement week when the seniors or the star orators from each of the
societies performed before large audiences. At Randolph-Macon, the
faculty dismissed the seniors from all classes for four weeks prior to
commencement to allow them to write, memorize, and polish their orations with one of the instructors. The student narrations served not only

as the climax of the literary society activities for the year but also as major public relations events for the colleges. The college presidents anxiously desired that the students perform ably and, above all, that they avoid any controversy that might embarrass college officials. Consequently, at Bucknell the president carefully monitored the orators during their preparation period, requiring them to submit their orations to him well in advance so that he might strike any objectional passages. If the student chose to use forbidden material on the day of graduation, he forfeited his degree.[39]

The literary societies maintained significant libraries to provide resource material for students preparing for their public performances. In some cases, the society libraries exceeded the college library in size. In 1839, for example, the Yale society libraries numbered 15,000 volumes while the college library stood at only 10,500. At Union College in the same year, the society libraries had 8,450 books, 300 more than the regular library collection. The two literary society libraries at Trinity (Duke) contained 2,200 volumes each in 1866, while the college library had only 650 books. The societies developed such extensive collections because the college libraries were almost without exception inadequate and inaccessible. The typical college library held a disproportionately large number of theological, legal, and medical books. The Dickinson library of 3,100 volumes in 1837 contained 700 works in theology, 600 in law and politics, and 400 in medicine and chemistry. Even worse, many of these studies were long outdated. Of the 400 volumes in medicine and chemistry, 35 had been printed in the sixteenth century, 244 in the seventeenth century, 53 in the eighteenth century, and only 4 in the nineteenth century. Furthermore, only 11 of the 400 volumes were in English.[40]

Even when a student demonstrated a special interest in an area in which the college library was strong, he faced considerable difficulty in gaining access to the collection because few college libraries held regular hours for students. The limitations at Columbia were by no means unique: "Freshmen and sophomores were allowed to visit the library only once a month to gaze at the back of books; the juniors were taken there once a week by a tutor who gave verbal information about the contents of the books, but only seniors were permitted to open the precious volumes which they could draw from the library during one hour on Wednesday afternoons." The society libraries, then, invariably exceeded the college libraries in the breadth of their collections and in their usefulness and availability to the students.[41]

It is difficult to exaggerate the positive influence the literary societies exerted upon student life. They provided some of the best intellectual activities—often better than those found in the classroom—and served as the only major organized social activity at the schools. They broadened the students' scope of information by emphasizing areas of knowledge that complemented more than duplicated the classroom work. They forced the students to analyze current events and to develop skill in precise reasoning and oral persuasion. Moreover, as the one aspect of campus life that was not dominated by the faculty, they provided students with a sense of participation in campus government and the opportunity to develop leadership skills. Many if not most colleges in this period could have echoed the experience of Hillsdale, whose historian wrote of the societies that "nothing else ever exerted so profound an influence upon Hillsdale students." Many students could have identified with the comment of William Seward, secretary of state under Abraham Lincoln, who stated about his years at Union College in New York in the early nineteenth century: "If I were required now to say from what part of my college education I derived the greatest advantage, I should say the exercises of the Adelphic Society."[42]

After the Civil War, the literary societies in colleges in the Northeast and Southeast began to decline, while those in the newer schools in the West reached their peak in the period just before 1900. The societies faded, in each case, for a variety of reasons. Many of the newer middle-class students began to prepare for technical vocations in which oral persuasion was not of major importance. In addition, other extracurricular activities such as musical organizations, athletic teams, and fraternities began to compete for students' time. And finally, the new electives added to the official curriculum in the late nineteenth century covered many of the areas of inquiry that society members had found most exciting.[43] While they lasted, though, the activities of the literary societies probably did more than any other campus activity to stimulate students to think creatively and develop the leadership skills that would be demanded of them as adults.

Such was life on the old-time college campus. The physical facilities were meager, the curricular and extracurricular options were limited, the instructors were minimally trained, and the supervision was intense. Yet the students received personal attention, they usually acquired an integrated worldview and a sense of purpose, and they probably enjoyed their experiences as much as today's students do. These schools' positive legacy of religious idealism, community service, and personal care is being reaffirmed, in whole or in parts, by a variety of educational leaders today.[44]

NOTES

1. See especially the writings of Richard Hofstadter, notably Hofstadter and C. De-Witt Handy, *The Development and Scope of Higher Education in the United States* (New York: Columbia University Press, 1952); Hofstadter and Walter P. Metzger, *The Development of Academic Freedom in the United States* (New York: Columbia University Press, 1955); Hofstadter and Wilson Smith, eds., *American Higher Education: A Documentary History* (Chicago: University of Chicago Press, 1961); Hofstadter, *Anti-Intellectualism in American Life* (New York: Knopf, 1963); and Hofstadter, "The Revolution in Higher Education," in *Paths of American Thought,* ed. Arthur M. Schlesinger, Jr., and Morton White (Boston: Houghton Mifflin, 1963).

2. See James McLachlan, "The American College in the Nineteenth Century: Toward a Reappraisal," *Teachers College Record* 80 (December 1978): 298-300; N. A. Naylor, "Antebellum College Movement: Reappraisal of Tewksbury's *Founding of American Colleges and Universities,*" *History of Education Quarterly* 13 (Fall 1973): 261-70; Douglas Sloan, "Harmony, Chaos and Consensus: The American College Curriculum," *Teachers College Record* 73 (December 1971): 224-26; David B. Potts, "College Enthusiasm as Public Response, 1800-1860," *Harvard Educational Review* 47 (February 1977): 28-30; James Axtell, "The Death of the Liberal Arts College," *History of Education Quarterly* 11 (Winter 1971): 341, 346; David B. Potts, "American Colleges in the Nineteenth Century: From Localism to Denominationalism," *History of Education Quarterly* 11 (Winter 1971): 366.

3. See McLachlan, "The American College in the Nineteenth Century," 295; George P. Schmidt, "Colleges in Ferment," *American Historical Review* 59 (October 1953): 19.

4. Clarence P. Shedd, *Two Centuries of Student Christian Movements* (New York: Association Press, 1934), 36, 48; Charles E. Cunningham, *Timothy Dwight, 1752-1817* (New York: Macmillan, 1942), 300-302.

5. John S. Brubacher and Willis Rudy, *Higher Education in Transition: A History of American Colleges and Universities, 1636-1976,* 2d ed. (New York: Harper and Row, 1968), 42-43.

6. Donald G. Tewksbury, *The Founding of American Colleges and Universities before the Civil War* (New York: Teachers College, 1932), 16, 69-73; Potts, "College Enthusiasm," 41.

7. Tewksbury, *Founding of American Colleges,* 104-5.

8. Ibid., 115-16.

9. See R. Freeman Butts, *The College Charts Its Course: Historical Conceptions and Current Proposals* (New York: McGraw-Hill, 1939), 118; Sloan, "Harmony, Chaos and Consensus," 231; James H. Fairchild, *Oberlin: The Colony and the College, 1833-1883* (Oberlin: E. J. Goodrich, 1883), 151-53; Colin B. Goodykoontz, *Home Missions on the American Frontier* (Caldwell, Idaho: Caxton Printers, 1939), 381; Ernest Earnest, *Academic Procession: An Informal History of the American College, 1636-1953* (Indianapolis: Bobbs-Merrill, 1953).

10. Naylor, "Antebellum College Movement," 270; Jurgen Herbst, *From Crisis to Crisis: American College Government, 1636-1819* (Cambridge: Harvard University Press, 1982), xi-xii; Charles D. Johnson, *Higher Education of the Southern Baptists: An Institutional History, 1826-1954* (Waco, Tex.: Baylor University Press, 1955), 47; William C. Ringenberg, "The Protestant College on the Michigan Frontier" (Ph.D. diss., Michigan State University, 1970), 63, 66, 72-73.

11. Potts, "American Colleges in the Nineteenth Century," 367-68; Potts, "College

Enthusiasm," 31-37; Timothy L. Smith, *Uncommon Schools: Christian Colleges and Social Idealism in Midwestern America, 1820–1950* (Indianapolis: Indiana Historical Society, 1978), 3, 21-29, 59.

12. *General Catalogue of Oberlin College, 1833–1908*, 117; *Oberlin College Catalogue, 1858–1859*, 38; *Oberlin College Catalogue, 1864–1865*, 6-34; Clyde S. Kilby, *Minority of One: The Biography of Jonathan Blanchard* (Grand Rapids: Eerdmans, 1959), 151-52; Charlie Brown Hershey, *Colorado College, 1874–1949* (Colorado Springs: Colorado College, 1952), 41; Smith, *Uncommon Schools*, 30.

13. Potts, "College Enthusiasm," 37-38; David F. Allmendinger, "New England Students and the Revolution in Higher Education, 1800–1900," *History of Education Quarterly* 11 (Winter 1971): 381-86; Allmendinger, *Paupers and Scholars: The Transformation of Student Life in Nineteenth-Century New England* (New York: St. Martin's, 1975), 1-22.

14. George P. Schmidt, *The Liberal Arts College: A Chapter in American Cultural History* (New Brunswick, N.J.: Rutgers University Press, 1957), 274; *Beloit College Catalog, 1860–1861*, 12; *Franklin College Catalog, 1847*, 5-7.

15. See Albea Godbold, *The Church College of the Old South* (Durham, N.C.: Duke University Press, 1944), 107-9; the quote is from Walter Havighurst, *The Miami Years, 1809–1959* (New York: Putnam, 1958), 32-33.

16. Godbold, *The Church College of the Old South*, 10-23; *Beloit College Catalog, 1860–61*, 19; Thomas LeDuc, *Piety and Intellect at Amherst College* (New York: Columbia University Press, 1946), 24.

17. Godbold, *The Church College of the Old South*, 71.

18. Hofstadter and Metzger, *The Development of Academic Freedom*, 152, 293.

19. George P. Schmidt, *The Old Time College President* (New York: Columbia University Press, 1930), 190-91; Shedd, *Two Centuries of Student Christian Movements*, 122.

20. Thomas J. Wertenbaker, *Princeton, 1746–1896* (Princeton: Princeton University Press, 1946), 165; Godbold, *The Church College of the Old South*, 128-30; George B. Manhart, *DePauw through the Years*, 2 vols. (Greencastle, Ind.: DePauw University, 1962), 1: 138.

21. Kilby, *Minority of One*, 84.

22. See Tewksbury, *Founding of American Colleges*, 83-84; Johnson, *Higher Education of the Southern Baptists*, 10; Godbold, *The Church College of the Old South*, chap. 2; William M. Glasgow, *The Geneva Book* (Philadelphia: Westbrook, 1908), 72; quote is from G. Wallace Chessman, *Denison: The Story of an Ohio College* (Granville, Ohio: Denison University, 1957), 117.

23. McLachlan, "The American College in the Nineteenth Century," 297; Goodykoontz, *Home Missions*, 362, 365; Shedd, *Two Centuries of Student Christian Movements*, 122; Godbold, *The Church College of the Old South*, 196; Ringenberg, "Protestant College on the Michigan Frontier," 159; Claude M. Fuess, *Amherst: The Story of a New England College* (Boston: Little, Brown, 1935), 22-43. For comparative data on the late eighteenth century see Donald O. Schneider, "Education in Colonial American Colleges, 1750–1770, and the Occupation and Political Offices of Their Alumni" (Ph.D. diss., George Peabody University, 1965); and Walter C. Bronson, *The History of Brown University, 1764–1914* (Providence: Brown University, 1914), 154.

24. *Ripon College Catalog, 1864–65*, 16. Mark Noll's first essay in this volume examines in detail the aims and content of these integrative courses, leaving it to this essay to focus on the other important curricular components.

25. Sloan, "Harmony, Chaos and Consensus," 240-42; Merle Curti, *The Growth of American Thought* (New York: Harper, 1951), 362; Earnest, *Academic Procession*, 22.

26. Stanley M. Guralnick, *Science and the Antebellum College* (Philadelphia: American Philosophical Society, 1975), viii-xii, 141-42, 158-59; Potts, "College Enthusiasm," 39; Godbold, *The Church College of the Old South*, 81; Sloan, "Harmony, Chaos and Consensus," 233.

27. Guralnick, *Science and the Antebellum College*, 153-55; Theodore Dwight Bozeman, *Protestants in an Age of Science: The Baconian Ideal and Antebellum American Religious Thought* (Chapel Hill: University of North Carolina Press, 1977), vi-xii, 76-81; Ralph Henry Gabriel, *Religion and Learning at Yale* (New Haven: Yale University Press, 1958), 113-16; Hofstadter and Metzger, *The Development of Academic Freedom*, 292; Wertenbaker, *Princeton, 1746–1896*, 95; Sloan, "Harmony, Chaos and Consensus," 227.

28. Earnest, *Academic Procession*, 95.

29. Cunningham, *Timothy Dwight*, 35-39.

30. Guy E. Snavely, *The Church and the Four-Year College: An Appraisal of Their Relation* (New York: Harper, 1955), 80-81; Norvell Young, *A History of Colleges Established and Controlled by Members of the Church of Christ* (Kansas City: Old Paths, 1949), 31; Glasgow, *The Geneva Book*, 20.

31. Wertenbaker, *Princeton, 1746–1896*, 198-99; John Barnard, *From Evangelicalism to Progressivism at Oberlin College, 1866–1917* (Columbus: Ohio State University Press, 1969), 25; Earnest, *Academic Procession*, 45; Johnson, *Higher Education of the Southern Baptists*, 10.

32. Sloan, "Harmony, Chaos and Consensus," 242-48; Earnest, *Academic Procession*, 75-77.

33. Butts, *The College Charts Its Course*, 129-31.

34. Henry D. Sheldon, *Student Life and Customs* (New York: D. Appleton, 1901), 89-93, 125-35; Thomas S. Harding, *College Literary Societies: Their Contribution to Higher Education in the United States, 1815–1876* (New York: Pageant, 1971), 22; Brubacher and Rudy, *Higher Education in Transition*, 46-48.

35. Sheldon, *Student Life and Customs*, 125-35; Godbold, *The Church College of the Old South*, 88.

36. Godbold, *The Church College of the Old South*, 85-88; Ringenberg, "Protestant College on the Michigan Frontier," 119; Earnest, *Academic Procession*, 86; Manhart, *DePauw through the Years*, 1: 129-30.

37. Kilby, *Majority of One*, 28-29; Barnard, *From Evangelicalism to Progressivism at Oberlin*, 21-22; Wertenbaker, *Princeton, 1746–1896*, 201-4.

38. Harding, *College Literary Societies*, 49, 101, 132, 158, 197-98, 232, 235-36; Codman Hislop, *Eliphalet Nott* (Middletown, Conn.: Wesleyan University Press, 1971), 181.

39. Godbold, *The Church College of the Old South*, 94, 168; Barnard, *From Evangelicalism to Progressivism at Oberlin*, 21; J. Orin Oliphant, *The Beginnings of Bucknell University* (Lewisburg, Pa.: Bucknell University Press, 1954), 66.

40. Harding, *College Literary Societies*, 56, 67-68; Godbold, *The Church College of the Old South*, 79. The largest college library collection was that at Harvard, which numbered 13,000 volumes in 1800 and 122,000 in 1854; for these figures see Theodore Hornberger, *Scientific Thought in American Colleges, 1630–1800* (Austin: University of Texas Press, 1945), 78; and Brubacher and Rudy, *Higher Education in Transition*, 94-95.

41. Harding, *College Literary Societies*, 56, 83.

42. Vivian Lyon Moore, *The First Hundred Years of Hillsdale College* (Ann Arbor: Ann Arbor Press, 1944), 93; Harding, *College Literary Societies,* 1.

43. Harding, *College Literary Societies,* 262, 296-98, 318.

44. This essay owes much to chap. 2, "The Old-Time College," in my book *The Christian College: A History of Protestant Higher Education in America* (Grand Rapids: Eerdmans, Christian University Press, 1984).

The University Arrives in America, 1870–1930: Christian Traditionalism During the Academic Revolution

Mark A. Noll

While the rest of the world has gone on its way, historians in recent years have been debating the relative merits of permanence and change. A select group of mostly French scholars has made the charge that so many of their colleagues are so mesmerized by change that more basic, more permanent realities escape their notice. This charge comes packaged with the appropriate foreign phrases—the failure to perceive reality results from myopic fascination with *histoire evenementielle*—and with a suitably spectacular demonstration of what research can do if it focuses on enduring rather than changing conditions.[1] There clearly are merits to this position, but not necessarily for the study of American higher education in the thirty years before and the thirty years after 1900. For this was a period absolutely and stunningly dominated by conditions of change.

A simple parade of figures suggests the dimensions of the change in American higher education from the end of the Civil War to the start of the Great Depression. From 1870 to 1930 the population of the United States more than tripled, from 40 million to 123 million. The number of colleges and universities in the country roughly kept pace with this increase: there were 563 in 1870, increasing to 1,407 in 1930. Yet every other measurable feature of American higher education far outstripped the growth in population. Twenty-three times more college degrees were awarded in 1930 than in 1870; colleges and universities employed over twenty-six times more faculty; student enrollment increased nearly twenty-nine fold over the same period; and the production of Ph.D.s in 1930 was greater than in 1870 by a factor of 3,290.

It is possible to humanize such sterile statistics with particular comparisons. In 1985 as many students were enrolled in Penn State University by itself as attended all the colleges and universities in the entire country in 1870. In 1985 many of the schools in the Christian College Coalition employed more faculty with earned doctorates than the nation as a whole produced in 1880 (54), and a few are home to more Ph.D.s than came forth from all American universities in 1890 (149). Two more comparisons are distorted because of monetary inflation since World War II, but they are still intriguing. In 1985 the income of Wheaton College very nearly equalled the income of all institutions of higher learning in the entire United States for the year 1890. Also in 1985, Wheaton's endowment was nearly three times larger than the endowment of Harvard University in 1909. To provide one more fiscal comparison not affected by inflation, the property values of American colleges and universities rose over twenty-one times from 1890 to 1930 while the country's population merely doubled.[2]

Suffice it to say, the sixty years after 1870 witnessed remarkable changes in the structure of American higher education. Yet the changes revealed by these statistics were probably not the most important events in education of the period. Even more dramatic alterations were underway, especially in assumptions about intellectual life and in conceptions of higher education itself.[3] Each of these matters deserves brief attention.

The intellectual change was associated with what George Marsden in a revealing essay has called "The Collapse of American Evangelical Academia."[4] Almost overnight, it seemed, realistic, static, and absolutist assumptions about learning gave way to the idealistic, developmental, and historicist. To be sure, intellectual changes had been occurring at a slow pace beneath the surface throughout the nineteenth century. While the dominant frame of reference in American colleges was a realist philosophy from Scotland, idealist notions were gaining ground through the speeches of the peripatetic lecturer Ralph Waldo Emerson, and through the efforts of several Congregationalist and Presbyterian ministers to publish the works of Samuel Taylor Coleridge.

This early American bent toward idealism, toward the constituting power of the mind, seemed more domestic and less recondite than the foreboding philosophy of Immanuel Kant; yet during the first half of the century it was never more than a minor eddy in comparison to the major currents that made up American thought. All this began to change, however, under the impact of two sets of circumstances. First of all, around mid-century when young scholars like Charles Eliot, president of Harvard, or Andrew Dickinson White of Cornell began to restructure the American university, they found various forms of philosophical idealism a useful ally in breaking the hold of older instructional forms. Second, when these new academic administrators sought highly qualified faculty, they instinctively looked to those who had done graduate study in Germany where prodigies of research and the assumptions of idealism went hand in hand.

Similar stories could be told for the replacement of static and absolutist assumptions by developmental and historicist ones. The newer theories seemed liberating; they offered means of breaking through the intellectual torpor of the old American college. Moreover, advocates of these conceptions—Charles Darwin in biology, Herbert Spencer in the new discipline of sociology, and from Germany the polymath Max Weber or the ethicist Albrecht Ritschl—were the most accomplished intellects of the day. In a time of technical innovation, demographic expansion, and—above all—educational revolution, these new forms of thought seemed just the thing to inaugurate a fresh era in the educational history of humankind.

Implications of this intellectual transformation for Christian higher education were immense. The old American college may not have been as explicitly Christian as it once seemed, but its efforts were still almost entirely in keeping with general Christian principles. The curriculum of the old-time American college had descended from the first collegiate instruction at Harvard in 1636 and in the late eighteenth century had been adjusted by adding selected principles of Enlightenment rationalism. In the past, its curriculum had consisted of a little mathematics, an introduction to empirical science, an exposure to philosophical reasoning, and a concentration on the classics. As I noted in my other essay above, its Christian structure was revealed most clearly by the capstone of instruction, the year-long course in moral philosophy. Now, after more than two hundred years continuous existence, this curriculum and its attendant values vanished almost without a trace. Disembodied pieces went on to serve as embryos for the new social sciences or as atomistic contributions to the offerings of philosophy departments. But the new university was far too secular, far too skeptical of Common Sense reasoning and Victorian conventions, to retain the Christian rationalism that had defined the intellectual life of American colleges since their beginning.

If change came swiftly in intellectual life, it came just as swiftly in the conception of higher education itself. The dawning age was professional and utilitarian, replacing an era of common sense and absolute ethics. While professors in the old colleges had taught students, those in the new universities taught subjects. Until after the Civil War it was customary for one or two instructors to oversee the entire education of particular students from their first days as freshmen to their graduation. To be sure, this instruction was supplemented by occasional lectures from a scientist, who might be given half-time to pursue a speciality, and by the senior course from the president. By and large, however, instructors in the old-time colleges were less like modern professors and more like the guidance counselors in our contemporary high schools who work with the same group of students throughout their academic careers. Trustees and faculty of the old college perceived no difficulties in this system because they considered themselves primarily the guardians of citizenship. Colleges did not exist to transmit knowledge, but to mold character. Learning was an important feature of that process, but the learning that mattered most was a knowledge of the classics, which were important because they illustrated virtue and vice in a time-tested fashion. (Greek and Latin—reading, writing, and speaking—made up the bulk of student instruction until the 1830s or 1840s, and still a vast portion of it until the 1870s and 1880s.)

Qualifications for faculty reflected this view of the academic life. Professors were to be patient, exemplary teachers of youth. They were to devote their days, and often nights as well, to the protection, guidance, assistance, and shepherding of the young men (and eventually young women) in their charge. If an occasional professor managed to free a little time for what we would today call research, it was a nice bonus that college authorities tolerated as long as it did not interfere with the main job of the institution. Not specialization, not technical expertise, not the ability to show the economic value of an education, but a calling to the training of young people was the essential ingredient of the academic life.

All this too was swept away in the coming of the new university. Research on the German model defined the road to success. The world was expanding, and scholars had to rush to keep pace. The new professors—soon women as well as men—enjoyed certifiable standing; they began to commit as much to their profession (as philosophers, chemists, historians, etc.) as to their institution. The training of undergraduates, especially freshmen and sophomores, could easily become a burden. Toward the end of the century one Harvard scholar went so far as to suggest that "the College [i.e., the undergraduate program] ought to be suppressed or moved out into the country where it would not interfere with the proper work of the University." President Eliot introduced his famous program of electives at Harvard (among other reasons) to encourage the faculty in the advancement of their research. He also tried to compress the B.A. program into three years in order to make more room for specialization, though this effort did not succeed. To the gimlet eye of George Santayana all of this was suspect. He felt that the Harvard faculty was becoming "an anonymous concourse of coral insects, each secreting out one cell, and leaving that fossil legacy to enlarge the earth."[5]

Whatever its actual character, the new university had a vastly different conception of its own role. It needed not the plain truths of plain people, not merely commonsensical contemplation of the world, not a disinterested concern for community welfare, but a focused, specialized, professional wisdom that acknowledged no master except Scientific Truth and Pragmatic Usefulness. New vistas of knowledge beckoned the academic; new visions of upward mobility entranced the graduate.

In sum, more than the mere passage of years and a mere growth in numbers separated the traditional college of 1870 from the trend-setting university of 1930. The new university was professional; it offered training useful for many professions. It was funded by large gifts from America's industrial giants instead of by small contributions garnered from the surrounding community. Its professors sought to become well known in their fields and to speak expertly to society as a whole. And its new science purported to illuminate a better way to truth, progress, and happiness.

The question for us today is how Christian education fared in this period of far-reaching change. Certain actions seemed of no great consequence in themselves yet spoke volumes about the direction in which the mainstream was flowing. At Harvard, compulsory chapel ceased in 1886. Ten years earlier the ceremonies that opened the Johns Hopkins University, the country's most professional center of higher learning, had included no invocation. And increasingly after the Civil War college presidents came from the ranks of faculty or even business, rather than from the pool of ministers who had filled almost all such posts before this time. But these were minor matters compared to the larger reorientation of the academic enterprise. When Christians lost control of science, when learning more generally was turned from a friend of faith to its enemy, when pragmatic intellectual fragmentation was thought to do a better job at preparing citizens than an integrative moral philosophy, what were the results for Christian higher education?

We must say first of all that a surprisingly large number of American institutions rejected, or remained ambiguously skeptical about, the revolution in higher learning. Some old-style colleges, a few institutions recently founded by Christian immigrants, a large number of newly-fashioned Bible schools, a growing network of Catholic colleges, and a sizable group of public institutions in the South and Midwest rejected many aspects of the academic revolution.[6] While all were influenced in subtle ways by the values of the new university, many rejected the agnostic science, the atomized curriculum, and the redefinition of citizenship promoted by the nation's academic pacesetters.

Yet it was by no means clear what course of action these schools, which the main current had left in a backwater almost overnight, should follow. Were they to be resolute naysayers, rejecting the learning of the world as in principle a contamination of civilization and Christianity? This was largely the choice of the new Bible schools. Or were they to maintain the academic integration of the early nineteenth century and thus promote an alternative vision of learning and a traditional certainty in the harmony of faith and science? This was the path that some Catholic and evangelical institutions followed. Or should the effort be rather to offer a miniaturized, Christianized version of the new university and thereby to reap a selective harvest from the new learning? While only a few Christian schools selected this response early in the century, it became a widespread pattern among Catholic, evangelical, and denominational colleges over the next seventy-five years.

Indecisiveness in the face of the academic revolution revealed a modicum of confusion in how Christian educators had pictured their own work. While they agreed on the necessity of preparing Christian citizens, they had not given extended thought to the role of learning itself toward that lofty goal. During the first sixty years of the nineteenth century, the heyday of evangelical religion in the United States, it had been all too easy to assume that science would always support the faith. As long as evangelical Protestantism served as the nation's unofficial established religion, there had been no particular reason to pay close attention to educational foundations. Now, when the rules of the game were changing fast, when pluralism and secularism advanced with a rush, the Christian colleges were confused. Institutions that had enjoyed the fruits of a Promised Land found themselves all of a sudden in Babylon. What should they do?

The report card for Christian higher education in this era of great change is mixed. Marks are high for citizenship, but decidedly worrisome for Christian scholarship. But both of these judgments deserve some amplification.

The great triumph of Christian colleges in the era of the new university was the preservation of a holistic ideal. In spite of the fragmentation and utilitarian pressure inherent in the new academic standard, Christian institutions continued to insist that education was for life. Colleges that retained a large measure of control over their student's courses, their extracurricular activities, and their mores did so for noble purposes. The justification for such authoritarianism may have sounded increasingly sectarian, but the motive behind it was sound. A college career, in the view of these colleges, was not meant primarily to show an individual how to benefit from the world but rather how the world could benefit from the individual. Christian educators had this motive, but an even higher one as well. Not just service to the world but service to Christ was the aim of a Christian education.[7]

As successful as the Christian colleges were in maintaining a holistic vision of Christian citizenship, they foundered in response to the specifically intellectual crises of the period. In what follows, my criticism of American Christian thought should be regarded as only part of the story, for the whole story involves a bit more than I am able to fill in here. The determination to educate people instead of consumers was, beyond doubt, the most important element of Christian higher education. But within that greater faithfulness there were serious intellectual problems, problems that had less to do with the contemporary revolution than with well-entrenched patterns of education. The old forms of education maintained by Christian colleges were now revealing their flaws: they contained serious weaknesses of two sorts—narrowly intellectual and more broadly structural.

The specific intellectual problems had to do with the Common Sense Realist content of courses in moral philosophy that dominated instruction in the old college. When removed from the hands of its Scottish authors and popularized in America, this perspective became, first of all, overly simplistic. It embodied a naive reliance upon intuition as a defense of morality, on science as an unequivocal road to truth, and on logical arguments as proof for the existence of God. Christian educators put these procedures to use for Christian purposes, even though each was only a thinly-veneered Christian adaptation of eighteenth-century rationalism. True enough, Christian education in America through the time of Jonathan Edwards employed these same arguments, but leaders like Edwards were also, at the same time, wrestling self-consciously with the problem of grounding supernatural beliefs on natural foundations. By the nineteenth century, however, the blithe assumption that these rationalistic arguments were fully compatible with Christian faith had replaced serious investigation of epistemological first principles.

A second difficulty of moral philosophy grew out of one of its strengths. In the hands of the nineteenth century's great educators, moral philosophy had been a tool for organizing people for battle against slavery, drink, and many other social evils, for advancing their conception of the kingdom of God on earth, and for preserving the virtues of the republic. Needful as such concerns continued to be later in the century, altered circumstances also called for an ethic applicable to institutions, not just individuals. Apart from an appeal to individuals to live honorably, however, moral philosophy offered little by way of institutional analysis. Since moral philosophers considered evil the result of individual choice, they had great difficulty in accounting for the detrimental effects of unregulated government, commercial giantism, or the national systems of communication. Yet these were the very structures that most desperately required the application of Christian ethics at the turn of the century. Where moral philosophy had failed, however, the new universities with their new models of education promoted, however inadequately, impressive theories and theoreticians devoted to the explanation of just these problems.

Finally, a third failure of moral philosophy was its captivity to a static view of science. "Facts" were unchanging elements of nature, perceived reliably through unbiased sense experience, organized inductively into generalizations, and summarized as natural laws. Christians who accepted this tradition were usually not prepared to see that science also rested on metaphysical foundations, that scientists were also moral actors, that the results of science deserved to be evaluated within the context of human life in its broadest extent. Precisely because science was such a treasured ally for leaders of the old college permeated by Christianity, it became a dreaded enemy when co-opted by secularists. In neither case did Christian educators realize how important it was to integrate science and technology into moral, philosophical, and theological frameworks.

These deficiencies in moral philosophy rendered Christian educators nearly mute before the spokesmen of the new universities. The crying need of the day was for intellectual resources that could analyze scientific, industrial, and social phenomena in relationship to worldviews. Yet strong as moral philosophy had been in other areas, it was weakest in providing such resources. Thus while Christian educators continued to call for full-orbed intellectual activity, few could say just what that activity should be like and how it should discriminate between the good and the bad in the new learning.

The failure of moral philosophy to respond to the new situation was the major intellectual problem for Christian higher education at the end of the century. A second, parallel, failure was structural, stemming from the hereditary division between theology and other forms of Christian learning. Americans had invented the independent school for theological education shortly after 1800. By mid-century a number of respected institutions were in place to prepare ministers, to defend the faith against its enemies, and to offer authoritative theological interpretations of the current scene. While a few of these seminaries sustained either formal or informal connections with colleges, most were under the direction of denominations or independent boards of trustees and were free to go their own way. As they did so they played an important part in the development of graduate education in the United States. In fact, for more than fifty years, they *were* graduate education in the United States. These seminaries often nurtured a lively academic life, and their periodicals provided Americans with the most intellectually challenging publications of the day. Under one masthead, these journals combined functions that are now the province not just of the religious press but also of such publications as *Psychology Today, Scientific American,* and the *New York Review of Books.* In more specifically Christian terms these seminaries did their jobs well—perhaps even too well in light of the larger purposes of Christian education.

The problem with the American seminary was not the school itself, for it had earned its place in the sun. The problem rather was the connection between theology and other forms of learning. The rise of the seminary had created a situation in which experts in Scripture and theology, working in the seminary, were widely separated from those who taught the wide range of academic subjects at the colleges. As colleges were transformed into universities toward the end of the century, it left a three-fold division: Christian colleges concerned for the liberal arts, Christian seminaries attempting advanced work in theology, and secular centers of research more generally. As a result of the institutional divisions, precious little cross-fertilization occurred between first-class biblical scholarship and first-class Christian thinking in the arts and sciences. Furthermore, when the universities emerged, they too, with their advanced scholarship in numerous areas, were separated from the most careful advanced thought in Bible and theology. The earlier development of separate theological training ruled out an ideal Christian learning, in which penetrating thinking about special revelation would coexist alongside penetrating thinking about revelation in nature, with each task fructifying the other. Also ruled out were the mutual benefits that could have resulted from a closer association of advanced scholarship in theology and Scripture and advanced scholarship in all disciplines at the secular institutions.

The presence of these two weaknesses—one in the intellectual content of thought, the other in the structure of academic institutions—largely prevented the Christian colleges from making an intellectual contribution to the wider world of higher education during the era of educational change. At a time when Americans needed to hear how human learning and the Christian faith could coinhere, when academic professionalization was fragmenting the life of the mind, and when urbanization and industrialization were making the Protestant ethic a dead letter, the Christian college had little to offer intellectually. Its practice of comprehensive Christian concern was a light in the darkness, but the beams from that light cast only a murky glow on the intellectual task at hand.

From our perspective near the end of the twentieth century it is clear that the character of Christian education one hundred years ago explains much about ourselves. Modern Christian colleges are distinctive in preserving a belief that character-formation is an essential part of higher education. They are likewise distinctive for preserving an ideal of education that integrates the academic with other spheres of existence. Yet the story of our past also helps to explain why institutions of Christian higher learning have done a better job of preserving an ideal of wholeness than of defining the actual intellectual content of that ideal. It is fair to say that work has only just begun on this task—or perhaps even that those of us who are committed to Christian higher learning have only just begun to sense the need for work on this task.

The story of Christian education in the face of the academic revolution is an honorable one. Outgunned intellectually, often outmaneuvered professionally, sometimes the object of public discrimination, always facing an intense pressure to conform to secular verities, the Christian colleges went on. As they did so, they preserved an institution with a mixed set of characteristics, including faithful Christian purpose, determined opposition to cultural fragmentation, a somewhat muddled legacy of nineteenth-century intellectual notions, and a persisting institutional division between academic work in sacred and secular subjects. Each of these was part of the history of American higher education during the coming of the university. Those who seek wisdom for Christian colleges at the end of the twentieth century could do worse than begin their search at the end of the nineteenth.

If the lessons of that era are taken to heart, it will encourage Christian educators to resist the atomization of the learning process as well as the definition and evaluation of that process simply in terms of economic relevance. It will also demonstrate the necessity for making their centers of Christian living into centers for Christian thought as well.

NOTES

1. For background, see *The Journal of Modern History* 44 (December 1972): 447-539, an issue devoted to the work of Fernand Braudel.

2. These figures are from *Historical Statistics of the United States: Colonial Times to 1957* (Washington, D.C.: Bureau of the Census, 1960), 210-12.

3. For further exploration of these changes and their implications for Christian higher education, along with documentation and sources for literature concerning many of the points made in this essay, see my "Christian Thinking and the Rise of the American University," *Christian Scholar's Review* 9 (1979): 3-16; and my essay "Christian Colleges, Christian Worldviews, and an Invitation to Research," which serves as the introduction to William C. Ringenberg, *The Christian College: A History of Protestant Higher Education in America* (Grand Rapids: Eerdmans, Christian University Press, 1984), 1-36. My other essay in this volume owes much to this introduction.

4. George M. Marsden, "The Collapse of American Evangelical Academia," in *Faith and Rationality: Reason and Belief in God,* ed. Alvin Plantinga and Nicholas Wolterstorff (Notre Dame: University of Notre Dame Press, 1983), 219-64.

5. Quoted in Robert A. McCaughey, "The Transformation of American Academic Life: Harvard University 1821–1892," *Perspectives in American History* 8 (1974): 306, 309.

6. See Ringenberg, *The Christian College,* chaps. 4 and 5, for a record of these institutions.

7. D. H. Meyer, *The Instructed Conscience: The Shaping of the American National Ethic* (Philadelphia: University of Pennsylvania Press, 1972), 65-66.

The Bible Schools and Conservative Evangelical Higher Education, 1880–1940

Virginia Lieson Brereton

Probably no other set of institutions was more important for the development of conservative evangelicalism in early twentieth-century America than the Bible schools. Yet for a variety of reasons they have largely escaped scholarly attention. Even conservative evangelicals themselves have had mixed feelings about the Bible school movement; from the very beginning Bible school educators had to answer evangelical critics who thought that these were "short cut" institutions that threatened efforts to sustain high standards of ministerial education.[1] The affinity of these schools to fundamentalism and other popular evangelical movements has dampened interest as well. Contemporary evangelical scholars have until recently found it difficult to examine their past in a detached manner; and when researchers in the more secular academic world have assessed twentieth-century evangelicalism, objectivity and interest have been in short supply. Scholars of education in particular have generally relegated Bible schools to the fringes of the American educational scene, finding them difficult to classify and even more difficult to understand.

The resurgence of conservative evangelicalism, however, has begun to command scholarly attention. Widespread adherence to traditional religious beliefs, in the face of the supposedly irresistible advance of secularization, commands such scrutiny. Fundamentalists and their kin seem to have an innate talent for attracting and convincing a popular audience and for disseminating their beliefs. Could it be that through a quiet work of education they have captured the hearts and minds of far more Americans than has hitherto been supposed? Such speculation is difficult to confirm, because evangelical educational efforts have been so totally ignored. Yet this much is clear: in the first half of the twentieth century, the Bible schools were the matrix of conservative evangelicalism. They trained its workers, nurtured and communicated its beliefs, and organized many of its activities. Furthermore, the dominant position of the Bible schools during these years allowed them to leave their stamp on the evangelical liberal arts colleges that have flourished since World War II.

My first task in this essay, then, is to formulate some understanding of the development and character of these institutions. After that, I will outline the impact of the Bible school movement in shaping conservative evangelical higher education since 1940. Because Bible schools figure so prominently in the history of conservative evangelicalism, their educational values and practices comprise an important legacy for evangelical higher education. As today's evangelical Bible and liberal arts colleges reassess their mission, they need to have an accurate idea of what they have inherited.

Origins and Early Development

The earliest Bible schools date from the 1880s and 1890s. The first of these, the Missionary Training Institute, was established in 1882 in New York City by A. B. Simpson, founder of the Christian and Missionary Alliance; in 1886 came Dwight L. Moody's Bible Institute in Chicago; and in 1889 the school that was to become Gordon College was founded in Boston as the Boston Missionary Training School. These schools took part in a broad mobilization to cope with what some Protestants of that era saw as desperate social and religious needs. They had become painfully aware of the millions overseas who, as they put it, had never heard the name of Jesus Christ. And on the home front they worried over the countless immigrants, many of them Catholic, living in destitution and ignorant of the evangelical Protestant faith. Even their fellow Protestants afforded them scant comfort; the typical congregation, they feared, was full of the lukewarm and comfortable who cared little about the church's mission.

This sense of alarm was shared by both theological liberals and conservatives; even the nature of their responses had much in common.[2] Like other Protestants before them, they resorted to the search for spiritual and educational renewal. Conservatives turned particularly to Bible and prophetic conferences, the first of which convened in 1868, where they met to pray and study God's word. They published journals and books that focused on Bible study, the second coming, missions, and Sunday school teaching. And they used the urban revival campaign, with Moody leading the way.[3]

The theologically conservative ministers and evangelists who conducted many of these activities were not particularly conservative in other respects. Indeed, they comprised an evangelical wing of what has come to be known as the "social gospel" movement. These reformers sought to reach beyond comfortable congregations to appeal to the urban masses by dispensing with pew rentals, elaborate sermon styles, and formal worship. Like their liberal counterparts, they widened their churches' scope of service, transforming them into virtual city missions.[4] They were also vitally linked to a massive "gospel welfare" network of urban evangelistic and social ministries, spearheaded by the *Christian Herald,* the Christian and Missionary Alliance, and especially the Salvation Army.[5]

If Protestants were to reach the unchurched in significant numbers, everyone agreed, they were going to have to field legions of trained workers, lay as well as ordained, female as well as male. Theological seminaries, primarily oriented toward producing relatively small numbers of male pastors, could not turn out enough workers. Into the breech came scores of "missionary training schools," modeled on European institutions and intended to attract lay people—including women—and to give them a short, practical course of one or two years that would enable them to become effective evangelists, home and foreign missionaries, Bible and Sunday school teachers, Y workers, pastors' assistants, and religious musicians.

There was nothing inherently conservative or liberal in the religious training these early students received, or in the activities they were trained for. The schools were conducted by a variety of denominations and groups, from Episcopal to Baptist, from Quaker to Advent Christian, and from the YMCA to the Salvation Army. The first Bible schools, then, belonged to this wider heterogeneous group of missionary training schools. Sometimes, in fact, except for the more conservative theologies of their instructors, Bible schools were virtually indistinguishable from the denominational training schools.[6]

It was not until the 1920s and the emergence of a fundamentalist movement proper that Bible schools began to be identified with conservative evangelicalism.[7] Fundamentalists had just as much faith in education as mainline Protestants had had before them, but they were concerned that most of the existing church colleges and theological seminaries had fallen into the hands of theological liberals. By 1924 many conservatives had lost confidence in all but a very few of the older Protestant colleges, notably Wheaton, Geneva, Houghton, and Taylor. But founding new, conservative evangelical colleges and seminaries was becoming increasingly expensive, as accrediting agencies and state departments of education set more and higher criteria for these institutions. Hampered by scarce resources, conservative evangelicals could manage to establish only a handful of liberal arts colleges and seminaries during the twenties and thirties.[8]

Faced with this educational vacuum, conservative evangelicals turned increasingly to a proven form of education that, by this time, they usually called the "Bible school" or "Bible institute." Although they showed strong parallels to the many normal schools, vocational training institutes, and business colleges then being founded, Bible schools confounded the categories established by accreditors and state officials. They were easy and cheap to set up, for they could be housed in a church or a commercial building and could be run with minimal full-time staff—at whatever academic level leaders saw fit.[9] Moreover, several of the pioneering Bible schools—notably Moody Bible Institute in Chicago, Gordon College of Theology and Missions in Boston, and the Bible Institute of Los Angeles (often called Biola)—had already become far more than schools; they were regional centers for conservative evangelicalism.[10] So, while evangelicals never stated a clearcut preference for Bible schools over colleges or seminaries, these institutes were a very practical choice. They were popular as well—between 1918 and 1945, evangelicals founded at least seventy Bible schools.[11]

Whatever the diversity among these institutions, they all tended to develop along similar patterns. This held true whether they were large like the Moody Bible Institute or small like the Advent Christian Church's Boston Bible School, whether they were interdenominational or sponsored by a particular church group. Bible schools looked a lot like each other because their leaders had frequent contacts, but also to an extent because the powerful Moody Bible Institute influenced and put its stamp on the entire movement.[12] The result was a distinctive Bible school curriculum and ethos. Three goals in particular infused the Bible schools' sense of purpose: they wished to offer popularly oriented, practical training; they demanded a curriculum centered on the Bible; and through the first two goals they hoped to prepare their students for service in Christian ministry.

A Popularly Based, Practical Education

The emphasis of Bible school educators on practical training stemmed from the spirit of urgency about social and spiritual needs that had impelled conservative evangelicals since Moody's day. The chief obstacle to the fulfillment of the evangelical vision of a converted world and a harmonious and Christian America appeared to be the lack of trained workers. So a broad summons went forth for trained lay people. Moody issued his famous plea for "gap-men to stand between the laity and the ministers," and C. I. Scofield echoed, "this is a layman's age." A. J. Gordon wanted "to call out our reserves—to put into the field a large force of *lay* workers," and A. B. Simpson asked for "irregulars," saying, "God is building windows for the cathedrals of the skies out of the rejected lives and fragments of consecrated service for which the wisdom of the world has not room."[13]

What part of the population did these lay people eventually come from? From the romantic rhetoric thrown about one would have expected them to come from the "toiling masses of our people . . . who are kept back by the feeling that they are not qualified. . . ."[14] But in reality, recruits for home and foreign missions were more likely to have been salesmen, store clerks, teachers, secretaries, skilled craftsmen, and small business owners than farmers or factory workers.[15] True, those entering the Bible schools were often not particularly well educated by present-day standards, but then very few Americans attended high schools, let alone colleges and seminaries, until the 1920s.[16] The most easily identifiable group of potential workers was women, who by the late nineteenth century had organized foreign missionary societies and taken on roles as pastors' assistants, Sunday school officers, Bible teachers, evangelists, missionaries, gospel musicians, and workers in city missions, settlements, and the YMCA. But all these callings demanded more skills, more knowledge, and more training than most women had, and which for the most part theological seminaries were unwilling to give them.[17]

If American lay men and women were to be quickly readied in sufficient numbers for the struggle ahead, a different kind of education was called for. First, it had to be abbreviated. According to missions leader Arthur T. Pierson, "If we would largely increase the missionary force, we must in some way lessen the time and cost of the preparation of the average workman."[18] The first schools thus required only one or two years of attendance, and occasionally even less. The brevity of the training was also intended to keep up the ardor of the recruits. Pierson argued that "long withdrawal from active work, and absorption in mere study, are not favorable to burning zeal."[19]

Another feature of the new education was that it should be "practical." Practicality demanded that classroom teaching concentrate on transmitting the skills and knowledge the students needed for their evangelistic work. Liberal or general education was considered an unwanted extravagance given the exigencies of the time. Practicality also dictated that students were to get plenty of actual experience in service to the poor, immigrants, and criminals. Because the new kind of education was briefer and more to the point, its supporters could suggest that it was more efficient, and that these efficiently trained religious workers had been taught only what they needed to know in order to perform their functions quickly and confidently—a claim that reflected the great enthusiasm for "efficiency" and new business methods in the late nineteenth and early twentieth centuries.[20]

All these elements—brevity, practicality, efficiency—were summed up in the word "training." The emphasis on training reflected the Bible schools' participation in a widespread educational revolt against the older classical learning. Many of the training school founders, to be sure, valued their own classical educations, but recruits to the mission fields and city ministries, like those training for careers in nursing and accounting, simply lacked time for this luxury. And often, leaders thought, such learning could be downright harmful. A. B. Simpson complained in 1897 that a liberal education was "often . . . merely intellectual, scholastic, traditional," and many Christian workers had been forced "to unlearn what man had crammed into [their] brains."[21] Moody complained that frequently a young preacher has learned "nothing about human nature, doesn't know how to rub up to common men and adapt himself to them, and then gets up a sermon on metaphysical subjects miles above these people. . . . What we want is men trained for this class of people."[22] Yet for all their anticlassicism, these educators neither opposed longer training nor judged theological seminaries to be outmoded. They simply wanted to provide shorter, more accessible avenues to Christian service and argued that the church would forfeit valuable talents by rigidly insisting on a traditional education.

A Bible-Centered Curriculum

But enough about the schools' rationale. We need to see what they taught. The heart of a Bible school curriculum was, naturally enough, study of the Bible; for above all else, Bible school educators wanted their students to have useful Bible knowledge. During the twenties, the Assemblies of God's Central Bible Institute in Springfield, Missouri, pronounced the Bible to be "the chief text-book," an assertion that the Bible Institute of Los Angeles echoed and applied to all Institute classes. The 1920 catalog description of Biola's department of Psychology and Sociology declared "that the best text book on psychology is the Bible," for it shows "man as he really is, and not as speculative philosophers imagine him."[23] When Bible school educators called their institutions "Bible-centered," they were not exaggerating.

Though their Bible courses were designed for conservative religious purposes, Bible school educators considered themselves reformers. They were responding to the growing inaccessibility of Bible knowledge for ordinary people caused by the professionalization of biblical studies. Bible teachers criticized the older practice of exegesis, the close scrutiny of a passage in the original language with minute attention to philological distinctions. Such an approach, they argued, fragmented and obscured Scripture. These teachers also rejected the idea that students must acquire Greek and Hebrew in order to grasp the meaning of the Bible. Instead, Bible school classes concentrated upon study of the Bible in English, a practice that made it possible for students to gain familiarity with the whole sweep of the Scriptures in a relatively short time.[24] Accordingly, C. I. Scofield advocated "A Panoramic View of the Bible"; and James M. Gray of Moody Bible Institute recommended his method of "synthetic Bible studies" as "giving a Bird's-Eye View of the Bible."[25]

This holistic approach to Scripture study was based upon the dispensational theology taught at the majority of Bible schools. Dispensationalists interpreted the Bible as a series of divine offers of salvation and a corresponding series of human rejections. Thus the Bible, considered as a whole, revealed God's grand and progressive scheme for human redemption, unified by the unchanging nature of God's purpose and by the consistency of human resistance. Moreover, dispensationalism claimed to reconcile the seemingly contradictory parts of Scripture, rendering them comprehensible rather than perplexing.[26]

Probably no approach to learning the Bible was more popular in

Bible schools than James Gray's "synthetic" and "inductive" method. As early as the first half of the 1890s it was in use at Moody Bible Institute and Gordon College of Theology and Missions, and in succeeding decades this method spread to many other schools and became the backbone of their Bible synopsis or Bible survey classes.[27] Gray's method instructed students to read a Bible book or a large chunk of it in a single sitting. After that, they were urged to reread the same book several times in the attempt to grasp its overall themes. They started with Genesis and went on to each book in the order of its appearance in the Bible.

Gray made Bible study seem a remarkably simple, inductive, matter-of-fact affair. The task of Bible study, he argued, was to grasp the facts first and then to interpret them. He insisted that "if we get the facts the interpretation will take care of itself, for the Bible is wonderfully self-interpretive."[28] This argument, besides making the Bible seem refreshingly accessible, also put it on much the same footing as the data of science, and implicitly compared the Bible student to the scientific investigator.[29]

But Gray was interested in more than simply classifying biblical facts, identifying the main outlines of biblical narrative, and fixing these in the students' minds. He also offered definitions of biblical terms, apologetics for the biblical account of history and natural events, guiding principles of interpretation, and, in fact, his own interpretations of the text. Some of these interpretive lines were decidedly dispensationalist. For instance, he incorporated the dispensationalist idea of the "rapture" of the church in his discussion of Isaac: "Isaac going out to meet his bride . . . is emblematical of Christ coming out from Heaven to meet the church, and the rapture of the latter . . . as we find in such places as John 14:1-3, and I Thessalonians 4:13-18."[30] In his interpretation of the Old Testament, Gray showed little interest in explaining the patriarchs in their historical context. Instead he treated their lives primarily as moral lessons for present-day Christians. And he was always anxious to add notes that demonstrated how natural science or archaeology corroborated the biblical record.[31]

A holistic introduction to Scripture was only the beginning of Bible study, which consumed the majority of classroom hours. Scripture could also be approached topically, sometimes in classes called "Bible doctrines," or students could concentrate their attention upon particular Bible characters, single books, "great chapters," "key words," "biblical prophecy," or the various "names of God." Once the whole Bible was mastered, students could also learn traditional exegesis, usually referred to as "Analysis" in the catalogs. A woman student at Moody Bible Institute commented that "after such 'telescopic' work [offered by Gray], Prof. Weidner and his 'microscopic' study of Genesis is delightful."[32] Other Bible classes, notably "Bible Geography," "Bible Atlas," or "Blackboard Drawing" served as auxiliaries. "Bible Introduction" usually had an apologetic purpose; at Moody it dealt with "the authenticity of the Bible including its history, the formation of the canon, and current criticism."[33] And finally, Bible study at Bible schools included a great deal of memorization, since evangelists were expected to quote Scripture verses at will. Louis Talbot, a student at Moody Bible Institute during the early teens, wrote home that he was thankful that he had a good memory.[34]

Such concentration on the Bible represented the apotheosis of American Protestant biblicism. In these schools Scripture became not only the center of the curriculum but also the focus of the student's life. For the Bible school student, to think, feel, react, and speak biblically was the ultimate goal. In the introduction to his *Synthetic Bible Studies,* James Gray expressed his desire that such study would "be something more than a feast of intellect."[35] At the Bible schools, the Bible classes were indeed much more.

In fact, the test of success in Bible study was practicality: could it be applied? Did students know the Bible well enough to create an expository preaching or Bible teaching series? Could they quickly quote verses they wanted? Could they grasp another's needs and sense which verse or passage would most likely meet them? In addition to their Bible classes, therefore, most Bible school students attended classes in "Personal Work," "Personal Evangelism," or "Personal Soul-Winning," which taught them how to approach others in the attempt to convert them. Much like classes in sales techniques, they were designed to identify personal approaches suited to the wants and needs of individual prospective "customers."

Teachers outlined the objections most frequently raised by potential converts and suggested standard responses. They identified scriptural passages that might prove effective in given cases, and they rehearsed techniques that had proven effective in the past.[36] Subjects for evangelization were classified as character types and matched to a set of methods for approaching them.[37] Despite the attempt to reduce personal work to sets of principles, however, the most important pedagogical tool was the anecdote. Instructors told stories of successful encounters, and from their own daily experiences students brought accounts of their attempts.[38] These courses often functioned as workshops, then, to discuss and evaluate students' practical work assignments.

The majority of students at Bible schools selected a program called the "General Bible Course," or some similar title. They studied Bible, evangelism, some theology, and perhaps a smattering of music and pedagogy. At many schools it was also possible to follow special programs, still based on the same core of Bible and evangelism courses, that taught the particular skills required of certain positions—pastor, Christian educator, religious musician, or foreign missionary. Prospective foreign missionaries, for example, might add to the General Bible Course the history and principles of missions, elementary medicine, linguistic principles, biographies of missionaries, and characteristics of particular fields. Christian education courses included child psychology, principles of pedagogy, storytelling techniques, and Sunday school teaching methods. Prospective religious musicians took classes in music theory and instrumental lessons. While many of these classes were new on the religious educational scene, the pastoral course often injected a number of subjects from the traditional theological curriculum: apologetics, systematic theology, homiletics, pastoral theology, Greek, and Hebrew. The retention of these courses in the curriculum reflected the lingering ideal of the learned minister, even though the old curriculum might be altered to fit the goals and clientele of the Bible schools. Greek or Hebrew were likely to be taught on a rudimentary level, and homiletics classes often included women who had no prospect of preaching from the pulpit.[39]

Bible school educators were cautious about introducing liberal arts subjects. One reason is obvious: the more of these courses in the curriculum, the less time and energy students and faculty would have left for Bible and missions studies. In addition, the liberal arts could also seem to endanger institutional goals in more fundamental ways. The social sciences posed the greatest threat to the Bible school view of the world, for in their focus on humanity they employed concepts of gradual development and human and material causation. This contradicted the fundamentalist insistence upon divinely superintended discontinuities in the affairs of culture and nature. Then, too, the separatist impulse of many evangelicals discouraged exploration of this-worldly human phenomena. Even when a school did teach the social sciences, it did so for the direct application to Christian work. Thus the Biola *Bulletin* described one Personal Work course as a study "in real and practical psychology, and not in mostly imaginary and theoretical psychology, so common today."[40] The "how" rather than the "why" predominated in instruction, the practice rather than the theory.

Contrary to what one might assume, natural science was not necessarily regarded as threatening, because it could be learned in its Baconian version—as facts, information, and techniques, and as a doxology for the design that flowed from the Creator's hand. Such was the approach of the Sermons from Science presented by Irwin Moon, a Moody Bible Institute extension evangelist in the late 1930s.[41] Science as a body of theory, or as a skeptical, inquiring approach to the world, was derided as "science falsely so called."[42] Nevertheless, most Bible schools simply lacked the time, personnel, and demonstration equipment necessary for teaching any kind of science until late in their development.

Among the humanities, English literature entered the Bible school curriculum quite early on, partly because the subject was linked to improving students' writing skills. Moreover, literary studies could bestow a little culture upon students whose backgrounds afforded little acquaintance with the arts. At Gordon College in the 1920s and 1930s, for example, classes were offered in English literature including the Victorians Arnold and Tennyson. In addition there were classes in rhetoric, philosophy, science, history, French, and mathematics. These classes gave a little polish to students who had come to Boston from maritime Canada and northern New England.[43] To be sure, literature was more for edification than for provoking thought; history and philosophy were for appreciating and defending Christianity and "Christian civilization" rather than for asking critical questions and inspiring new creativity. Gordon College's efforts to incorporate the liberal arts were more vigorous and successful than those of other Bible schools, though in fact not all Bible school educators would have wanted to emulate Gordon. But the model existed and pointed the way for at least some others.

There were many consistencies and constancies in the Bible school curriculum, then, whatever the time period or the school: an emphasis on Bible study and certain interpretations of Scripture; a preoccupation with the practice of evangelism and missions; and the five-course division (General Bible, the Pastorate, Christian Education, Missions, and Music). Yet if we were to end our exploration here, we would have a distorted picture, for the "extracurriculum" was also a crucial part of what students learned.

Preparation for Service

Bible school students typically spent several hours a week in actual religious work outside the school. So important was this practical-work experience in some schools that it might be argued that classroom learning was the supplement rather than the core. The Bible Institute of Los Angeles, for instance, described itself in 1915 not so much as a school as "a soul saving station whose workers were busy night and day reaching unsaved people in all walks of life."[44]

The requirement that students obtain practical training served several purposes. First, it followed the principle of then-current educational theory that students learned best by doing. Practical work outside the school also helped students develop sympathy with the working classes and taught them how to deal effectively with them. As a Moody Bible Institute writer warned, "If you cannot make a corking good speech from a soap box; . . . if you do not know the problems of the working class and cannot speak of them . . . you had better not go."[45] Practical work also provided a welcome outlet for students who were impatient to "win souls." Many eagerly regarded it as the core of their training, the most challenging part.

Students could choose from a variety of work assignments. At the Bible Institute of Los Angeles, these were purposely rotated to afford each student a variety of experiences. It was usual for Bible school students to lead church choirs, teach Sunday school classes, or advise young people's groups. Others chose to serve in asylums, almshouses, "old people's homes," hospitals, prisons, industrial homes, rescue missions, settlement houses, and city missions—settings where they mixed social and evangelistic ministries. Some set out to distribute Bibles and tracts or to witness door-to-door, while others served in street meetings, tent services, or mass revival meetings. In 1917, Gordon College students were out in force at the Billy Sunday meetings in Boston.[46] Work with immigrants often fell to students with foreign missionary aspirations. If they proved effective with Mexicans in Los Angeles or Italians in Chicago who knew neither the English language nor the evangelical faith, surely they could succeed with Chinese, Sudanese, or South Americans. One alumnus of Moody Bible Institute testified that his work with Chinese immigrants in his first year at school prompted a lasting interest in foreign missions.[47]

Practical-work programs were not without their problems, notably their conflict with schools' efforts to raise academic standards,[48] but they nonetheless afforded students valuable opportunities. They could test and prove themselves and add to their skill and self-confidence as evangelists. Furthermore, while Bible school educators tried to shelter their charges from the world's corruption, practical work rendered the students streetwise in acceptable and functional ways. Indeed, since most early Bible schools were located in cities, practical work introduced the students, many of whom came from rural and small-town backgrounds, to the city and to typically urban groups that they might not otherwise have known—immigrants, blacks, Jews, and working-class people. Thus Bible schools helped fundamentalism adapt to urban America, and thereby contributed to the movement's effectiveness.

In addition to encouraging students to acquire useful knowledge and practical skills, the Bible school was also expected to shape their spiritual and emotional lives. The struggles common to life at Bible school—for more meaningful spiritual experience, for a worthy and definite calling, for greater righteousness, and for the boldness required by evangelists—were encouraged, even if the attendant strain made the Bible school something of an emotional pressure cooker. Many elements of Bible school life were designed to promote and intensify those strivings but also to foster satisfactory resolutions.

In helping students to spiritual maturity, nothing was more important than emulation. The faculty, occasional speakers, graduates, and admired evangelicals of the past all served the goal of inspiring students and demonstrating what roles they too might play in furthering "the King's business." Generally speaking, the faculty of Bible schools were chosen for the quality of their spiritual lives. Teachers endowed with vital faith, it was hoped, would transmit their visions to their students. The faculty also served as models of active service, for they often worked simultaneously as pastors, evangelists, missionaries, writers, and administrators of religious agencies. A. E. Thompson, of the Nyack Missionary Training Institute, had spent much of his life in Palestine, while his colleague Robert Glover had served in China. Students under such tutelage often resolved to emulate their teachers' achievements as well as their piety.[49] More than emulation was involved, however, as Bible school teachers often served their students as spiritual parents. Customarily described as "homes," many Bible schools were small enough for everyone to know everyone else well. Bible school work was often a family affair, with husband and wife both on staff. Full-time faculty participated in worship services, prayer meetings, and social events and counseled students who needed help. Students responded in turn by fondly calling their mentors "pappy" and "mother."[50]

A stream of visiting speakers, male and female, modeled faith and activism as well. Students at the Nyack Institute, for instance, heard many missionaries and evangelists. Among the most colorful were "Mother" Whittemore, founder of the Door of Hope rescue mission for prostitutes in New York City,[51] and "Brother" Crawford, representing the Christian Alliance in Boone, Iowa, who spoke in 1912 on 1 Corinthians 4:9: "Appointed to Death," the call to be "a minister of Christ after the apostolic type."[52] Regularly scheduled religious conferences, like Moody's annual Founder's Week, brought together the movement's stalwarts and devoted graduates now in religious service to stir students' aspirations.

Finally, students drew inspiration from heroes of the past. Accounts of mission pioneers Hudson Taylor and George Muller brought edification, as did those of the Bible school movement's own patrons, notably Dwight L. Moody, A. J. Gordon, and A. B. Simpson. Exemplary lives of earlier generations were recounted in biographies: among the better known were of British evangelicals Charles Haddon Spurgeon and H. Gratton Guinness, and those of Martin Luther, David Brainerd, Adoniram Judson (and his wives, Ann Hasseltine Judson and Sarah Boardman Judson), Charles Grandison Finney, John Wesley, and John Woolman. The world of the Bible school student was populated with saints, both living and dead, who taught that all things were possible to those who had faith.

Other facets of Bible school life directed the students toward greater devotion. Frequent prayer meetings, missionary zeal, and behavioral strictures enveloped these earnest communities, but probably nothing distinguished the Bible school more than the pervasiveness of evangelical music. Their halls resounded with the strains of practicing singers, pianists, trumpeters, and organists. Anthems and choruses rang out from devotional gatherings, classes, mealtimes, picnics, and other student outings. At the Nyack Institute, the "quiet hour" each night was announced "by the singing or playing softly of a devotional hymn, by a group going from floor to floor." Students and faculty often wrote songs in their spare hours, giving several schools their own native hymnodies.[53] Hymns could be powerful teachers of service, devotion, and piety. When students at Nyack sang Kenneth Mackenzie's "Here Am I, Oh Lord, Send Me," for instance, they confronted the missionary's radical commitment: "Jesus, use me now and ever, / I will give myself to Thee, / Thine to be in body, soul and spirit, / Here am I, O Lord, send me."[54]

Prayer also prevailed at Bible schools. Prayer meetings took many forms: formally scheduled occasions arranged by the faculty or administration or meetings held by the students themselves, all-day intercessions for a particular concern or impromptu gatherings involving anywhere from a handful to everyone. A student at Boston Bible School recalled "gathering in small groups to take some special burden to the Lord." At the Christian Workers Training Institute in Los Angeles, a Quaker institution, "sometimes the 5 A.M. Thursday prayer hour would last until 9 A.M." Biola students gathered daily for the "superintendent's half hour" right after breakfast, for a student-led meeting after supper, and for daily "corridor prayer meetings" to discuss personal problems and "present them to God for solution." At Moody Bible Institute in 1922, Institute leaders reported 1,324 "stated prayer meetings" per month, "besides innumerable gatherings . . . that . . . cannot be tabulated."[55]

One of the most important ingredients of such gatherings was the giving of testimony. When students testified, they told and retold the story of their spiritual journeys. Testimonies often sounded as though they had been learned by heart, and they frequently incorporated the same phrases and Scripture verses. The formulaic style of the testimonies prevented the experience from becoming too painfully personal and enabled nearly everyone to participate. The ritual of testimony sharing could bring on a powerful experience of emotional bonding, a sense of kinship in Christ's family—and in the family of the Bible school.[56]

Occasionally, a student's remarks or a sermon would elicit a particularly intense response from other students, and revival would break out. At the Nyack Institute, one early report recalled, the Holy Spirit "came suddenly one Sunday noon at the Missionary prayer meeting." The meeting did not end until six o'clock the next morning, and the revival then "superseded regular class and study time" and continued for three weeks.[57] A similar revival occurred in 1938 at the Central Bible Institute in Springfield, Missouri, when "for two days He visited us in an unusual manner, during which time classes were suspended." Before the revival was ended, the reporter testified, "we were feeling clean and refreshed . . . and God, just as good as His Word, had imparted new blessing to our souls."[58] Revivals such as these offered students the chance to get rid of their frustrations and begin again with a clean slate, a sense of empowerment, and restored community solidarity.

The Bible schools' inner culture was devoted to the missionary enterprise. Many of these schools had been founded specifically to train missionaries, and if their purposes had broadened a bit by the 1920s and 1930s, the missionary ethos still filled their corridors. It was not uncommon that Bible school students had parents or some other close relatives already working as foreign missionaries. Many students had early on pledged their future to the foreign mission fields, and some had even selected a particular field for service. Alumni who had become foreign missionaries sent stirring reports of their experiences, and in frequent recruiting visits they regaled students with accounts of missionary endeavors. Foreign missions work was often risky, and it was not unusual for graduates to die in the field. News of such "martyrs" often galvanized students to pledge themselves to take the place of the fallen.[59] Student publications exhorted classmates in urgent, elevated, Scripture-laced prose: "Hear the voice of Jesus say, 'Who will go and work for me?' . . . Who, who, will answer gladly saying, 'Here am I, O Lord, send me.'"[60]

Each Bible school had at least one foreign missionary organization, perhaps a branch of the Student Volunteer Movement or, after its founding in 1936, the Student Foreign Missions Fellowship. Many schools were divided into "prayer bands," each of which met weekly to study a particular field, track its progress, pray for its missionaries, and raise money.[61]

The extent of this emphasis on foreign missions is reflected in the statistics. By 1927, less than two decades after the founding of the Bible Institute of Los Angeles, 300 graduates had gone to the foreign mission fields. In 1928 Moody Bible Institute reported that it had by that time sent out 1,440 missionaries, 1,096 of whom were still active. By 1962, Safara Witmer of the Accrediting Association of Bible Colleges estimated that at least half of the 27,000 Protestant missionaries then in the field had prepared at Bible schools. Some 2,700 of these were Moody graduates.[62]

Bible school leaders took pride in such figures, which reflected their schools' highest aspirations. But in order to maintain an environment that they believed would be conducive to such ends, they moved, after the second or third generation of students, to impose regulations on community behavior. The early Bible school students had been largely unregulated, probably because most of them were already in their twenties and highly motivated; they hardly had time or energy for the mischief characteristic of younger students. Student bodies tended to get younger as the school got older, however. At Biola, for example, the average age of the students declined from twenty-five between 1908 and the early 1930s to twenty by the early 1940s.[63] Evidently, the new dependence of conservative evangelicals on Bible schools as the bastions of orthodoxy pressured the schools to enroll younger and less committed students. As the 1928 catalogue of Moody Bible Institute explained, "parents are asking the Institute to accept their sons and daughters though under age, in order that they may be equipped . . . to meet the attacks upon their faith" at secular colleges and universities.[64] It seems that Bible schools began to admit younger students simply because their parents thought attendance would do them good. Inevitably, some of these students were not committed Christians and found themselves in Bible school against their will.[65]

As the character of the student body began changing, then, and students as a rule were less mature spiritually and emotionally, the schools began to regulate student lives more closely. A necessary ingredient for creating the "total environment" Bible schools sought was the dormitory or residence hall, where oversight could be maintained and rules enforced twenty-four hours a day. By the early 1930s, the New England School of Theology imposed mandatory study hours each weekday evening as well as spot inspections of student rooms. The dean's list there rewarded not only academic achievement but also "general deportment," "orderliness in person and room," "school spirit," and "unsolicited cooperation."[66] Nothing, it seemed, escaped the purview of school authorities.

Rules regarding recreational activities and relations between male and female students were becoming especially stringent. Sexual segregation or close supervision became the norm. The codes of behavior generally outlawed smoking, drinking, theater attendance, dancing, betting, and card playing, and they also dictated what constituted "decent" student appearance. A male graduate of the Nyack Institute recalled the strictness of Dean Cora Turnbull during the teens and twenties with these words: "There was no integration of sexes in those days. Boys must walk south on the days the girls walked north, and vice versa. . . . Any couple whose courses crossed on the Nyack-Tarrytown ferry were sure to be limned in her telescopic eye."[67]

Individual schools had their own procedures for dealing with those who broke the rules. At Biola, disobedient students were summoned to the superintendent or dean, where they might hear: "What are you here at school *for?* You come from wonderful dedicated Christian parents. . . . It would break their hearts if you were thrown out. What do you think is wrong with Biola? Maybe something is really wrong with *you.*" For serious offenses students might face probation or even dismissal, but transgressors often received chances to reform. It was difficult to give up on students considered "spiritually not right with the Lord."[68]

Enveloped in such an intense community, students would have had a difficult time voicing dissent, remaining aloof, or only pretending piety. Indeed, at Biola it was even forbidden to "talk against the school."[69] Nonetheless, the records here and there show glimpses of students who were unwilling or unable to cope with the highly charged and highly regulated atmosphere. Those who found the pressure too great to bear either departed voluntarily or were forced to leave. One revival at Nyack evoked both "all kinds of confessions" and also some resistance; evidently the unrepentant were accused of causing "confusion," and several left school.[70]

It would be a mistake, of course, to suggest that Bible school students never had fun. After a Thanksgiving Day turkey dinner in 1927, for example, Biola students spent the rest of the holiday boating in Westlake park, singing gospel choruses accompanied by a saxophone, and playing games. Bystanders, it was assumed, must have been surprised to see "a group of young people so happy without having hired an orchestra and executing a fox trot."[71] Furthermore, the rules never meant that the only students engaged in high jinks were malcontents; others were quite as capable of having their fun, such as a parody at Biola of R. A. Torrey, a dean who was notorious for his formal manners and attire.[72] Moreover, despite abundant restrictions on courting, many students managed to carry on romances and later to marry.

On the whole, Bible school students fully merited the adjectives wholesome, earnest, and pious. In an era that was tending to give more rather than less latitude to its young people, Bible school leaders succeeded in imposing even greater oversight upon their charges. The students in turn seem to have accepted and even embraced the system set out for them. If much of the outside world seemed indifferent and even inimical to evangelicalism, the schools were safe, supportive havens—"plausibility structures," as sociologist Peter Berger puts it.[73] No troubling pluralism confused students and required choices of them; the curriculum and extracurriculum taught the same evangelistic goals and fostered the same evangelical subculture.

The Impact of the Bible Schools

The survival and recent renaissance of evangelicalism is simply impossible to understand without taking into account the role of the Bible schools. As perhaps the most powerful terminals in the conservative evangelical network, the Bible schools helped the movement thrive. Functioning much like denominational headquarters, as historian Ernest Sandeen points out, they trained workers and leaders for the movement, helped shape its basic ethos and style, operated as regional organizing centers, and served as bases of operation and innovation for dozens of religious enterprises.[74] No wonder that one observer half-seriously defined fundamentalism as "all those churches and persons in communion with the Moody Bible Institute."[75] The Bible schools' lengthy domination of evangelical higher education, then, made them a major force in shaping the evangelical college movement of recent decades.

The fortunes of conservative evangelicalism have improved greatly since the 1940s, and the Bible school movement has shared in the general prosperity. Indeed, these institutions have entered an important new stage of development. Bible schools and institutes responded to growing evangelical demands for academic respectability by lengthening their programs of study, requiring high school diplomas of applicants, offering more courses in the arts and sciences, granting degrees, expanding their libraries, and insisting that their faculty pursue postgraduate studies. In short, many Bible schools and institutes have become Bible colleges. They have also been willing to impose guidelines upon themselves: in 1946, some of the leading schools founded the Accrediting (now American) Association of Bible Colleges to encourage themselves and other Bible schools to raise academic standards. By the mid-1980s, twenty-one of the AABC's ninety-seven institutions had also earned regional collegiate accreditation from secular accrediting organizations. All of this has contributed to the growth of the Bible school movement, which now includes over five hundred institutions.[76]

These changes came at a cost, though. A more diversified curriculum normally raised expenses, so schools began to charge or increase tuition fees, and many curtailed enterprises outside of the classroom that drained resources. Some schools exchanged their urban location for the cheaper land, tranquil streets, and growing evangelical constituency in the suburbs, but in the process they also left behind the practical training in hands-on ministries among needy groups in the city and isolated themselves from much that had been so important to them earlier in their history. As evangelicals sought and achieved new levels of respectability, some Bible colleges converted into liberal arts colleges, and sometimes into graduate seminaries as well. The growing number and prestige of these alternative forms of Christian higher education paralleled the growth of the Bible colleges, so while the Bible colleges prospered with the larger evangelical movement, their relative power and influence within that movement as organizers, innovators, and providers of leadership faded.

Despite this shift in status, the Bible school movement continues to powerfully influence evangelical higher education. As the dominant evangelical institutions for the first half of the twentieth century, the Bible schools have provided both a standard of comparison and a shaping force for evangelical liberal arts colleges. Take, for example, their impact on the study of the English Bible. In the nineteenth century, as William Ringenberg points out, biblical studies were rarely a part of the curriculum of evangelical colleges.[77] But thanks to the insistence of Bible school leaders that education be Bible-centered, Christian College Coalition schools today characteristically require courses in biblical studies. Similarly, the service and internship programs of evangelical colleges reflect the Bible schools' stress on practical Christian work. For the alumni and supporters of liberal arts colleges that began as Bible schools, these two legacies plus a third—an emotionally intense and behaviorally constraining religious atmosphere—are the true marks of a Christian college.

Constituents with such an idea in mind about what characterizes the Christian college often have trouble appreciating attempts on the part of some schools to assert their Christianness in other ways, as in submitting every discipline to a Christian worldview. Adding courses in the arts and sciences while subtracting hours required in Bible and doctrine seems like secularization to many constituents. So does the typically less-directive approach to spirituality and godly living taken by liberal arts colleges. These differing visions have, on occasion, resulted in conflict.[78]

Although Bible school educators did not explicitly wish to inhibit the development of a full range of Christian scholarship, their domination of the field from 1920 to 1950 probably has something to do with the evangelical hesitation to envision and develop Christian thinking at the very highest levels. The Bible schools' success at promoting pragmatic and popular goals for education has reinforced the tendency of American evangelicals to avoid thought that is theoretical as well as practical, critical as well as appreciative, and creative as well as derivative.[79]

Nevertheless, Bible colleges and liberal arts colleges have played complementary roles in recent decades. The former is not an underdeveloped version of the latter, nor is the latter a secularization of the former. Bible colleges still excel at making the Bible accessible to the general public and training workers for immediate service to the church. They are effective popular educators and are the most prolific producers of evangelists and missionaries. Yet they have learned to show their students, through study of the arts and sciences, the insights for ministry to be gained from the wider range of human thought.[80] Liberal arts colleges are designed to engender a Christian worldview more than religious vocational competency. Yet they have learned to teach their students to study the Bible and to put their faith to work. So, as evangelical colleges of these two kinds consider the need for both praxis-oriented education and detached reflection in the years to come,[81] let us hope that their partnership will grow.[82]

NOTES

1. A. J. Gordon, "Short Cut Methods," *The Watchman* 70 (7 November 1889): 1; "The Nyack Corner," *Alliance Weekly* 38 (17 August 1912): 317.

2. Grant Wacker argues this point compellingly in "The Holy Spirit and the Spirit of the Age in American Protestantism, 1880–1910," *Journal of American History* 72 (June 1985): 45-62.

3. Ernest R. Sandeen, *The Roots of Fundamentalism: British and American Millenarianism, 1800–1930* (Chicago: University of Chicago Press, 1970); see esp. chap. 7, "The Millenarian Meridian," 162-87, which documents these efforts. Moody's leading role in this movement is shown by James F. Findlay, Jr., *Dwight L. Moody, American Evangelist, 1837–1899* (Chicago: University of Chicago Press, 1969).

4. See, for example, Ernest B. Gordon, *Adoniram Judson Gordon: A Biography* (New York: Fleming H. Revell, 1896); and A. E. Thompson, *A. B. Simpson: His Life and Work* (1920; Harrisburg, Pa.: Christian Publications, 1960).

5. Norris Magnuson, *Salvation in the Slums: Evangelical Social Work, 1865–1920* (Metuchen, N.J.: Scarecrow, 1977).

6. Warren Palmer Behan, "An Introductory Survey of the Lay Training School Field," *Religious Education* 11 (1916): 47-52; Virginia Lieson Brereton, "Preparing Women for the Lord's Work: The Story of Three Methodist Training Schools, 1880–1940," in *Women in New Worlds,* ed. Hilah F. Thomas and Rosemary S. Keller, vol. 1 of Historical Perspectives on the Wesleyan Tradition (Nashville: Abingdon, 1981), 178-99.

7. During the 1920s most of the missionary training schools maintained by established denominations closed, merged with seminaries, became colleges, or otherwise lost their training-school identity. For a more extensive treatment of the fate of these schools see Brereton, "Preparing Women for the Lord's Work."

8. Consider the hard times recorded in the histories of three prominent examples: on Eastern Baptist Theological Seminary's early years see Gilbert L. Guffin, ed., *What God Hath Wrought* (Philadelphia: Judson, 1960); on Dallas see Rudolf A. Renfer, "A History of Dallas Theological Seminary" (Ph.D. diss., University of Texas, 1959); and on Bob Jones University see Melton Wright, *Fortress of Faith* (Grand Rapids: Eerdmans, 1960).

9. The early history of the Detroit Bible Institute, for example, displays this pattern. See the research notes and documents compiled on this school by Maureen W. Le-Lacheur, on file at William Tyndale College, Farmington Hills, Michigan.

10. See Joel A. Carpenter, "Fundamentalist Institutions and the Rise of Evangelical Protestantism, 1929–1942," *Church History* 49 (March 1980): 66-68, 73. William Vance Trollinger carefully details this role at yet another Bible school; see his "One Response to Modernity: Northwestern Bible School and the Fundamentalist Empire of William Bell Riley" (Ph.D. diss., University of Wisconsin, 1984).

11. Virginia Lieson Brereton, "The Formation of American Bible Schools, 1880–1940," author's typescript, 180-180e; much of this data was drawn from Hubert Reynhout, Jr., "A Comparative Study of Bible Institute Curriculums" (M.A. thesis, University of Michigan, 1947), 43-54. These works probably do not account for all such schools.

12. Don O. Shelton, "Instrumentalities God Chooses *and* Uses," *Moody Bible Institute Monthly* 33 (June 1933): 44-49. Shelton, the head of the National Bible Institute of New York City, acknowledged MBI's nationwide influence.

13. Moody quoted from an address at MBI's Farwell Hall, Chicago, 22 January 1886, by Gene A. Getz, *MBI: The Story of Moody Bible Institute* (Chicago: Moody Press, 1969), 36; Scofield quoted by Renald Showers, "A History of Philadelphia College of the Bible" (Th.M. thesis, Dallas Theological Seminary, 1962), 62; Gordon quoted by

Ernest B. Gordon, *Adoniram Judson Gordon,* 171-72; Simpson quote is from A. B. Simpson, "The Training and Sending Forth of Workers," *Christian and Missionary Alliance* 18 (30 April 1897): 419.

14. J. N. Murdock, in "Missionary Training Schools—Do Baptists Need Them? A Discussion," *Baptist Quarterly Review* 12 (January 1890): 81.

15. Commencement bulletins from the Moody Bible Institute often listed the previous occupations of the graduates (Moodyana Room, Moody Bible Institute, drawer G). The Institute also retains in its vaults the files of each graduate. These contain valuable information and are available to researchers on a restricted basis by special permission.

16. Edward A. Krug, *The Shaping of the American High School,* vol. 2, 1920–1941 (Madison: University of Wisconsin Press, 1972), 41.

17. See Virginia Lieson Brereton and Christa Ressmeyer Klein, "American Women in Ministry: A History of Protestant Beginning Points," in *Women of Spirit,* ed. Rosemary Ruether and Eleanor McLaughlin (New York: Simon and Schuster, 1979), 301-32.

18. A. T. Pierson, *The Crisis of Missions; or, The Voice Out of the Cloud* (New York: Robert Carter & Bros., 1886), 331.

19. Ibid., 340-41.

20. Samuel Haber, *Efficiency and Uplift: Scientific Management in the Progressive Era, 1890–1920* (Chicago: University of Chicago Press, 1964); Ben Primer, *Protestants and American Business Methods* (Ann Arbor: UMI Research Press, 1979).

21. Simpson, "The Training and Sending Forth of Workers," 419.

22. Getz, *MBI,* 37.

23. Central Bible Institute quote is found in Thomas F. Henstock, "A History and Interpretation of the Curriculum of Central Bible Institute" (M.A. thesis, Central Bible Institute, 1964), 52; Biola quote is in the school's *Catalog, 1920.*

24. Conservatives were not alone in seeking to reform Bible education. Liberal higher critics also sought to synthesize biblical themes and foster English Bible instruction. See Glenn Miller's insightful essay on the crisis of biblical accessibility in the late nineteenth century, "The Only Guide to Faith and Practice," paper presented to the Homewood Seminar of the Program in American Religious History at the Johns Hopkins University, February 1977.

25. C. I. Scofield, ed., *Scofield Reference Bible* (New York: Oxford University Press, 1909), v; James M. Gray, *Synthetic Bible Studies* (Cleveland: F. M. Barton, 1900), title page.

26. Timothy P. Weber gives a helpful overview of the dispensational system and describes how it was used to reconcile Scripture into a harmonious whole in *Living in the Shadow of the Second Coming: American Premillennialism, 1875–1925* (New York: Oxford University Press, 1979), 9-42.

27. As a matter of fact, Gray's ideas and methods were not exclusively his. Many of them were in the air, and a number of teachers were advancing one of his principles—the study of the Bible by books rather than by random passages. See Scofield, *Scofield Reference Bible,* v; and I. M. Haldeman, *How to Study the Bible: The Second Coming and Other Expositions* (Philadelphia: Philadelphia School of the Bible, 1904).

28. Gray, *Synthetic Bible Studies,* 15.

29. Gray's strong insistence on "facts," "laws," and the Bible's agreement with scientific evidence confirms George M. Marsden's point that fundamentalists were champions of Baconian science and saw Scripture in that context. In their opinion, true science consisted of "facts," observable data, and proven laws—not theories. As Marsden argues, Baconians were taxonomists, categorizers, and classifiers rather than

theorists. So also were fundamentalists: when they turned to the word of God, their views of it reflected the certitude of Baconian science with its fixed classifications and laws. See George M. Marsden, *Fundamentalism and American Culture: The Shaping of Twentieth Century Evangelicalism, 1870–1925* (New York: Oxford University Press, 1980), 55-62; and idem, "Understanding Fundamentalist Views of Science," in *Science and Creationism,* ed. Ashley Montagu (New York: Oxford University Press, 1984), 95-116. See also Gray, *Synthetic Bible Studies,* 17.

30. Gray, *Synthetic Bible Studies,* 21.

31. Ibid., 15-21.

32. Edith Metcalf, *Letters to Dorothy* (Chicago and New York: Fleming H. Revell, 1893), 11.

33. *Catalogue of the Moody Bible Institute of Chicago, 1911–12,* 37; see also *Bulletin of the Bible Institute of Los Angeles* 5 (1920): 35.

34. Carol Talbot, *For This Was I Born: The Captivating Story of Louis T. Talbot* (Chicago: Moody Press, 1977), 26.

35. Gray, *Synthetic Bible Studies,* 11.

36. For example, when Samuel H. Sutherland was teaching personal evangelism at the Bible Institute of Los Angeles in the thirties, he had his students memorize—"word perfect"—130 Scripture verses. Conversation with Samuel Sutherland, 28 July 1983.

37. *Bulletin of the Bible Institute of Los Angeles* 5 (October 1920): 30; *Catalogue of the Moody Bible Institute of Chicago, 1911–12,* 36.

38. For a good anecdotal example, see *The King's Business* 6 (1915): 78.

39. The Biola *Bulletin* said this of the school's Homiletics Department: "The object . . . is to qualify men and women to deliver sermons, Gospel addresses, Bible readings and expositions of God's Word wherever needed—for pulpit, street, jail, shop, or cottage." *Bulletin of the Bible Institute of Los Angeles* 5 (1920): 31-32.

40. Ibid., 30.

41. Getz, *MBI,* 318-21, 344.

42. 1 Timothy 6:20, KJV. See on this point William Bell Riley, *Are the Scriptures Scientific?* (Minneapolis: published by the author, n.d.), 5; Harry Rimmer, *The Theory of Evolution and the Facts of Science* (Grand Rapids: Eerdmans, 1935), 15; and "The Deicides," a cartoon by E. J. Pace in *The King's Business* 16 (May 1925): 197, reprinted in Marsden, *Fundamentalism and American Culture,* 209.

43. The catalogs for the teens, twenties, and thirties reveal three course offerings, and also that a large number of Gordon students of the time came from small towns in Maine, New Hampshire, and the eastern provinces of Canada.

44. *The King's Business* 7 (1916): 74.

45. *The Christian Worker's Magazine* 13 (July 1913): 691.

46. Nathan R. Wood, *A School of Christ* (Boston: Gordon College, 1953), 94-99. For accounts of student work assignments more generally, see G. Jennings, "Students' Evangelistic Work," *Alliance Weekly* 38 (29 June 1912): 204; and *Brief Facts about the Moody Bible Institute of Chicago* (Chicago: Moody Bible Institute, 1928).

47. Talbot, *For This Was I Born,* 27.

48. Several articles document this tension at the Missionary Training Institute; see "Notes from Nyack Institute," *Alliance Weekly* 38 (29 June 1912): 203; "The Nyack Corner," *Alliance Weekly* 38 (17 August 1912): 317; and "The Nyack Corner," *Alliance Weekly* 38 (24 August 1912): 381.

49. John H. Cable portrays the inspiration that A. B. Simpson's students drew from his example in *A History of the Missionary Training Institute: The Pioneer Bible School of America* (Harrisburg, Pa.: Christian Publications, 1933), 12.

50. See, for example, M. Stetson Lincoln, "A Day at the Institute," *Victory* 1 (April-May 1934): 10, which portrays daily life with the Providence (R.I.) Bible Institute "family," where chapel was a "family service," and "Mother Mathison" cooked the meals.

51. *Christian Alliance and Missionary Weekly* 6 (17 April 1891): 249. For a biographical sketch of Whittemore see David J. Fant, "Early Associates of A. B. Simpson," *The Southeastern District Report of the Christian and Missionary Alliance,* January-February 1977, 4.

52. W. C. Stevens, "Notes from Nyack Institute," *Alliance Weekly* 38 (27 April 1912): 55.

53. Charles C. Washburn, "The Ministry of Music," *Alliance Weekly* 55 (6 August 1921): 330; see *WMBI Song Favorites* (Chicago: Moody Bible Institute, n.d. [circa 1930]), nos. 1, 2, and 3; this work features compositions by MBI staffers Arvis Christiansen, Wendell Loveless, and William Runyan.

54. Washburn, "Ministry of Music."

55. On the Boston Bible School, see Florence L. Bartlet, "The Spiritual Life of the New England School of Theology," *World's Crisis,* 16 September 1923, scrapbook, Berkshire Christian College Library; on the Christian Workers Training Institute, see Charles H. Brackett, "The History of Azusa College and the Friends" (M.A. thesis, University of Southern California, 1967), 55; on Biola, see the school's *Catalog, 1920,* 13; on MBI, see *Moody Bible Institute Monthly* 22 (March 1922): 844.

56. See Ellen C. Coburn, "How I Came to the New England School of Theology," *World's Crisis,* 1 August 1923; and Christina E. Lang, "My Call to India," *World's Crisis,* 18 October 1922, scrapbook, Berkshire Christian College Library. See also "Student Testimonies," *Alliance Weekly* 55 (6 August 1921): 329. The testimonies in Shirley Nelson, *The Last Year of the War* (New York: Harper and Row, 1978), passim, although fictional, are authentic in tone.

57. *Tenth Annual Report of the Christian and Missionary Alliance* (1907), 77.

58. Yearbook from the Central Bible Institute (1938), 39.

59. For reports of missionary experiences, see W. C. Stevens, "Notes from Nyack," *Alliance Weekly* 37 (13 April 1921): 27; see also the missionary news feature in each issue of the *Moody Bible Institute Monthly* during the 1930s and 1940s. For artifacts, see those collected in Zaire by Titus Johnson, a pioneer Free Church missionary, and now on display at Trinity College (formerly a Bible school), Deerfield, Illinois. For accounts of mission work, see Mary Guinness Taylor, *Borden of Yale '09: "The Life that Counts"* (London: China Inland Mission, 1926); Rowland V. Bingham, *Seven Sevens of Years and A Jubilee! The Story of the Sudan Interior Mission* (Toronto: Evangelical Publishers, 1943); Marshall Broomhall, *Hudson Taylor: The Man Who Dared* (London: China Inland Mission, 1925); Rosalind M. Goforth, *Goforth of China* (Grand Rapids: Zondervan, 1937). On martyrs in missions, see Mary Guinness Taylor, *The Triumph of John and Betty Stam* (Philadelphia: China Inland Mission, 1935).

60. "Student Volunteers," *Hypernikon* 1 (1923): 71.

61. Ibid.; see also Bible Institute of Los Angeles, *Catalog, 1929,* 41; H. Wilbert Norton, *To Stir the Church: A Brief History of the Student Foreign Missions Fellowship, 1936–1986* (Madison: Student Foreign Missions Fellowship, 1986).

62. See *The King's Business* 18 (March 1927); *Moody Bible Institute Bulletin* 8 (December 1928): 5; S. A. Witmer, *The Bible College Story: Education with a Dimension* (Manhasset, N.Y.: Channel Press, 1962), 111.

63. Robert Williams and Marilyn Miller, *Chartered for His Glory: Biola University, 1908–1983* (La Mirada, Calif.: Associated Students of Biola University, 1983), 71.

64. *Catalogue of the Moody Bible Institute of Chicago, 1928–29.*

65. Nyack alumna Ella M. Brettell, for example, reported in an interview on 4 May 1978 that although she had gone to Nyack at her parents' insistence, it was not until after she had entered the school that a friend "led me to the Lord."

66. See New England School of Theology, *Catalog, 1931–1932*, 35; and "New England School of Theology," *World's Crisis*, 8 November 1939.

67. On Cora Turnbull see David J. Fant, "Early Associates of A. B. Simpson," *The Southeastern District Report of the Christian and Missionary Alliance*, May 1977 (special edition), 14.

68. Interview with Samuel H. Sutherland, 25 July 1982.

69. Ibid.

70. David J. Fant, "Early Associates of A. B. Simpson" (W. C. Stevens), *The Southeastern District Report of the Christian and Missionary Alliance*, January-February 1976. This is only a tantalizing glimpse; one wishes that Fant had furnished more details.

71. *The King's Business* 18 (1927): 108.

72. Williams and Miller, *Chartered for His Glory*, 40-41.

73. Peter L. Berger, *The Sacred Canopy: Elements of a Sociological Theory of Religion* (Garden City, N.Y.: Doubleday, Anchor Books, 1969), 46-51.

74. Sandeen, *Roots of Fundamentalism*, 241-43.

75. Daniel P. Stevick, *Beyond Fundamentalism* (Richmond: John Knox, 1964), 45.

76. Kenneth Gangel, "The Bible College: Past, Present, and Future," *Christianity Today* 24 (7 November 1980): 1324-26; William C. Ringenberg, *The Christian College: A History of Protestant Higher Education in America* (Grand Rapids: Eerdmans, Christian University Press, 1984), 170-73; American Association of Bible Colleges, *Directory, 1985-86*.

77. See Ringenberg's essay "The Old-Time College, 1800–1865," above.

78. For example, Trinity College (Deerfield, Illinois) recently weathered a crisis of confidence with its constituents that was prompted in part by differing perceptions of the proper spirit and goals for Christian higher education. Alumni remembered Trinity as a Bible school and had corresponding expectations for its present and future ethos, while faculty and administrators followed a more "integrationist," academic model of Christian distinctiveness. See "A Christian College Steps Back from the Brink of Closure," *Christianity Today* 27 (8 April 1983): 58; Joel A. Carpenter, "Trinity College, the Free Church, and the American Evangelical Mosaic: The Roots of Our Identity and Mission," paper presented at the Trinity College Faculty Workshop, Deerfield, Illinois, 28 August 1980; and several articles in *Evangelical Beacon* 56 (15 May 1983), including George M. Keck, "Conferences, Colleges and Manatees," 18; Keck, "Trinity College Reaffiliation Wins Delegate Approval," 8; Thomas A. McDill, "Important Changes at Trinity College," 16-17; and Kenneth Kantzer, "Critical, Challenging Days in the Life of Trinity College," 22.

79. The lack of evangelical support for advanced scholarship has other powerful sources as well, which are rooted deeply in the movement's history and character. See the essays by Nathan O. Hatch, "Evangelical Colleges and the Challenge of Christian Thinking," and George M. Marsden, "Why No Major Evangelical University? The Loss and Recovery of Evangelical Advanced Scholarship," both in this volume.

80. Kenneth O. Gangel, ed., *Toward A Harmony of Faith and Learning: Essays on Bible College Curriculum* (Farmington Hills, Mich.: William Tyndale College Press, 1983), presents the current educational philosophy of the Bible college movement.

81. See the essays by Nicholas Wolterstorff, "Teaching for Justice," and Richard J. Mouw, "Knowing and Doing: The Christian College in Contemporary Society," both in this volume.

82. This essay is based on my unpublished doctoral dissertation, "Protestant Fundamentalist Bible Schools, 1882–1940" (Columbia University, 1981).

The Shaping of Evangelical Higher Education Since World War II

Thomas A. Askew

Surveyors of the landscape of higher education have observed that in the last decade conservative or evangelical Christian colleges have surged as a group into a more visible profile. When *New York Times* education editor Edward Fiske noted in 1983 that these colleges are among the fastest growing in America, he affirmed what other pundits were beginning to suspect: evangelical colleges occupy a growing place in American higher education.[1] As these colleges, like the evangelical religious movement in general, receive more public scrutiny, some now wonder what public role they, like the larger movement, will play in society in the future.

The new strength of evangelical higher education derives, no doubt, from the resurgence of conservative Protestantism. Thus a dissertation currently under preparation at the University of Chicago confidently asserts that "these . . . colleges have fared well by appealing to the growing number of conservatives and providing them with a religiously based liberal arts curriculum which seeks to prepare students for careers."[2] Yet the trends that prompted a new vitality among evangelical colleges are more complex than commonly assumed. Given the dearth of quantitative studies,[3] however, my approach depends heavily on impression and experience drawn from numerous institutional chronicles, as well as on thirty-six years of personal association with Christian colleges.[4] Thus I take encouragement from Ralph M. Besse's observation in *The Invisible Colleges:* "Someone has pointed out that most people's views of colleges are autobiographical."[5] In this essay, then, I seek to analyze those factors, external and internal to the campuses, that have shaped conservative Christian higher education since 1945.

Certain factors after World War II—including the postwar pattern of economic growth, expansion of government aid (beginning with the

GI Bill), growing demand for a more credentialed work force, and the ever-rising popularity of attending college—benefited higher education in general and also enhanced the development of Christian colleges. Unfortunately, few comparative analyses,[6] longitudinal studies, or control-group samplings are available to provide the insights or quantitative data necessary to evaluate the last forty years of Christian higher education. William Ringenberg terms this period "The Reconstruction of Christian Higher Education" and supplies a detailed, descriptive analysis in his book on the Christian college.[7] I will not summarize what Ringenberg has already compiled. Rather, to stimulate reflection and to provide a context for raising certain pertinent themes, I propose an interpretive paradigm for understanding the tremendous changes in the evangelical college movement since 1945. Something substantial occurred over the last several decades, but it is difficult to project exactly what it was or how it transpired unless we have a framework for analysis. Such a paradigm or framework should apply to the evolution within individual institutions yet also open perspectives on the movement as a whole.

My paradigm is actually double layered. The first layer involves the chronology of the emergence of Christian colleges since World War II. Here I have delineated three phases, or tendencies, that have earmarked the rise of these colleges in this period. Not all follow exactly the same pattern, of course. Some colleges have telescoped or overlapped the phases; others have worked longer at the process, some of them beginning back in the 1930s or 1940s.

The first phase finds the college as an insular, church-focused institution. This accurately describes most of the Christian College Coalition schools at the close of World War II, when little cross-fertilization among unlike schools occurred. The second phase is a time of corporate definition, consolidation, and credentialing. Characteristic of this phase are increased self-understanding, clarification or broadening of mission, and limited cooperation with other colleges. Some schools started the process before World War II; most, however, since 1945. And in the third phase the colleges experience professionalization, expansion of networks, and theoretical development. This is most characteristic of the last fifteen or twenty years in the more developed institutions.

The first layer of my paradigm, the chronology of change, is rather clear. The second, however, is perhaps more elusive, for it concentrates on the ferment of ideas and convictions that have accompanied these institutional changes. In his 1982 book *A College of Character,*[8] Warren Bryan Martin highlights the vitality unleashed by the struggle for ideals and values, by the pursuit of visions of truth, and by attempts to permeate the institution with a core philosophy. These struggles are characteristic of Christian higher education. In recent decades, as the trend in American higher education moved toward fragmentation and pluralism, the Christian colleges strove to maintain a synoptic vision. Working out this vision, however, continues to involve more tension and creative struggle than many recognize. Simple reductionistic moralisms or sloganeering do not provide the answers. It is a challenging and often perplexing undertaking for a college to take seriously both its scholarly task and its spiritual responsibilities, while at the same time operating as a corporation in the world around it. Those Christian colleges that show the greatest potential for distinction and maturity have worked consciously to balance or juxtapose these forces, thus unleashing a substantial creative drive.

I. Three Phases of Development

Phase One:
The Insular, Church-Focused Institution

At the end of World War II, Christian colleges, Bible colleges, and Bible institutes faced a changed and changing environment after a quarter century of tension caused by numerous factors, including a revolution in higher education, the fundamentalist-modernist controversy, and the vicissitudes of economic depression and global war. During those past twenty-five years, institutional survival was the issue; it was not until after the war that many of them could even begin to think again about their role in the world. The most striking characteristic of these postwar campuses, however, was their individuality and distinctiveness despite the similarity in their stated goals. Shaped by the needs of their constituencies, the denominational schools kept close company with their ecclesiastical home base, especially if an ethnic or special heritage was also at stake—as was true at Calvin, Bethel, and the Mennonite and Lutheran schools. In similar fashion, the Nazarenes and other Wesleyans drew from their own networks. Interdenominational institutions of fundamentalist lineage, notably Wheaton and Bryan, also cultivated special constituencies. Some schools, such as Spring Arbor, Northwestern, and North Park, were two-year institutions while others, including Gordon, Nyack, Barrington, Malone, and

Westmont, were undergoing the transition from Bible college to liberal arts college. The strongest were regionally accredited; many were not. Some reflected a fundamentalist ambivalence about modern thought while others, secure in their scholarly traditions, showed more familiarity with cultural issues. Until additional comparative research is conducted on each school, it is difficult to generalize about intellectual trends with much confidence, especially since the available institutional histories usually provide little of the needed insights. Nevertheless, we can offer a few observations on leadership styles, faculty characteristics, curricula, and institutional identities.

At the head of the college was indeed an "old-time college president," operating in the manner described by George P. Schmidt in his 1930 classic, *The Old Time College President.*[9] Typically a clergyman, or quasi clergyman, the president solicited funds, discipled students, recruited faculty, befriended parents, wooed the public, and administered the entire enterprise; often the college became an extension of his personality.

Gathered about the president was an indefatigable faculty, the backbone of which was a coterie of veterans, loyal to and trusted by the president. These were assisted by younger and often more transient instructors, some of whom eventually evolved into the committed coterie. To these doughty pedagogues, teaching was ministry, the fulfillment of a special call for which they were willing to sacrifice, with missionary zeal. Specialized educational credentials varied, with some exhibiting considerable graduate preparation at universities. Most instructors, however, were oriented more toward the church than to the broader life of American higher education or the scholarly societies, and so did not consider advanced training as important as their fellows in secular institutions did. Their teaching, moreover, tended to be largely descriptive rather than analytical and exploratory.

Despite commonalities, curricula were diverse, with liberal arts courses sometimes found in Bible college class lists and considerable vocationalism present in liberal arts colleges—a secretarial science major persisted at Wheaton College into the 1950s, for example. Felt and perceived needs of the constituents, along with presidential inspiration, heavily defined the course of study. Obviously, a high priority was preparation for religious vocations, including the training of parochial school teachers in the Reformed and Lutheran colleges.

Conceptual distinctions relating to church connections and religious ideals, higher educational mission and obligations, and corporate policy and identity were often unclear. Few schools enjoyed substantial endowments, depending instead on donations or denominational appropriations along with tuition income from their largely first-generation college students.

This is not to speak condescendingly about the minds enriched, the lives changed, the world visions enlarged for legions of graduates sent forth to serve. In the postwar era, however, evangelical families and communities were demonstrating upward social mobility, and their educational ambitions and expectations were rising with them. Thus in order to offer credible and competitive higher education to their constituents, and to fulfill the expanding vision of key faculty and trustees, evangelical educators sought to upgrade their curricula and credentials. This was especially true in institutions lacking full accreditation and featuring constricted courses of study.

Phase Two:
Corporate Definition, Consolidation, and Credentialing

For most of the evangelical colleges the process of definition, consolidation, and credentialing took place during the rapid expansion of American higher education in the 1950s and 1960s. A few schools, notably Calvin and Wheaton, began this transition before World War II and refined it in the postwar epoch. Others began much later and are still in the process.

Whatever the particular ingredients in a given school's evolution, goals usually included increasing enrollment, raising academic standards, improving faculty qualifications and salaries, strengthening financial resources, fine tuning public relations, expanding the physical plant, and developing profitable relationships with educational associations and government agencies. Various schools also engineered upwardly mobile changes in location.[10]

Formal accreditation was the objective for those lacking it; others sought different accreditation, especially for public school teaching certification, including review by the National Council for the Accreditation of Teacher Education and by the National Association of Schools of Music. Furthermore, even accredited institutions had to undergo ten-year accreditation reviews and seek credentials for any new programs added to the curriculum. There is no stimulus like an impending visit from an evaluation team, with the attendant self-study, for clarifying goals, sharpening administrative procedures, and reviewing faculty committees. On a more subtle level, for these schools with definite religious commitments, external evaluation necessitated communicating their religious stance to outsiders in a civil and comprehensible manner.

The importance of teacher education programs for the growth of evangelical higher education cannot be overemphasized, especially for their impact on recruiting women as students. During the bull market of teaching opportunities in the 1950s and 1960s education departments in many schools more than carried their share in attracting and educating students. For schools such as Taylor, which by the mid-1950s was certifying half its graduates as teachers, education was the bread and butter program. [11] Teacher training fit well with the aspirations of many first-generation college students and with the ideal of service at many schools. At the same time, teacher training also became a vehicle for fulfilling community needs and demonstrating similarity with other colleges.

In defining mission and developing curriculum, each institution followed its own traditions, obligations, ideals, and momentum. Wheaton, for instance, decided to hold its undergraduate enrollment below two thousand, added ROTC, dropped majors in secretarial science and home economics, yet postponed temporarily a separate philosophy department. Calvin, in contrast, elected to expand to several thousand, forego ROTC, include applied majors such as engineering, and permit relatively open admission for students from denominational homes. Messiah, Barrington, and others introduced vocationally oriented majors while Gordon canceled a graduate program in education and defined its curriculum as closely as possible around the liberal arts. Seattle Pacific, following a university model, eventually launched schools of education and business. Each college represented in the Christian College Coalition thus has its own special interplay of interests, ideals, clientele, and personalities.

As federal funds for education became available in the 1950s and 1960s, leaders of Christian colleges had to decide whether to apply. Fearing government control, Wheaton and Grove City rejected direct assistance, but most schools could not afford to build new facilities without low-cost federal loans. Without these federal subsidies, the skyline of Christian higher education would appear quite different.

For the smaller and unaccredited schools the formation in 1955 of the Council for the Advancement of Small Colleges (now the Council of Independent Colleges) proved pivotal. [12] A glance at the charter membership of fifty-three colleges and the expanded roster of one hundred by 1970 reveals that several dozen schools now in the Christian College Coalition have been active in CASC efforts. In addition to the obvious goals of obtaining newly appropriated federal funds and achieving regional accreditation, other benefits accrued. For the first time, lasting institutional and personal linkages developed across theological, denominational, and geographic boundaries. Furthermore, leaders from disparate evangelical campuses were called on to share common concerns with counterparts from Catholic institutions and those that made no religious claims.

A bevy of newly founded schools drew special benefit from the Council.[13] Their leaders found help in the proliferating workshops and access to the rapidly growing literature on higher education.[14] Precedents were set for future Consortium and Coalition formation, and lines of access were opened to the Washington associations and governmental bureaucracy. In short, participation in CASC edged all the Christian member colleges closer to the mainstream while propelling individual colleges toward their goals. All of this took place, of course, in a rapidly changing educational and social context. Increasing affluence, the paperback publishing revolution, the arrival of television, heightened mobility, and easy air travel all had dramatic effects on the general society as well as on religious communities and their collegiate institutions.

During these years, evangelical colleges followed their nonevangelical counterparts in the liberal arts by strengthening the credentials of their faculties. There is a considerable lack of research on the development and professionalization of evangelical college faculties from 1950 to 1980, but we can still make some observations. First, common wisdom dictated to deans and administrators of both secular and religious schools that a faculty boasting an increased number of earned doctorates could only stimulate progress to quality and enhanced institutional reputation. In response to the nationwide shortage of Ph.D.'s entering the market, the Danforth Foundation launched a grant program in 1955 to assist deserving scholars toward completion of their doctorates. Hundreds of young professors, myself included, greatly benefited from Danforth's generosity. For many other instructors in evangelical colleges, entry into college teaching came by way of a circuitous route, often following a period in the pulpit or a stint in a high school classroom. Except in the more prestigious colleges and universities, career patterns everywhere were more fluid than they are today.

Despite new aid programs, many members of evangelical college faculties did not earn their doctorates until mid-career, and occasionally even later in life. Completing the degree became a credentialing for both teacher and institution, a confirmation of scholarliness (not so much an initiation into scholarliness, as it is today). If one earned a doctorate in early career, it was usually in one of the natural sciences, not in the humanities or the social sciences. This evangelical attitude toward the advanced degree was matched by a similar attitude toward advanced scholarship. While some faculty did attempt to interact with disciplinary peers elsewhere and did do research and publish, the majority were more concerned with building their institutions and with the ministry of teaching than with nurturing external disciplinary recognition. Institutional loyalty and a pastoral spirit were recognized and rewarded. This was then a transitional faculty generation, in their values and loyalties half-way between the old-time coterie of less-credentialed instructors on the one hand and the baby-boom generation of cosmopolitan, aggressively professional faculty on the other.

This transitional corps of faculty grappled long and hard with the question of what it meant to have a creditable, competent liberal arts college that at the same time held to a conceptual synthesis based on Christian theism. In most categories of institutional advance the evangelical campuses were marching in line with a host of other colleges and small universities, but it was the persistant quest for an integrating religious philosophy that set apart these largely unknown or "invisible" conservative institutions.[15]

Immensely helpful to the discussion was the publication in 1959 of Elton Trueblood's *Idea of a College,* which had evolved out of an address to the Association of American Colleges in 1950. Emphasizing the importance of the religious assumptions of the faculty, Trueblood claimed "that the Christian character of the college is attested, not by what goes on at the fringes and not even by the existence of scholarly courses in Biblical studies . . . [but] by the morale and conviction of the major teaching of the institution."[16] Trueblood thus helped clarify and define more adequately the nature of committed Christian higher education, which was an increasing topic of concern. As early as 1948, Dean Bertha Munro of Eastern Nazarene College had been authorized by the General Assembly of her denomination to draft a statement of educational philosophy for all colleges of the Church of the Nazarene. Likewise, between 1953 and 1965 special study committees at Wheaton, St. Olaf, and Calvin produced insightful and historically oriented explications of Christian higher learning and curriculum philosophy.[17]

We should not forget that during the 1950s and 1960s much was being written on the proper role of religion in the older, mainline, denominational colleges. Numerous publications appeared, ordinarily reflecting a pluralistic and liberal theological stance.[18] Religiously affiliated colleges of all sorts took encouragement from the manifold speeches and writings of Earl McGrath. Finally, in 1966, M. M. Patillo and D. M. MacKenzie's *Church Sponsored Higher Education in the United States* presented a taxonomy of church-college relationships that suggested a legitimate positioning for the emerging evangelical colleges, separating them out from more fundamentalist ones. Among the Christian colleges themselves and within the higher education community in general, distinctions began to be made between "faith-affirming" and "defender-of-the-faith" institutions, the latter group including those that were more defensive, sectarian, and reductionist in their approach to learning.[19]

That by the 1960s a distinction could be made between "faith-affirming" and "defender-of-the-faith" colleges points to a much deeper realignment that had occurred within the ranks of the evangelical-fundamentalist wing of Protestantism. This, however, is not the occasion to delve into the episodes that precipitated the move to moderation by some leaders and institutions, a shift roundly criticized by the more separatistic and suspicious fundamentalists. Some campuses, such as Wheaton on the evolution issue, suffered repeated attack.[20] Nevertheless, the evidence is clear that the evangelical colleges contributed substantially to the resurgence of evangelical thought in modern America, and their importance was increasingly recognized in conservative church circles. A cascade of articles appeared in such popular periodicals as *Christianity Today, Eternity, United Evangelical Action, Alliance Witness, Reformed Journal,* and *Christian Life* extolling the importance of the Christian colleges for both church and society and featuring their professors' insights on a variety of topics.[21]

Indeed, the evangelical institutions had convinced parents that their children could receive intellectual grooming and credentialing for professions without eschewing moral and spiritual nurture. And, on a larger scale, wider constituencies began to grasp the practical and theoretical necessity of developing distinctly Christian views of the world.[22] In securing the confidence of the evangelical public, the conservative Christian colleges also recaptured a historical legitimacy, claiming origins in the colonial and nineteenth-century colleges, and ultimately reaching back to Geneva, Cambridge, Oxford, and the medieval heritage of Christian learning. In doing so these campuses sought an identity, not as something novel on the educational scene, but as the inheritors of a long, noble tradition.

Phase Three:
Professionalization, Networks, and Theoretical Understanding

Whether or not phase three may in fact be an extension of phase two, we can discern some subtle but discernable changes that have transpired in this area in the last fifteen or twenty years. The first is increased professionalization at every level of the institutional life of evangelical colleges, which reflects a larger trend occuring throughout academia. The professionalization of administrative leadership is just as significant as that of faculties. As institutions have become larger and more complex, or as modest ones met perplexing budget problems, they sought managerial expertise. Dealing with government agencies became virtually a profession in itself. No longer could that beloved professor or pastor be tapped for the presidency, put down his textbooks or commentaries, read Peter Drucker's latest book, and step confidently into the executive office. University graduate schools of education consequently began preparing a whole cadre of young specialists whose goal was not to teach but to enter directly into administrative careers.

No one has yet undertaken the quantitative, longitudinal, and comparative analyses necessary to understand the professionalization process in evangelical faculties and administrations, though there are some useful models available.[23] Leaving aside the complexities of professionalization theory, I use the term in a straightforward sense in reference to the growth of credentialed, self-consciously distinct occupational subcultures, whose development and distinctiveness is based on specialized training and methodological expertise.

Professional administrators—executives in many respects—have set the pace and administrative style for others who joined them by way of the classroom. Whether in administrative or faculty appointment, they insist that increasing attention be focused on a candidate's credentials and curriculum vitae, and that there be at least the appearance of an open search for the best. Professionalization of staff is also apparent in the sometimes rapidly changing student services field and counseling services. It is evident in the evolution of the campus chaplaincy and much more careful approaches to chapel services and nurturing spirituality. It was a long, slow evolution from campuswide evangelistic revival campaigns to the observation of Spiritual Emphasis Weeks and the establishment of psychological counseling centers. Indeed, professionally trained residence hall directors, state certified mental health counselors, and cross-culturally experienced advisors constitute only part of the well-staffed student services office today. No longer is the missionary brother-in-law on furlough a suitable fill-in candidate for the dean of students.

Several developments point to increasing professional self-consciousness in evangelical faculties. Colleges have fostered this trend with their attention to the proportion of earned doctorates on the staff, pride in the prestige of graduate schools represented, faculty development programs, and stricter promotion and tenure guidelines. At the same time, the quality of many young faculty candidates is outstanding. They come with degrees in hand, or almost so, they are sophisticated on epistemological and methodological issues, and they are committed to meaningful participation in the life of their discipline beyond their teaching responsibilities and even beyond the confines of the campus. They tend to be cosmopolitan and have a broad view of Christianity, one that appreciates the various traditions that are represented in the church. Because of heavy teaching loads, only a few may achieve national prominence for their publications and innovations; yet most of them do not seek it either. Much more than their predecessors ever did, they measure their own worth and achievement by meaningful, not necessarily prominent, participation and publication within the discipline.

Such attitudes directly influenced this new faculty generation's loyalty to and attitudes toward the employing institution. These younger professors expect remuneration, working arrangements, and fringe benefits more typical of academic than of missionary enterprises. They bring with them an intellectual zest, an international perspective including contact with continental forms of Christian orthodoxy, and an expertise that provides an enormous resource to the church, if it can be cultivated and directed.

Professionalizaton in evangelical colleges is inevitable and the benefits evident; yet some cautions need to be raised. As institutions become more complex, and bureaucratic layers evolve, will loss of community result? Does career orientation and professionalization weaken Christian vocation and institutional loyalty? Is there danger of professional identities becoming too tied to the interests of Peter Berger's "New Class"—the symbol-manipulating, information-dispensing elite? Do we run the risk that the development of an entire network of interinstitutional professional relationships and commitments will lead to the domination of an ingroup establishment?

The development of just such networks has inevitably accompanied the trend toward professionalization. Formal cooperative associations flow out of informal linkages and mutual interests. Actually, the impetus for formalized collaboration between institutions derived largely from faculty disciplinary networks that eventually evolved into chartered professional associations. Among the earliest and most vital are the American Scientific Affiliation, the Conference on Faith and History, the Conference on Christianity and Literature, the Evangelical Theological Society, and the National Associaton of Christians in Social Work—all of which developed their own journals or newsletters. Undoubtedly the most significant interinstitutional collaborative efforts to date are the Christian College Consortium, formed in 1971, and the geographically and ecclesiastically broader Christian College Coalition, an overlapping outgrowth of the former organized in 1976. The work of these associations has been pivotal to the emergence and vitality of Christian higher education in the 1980s. Sponsored by Consortium, Coalition, and other schools (Baylor, for example), *The Christian Scholar's Review* has served as a forum for integrative, academic dialogue since 1971. It is but one product of institutional cooperation.

II. The Ferment of Ideas

The search for a consistent theoretical basis for Christian higher education has increasingly commanded the attention of evangelical professors and administrators since the 1940s. It persists, all the while marked by the aspirations and frailties of the larger American evangelical pilgrimage. As Warren Bryan Martin suggests, it is this quest for philosophic and theoretical synthesis that generates a school's vitality and defines its distinctive mission. Combining theological integrity, moral nurture, and academic analysis creates formidable challenges, both internally and externally—especially so because, as many now insist, it involves deeds as well as rhetoric. Many of the other essays in this volume examine the issues of building a thoroughly Christian outlook and cultural witness, however, so my treatment here will be very brief.

The paramount internal demand for a Christian foundation rises from the need to apply biblical ideals to daily campus life and operations. This problem, held in common with other parachurch corporations, is compounded in an academic setting. Simply stated, how are New Testament models of ethics and piety for individuals to be adapted to multifaceted institutions serving diverse constituencies and run as corporations? Complementary—and perhaps more often competing— sets of values, procedures, and ideals emanate from the college's various goals and obligations. The principles of effective corporate management—reflecting hierarchy of authority, business techniques, and market orientation—often run counter to the intellectual heritage of academia, which insists that collegiality and the pursuit of truth define the curriculum, the learning process, and professorial identity. Moreover, both of these clusters of values must be conformed to the call for biblical faith, service, and fellowship, which builds community and provides the unifying philosophy. As of yet, only a few evangelical colleges have responded to this issue with systematic self-evaluation and structural reform.

On the level of the academic disciplines, theoretical concerns are now being addressed in the Christian College Consortium's faith-and-learning seminars and the Christian College Coalition's National Endowment for the Humanities workshops. These enterprises are significant. No longer can the informed instructor ignore epistemological dilemmas or offer simplistic analyses. Yet evangelical education still depends all too frequently on assumptions from the old Enlightenment-Protestant cultural synthesis of nineteenth-century American thought forms. As the professors of the new generation participate in contemporary scholarly debate involving more complex analytical paradigms, however, they are bringing the issues of postmodern epistemology to bear on what it means to think Christianly. Furthermore, constructing a Christian worldview, Christian scholars recognize, requires bringing all thought and practice under the lordship of Christ. Such a response to contemporary intellectual, societal, and global issues means examining hoary assumptions and addressing unsettling questions—in short, dealing with modernity. The essays following in this volume reflect the nature of these discussions, and so recent history now gives way to current debate.

In closing, let me direct a few words to present and future opportunities. In a recent penetrating essay, "Toward a New Public Philosophy," Robert B. Reid of Harvard's Kennedy School of Government adds his voice to a variety of contemporary witnesses in observing that the old liberal ideology of the twentieth-century West "no longer compels widespread belief, but its conservative counterpart is at odds with the new realities of the world economy" and minority aspirations.[24] If this is indeed true, then evangelical colleges now serve and educate in a particularly uncertain era, one in which traditional social institutions are losing their ability to meet individual and societal expectations. How should they respond to this challenge? It would be presumptuous for these schools to thrust themselves forward as agents of cultural renewal, but if they would commit themselves to building a new Christian cultural synthesis and finding fresh ways of contributing to public discourse, perhaps they could help. At a time when Christian colleges are beginning to be heard from, and voices of hope and direction are scarce, perhaps we can answer—indeed, contradict—the complaint of Aleksandr Solzhenitsyn that America cannot hear "highly intelligent persons, maybe a teacher in a far away small college, who could do much for the renewal and salvation of his country."[25] Thus it is fitting, now more than ever, that the avowedly Christian colleges echo the ancient Psalmist who prayed, "Let the favor of the Lord our God be upon us, and establish thou the work of our hands upon us, yea, the work of our hands establish thou it" (Ps. 90:17).

NOTES

1. Edward Fiske, *Selective Guide to Colleges* (New York: New York Times, 1983); see also Kenneth Briggs, "Evangelical Colleges Reborn," *New York Times Magazine*, 14 December 1980, 140-44; C. Robert Page, *Education and Evangelism* (New York: Carnegie Commission, 1972); David Riesman, "The Evangelical College: Untouched by the Academic Revolution," *Change* 13 (January-February 1981): 15.

2. Abstract from Cynthia Benn Tweedell, "The Conservative Protestant College: Who Comes and Why" (Ph.D. diss., in preparation, University of Chicago).

3. Even the cascade of publications from Jossey-Bass Publishing Co. in San Francisco and McGraw-Hill's Carnegie Commission series offers little assistance.

4. Among the most useful institutional histories are Paul M. Bechtel, *Wheaton College: A Heritage Remembered, 1860–1984* (Wheaton, Ill.: Harold Shaw, 1984); James R. Cameron, *Eastern Nazarene College: The First Fifty Years, 1900–1950* (Kansas City: Nazarene Publishing House, 1968); Gerald F. DeJong, *From Strength to Strength: A History of Northwestern, 1882–1982* (Grand Rapids: Eerdmans, 1982); Byron L. Osborne, *The Malone Story: The Dream of Two Quaker Young People* (Newton, Kans.: United Printing, 1970); J. Winston Pearce, *Campbell College: Big Miracle at Little Buies Creek 1887–1974* (Nashville: Broadman, 1978); William C. Ringenberg, *Taylor University: The First 125 Years* (Grand Rapids: Eerdmans, 1973); John J. Timmerman, *Promises to Keep: A Centennial History of Calvin College* (Grand Rapids: Calvin College and Seminary, Eerdmans, 1975).

5. Ralph Besse's commentary is in A. W. Astin and C. B. T. Lee, *The Invisible Colleges: A Profile of Small Private Colleges with Limited Resources* (New York: McGraw-Hill, The Carnegie Commission, 1972), 112.

6. H. L. Hodgkinsons's *Institution in Transition* (New York: McGraw-Hill, 1971) is the best of these.

7. See chap. 6 of Ringenberg, *The Christian College: A History of Protestant Higher Education in America* (Grand Rapids: Eerdmans, Christian University Press, 1984).

8. Warren Bryan Martin, *A College of Character* (San Francisco: Jossey-Bass, 1982).

9. George P. Schmidt, *The Old Time College President* (New York: Columbia University Press, 1930).

10. Gordon moved from urban Boston to exurban Wenham, Malone from inner city Cleveland to the outskirts of Canton, Calvin and Bethel to the suburban edge of town, while Taylor flirted with migration but stayed in rural Upland.

11. Ringenberg, *Taylor University: The First 125 Years*, 151. More research is called for on the role of teacher training in the growth of the Christian colleges, especially since education departments have not always enjoyed the same prestige received by other disciplines.

12. CASC was initially led by Roger J. Voskuyl, a former president of Westmont and dean at Wheaton. For more information on CASC, see the *Directory of Member Colleges* (Washington: CASC, 1971); and Alfred T. Hill, *The Small College Meets the Challenge: The Story of CASC* (New York: McGraw-Hill, 1959).

13. Such schools include Le Tourneau (founded in 1946), Bethel of Mishawaka (1947), Oklahoma Christian (1950), Eastern (1952), Judson (1963), and Oral Roberts (1963).

14. See Thomas A. Askew, *The Small College: A Bibliographic Handbook* (Washington: CASC and the U.S. Office of Education, 1973).

15. See Astin and Lee, *The Invisible Colleges*.

16. Elton Trueblood, *The Idea of a College* (New York: Harper and Brothers, 1959), 25.

17. On Eastern Nazarene's statement see J. A. Cameron, *Eastern Nazarene College*, 371. In 1953, drawing on the work of a special study committee and personal research, Earle Cairns at Wheaton published a *Blueprint for Christian Higher Education* (Wheaton, Ill.: Wheaton College, 1953). Though prepared only for in-house use in 1956, St. Olaf's *Integration in the Christian Liberal Arts College* (St. Olaf College) proved immensely useful to others able to obtain a copy. Hammered out in several years of vigorous and thorough committee effort, *Christian Liberal Arts Education* (Grand Rapids: Eerdmans, 1970) was initially released in 1965 by Calvin College.

18. See, among others, Richard N. Berder, ed., *The Church-Related College Today: Anachronism or Opportunity?* (Nashville: United Methodist Board of Education, 1971); Lloyd J. Averill, *A Strategy for the Protestant College* (Philadelphia: Westminster, 1966); W. A. Geir, ed., *Campus Unrest and the Church-Related School* (Nashville: United Methodist Board of Education, 1970); Charles S. McCoy, *The Church-Related College in American Society* (Washington: Association of American Colleges, 1970); W. A. Koelsch, "Should the Christian College Survive?" *Soundings* 52 (Summer 1969): 218-32; and C. E. Peterson, Jr., *The Church-Related College: Whence before Whither* (Washington: Association of American Colleges, 1970).

19. M. M. Patillo and D. M. MacKenzie, *Church Sponsored Higher Education in the United States* (Washington: American Council on Education, 1966), 30-101; this comprehensive study was sponsored by the Danforth Foundation. See also Merriman Cunningim, "Categories of Church Relatedness," in *Church-Related Higher Education*, ed. R. Parsonage (Valley Forge, Pa.: Judson, 1978); and Ringenberg, *The Christian College*, chap. 6.

20. Bechtel, *Wheaton College*, 211-13.

21. For a list of articles extolling the contributions and possibilities of the evangelical colleges, see the annual index of each journal. The articles are numerous. Between 1960 and 1974, for example, *Christianity Today* carried at least 21 articles supporting Christian higher education; *Christian Life*, 12; *United Evangelical Action*, 8; *Eternity*, 7. In addition, these and other periodicals regularly featured articles on other topics written by Christian college professors, which helped to keep the schools and their task before the Christian public. In this vein, see also Arthur F. Holmes, *The Idea of a Christian College*, rev. ed. (1975; Grand Rapids: Eerdmans, 1987), who also tries to communicate this vision to a broader audience; and Bernard Ramm, *The Christian College in the Twentieth Century* (Grand Rapids: Eerdmans, 1963).

22. See Mark A. Noll's introduction, "Christian Colleges, Christian Worldviews, and an Invitation to Research," in Ringenberg's *The Christian College*, 34-36.

23. See, for example, Martin Finkelstein, "From Tutor to Specialized Scholar: Academic Professionalization in Eighteenth and Nineteenth Century America," *History of Higher Education Annual* 3 (1983): 99-121; Sheila Slaughter and Edward T. Silva, "Against the Grain: Toward an Alternative Interpretation of American Professionalization," *History of Education Annual* 2 (1982): 128-70; and Burton L. Bledstein, *The Culture of Professionalism: The Middle Class and the Development of Higher Education in America* (New York: Norton, 1977).

24. Robert B. Reid, "Toward a New Public Philosophy," *The Atlantic*, May 1985, 68.

25. Aleksandr Solzhenitsyn, *A World Split Apart: Commencement Address Delivered at Harvard University, June 8, 1978* (New York: Harper and Row, 1978), 29.

II
Refining the Vision

Evangelical Colleges and the Challenge of Christian Thinking

Nathan O. Hatch

There is an impression somewhat general . . . that a vigorous and cultivated intellect is not consistent with distinguished holiness; and that those who would live in the clearest sunshine of communion with God must withdraw from the bleak atmosphere of human science.

Bela Bates Edwards, 1853

Academics who are committed to the vitality of the church come up against a rude stumbling block in the record of the last century and a half. In the Western democracies, at least, there is strong evidence that the vitality of churches, Catholic or Protestant, has been inversely proportional to the influence of intellectuals in church life. In Europe and Great Britain, where succeeding generations of university theologians have kept the church abreast of the contemporary intellectual ferment, the overall influence of the church in society has declined precipitously, leaving a coterie of erudite theologians talking largely to themselves. In the United States, by contrast, Protestant and Catholic churches have not taken intellectual moorings quite so seriously. They have tacked to far more popular winds. The result is that churches here are still remarkably filled on Sunday mornings—with over 40 percent of the population—even as intellectuals bemoan the lack of respect for Christian thinking within and without the churches.[1] Such evidence led William Buckley to exclaim that he would sooner be governed by a church whose bishops were chosen by the first five hundred names of the Chicago phone directory than by a church whose bishops were a bunch of university professors.

Does careful thinking necessarily have a doleful influence upon religious life? Do intellectuals in the Lord's vineyard end up sowing weeds rather than gathering grapes? One would be hard pressed to maintain that argument in the face of the examples of scholarly saints such as Augustine, Anselm, Aquinas, Calvin, Wesley, Edwards,

Chesterton, Maritain, and C. S. Lewis. These certainly point to a different, even opposite, conclusion. Yet in America the importance of serious Christian thinking often seems a difficult argument to support, given the manifest success of religious groups that disparage or simply neglect rigorous intellectual life. The rift between spirituality and thinking is broad and deep in America as Catholics such as John Tracy Ellis and more recently Andrew Greeley have noted. Roman Catholics in America, so the critique goes, have been pragmatic activists, intent on getting institutions in place initially to defend the faith for new immigrant groups and then to train Catholic leaders within the various professions. Scholarship as such has long seemed a luxury American Catholics simply could not afford. As Andrew Greeley noted recently: "The slow methodical poking around of the scholar, his dispassionate suspension of judgement, his proclivity for nuance and qualification and his refusal to provide the kind of answers that are wanted when they are wanted are intolerable if the enemy is at the gates. Indeed it is not at all clear that the scholar might not be on the side of the enemy."[2]

Among American evangelicals, respect for learning has been an even rarer commodity over the last 150 years. In addition to the strains of pragmatism and activism shared with Catholics, the structures of evangelical life have been characteristically democratic, a positive virtue in many respects but one that hampered mature Christian reflection. In suggesting that evangelicalism is a democratic movement, I mean three things: that is has been audience centered, intellectually open to all, and organizationally pluralistic and innovative.[3]

The genius of evangelicals has long been their firm identification with people above all else. While others worried about confessional orthodoxy or building institutions to weather the storms of time, evangelicals have been passionate about communicating a message to their fellow human beings. This required an idiom in touch with the people and often resulted in definitions of the faith organized around the issue of communicating the gospel. It is no accident that when evangelicals have gathered for a major concerted purpose, it is the subject of world evangelization that has occupied their attention.

Such audience orientation has had profound effects on the way American evangelicals came to organize and carry out religious thinking. Directing attention principally to the common man and woman meant that evangelical expression would have less currency with people of ideas, the uncommon ones. Democratic America would never produce another theologian to rank with Jonathan Edwards. Nor would evangelical expressions of faith have much appeal for people of an intellectual bent. While evangelicals in America are generally less educated than people in more liberal mainline denominations,[4] they do not tend to be overtly anti-intellectual. Instead, they have merely followed their impulse to throw open theological questions to any serious student of Scripture, trusting the commonsense intuition of people at large to be more reliable than the musings of an educated few. The primary impulse of the Bible school and missionary training movement, which was behind the foundation of so many of today's evangelical liberal arts colleges, was to make Christian education available for the widest possible audience. This strategy rested upon an assumption deep within the evangelical soul that breadth of audience shows a high correlation with depth of insight.

The sorting out of evangelical churches under American democracy has produced a striking degree of pluralism and diversity. Whatever common spirit has bound evangelicals together, it has assumed few institutional manifestations. The seventy-five or so institutions in the Christian College Coalition are ample testimony to this diversity. They represent an enormous range of denominations, styles, and constituencies: Independents, Baptists, Presbyterians, Reformed, Pentecostals, Nazarenes, Brethren, Mennonites, Quakers, Lutherans, and nonaffiliated Christians. Some of the schools "are the lengthened shadow of one person or one family. Others rest securely within a particular denomination, and still others serve complex interdenominational networks."[5] Taken as a whole, these colleges suggest that evangelicals spend enormous sums of money on higher education. But while much money is spent, it is nowhere concentrated: the diffusion of resources means that almost none of these colleges can afford a research faculty or a substantial library or dream of becoming a university in the finest sense of the word.

What, then, do we make of the state of evangelical higher education in America? Like the religious communities they represent, evangelical colleges at one level have never seemed stronger. Most have loyal constituencies, committed faculties, and satisfied students. Their record of academic improvement since World War II is quite remarkable. Like many Catholic colleges and universities, they are successful in opening up the liberal arts for students in a way that is faithful to a given religious tradition.

Yet from a different vantage point it is fair to raise a more unsettling question. What responsibility do evangelical liberal arts colleges have for the careful articulation of Christian thought in the broader intellectual world—among those for whom Christian convictions are not a given? In recent years evangelicals have come to raise the alarm about the pervasive secularism of modern intellectual life and its repercussions in legislation, ethics, and jurisprudence; yet they have done almost nothing to address the root of the problem. The battle for the mind cannot be waged by mobilizing in the streets or on Capitol Hill, nor by denouncing more furiously the secular humanists. If we are to help preserve even the possibility of Christian thinking for our children and grandchildren, we must begin to nurture first-order Christian scholarship. This means, of course, freeing Christian scholars to undertake what is a painstakingly slow and arduous task, one that has almost no immediate return on investment. The support of Christian scholars is a selfless enterprise indeed, because it is investing current resources to ensure that we do not mortgage the future intellectually for the next generation. Neither as Americans nor as evangelicals are we accustomed to undertaking this kind of long-range and indirect plan.

While nurturing Christian thinking is certainly not the only task in our lives, it is still vitally important if evangelicals today are to be able to establish a beachhead, however tiny, in territory that has become pervasively alien during the last century. Among contemporary intellectuals, the sway of secularism reigns virtually unchallenged, and its attack against the Christian faith remains heavy and sustained. Yet on the campuses of evangelical colleges one is likely to find a heady confidence that things have never been better. The jarring disparity between these two worlds indicates how rarely the evangelical college serves as a bridge to issues and audiences beyond the safe confines of the evangelical world.

Consider again the question of responsibility. If evangelical colleges do not begin to shoulder the burden of Christian scholarship, who will? To phrase the question differently, what other institutions have a greater responsibility in this area? Significant scholarship and reflection certainly cannot be done by individual churches or even denominations, or by mission boards, evangelistic organizations, magazines, or professional societies. Christian colleges, on the other hand, obligate themselves by their own professions. It is simply a contradiction in terms for Christian scholarship to languish at institutions that call themselves Christian liberal arts colleges. This is not to propose that small colleges blossom into universities or that research supplant undergraduate teaching; rather, that among a college's chief aims must be the development of a faculty of Christian intellectuals and the nurturing—among the entire evangelical community—of the attitude that intellectual activity can be a fundamental part of service to the Lord.

That, of course, is a challenge that involves every dimension of a college's life: constituents, board, administration, faculty, and students. To make this challenge more concrete, I will address two issues: the institutional obstacles to Christian thinking within evangelical colleges, and then the crisis of authority for the evangelical scholar. I put forward my proposals primarily to stimulate discussion and debate; what I have to say is intended to raise questions rather than nail down answers.

Institutional Obstacles to Christian Thinking

Can one expect evangelicals at the end of the twentieth century to take up the challenge of Christian thinking? Unfortunately, one finds deeply entrenched obstacles to this goal within the values of evangelical communities and within the structures of evangelical organizations. Fear persists that strengthening academics will set an institution upon the same course of spiritual decline that once beset Harvard and Yale. The inertia is considerable and the available levers for change are weak and often ineffective. Yet complacency on this front is unacceptable, and we must attempt some assessment of the current state of affairs before making proposals for change, even if the results of that diagnosis are discouraging.

The first and most difficult problem for evangelical colleges is in some sense their own history. A pattern continues throughout the twentieth century of alienation from main centers of learning and a failure to appreciate, or even to understand, the costs and demands of serious scholarship. By any measure, most evangelical colleges have been struggling institutions, more concerned with issues of survival than of quality. Now that some of these colleges are stable and prospering, the danger is twofold: that board members, constituents, and administrators will not raise their sights, and that even if they did, they would be hard pressed to recruit a more able faculty.

Let me suggest somewhat whimsically that for evangelicals the heritage of fundamentalism in Christian learning was akin to the impact of Chairman Mao's "Cultural Revolution" on Chinese academia. Both divorced a generation of academics from the mainline, thus making reintegration a difficult and bewildering task. For too long the Wheatons, Calvins, Asburys, Westmonts, and Gordons have compared themselves only with each other, if with anyone else at all, instead of with Oberlin, Swarthmore, Georgetown, and Notre Dame. The point is not to ape whatever is in vogue in higher education. Yet at least we ought to know more about the requirements of an institution of quality in the modern world.

A second and related difficulty is that the development of the Christian mind receives anything but commanding support among evangelical people at large, the broad constituency of Christian colleges. It is here that one sees most directly the continuing divorce between piety and learning. How many Christians do you know who would tithe so that a Christian scholar can go about her work? It is much easier for large ecclesiastical organizations than for individuals to make such commitments of support. Yet evangelical organizations by and large depend upon a support base of individuals, each of whom weighs the merits of the endeavor at hand. Moreover, evangelical agencies that do distribute financial resources are controlled in the main not by denominations but by boards comprised of ministers and business executives who are always comparing the needs of a college with those of endeavors that manifest a greater sense of urgency and the promise of more immediate success: mission boards, relief agencies, or evangelistic crusades, for instance. Among such a democratic constituency, the call to support abstract thinking, intensive reading, and careful research—all of which often leads to further questions and complexity as much as to certainty and action—falls on deaf ears.

A third institutional obstacle is the sheer number of different colleges that are competing for scarce resources. The diversity of these institutions and their contrasting constituencies certainly expand the overall influence of evangelical higher education, but very few of these institutions can plan for genuine excellence rather than mere survival. Can these schools afford to be selective in student admissions so as to obviate setting the curriculum to catch every vocational breeze?[6] How can they accumulate a reasonable endowment? How can they attract the best faculty rather than those who come at bargain rates? Which of these can offer the kind of environment to retain first-rate scholars? In an age of reducing college enrollments, of deep concern about the escalating cost of private education, and pessimism and loss of intellectual morale among faculty, the greatest age of American higher education may be over, as Laurence Veysey has suggested.[7] The present climate does anything but invite small liberal arts colleges to think of setting grand agendas—particularly when most of them service a limited geographic or denominational constituency and have little vision for serving the church universal.

A fourth institutional obstacle concerns the issue of boundaries and identity. What are the criteria for being evangelical? Who defines such boundaries and how are they applied to faculty members and to their ongoing scholarly work? The problematic nature of evangelical boundaries is best seen when they are contrasted with other traditions. Roman Catholics, who have a much more inclusive definition of the church, tolerate within their educational institutions a broad spectrum of opinion. The glue that holds Catholicism together is less a rigid doctrinal system than the institutional church with its designated structures of authority, its sacramentalism, its system of parochial education, and its traditions, diverse as they are. These bonds involve much more than what one believes and experiences at any given point in time and are often strengthened by deep ethnic, community, and family ties. Denominations that are confessionally orthodox and ethnically distinctive, such as the Missouri Synod Lutheran Church or the Christian Reformed Church, manifest many of the same complex strands that bind people to the tradition.

Many American evangelicals, however, profess to live without ecclesiastical, denominational, ethnic, or theological traditions. What they sustain, instead, is an ideological traditionalism that orients thinking around a set of principal ideas or practices rather than around institutions or creeds.[8] The problem for educational institutions serving such evangelical constituents is that their faculties are subject to vigilant scrutiny. Indeed, evangelical people have historic reasons to fear that scholars might lead the faithful astray. While such scrutiny is less fearful and reflexive than it once was, its searchlight can still appear with frightening intensity if the orthodoxy of a faculty member is ever questioned.

In such cases, the democratic structure of evangelical life comes to the fore. Even when facing the most serious and complex intellectual issues, evangelicals have the instinct to play them out before a popular audience—though this does not mean that they are played out fully and in all their implications. In fact, issues are more likely to be treated in ways that rally a large constituency than in ways that admit to the genuine complexity involved and that allow scholars to carefully weigh and clarify the issues at hand. In this sense, it is the people who are the custodians of orthodoxy and who at any time can blow the whistle on an individual or institution that is judged out of bounds. This instinct can certainly function in very positive ways; but it also retards creativity and makes going to the intellectual frontier a very risky business. Christian scholars need to preserve the tension between openness and commitment, a problem that John Stott recognized in calling for Christian scholars "to accept some measure of accountability to one another and responsibility for one another in the Body of Christ. In such a caring fellowship I think we might witness fewer casualties on the one hand and more theological creativity on the other."[9]

The fifth, and last, institutional problem I plan to discuss concerns the prospects for evangelical colleges' being able to build competent and creative faculties. While there are some positive signs on the horizon, there is also considerable evidence to suggest that the profession of learning is increasingly troubled. Academic life has become less attractive to our brightest students: the proportion of college freshmen preparing to pursue careers in college teaching is now only one ninth what it was fifteen years ago.[10] There is little reason to think that gifted evangelical students have run counter to this trend. A related issue is whether evangelical colleges are willing to recruit outstanding talent and then provide the kind of compensation and work environment that will keep their most gifted faculty members from going elsewhere. Are there compelling reasons that a scholar should stay at a place like Wheaton rather than accept an offer from the likes of the University of Illinois? Are evangelical colleges willing to put up with the eccentricities characteristic of intellectuals? Those who excel at the life of the mind generally do not win awards for sociability—and certainly not for conformity. This is really a twofold question: do evangelical colleges sincerely want intellectuals on their faculty, and if so are they willing to provide an inviting academic home?

Evangelical Scholars and the Crisis of Authority

Added to these institutional hurdles is today's troublesome intellectual world and the challenge to evangelical scholars to come to grips with it in constructive ways. The most acute problem that thoughtful Christians face today is the profound crisis of authority in the modern world. Where does one find a solid position from which to assess the fluid instability all around? As Harry Blamires suggests in his book *Where Do We Stand?* "today's boundary between Christian fidelity and treachery is no floodlit Berlin wall, set about with watch-towers and man-traps, and patrolled by jealous guardsmen; it is a frontier barely recognizable on the terrain over which it runs. To locate it, you have to consult a map; and reliable maps, alas, are not easy to come by."[11]

There are at least three reasons why it is difficult—much more difficult than even a generation ago—for evangelical Christians to locate trustworthy maps or compasses in the contemporary world. One might think of these as three concentric circles. The first and broadest dimension of the problem is the underlying crisis of authority in the contemporary academic world. The second is the theological instability that besets the Christian church. And the innermost circle is a problem specific to evangelicals: the lack of intellectual and spiritual depth in their own particular heritage of faith.

The modern intellectual world is adrift, incapable or unwilling to allow any claim of certainty to set the coordinates by which ideas and commitments are to be judged. The positive side of this situation, of course, is that toleration and subjectivity have become the principal virtues of our age, meaning that marginal groups—even evangelicals—are accorded far more respect than they were earlier in the century. The danger of course is that the gentle lamb of toleration often returns as the wolf of relativism. Christians, then, are both better off and worse off: better in that they are tolerated like everyone else, worse in that no claim to truth carries weight any longer.

In this context, academic disciplines in recent years have become increasingly fractured as competing methodologies and ideologies clamor for attention. While I lack the competence to trace this problem through the various disciplines in the liberal arts, two matters seem clear: a graduate student today will find few firm footings as she attempts to bring some coherence to her understanding; and many of these methodological perspectives—Marxist, Freudian, behavioralist, structuralist, deconstructionist, or whatever—have shrouded the academic world with such fog that losing one's way is easy without clear theological bearings.

The problem is compounded by the rapid disintegration of church authority in recent years, of which the Roman Catholic church provides the most vivid example. Since Vatican II, just over two decades ago, the largest Christian church in the world has set out to update its witness to the gospel and in the process has overturned patterns of language and liturgy going back fifteen hundred years, of church polity going back a thousand, and of theology going back over five hundred. The subsequent turmoil is something to behold, heartening in its return to Scripture and lay involvement, heart-rending in the confusion and bitter recriminations among the various parties.[12] Shattered is the Thomistic intellectual synthesis that had been the dominant and unifying force in Catholic intellectual life. In its place, one finds claimants to intellectual authority that are as diverse as the spectrum between Protestant fundamentalists and liberals. A century ago Protestants like John Henry Newman who were troubled by a crisis of authority could find a safe haven in the Church of Rome. Today, the full force of the tempest has reached even those shores, leaving thoughtful Catholics few stable intellectual moorings amid a bewildering range of theological options.

The Catholic experience is symptomatic of a broader trend: powerful and synthetic theologies are everywhere on the wane. A similar, if less drastic, toppling of a given systematic theology is taking place within the Christian Reformed Church and among other Calvinists. A stable theological system that for generations had been the core of broader intellectual life has been losing its grip over the last twenty-five years, some parts being consciously laid aside, others simply ignored. Creedal orthodoxy is on the wane, biblical exegesis on the rise, but no new synthesis is on the horizon. Lutheran orthodoxy has been even less successful as an intellectual force, as the split in the Missouri Synod Lutheran Church graphically demonstrates. Christian scholars will find few stable points of reference either in disciplines they are studying or in current theological frames of reference.

Evangelical scholars in America also face a more particular difficulty: their own heritage. Those who are heirs of fundamentalism or other kindred movements have difficulty going beyond or transcending the long-standing dichotomy between religious experience and rigorous and critical thought. The problem, simply put, is that the traditions of faith in which many of us were raised have been powerful enough to maintain their hold but not powerful enough either intellectually or spiritually to provide an orienting vision for all of life. Christian scholars will never speak with authority in the various disciplines of the liberal arts until their faith becomes as profoundly intellectual as the disciplines to which they are called. And we will never encourage bright and talented students to fear God and serve him in humility until we put aside piety that is sentimental and human-centered and bend all of our mental gifts to understand the riches of the Christian faith that we profess.

Evangelical faith strikes many of us as anything but rich and profound. We spend more time avoiding our heritage than devoting ourselves to laying claim to it. Evangelical academicians are often children of reaction against the stern parent of fundamentalism—its inbred suspicion of the intellect, its retreat from liberal arts education, its hostility to aesthetics, its inability to confront modern science in constructive ways, its crabbed legalism, and most importantly its parochial religious vision. Too few can savor the faith committed to us as grand and majestic, can revel in its intellectual depths, or can find therein a point of departure for serious study. It is this deep ambivalence, this nagging self-doubt about our heritage that leads some to a stance of cynicism and others to seek a foundation in other traditions: Anabaptist, Kuyperian, Roman Catholic, or whatever.

Many evangelical scholars are historical orphans who have not reached back to recover an evangelical—even a broader Christian—heritage more profound than what they know in the twentieth century. We have not had solid vantage points from which to assess our own times. We have failed to traffic in Luther, Calvin, the Puritans, Wesley, and Edwards—what might be called a tradition of classic evangelical orthodoxy. That we have not mined such rich veins is striking, given the fact that in the last thirty years secular intellectuals like Perry Miller and neoorthodox theologians like H. Richard Niebuhr have found in these figures of the past profound insights for understanding the modern world.

The faith of Luther, Wesley, and Edwards was deeply intellectual and profoundly pious at the same time. For Jonathan Edwards, the issue was never piety versus the intellect, as if they were inversely proportional. Edwards realized full well the danger of rationalism but assumed that a more serious problem was that people had forgotton Christian truth or refused to submit to it. The purpose of life in his view was to fear God and serve him with abandon; yet people would become God-fearing only as they came to think in genuinely Christian ways. The problem was not too much thinking but the erroneous thinking that stemmed from pride. His proposed antidote for the decline in religious commitment, then, was an attempt to correct this muddled thinking.

A tradition of classic evangelical orthodoxy offers at least two perspectives that would strengthen evangelical engagement with the intellectual issues of our day. In the first place, this tradition, like all Christian theology worth its salt, began from the assumption that all of life must take on a theological orientation. To read Edwards—or Luther, Calvin, or Wesley—is to witness a believer enraptured with the power and majesty of God, struck dumb at the wonder of redemption, and jealous to uphold that name which is above every other. If fundamentalism in America is deserving of indictment for anything, it is for failing to maintain a lofty view of the triune God. Its pragmatic theology of salvation had neither intellectual bite nor a deep sense of reverential awe. Its legacy is that evangelicals are not in the habit of "living to God" or "working toward God," William Ames's definition of theology.[13] They do not plot their paths through life with a theological compass. Even today, evangelical colleges are much more likely to be enamored of pragmatic causes such as living simply, feeding the hungry, banning the bomb, or challenging abortion than they are to be concerned with learning to think seriously and theologically.

A flimsy theological foundation bedevils evangelicals in two particular respects. First they lack the resources to serve as theological prophets. Progressive evangelicals today are quick to take a "prophetic" stand against cultural conformity, against materialism, and against smug middle-class complacency. Yet the danger is that they are merely following the lead of what has become fashionable within the contemporary academic and theological world. What is desperately needed is tough-minded, historically informed theology to serve as ballast so that we will not proclaim as Christian whatever cause surfaces next.

Even more, Christian scholars need a theological framework to suggest the kinds of issues that they alone can raise. "The fact that it is respectable and fashionable nowadays to be socially conscious does not prove it the most urgent priority of Christian witness," Harry Blamires has said. "It may by contrast be a forbidding task to turn from the social to the intellectual front, and to attack established modes of thought which have the backing of contemporary academic circles with their vast intellectual authority and influence. . . . Is it not therefore incumbent upon us to adjust our priorities, and to strive to counter intellectual apostasy with the same buoyancy and relish with which we confront social injustice?"[14]

The absence of a compelling theological vision also affects Christian scholars in a second way. It leaves them without the means to compensate for the feelings of intellectual inferiority that plagues once-marginal religious groups as they seek to move back into the mainstream. This keen sense of wanting to be accepted by professional peers has been evident in recent times among Catholics, among confessional groups like the Christian Reformed, and most acutely among evangelicals. Like children long rejected, evangelical scholars are still too anxious to be accepted by their peers, too willing to move only in directions that allow them to be "relevant." The result is that we have been far more inclined to speak up when our Christian convictions are in tune with the assumptions of modern academic life than when they are at odds. It is much easier, for instance, to set oneself in the vanguard of social progress than it is to defend those Christian assumptions that the established and fashionable intellectual circles of our day regard as obscurantist and fanciful. Yet it is this tougher mental fight that we must not avoid.

Another helpful theme is replete in the tradition of classic evangelical orthodoxy: a "bearish" view of human nature that comes to terms with what Augustine called our "radical apostacy." Evidence abounds that evangelicals in the twentieth century are in danger of losing sight of the very mainspring of the Reformation, which taught that sin was no mild disease of the soul but a deep-seated and foul revolt. The evangelical awakenings of the eighteenth century again brought into sharp relief the paradox of the gospel: that it must crush self-sufficiency before uplifting the contrite, root out self-centeredness before offering consolation.

In the past, a sober view of human nature offered evangelicals engaged in intellectual matters great insight into the dynamics of life and the only plausible intellectual foundation for comprehending the horrors and tragedies that wrack human existence. Such realism gave Christians in the past a much better handle on the explosive potential that the life of the mind had for both evil and good. This kind of discrimination about intellectual pursuits is even more essential in our own day. While earlier evangelicals were, in the main, more intellectual than their descendants in the twentieth century, they were also more realistic about the blind spots and besetting sins of the intellectual. Two of these occupational liabilities are worth noting.

Evangelicals in the past noted that a commitment to reason very easily becomes tainted with rationalism, or the belief in rational autonomy and self-sufficiency. No one, to be sure, would pursue the life of the mind without hoping to increase his or her power of understanding, to make sense of complexity, to become, in some sense, an arbiter of truth for others. Yet intellectuals very easily cross the fine line and begin affirming their own intellectual self-sufficiency, trusting in their own wisdom rather than submitting the mind humbly to the truths of holy Scripture. Given their well-honed intellectual skills, academics are always prone to move in the direction of an unwarrantably high opinion of human natural powers.

It was for this reason that Luther, the Puritans, Wesley, and Edwards all embraced a prophetic onslaught against the reigning intellectual culture of their day—not because they hoped to substitute piety for reason but because they detected a pride and self-sufficiency among intellectuals that was 180 degrees from the call of the gospel: to confess the blindness of the heart, to renounce treating oneself as the measure of all things, and to receive with thanks the enlightening word of God. The problem with so many intellectuals, then and now, is very much a problem of rationalism—the refusal to acknowledge that they are creatures who do not stand on an even footing with our Creator and the refusal to admit to the truth of the biblical indictment that they are ruined and helpless rebels. The difficulty, obviously, is that the cross calls people who are trained to speak as intellectual authorities to admit their ignorance and foolishness. This was the message that Luther had for Erasmus, the Puritans for smug Anglicans, Wesley for his Oxford colleagues, and Edwards for the Harvard theologians of the 1740s.

The danger of intellectual pride, of the smug professionalism of the academic, is a theme that Christian scholars cannot dwell upon too often, both as we pursue our own calling and as we train students. Teachers must ground students firmly in the truth that the worst forms of evil parallel the original sin: our denial of our creaturehood, our hopeless striving to gain the knowledge that would put us on a par with God. If teachers fall into this trap, their students will be perplexed at the paradox of scholars of good will, people of unimpeachable integrity and sincerity, who have no use for Christian claims. This is not to condemn the genuine brilliance and creativity of many non-Christian scholars, but it is to suggest that sincerity and good intention do not necessarily put one on the road to life. The Christian scholar walks a precarious path because the deadliest vices of all, autonomy and pride, are so pervasive and so beguiling within academe.

With this sobering truth in mind, evangelicals of a different era were quick to point out a second characteristic of intellectual endeavor: that intellectual life is not something neutral, an evenhanded and objective exploration. It is instead an activity channeled by deep, and often unrecognized, personal assumptions. In his profound treatise *The Religious Affections,* Jonathan Edwards demonstrates that people do not approach the important issues of life as "indifferent unaffected spectators" but pattern their lives and their thoughts according to what they love, cherish, and value: the orientation of the will. A deep sense of the subjectivity of intellectual endeavor is a liberating insight. Christians, of all people, should not automatically defer to intellectuals, for their endeavors will reveal, to one extent or another, their own orientations and preconceptions. "So convenient a thing it is to be a reasonable creature," quipped Benjamin Franklin, "since it enables one to find or make a reason for everything one has a mind to do."

One reason that evangelicals today are less discerning than they should be about the pretensions of academic culture at large is that they have been too far removed from it. We will never penetrate the foundations of modern intellectual life and be able to discriminate between wheat and chaff until we too are deeply involved in academic culture. As long as we maintain our distance, it is too easy to be enamored of those who rule the academic roost. Unless we traffic regularly in the same world of ideas, we will never sort out the ample measure of pretentious folly that issues from the mind of even the wisest scholar. Our danger has not been too much thinking, but not enough.

Understanding the intimate correlation between one's commitments and the contours of one's thinking is also a pointed reminder of the danger of assuming that scholars can weigh issues as indifferent spectators. Cool detachment from issues of faith will have intellectual consequences, as Jonathan Edwards was well aware. That is why he decried smug Christians who approached their faith as an important intellectual puzzle. "That religion which God requires and will accept does not consist in weak, dull, and lifeless wishes, raising us but a little above a state of indifference." In the same vein, Harry Blamires comments about the vital link between the piety and the intellectual depth of C. S. Lewis: "The fact that he was a man of rare personal spirituality and saintliness and that he also, intellectually, had perhaps the most deeply dyed Christian understanding of our times, raises serious questions. Can the mind attain true Christian insight unless the will is comparably consecrated? Is built-in Christian mental orientation inseparably interconnected with moral obedience?"[15]

I recently visited an excellent liberal arts college in the Midwest to evaluate a new academic program. The president and dean took me through a newly opened Campus Center, a magnificent restoration of a science hall originally built in 1892. At the entrance of the building was set the original plaque which read: "This hall for the study and teaching of the works of God in nature." I have high admiration for this college. It has a dedicated faculty and an excellent tradition of study and teaching. Yet as I paused by that plaque for a moment I was struck with a deep sense of loss. That plaque brought home to me what has happened to higher education in twentieth-century America. Like most of academic discourse, the study and teaching of science at schools like this have over time been drained of any distinctive Christian worldview.

The easiest way to explain this loss of faith is to attribute it to the pursuit of academic excellence. Christian colleges lost their way because of their academic ambitions. If an institution is to avoid the same slippery slope, the argument goes, it must "withdraw from the bleak atmosphere of human science" to cultivate piety at the expense of learning, or to claim to hold them together while relegating the task to a faculty that is distinguished for neither.

Let us ascend a more narrow and dangerous path: higher education that is unflinching in its commitment both to Christian values and to serious learning. Evangelicals should accept this challenge not so that they will be accorded more respect within the academic world; nor because the American experience offers many models of colleges that have retained their Christian convictions while pursuing academic excellence; nor simply because they may succeed. Rather, we should do so out of a deep responsibility to the church, whose vitality in the future will depend upon how well you and I cultivate the mind today.

NOTES

1. Laurence Veysey, "Continuity and Decline in American Religion Since 1900," Kaplan Lecture, University of Pennsylvania, 1980.

2. Andrew Greeley, "Why Catholic Higher Learning is Lower," *National Catholic Reporter*, 23 September 1983, 1-7.

3. This is a condensation of the argument I made in the essay "Evangelicalism as a Democratic Movement," in *Evangelicalism and Modern America*, ed. George Marsden (Grand Rapids: Eerdmans, 1984), 71-82.

4. A Gallup poll in 1979 estimated that about 19 percent of persons holding evangelical beliefs were college graduates. This compares with 55 percent for Episcopalians, 50 percent for Presbyterians, 50 percent for members of the United Church of Christ, and 42 percent for United Methodists. See Robert Wuthnow, "Religious Movements and Counter-Movements in North America," in *New Religious Movements and Rapid Social Change*, ed. James A. Beckford (Paris: UNESCO, 1984).

5. Mark A. Noll, "Christian Colleges, Christian Worldviews, and an Invitation to Research," the introduction to William C. Ringenberg, *The Christian College: A History of Protestant Higher Education in America* (Grand Rapids: Eerdmans, Christian University Press, 1984), 33.

6. Laurence Veysey, a distinguished historian of higher education, believes that catering to the vocational interests of students threatens to dilute the quality of education in the liberal arts at all but the most stable institutions. See "Higher Education as a Profession: Changes and Continuities," in *The Professions in American History*, ed. Nathan O. Hatch (South Bend: University of Notre Dame Press, forthcoming).

7. Ibid.

8. See Mark A. Noll, "Evangelicals and the Study of the Bible," in *Evangelicalism and Modern America*, ed. Marsden, 118.

9. John R. W. Stott, *Between Two Worlds: The Art of Preaching in the Twentieth Century* (Grand Rapids: Eerdmans, 1982), 87.

10. The Study Group on the Conditions of Excellence in American Higher Education reported in the fall of 1984 that the proportion of entering college freshmen intending to pursue careers as college professors dropped from 1.8 percent in 1966 to 0.2 percent in 1982. This 89 percent decline bodes ill for the future of higher education; see *The Chronicle of Higher Education*, 24 October 1984, 37.

11. Harry Blamires, *Where Do We Stand?* (Ann Arbor: Servant, 1980), 4.

12. Much of this section draws on an essay by John Van Engen, "The Problem of Tradition in the Christian Reformed Church," *Calvin Theological Journal* 20 (1985): 69-89.

13. See Geoffrey W. Bromiley's summary of Ames in *Historical Theology: An Introduction* (Grand Rapids: Eerdmans, 1978), 308.

14. Blamires, *Where Do We Stand?* 39.

15. Ibid., 46.

The Contribution of Theological Studies to the Christian Liberal Arts

William A. Dyrness

This topic resembles a famous final exam some philosopher is supposed to have given: Please explain the world and give three examples. I say that because discussing "the contribution of theological studies to the Christian liberal arts" opens up questions that are rich in their potential for oversimplification and misunderstanding. In order to get some bearings, then, I will take some initial soundings and attempt a basic definition. After that, having explained the world, I will then offer three examples.

I

The soundings relate to the conjoining of theology and Christian liberal arts. To argue for this may be either unnecessary or impossible. It may be unnecessary because the history of the liberal arts has been so intimately connected with religion that one might argue that liberal arts are inconceivable without theological study. In the ancient roots of the liberal arts, in Egyptian and Hindu thought, the arts were essentially religious. The medieval development of the seven liberal arts continues this perspective and reflects a deeply theological view of the world. In fact, the very order of the quadrivium reflects a movement from earth to heaven: geometry studies actual objects, mathematics examines numbers, astronomy explores space, and music is meant to reflect the heavenly spheres. Moreover, study of the liberal arts was understood as propaedeutic: it was intended to assure the intellectual formation necessary for the proper study of Scripture and theology.[1] As other essayists have pointed out, even modern higher education in America received its original impulse from the Christian world and life view.

Against this background, the very fact that I am addressing the relationship between theology and the arts and sciences indicates that the conception of the liberal arts has changed, a process that began as early as the eleventh century, when the independent powers of dialectic began to be defended by Peter Abelard. These developments came to fruition during the Enlightenment and have been institutionalized in the modern secular university. My inquiry seeks to challenge some of these modified conceptions of the arts and sciences and to reestablish these fields on their proper and original foundation.

But thinking along these lines has some problems, for the liberal arts and theological reflection are often in serious tension. Reflection on the purpose of human life—enjoying God and serving him and his creation—and personal experiences of living in the Third World have led me to the view that studying the liberal arts may not always be an asset to Christian obedience. This is not to say that the study of these profane subjects is useless because of the absolute incapacity of the sinful mind and the inevitable failure of human thought, or that such study is a distraction from the real work of proclaiming the gospel. Rather, study of the liberal arts may reflect a human goal of contemplation rather than the divine call to obedience. When they emphasize reflective study, champions of the liberal arts may hold up an ideal of human life that is essentially Greek rather than Christian. It may be, moreover, that received notions of the arts and sciences need to be broadened by interaction with non-Western modes of thinking, and that their passive, text-oriented character needs to be supplemented with a more active, interactionist model of learning.[2] The liberal arts might reflect a religious impulse, but their history might have given a peculiar, even harmful, shape to that impulse.

One does not have to read far in the literature on higher education in America to know that not all is well, especially from a Christian point of view. Edward Farley in fact has recently suggested that theological education itself in America is in something of a crisis. His point is that faith is no longer the agenda-setting power in theological education. He argues that because of a heritage of rationalism and historical criticism, theology has been dispersed into various incoherent sciences that have little relation either to each other or to real life.[3] One could argue that his case applies to Christian colleges as well. Can one claim that Christian theology actually functions as an integrating element? When the faculties of Christian colleges and institutions of theological education are trained in today's radically fragmented universities,[4] it is no wonder they bring back not an impulse to integration but a mentality of specialization and mutual suspicion. Indeed, this tendency toward intellectual balkanization often occurs unconsciously, even in the presence of a strong personal faith.

If this picture has any truth in it, Christian liberal arts colleges are entering troubled and uncharted waters. The contribution of theological studies to liberal arts in this case may be less like giving aid and support than like bringing lifeboats around a foundering ship and providing survivors with alternative means of transport. A fresh understanding of what theological reflection is, then, may also disrupt rather than support the more commonly understood nature of a liberal arts education.

What does theological reflection look like today? It strikes a careful observer immediately that, as I have already mentioned, theological studies today are not exempt from the confusion plaguing higher education. Theology too seems captive to a tradition of abstraction and criticism, and it seems unable to respond creatively to the compelling issues of the modern world in a way that carries weight with either the church or its unbelieving neighbors. The reasons for this are many and complex. P. J. Cahill believes that theological studies have not flourished because they have been unable to go beyond their foundational presuppositions, which he identifies as "the pythagorean theory of harmonic ratios and the chain of being."[5] Lesslie Newbigin suggests, echoing Farley, that Western theological thinking since Descartes has replaced faith with doubt, an attitude that has become a central trait in our intellectual tradition. Interestingly, he proposes this as one of the reasons that the Western church is moribund and needs the life (and hope) that is represented by the church in the Third World.[6]

One of the signs of theology's malaise is the recent proliferation of religious studies in major universities, even while theological study done from the standpoint of faith seems to be in decline. Why is it, Jacob Neusner asks wryly, that we prefer the study of dead religion to that of living faith? "An old Christian text," he notes, "one from the first century, for example, is deemed a worthy subject of scholarship. But a fresh Christian expression . . . is available principally for ridicule, but never for study."[7] Meanwhile, Farley notes, even seminaries reflect the poverty of theological study in their focus on specific skills that enable one to function in some professional religious capacity. He concludes that theological study today seems to be for ministers as a professional group, not for human beings.[8]

Ironically, an emphasis on ministry skills might provide a way to integrate academic disciplines theologically. But the view of theology as the development of certain special skills, rather than an integral part of the curriculum, simply creates one more subspecialty. Even when curricular cohesion is discussed, it is almost always thought of in theoretical rather than practical terms. Meanwhile recent research in medical and ministerial education indicates that programs that try to work out a theoretical model—a "theological tradition"—are less effective in developing well-rounded practitioners than are those that focus on specific skills (equivalent to what we might call "servant ministries"). This is not to say that theoretical models are unimportant, only that they provide an inadequate integration point for curriculum planning.[9]

But the ferment that has led to this probing may itself be a sign that new options are opening up. Neusner's comments indicate that reflection on living faith may again become an integral part of theological study; and Farley's book may provoke a rethinking of theological education. William F. May has proposed a problematic rather than a systematic theology, a theology that focuses on common human problems such as meaning, marriage, death, and evil, which it shares with other disciplines of the liberal arts.[10] This emphasis on fundamental questions may provide evangelicals with a unique opportunity to contribute to renewal in theological education, for it is especially the Christian perspective on the liberal arts that makes faith an agenda-setting force. If, as seems clear, the crisis in education is part of a deeper crisis of faith, then the Christian dimension becomes crucial.

This background suggests the following definition of theological studies appropriate to Christian higher education. Theological reflection is the dynamic interaction between a prayerful listening to Scripture and a responsible involvement with the issues of our world that has as its goal a maturity of Christlikeness. Note that the questioning involved in this reflection goes in two directions. On the one hand Scripture speaks to us and enlarges our conception of things. On the other hand it confronts the issues of our lives and world—a confrontation that in turn affects us and calls for responsible interaction. By the working of the Holy Spirit, the whole process leads us individually and communally to a maturity of life and thought that the New Testament calls Christlikeness. That is, theological studies in Christian colleges should aim ultimately at Christian formation, not at research or scholarship merely for their own sakes.

This definition needs to be fleshed out more before we test its relevance to the study of the liberal arts. Martin Luther used three words to describe the activity of theology: *oratio, meditatio,* and *tentatio* (prayer, meditation, and testing). First, theological studies presuppose an environment of faith and prayer—*oratio.*[11] Since "Scripture makes folly of all other books," Luther notes, "you must begin by despairing of your own wit and enter into your closet and implore the Holy Spirit to guide you and give you understanding." Likewise, Karl Barth frequently said that theology is simply a matter of prayer and answer to prayer. "Praying, asking of God, can consist only in receiving what God has already prepared for us, before and apart from our stretching out our hands for it. It is in this praise of God that the children of God live, who love God, because he first loved them."[12] This presupposes that the only truthful, accurate response to the world and to God's love is faith and trust.

Growing out of this faithful trust and reflective of it is the need to listen carefully to God's word found in Scripture and to reflect on what our traditions have learned from it. This is *meditatio,* the second aspect of attaining theological aptitude. Continually hearing and submitting to Scripture is the heart and core of a trustful response to God.

A third characteristic of theology actually precedes faith: theology always happens in a social and historical context. Luther referred to this element with the word *tentatio,* by which he meant that only through affliction do we experience how good and true God's word is. Even prayer is often a cry to God out of the depths of some experience of suffering. In fact, the illumination of Scripture takes place only in vital interaction with the questions and problems that we bring to it.[13]

It is here that theological studies provide the greatest challenge and allow the largest scope to the arts and sciences: theological understanding takes place only within the grid of life itself. As Farley puts it, "The dialectic of theological understanding is set in motion here, by the matters which evoke response and interpretation."[14] By and large our students will be practitioners rather than theoreticians, so they must learn to practice their faith in their life settings. It is this context that provides the impetus for both understanding and active Christian response, which must be normed by Christian truth. All Christians, not just theologians, engage in this process. Theology, then, should provide travel guides for pilgrims rather than monuments of previous (or possible) journeys.[15]

Our final goal is true Christian maturity: "we are to grow up in every way into him who is the head, into Christ" (Eph. 4:15). In its dual emphasis on the importance of both the process of growth and the final goal to be sought, this conception recalls the ancient aim of learning as *paideia*—an education and cultivation that has to be traversed and also the goal that is to be attained, maturity.[16] It also reflects the biblical ideal of the wise person who has mastered ideas in the context of a joyful and consistent discipline.

Theological study, as an integrated part of the educational process, must involve actual experience with life as well as a breadth of understanding about the world. Thus it already calls for the perspective of the arts and sciences. By implication, this means that any study that values intellectual formation over character formation is not what the Bible holds up as Christian growth. This may mean that theological study in some formal sense should be provided for all of God's people throughout their lives so that understanding, experience, and responsible obedience can develop in creative interaction.

II

In what specific ways will theological reflection influence study of the arts and sciences? And, because the influence will not be all in one direction, how will study of the arts and sciences influence theological studies? What will the mutual interactions and influences be? Building on our definition of theological studies—a dynamic interaction between listening to Scripture and wrestling with the issues of our world—we can elaborate three foundational ways that theological studies can contribute to the arts and sciences. I do not propose here to formulate any hard and fast principles that can be applied to various fields, but rather to illuminate more general situations or contexts in which these fields must be construed. Perhaps in following this path we can come to a more articulate and integrated understanding of all human endeavor. The impact of these contributions is in two directions: on the one hand they shape personal habits of thought and life while on the other they confront the larger world by wrestling with the issues it raises.

The primary contribution of theological studies to the liberal arts—and to our understanding of the world around us—is the provision of a source and ground for all that exists. Where do things come from? This basic question has long furnished stimulus for the arts and fascination for scientists. But there is a further question that needs emphasis: What is the *continuing* ground of existence? What is the source of the wellsprings of life and all there is around us? The Scriptures portray this source as a personal God who superintends this created order and calls it to account. Moreover, as the order's creator he has placed within it signs of his lordship that must be noted and observed. All of this has traditionally been discussed under the doctrine of creation, but today we must elaborate our thoughts in a much more comprehensive way to include not only questions of beginnings but also questions about the nature of present structures and processes.[17]

Characteristic of the created order is that it stands responsible to God and images this responsibility in objective ways. Creation itself calls persons to act in ways faithful to the order that reflects God's purposes; our proper response must be personal and moral. We may describe this first situation as follows. This order is a personal matrix in which one exists as a responsible agent. Let me note that this is not a view that only a theist can endorse. Indeed, it is based on the assertion that religious and moral issues are related to the very structure of things and are ultimately essential to their reality. Karl Rahner expressed the same thought from another direction: "A tranquil atheism which behaves as if the religious question no longer existed either does not know what we mean by God or is a transparent technique of flight from God—and a pose."[18]

A further dimension of this sense of responsibility is added by the incarnation and resurrection of Christ and the pouring out of the Holy Spirit at Pentecost. Now there is a permanent dimension to reality, which makes real personal and social change possible, and a permanent source of hope that something new can happen. This hope is grounded in Christ's resurrection and the pouring out of the Holy Spirit, but it also anticipates Christ's personal bodily return and the new heaven and earth he will bring.

There are at least two ways this should affect our study of the arts and sciences. First, we will see the study of the physical or biological sciences in a different light. Observation and analysis will remain essential because scientific knowledge has intrinsic value, but they alone will not be enough. The student will be called to *respond* to nature as well as understand it; indeed, the one will not finally be possible without the other.[19] The survival of a particular species of bird, or the power latent in a chemical process calls us to responsible stewardship. This is not yet a call to act with theological intention, but simply to act responsibly—the situation itself implies it.

A sense of responsibility must also affect our study when we encounter human suffering, whether economic or physical. Here is a problem, or rather a cluster of problems, that must be addressed in many disciplines. Underlying this study, moreover, will inevitably lie transcendent questions of source and ground: Why does such a reality exist? What has been—and what can be—done about it? In the end, as Jürgen Moltmann notes, "it is in suffering that the whole human question about God arises. . . . [Suffering] is not really a question at all, in the sense of something we can ask or not ask, like other questions. It is the open wound of life in this world."[20] It is not simply that we have various ideas about suffering that we may usefully study—economic, physiological, sociological—but that life in this world brings suffering upon us and that, as it raises ultimate questions of source and ground, it forces us to respond. These questions can no more be ignored than the experiences themselves. Something of the dialectical relationship between theological convictions and study in the liberal arts now becomes clear. Not only do we bring theological convictions to our study, but the material we study itself calls forth a personal and even a moral and religious response. We bring our convictions of historical meaning to our study of history, but this study in turn forces patterns and meanings on us that we must deal with.

A second way theological reflection should affect study of the arts and sciences has to do with the nature and contour of reality. Reality is a dynamic project that God—its personal source—has initiated and in which humanity is inevitably involved. Questions arise at many points in the study of the arts and sciences: What is the point of this process? How does one discern signs and markers that will measure what one sees? What is happening here anyway?

When we ask such questions we are asking not about the source and ground, but about how to capture the real story. If the one determines the fact of responsibility, the other describes the contour of that responsible life. The fundamental theological conviction one should bring to study in the arts and sciences is that the ultimate shape of things is God's project of wooing a fallen order back to its original purpose to glorify and reflect him. This discovery demands an active response, a *mission:* we must make God's task our task; we too must be involved with God's purpose to redeem the world and thus glorify him.

How Christian scholars define this project and how they see themselves involved in its realization will have incalculable effects on their patterns of thought and approach to study. The importance of such patterns of thought are now recognized even in the shaping of scientific hypotheses, examples of which abound in the history of thought.[21] It has been argued, for example, that the modern faith in biological evolution ultimately derives from the previous acceptance of the materialistic habit of thinking. In *Ever Since Darwin*, Stephen Jay Gould suggests in fact that Darwin delayed publishing his theory of evolution by natural selection until the climate of materialism was more firmly established.[22]

Alasdair MacIntyre provides another example in his book *After Virtue,* in which he argues that since the Enlightenment, patterns of individualism and ethical emotivism have become so embedded in our culture that bureaucratic and manipulative modes of social life are the natural and necessary consequence. As a result, the study of morality and ethics is presently in a shambles. Because of these deeply embedded habits of Enlightenment thought, the communal and teleological language of traditional morality simply makes no sense. MacIntyre believes that only a return to previous habits of thought offers any prospect of escape from the current impasse in ethics. In particular, we must return to the understanding of human life and community as a narrative unity. "Any specific account of the virtues," he insists, "presupposes an equally specific account of the narrative structure and unity of a human life."[23] The study of both politics and ethics, then, is possible only within a previously defined communal and narrative structure.

It is just such a structure that theological study provides. The Scriptures tell us how we are called to involve ourselves in God's great program of redemption, defined by Christ's death and resurrection and inaugurated by the pouring out of the Holy Spirit. Note, however, that the claim of revelation is that these events have altered the actual character of creation and have marked this period of history. They suggest how real change is possible and how it may be measured. Any study, therefore, of human life and community must be approached in the light of this pattern of thinking, and alternative patterns must be confronted and evaluated in relation to this fundamental conception.

But liberal arts provide more than a confirmation of faith. Our definition of theological study has proposed that the events and behavior studied in the liberal arts must become the materials in which the basic pattern of reality manifests itself. The questions and challenges of history and the arts must be the context in which the Christian story is told. To pray that God's will be done on earth as it is in heaven is to distrust any theological study that responds to issues of no contemporary relevance.

The New Testament illustrates how life serves as the context of theological reflection. In the New Testament accounts, theological thinking was never done in isolation from the life of the church and its mission but rather as a reflection upon that reality. The decisive pattern of reality was Christ's life and action and the need to respond to them. Early Christians did not set out to think theologically in any formal sense but tried simply to obey God in their own situations. In his study "The Birth of Theology," Daniel van Allmen discusses how the gospel was brought into a Greek context. He argues that the "Hellenists did not set out with a theological intention. Rather they simply obeyed the call to mission which they heard in the facts of persecution and their scattering to the four corners of the earth."[24] Their convictions about the shape of the present time and its import led them to respond and think the way they did.

The "project of God," then, provides the study of the arts and sciences with a frame of reference for evaluating the present state of things. While this may seem more immediately relevant to the arts than the sciences, we should recall how thinkers like Teilhard de Chardin—or, closer to home, Thomas F. Torrance—have shown the potential importance of Christian patterns for scientific theory.[25] Believing scholars have seldom thought in radical Christian patterns such as these; they seldom examine and interpret all of life around them from the reference point provided by the "project of God." Perhaps they fail to do so because they lack something that theology can also provide them: hope.

Hope is vital to the Christian life, but it is something that we do not always have our hand on, that we do not always see around us. Indeed, Lesslie Newbigin, the former mission worker in India, has stated that the greatest difficulty he now faces in England is "the disappearance of hope." When he left England for India in 1936 he was leaving the pinnacle of Western civilization. By the time he returned home in 1974, however, he had grown accustomed to seeing young people from affluent English and American families roaming the streets of India in tattered clothes in quest of something that would make life worth living. The youth of England have no hope. Yet today, Newbigin notes, people in even the most squalid slums of Madras believe that things can get better.[26] A bright Filipino woman I know conveyed the same sentiments upon her return home after a year of study in America and England. How invigorating, she wrote, to come back to a place where history is beginning, rather than bearing the weight of a long and tired past.[27]

Hope, this third contribution that theological studies can make to the liberal arts, is not a vague wish that things can be better but a specific vision of what things *will* one day become when Christ comes to reveal his kingdom. Although evangelicals in the West have often argued about prophecy, they have seldom allowed the earth-shattering Christian hope to penetrate very deeply into their thinking. Not that they have been without certain kinds of hope; indeed, Americans are incurably optimistic. But their hope is almost always a thoroughly secular one: the market will rise, one's health will improve, another (better) job will come along, there will be another chance to prove one's worth. But these things are seldom tied to a belief that God will make all things new and that he has already given us the taste and appetite for this newness in the gifts of the Holy Spirit.

Let us reclaim this belief; let us acknowledge that the world is open to God and is not a closed system. It is emphatically this world and its people that will be the object of God's renewing work (Rom. 8:19-21). It is hard to understand how some can insist the Christian faith puts people in a box. The opposite is in fact true—the faith is not a box but a window. Christian convictions about creation and redemption make the world open to its transcendent purpose and to the future that God has planned for it. Through his Spirit, God has revealed to us "what no eye has seen, nor ear heard, nor the heart of man conceived . . ." (1 Cor. 2:9).

Because Christian hope is tied in the closest way to this world, it has great implications for the liberal arts. It prompts the exciting discovery of the possibility of novelty in human events. It inspires patience and levelheadedness in the midst of even the darkest social or scientific problems. And it impels us to respond carefully and thoughtfully to these problems—while we wait in hope.

III

Having surveyed three areas in which theological reflection is essential to education—areas we usually refer to as creation, redemption, and eschatology—we may again ask whether this way of conceiving things helps with current discussions about the scope and form of the liberal arts and the arid specialization of theological studies. In response I can say that it will help only if we as Christian scholars are willing on the one hand to conceive of the liberal arts in a more radically Christian way and on the other hand to direct our theological reflection more to our world context.

First, we must conceive of the liberal arts in a thoroughly biblical way. In an address at Wheaton College in 1982, Nicholas Wolterstorff argued that Christian liberal arts colleges are entering a new stage of their history: they must now move from the appropriation of a stream of culture to address society directly. They must equip Christians to hear and respond to the cries of a suffering world. Even as evangelical colleges in the past have cultivated piety and learned to appreciate the arts and sciences, they must now cultivate peace and the care of the earth.[28] The challenge to all Christian scholars today is to make this process determinative for the shape and nature of their institutions. We need not imitate the models of secular academia, though we must certainly learn from them. Rather, we must allow our basic convictions to point the way ahead. We must accept our call to respond to the world as part of the project in which God is working out his redemptive purposes for humanity and the world.

Second, if liberal arts are to be more Christian, we must address theological studies to this world. Theological inquiry cannot be passive; it is to be the reflective interaction of God's people with the issues of the day in which all the people hear and respond to the call of the gospel in very concrete ways—whether it be in caring for prisoners or visiting the children of the slums. Mary Stewart Van Leeuwen challenges theologians to get their act together and even proposes a moratorium on criticism while they do it. Theologians need all the help they can get, but the world cannot wait for evangelicals to get their act together. Indeed, it is not the theologians' "act" that should matter so much as the actions of all God's people. We all have a mission and we all need to be challenged and equipped to think about what we do in the light of God's love and justice. We should view the theologians among us more as tutors and aides in this reflective interaction than as sages who will eventually solve all our theological dilemmas.

Who knows whether Christian higher education might yet be the creative force in higher education it has been so often in the past. For this we earnestly work and pray. But for this to happen, both theological studies and liberal arts must be open to rethinking and even radical restructuring. Theological realities have large implications for the subject matter of the liberal arts, but even more significant than this is the impetus they can provide and the goal they can point to. Faith convictions provide a field in which the liberal arts can find their energy and meaning; and the arts and sciences in turn furnish the material in which this faith must be displayed. They offer, in Calvin's sense, a theater for the glory of God. The liberal arts can open up the world to theological reflection, but only a theological understanding makes it a "world." In the midst of today's specialization and mutual suspicion such a vision is bound to sound either strange or wonderful. But if it is indeed true, what we pursue in the Christian liberal arts not only remakes the arts, but also regains some of their earlier splendor.

NOTES

1. See R. M. Martin, "Arts Liberaux," in *Dictionnaire d'Historie et de Geographie, Ecclesiastiques,* A. Bandrillart, directeur, 2d ed. (Paris: Letouzey et Amé, 1930), 827-43, esp. 834. See also Arthur F. Holmes, *The Idea of a Christian College,* rev. ed. (1975; Grand Rapids: Eerdmans, 1987), esp. the chap. "Theological Foundations."

2. I have argued along these lines in "Christian Liberal Arts Education in a World Community," *Reformed Journal* 34 (February 1984): 13-19. Nicholas Wolterstorff similarly argues that Christian colleges up to the present have "ignored society and concentrated on culture." "The Mission of the Christian College at the End of the Twentieth Century," *Reformed Journal* 33 (June 1983): 16; this article is a revision of a convocation speech he gave at Wheaton College in September 1982.

3. "Theology has long since disappeared as the unity, subject matter and end of clergy education, and this disappearance is responsible more than anything else for the problematic character of that education." Farley, *Theologia: The Fragmentation and Unity of Theological Education* (Philadelphia: Fortress, 1982), ix.

4. See Charles Malik's attempt to expose the related religious vacuum in today's universities in *A Christian Critique of the University* (Downers Grove, Ill.: InterVarsity, 1982).

5. P. J. Cahill, "Theological Studies, Where Are You?" *Journal of the American Academy of Religion* 52 (December 1984): 745.

6. Lesslie Newbigin, *The Other Side of 1984: Questions for the Churches* (Geneva: World Council of Churches, 1983), esp. chap. 1, "Is There a Future?"

7. Jacob Neusner, quoted in Laurence O'Connell, "Religious Studies, Theology and the Humanities Curriculum," *Journal of the American Academy of Religion* 52 (December 1984): 736.

8. Farley, *Theologia,* 134.

9. Most interesting here is a book that is now making an impact on nursing education: Patricia Benner, *From Novice to Expert: Expertise and Power in Clinical Nursing Practice* (Reading, Mass.: Addison Wesley, 1984); Benner is a Christian professor at the University of California, San Francisco. For help in applying this to theological education, I am grateful to Robert Ferris, whose doctoral dissertation showed that commitment to leadership as servanthood made no appreciable impact on the five evangelical seminaries he studied. Ferris, "The Emphasis on Leadership as Servanthood: An Analysis of Curriculum Commitments" (Ph.D. diss., Michigan State University, 1983; Ann Arbor: University Microfilms, 1983).

10. William F. May, "Why Theology and Religions Need Each Other," *Journal of the American Academy of Religion* 52 (December 1984): 748-57.

11. See *Luther's Works* (St. Louis: Concordia, 1958), 14: 434; see also Francis Pieper's discussion of Luther on theology in *Christian Dogmatics* (St. Louis: Concordia, 1950). Interestingly, Farley, *Theologia,* 186ff., proposes Luther's three words as a possible framework for theological study.

12. Karl Barth, *Church Dogmatics* (Edinburgh: T. & T. Clark, 1957), I, 11, 454.

13. I have proposed an interactionist model of hermeneutics. Note that this interaction is a function of the whole body of Christ, not just of the biblical scholars among us, who are supporters and instructors in this ongoing process. See my essay "How Does the Bible Function in the Christian Life?" in *Evangelicals and the Bible,* ed. Robert Johnston (Atlanta: John Knox, 1985).

14. Farley, *Theologia,* 165.

15. George A. Lindbeck develops this model in *The Nature of Doctrine* (Philadelphia: Fortress, 1984).

16. See "Paideia," in the *Theological Dictionary of the New Testament*, ed. G. Kittel and G. Friedrich, abridged in one volume by Geoffrey Bromiley (Grand Rapids: Eerdmans, 1985), 753-58; or see the unabridged version (Grand Rapids: Eerdmans, 1967), 5: 596ff.

17. See George Hendry, *A Theology of Nature* (Philadelphia: Westminster, 1980); and Gustaf Wingren, *Creation and Gospel* (New York: Edwin Mellen, 1979).

18. Karl Rahner, "Philosophy and Theology," in *Encyclopedia of Theology* (New York: Seabury, 1975), 1230. I develop this view of history as God's dramatic movement to which we must respond in *Let the Earth Rejoice: A Biblical Theology of Holistic Mission* (Westchester, Ill.: Crossway, 1983),

19. See Jerry H. Gill, *The Possibility of Religious Knowledge* (Grand Rapids: Eerdmans, 1967), chap. 6.

20. Jürgen Moltmann, *The Trinity and the Kingdom*, trans. Margaret Kohl (New York: Harper and Row, 1981), 47, 49.

21. See Thomas Kuhn's discussion of how such thought patterns influence the formation of scientific paradigms in *The Structure of Scientific Revolutions* (Chicago: University of Chicago Press, 1970).

22. Stephen Jay Gould, *Ever Since Darwin: Reflections in Natural History* (New York: Norton, 1979). Tom Bethel also discusses this issue in "Agnostic Evolutionists: The Taxonomic Case against Darwin," *Harper's*, February 1985, 49-61, esp. 60-61.

23. Alasdair MacIntyre, *After Virtue: A Study in Moral Theory* (South Bend: University of Notre Dame Press, 1984), 243.

24. Daniel van Allmen, "The Birth of Theology: The Dynamic Element in New Testament Theology," *International Review of Mission* 64 (January 1975): 51.

25. See Teilhard de Chardin, *Le Milieu Divin: An Essay on the Interior Life* (London: Collins, 1960); and Thomas F. Torrance, *The Ground and Grammar of Theology* (Belfast: Christian Journals, 1980), esp. chap. 5, "Theological Science." One must not overlook the importance and influence of books like Fritjof Capra's *The Tao of Physics* (New York: Random House, 1975), which proposes fundamental patterns quite opposed to the Christian faith.

26. Newbigin, *The Other Side of 1984*, 1-2.

27. In the same vein is Gustavo Gutiérrez's testimony from Latin America: "We are not now in the evening of the history of the Church, but are beginning the new day of an opportunity for evangelization that we never had before." *We Drink from Our Own Wells* (Maryknoll, N.Y.: Orbis, 1984), 24. This openness to the future seems naive to Americans recalling the *Novis Ordo Seclorum* of the early republic, but it nevertheless has an interesting compatibility with Christian truth: new things can happen.

28. Wolterstorff, "Mission of the Christian College," 16-17.

Bringing Christian Criteria
to Bear on Academic Work

Mary Stewart Van Leeuwen

In dealing with a topic as far-ranging and controversial as the role of Christian criteria in academic work, it is wise to stake out the territory at the outset—to clarify what is *not* going to be addressed as much as what is. I do not claim to have erected a monument in this essay that can portray the generic Christian scholar for all seasons and all disciplines—indeed, such a task is at best premature, and at worst hopelessly idealistic. Instead, I will outline several forces that currently and unavoidably divide Christian scholars into subgroups; then I will comment on the problems generated by two of these subgroups in particular.

In light of Thomas Askew's essay in this volume and a recent essay by Philip Gleason on Catholic higher education, such an approach need not be viewed solely as an exercise in pessimism.[1] Gleason suggests that Catholic higher education is in a state of partial disarray because nothing has yet replaced the pre–Vatican II, neoscholastic vision of Christian integration, while Askew concludes that Protestant Christian colleges are still too busy "unlearning" their parochial and schismatic attitudes of the past to have yet developed a synoptic, unifying vision for all of Christian scholarship. For these historical reasons alone, then, pluralism and even contentiousness are bound to be present whenever Christian scholars debate the appropriate way to bring religious criteria to bear on academic work. Nevertheless, after dealing with the agenda mentioned in my opening paragraph, I will conclude by suggesting some policies—or better, perhaps, attitudes—that might generate somewhat more unity among Christian scholars than there seems to be at present.

A noted personality theorist has described his own area of psychology as centered around the recognition that each human being is in some respects (a) like all other persons, (b) like some other persons, and (c) like no other person.[2] The same might be said of the Christian scholar. Hopefully, he or she is in some respects like all other Christian scholars, past or present, Catholic or Protestant, Calvinist or Arminian, rationalist or mystic. At a minimum, we would want the self-styled Christian scholar to accept, both intellectually and experientially, the basic contours of the biblical drama as it speaks to the nature of God and his relationship to the world and its inhabitants, the reality of the Fall and our continued participation in its aftereffects, the work of Christ in atoning for the sins of humanity, and the promise that human history will see the reassertion of his lordship over all principalities, persons, and things. We would expect, moreover, that such commitments would not be compartmentalized from the scholar's intellectual life but that they would make a recognizable difference to the way in which his or her scholarship is conducted.

But having claimed this real, if fragile, basic unity among Christian scholars, we must immediately concede that a host of factors will divide them into myriad subgroups that, though not always in overt competition, seem often enough to be speaking mutually unintelligible languages. At this point, advances to the cause of Christian scholarship may come more by acknowledging and examining some of these differences than by rushing prematurely, and perhaps unrealistically, toward an enforced and superficial unity.

To begin with a most obvious example, Christian scholars are divided not only by the different disciplines they represent but also by different specializations, theoretical allegiances, and methodological preferences within each discipline. Cutting the pie slightly differently, we see that these scholars are also divided according to the apparent importance of a Christian worldview to the conduct of each discipline. For the social scientist, worldview concerns seem to permeate psychology right from the very first page of an introductory college textbook. To many in mathematics, by contrast, it is not until students have wrestled their way up to metamathematics, and demonstrated the validity of, say, Gödel's theorem, that faith and learning begin to interpenetrate in any significant way.

Another, peculiarly recent, division among Christian scholars runs between those who see in the methods of their disciplines—particularly the sciences and social sciences—the guarantors of objective truth and those who claim in contrast that such methodological orthodoxy conceals at least as many prejudices as it eliminates. This, of course, is part of the more general intellectual fallout produced by the philosopher of science Thomas Kuhn and his successors.[3] Thus, for example, in my own area of social psychology, a recent international survey revealed two distinct subcultures within the discipline. There is, on the one hand, a distinctly postmodern group that believes that experiments are used largely to demonstrate the obvious, that fads and fashions govern research topics and funding, that social knowledge is historically contingent, and that knowledge in general is ideologically based. On the other hand there is the traditionally positivistic group, still engaged in hypothesis testing (experimentally, wherever possible), convinced that cumulative social knowledge is possible through the application of traditional methods, indignant about ethical constraints placed on their use of human subjects, and, by their own self-report, sick and tired of hearing about the so-called crisis in social psychology.[4]

But such paradigmatic conflicts, significant enough in themselves, take on added weight when Christian adherents of each camp begin to speak out. For the Christian in the postmodern camp, the recognition that ideology permeates the theories and methods of even the "hardest" sciences is at one with the ideas that all of life is religion and that metaphysical convictions—theistic or otherwise—not only do, but should openly interact with theoretical and methodological concerns. Such a position has a great deal of significance for some Christians in the social sciences, for it means in a sense that the tables have turned. Christian conviction has long been regarded (even by many Christians) as an impediment to the practice of sound objective social science— rather like a personal quirk one must labor to control in polite company. But postmodern philosophy of science, as expressed by Kuhn, Michael Polanyi, and others, seems to imply that the reverse is more likely the case. Metaphysical worldviews affect the scientific practice of both confessing believers and professed atheists, the argument goes. Surely, then, it is an advantage to have a worldview that is articulated, recorded, and subject to ongoing discussion rather than one that remains unacknowledged. Not only is it more honest, it is also potentially more promising as a scientific catalyst. A professed believer in the social sciences allows social scientific thinking and theological thinking to openly cross-fertilize each other, rather than leaving the connection ephemeral and unarticulated yet still powerfully influential, as the naturalist or materialist social scientist does.[5]

For other Christian scholars in the sciences and social sciences, however, this view of science as necessarily permeated by ideology points the way to a rampant subjectivism in which a high view of both general and special revelation will necessarily suffer. Thus the neuroscientist Donald McKay recently wrote in the *Journal of the American Scientific Affiliation* that the Christian case for objectivity, as that term is traditionally understood, "is (and has always been) so obvious as hardly to need stating." In McKay's understanding,

> If God is the author of the book of nature, our obligation is to read it and do justice to it as He has in fact written it, whether we like it or not. If we publish results of our investigations we must strive to "tell it like it is," knowing that the Author is at our elbow, a silent judge of the accuracy with which we claim to describe the world He has created. In this sense our goal is objective, value-free knowledge.[6]

To do other than this, McKay suggests, is to give way to an intellectual laziness just as dangerous as moral laxity. He grants that our limitations, both intellectual and moral, will predictably limit our achievements in each sphere. Even so, he holds that dismissing the ideal of value-free knowledge as an unrealizable myth is as dangerous and misguided as dismissing the ideal of *righteousness* as a myth solely on the grounds that it is unattainable in its perfect form. In McKay's view, Christians who embrace the current fashions of postmodern philosophy of science are "radically inconsistent. They forget that, whatever their difficulties in gaining objective knowledge, they are supposed to be in the loving service of the One to whom truth is sacred, and carelessness or deliberate bias in stating it is an affront."[7]

Here then is a distinct example of Christian scholars, alike in their basic commitment to the faith, who diverge into conflicting subgroups over the meaning of that shared faith for one aspect of the conduct of a discipline. This particular controversy in the ranks of Christian behavioral scientists parallels an analogous controversy in the humanities—namely, the tension that exists between positivistic and postpositivistic approaches to literary, historical, and religious texts. Put simply, while those committed to the former approach hold that the application of appropriate analytical methods ought to yield a single, true meaning of a text, those in the latter category keep pointing out that textual interpretation is necessarily conditioned by historical, linguistic, literary, sociological, and other factors. Consequently, they say, the search for one, correct textual meaning is at least a terribly complex, if not totally vain, undertaking.

This, of course, leads back to what is perhaps the biggest and most divisive problem facing Christian scholars in all the disciplines. Historic Protestant orthodoxy has always held that one particular set of texts, namely, the received canon of the Bible, is the sole, authoritative guide to Christian belief and conduct. But if this is the case, how are Christian scholars who strive to integrate faith and learning—let alone mere Christian laity who attempt to do so—to contend with the confusion of voices in the world of evangelical theology and biblical scholarship, the very foundations upon which any respectable Christian academic work must be done? To bring Christian criteria adequately to bear on academic endeavors, scholars need not just minimal biblical literacy, not just statement-of-faith-based orthodoxy, not just a record of faithful attention to sermons and Sunday school lessons, but intellectual sophistication and discernment in their understanding and application of Scripture. Yet this, with rare exceptions, is just what Christian scholars lack—in part because they do not have the time or the motivation to pursue the required interdisciplinary training, but also in part because the relationship of evangelicals to the Bible they claim to hold so dear has never been as confused, or as confusing, as it is today.

Mark Noll has recently provided a long-needed analysis of American evangelical study of the Bible, past and present, pastoral and academic, denominationally centered and para-ecclesiastical. He points out that although evangelicals have always nourished a deep attachment to the Bible, theirs has not, until recently, been a particularly academic attachment. "In the past," he writes, views of the Bible "as a magical book unrelated to the normal workings of the natural world" powerfully shaped evangelical public opinion and the attitudes of some evangelical scholars. He insists that "such docetism has often made it difficult for evangelicals to see how academic studies of the Bible and its world could contribute to a better comprehension of this intensely spiritual book."[8] Even though in the years since World War II evangelical Bible scholars have obtained progressively better academic credentials and produced a tremendously diverse literature on Scripture, the bulk of their writing has remained pastoral, sermonic, and devotional. "To put the problem in general terms, the depth of evangelical commitment to the truth-telling and life-giving character of Scripture has not been matched by an equally firm understanding of the relationship between the Bible and modern learning."[9]

As a result of this common evangelical heritage, most Christian scholars come to their tasks with a decidedly lopsided training. On the one hand, their highest academic credentials have usually been obtained in intellectually sophisticated yet highly secularized university settings. On the other hand, their biblical training has largely been con-

fined to what they get from sermons, Sunday school lessons, and lay
Bible studies, all of which are aimed at the strengthening of faith but
not in a particularly intellectual way.

Even so, if the need to bring the Bible under more abstract and
analytical scrutiny were their only problem, Christian scholars might
not be so badly off. They would be no worse off, perhaps, than the
young native speaker of a language who suddenly, in school, must learn
to see that already-familiar language in terms of its formal grammar and
its literary uses. Granted, Christian scholars would still have the
problem of finding both the time and motivation to pursue biblical
studies in this more intellectually demanding way. But with the right
kind of institutional support from church and academy alike, both the
time and the enthusiasm for such expanded intellectual efforts would
likely be forthcoming.

But of course coming to grips with new rules for biblical studies is
not the only problem. As Noll graphically documented, the larger
problem is that the present world of evangelical theology and biblical
scholarship, reflecting the American evangelical mentality as a whole,
speaks with such divided and contentious tongues. It is largely incapable of giving unified guidance even to the most motivated of Christian academics in the other disciplines. Evangelicals at large, Noll
points out, are often more knowledgeable—and concerned—about
competing theories of biblical authority than they are about what the
Bible actually contains. They can argue endlessly about the proper
translation of a few select biblical texts while at the same time embracing the *Living Bible,* a nonscholarly paraphrase that is "rife with
eisegesis and marked by considerable disregard for the underlying
Hebrew and Greek texts."[10] Evangelicals in academic circles have
failed to develop the kind of overarching theology that would enable
them to separate wheat from chaff—the fruit of common grace from
the fruit of unbelief—in the burgeoning literature of biblical criticism.

Finally, Noll concludes, the peculiarly American traditions of individualism, egalitarianism, and antitraditionalism would make it hard
for evangelical theologians and biblical scholars to provide leadership
to the rest of the evangelical academic community even if they could
speak a unified message. While acknowledging that these American
traditions have helped preserve a sense of the priesthood of all believers
and the recognition of the necessity for all Christians to be immersed
in the Bible, Noll also observes that "the American myth that one man's
testimony is as good as another's destroys the proper respect which, all

things being equal, sophisticated scholarly investigation deserves to receive. . . ." Moreover, he argues, America's "antitraditional attitude . . . robs evangelicals of an historical sense. And this is a debilitating handicap when one is attempting to understand an ancient text. . . . Meanings that appear to lie on the surface are the [only] ones that count."[11]

Christian scholars, then, come to their task with a common commitment to a high view of Scripture but little if any agreement as to how it should be interpreted and used with regard to our various disciplines. I myself can remember vividly when the seriousness of this problem first came home to me. I had been teaching for ten years in a large public university—the kind of setting in which in-house differences between Christians usually seem insignificant compared to the gulf that separates the tiny Christian minority from the non-Christian majority. Consequently, when I was given a fellowship to join a group of Christian scholars for a year, specifically to discuss and write about the nature and role of the behavioral sciences, I naively anticipated getting the best of both worlds: an atmosphere of Christian unity in conjunction with depth of Christian scholarship.

I still look back on that year as one of stimulating intellectual interchange in a context of strong Christian motivation on the part of all involved. Yet, as it turned out, the broad commonality of Christian commitment was not enough to unify us around the stated aim of the study center—producing a communally written volume. As the year wore on, it became apparent that despite our attempts to halt or minimize the process, we were dividing into two opposed camps—not with respect to competing paradigms of social science, nor even with respect to competing basic theologies, but simply with respect to how we believed the biblical record, as a whole and in its various parts, should be brought to bear on theory and criticism within our respective disciplines.

All of us, it was clear, opposed the sort of naive biblicism that makes of the Christian communitarianism of Acts 2 a binding rule for all Christians at all times, or that imposes on the concept of the Holy Spirit as "counselor" a full-blown theory of modern psychological counseling. We were also uniformly uneasy about any social science theorizing that glibly translates the Bible into the language of one's own favored theory—behaviorism, symbolic interactionism, Jungian archetypes, or whatever—without regard for literary genre, historical context, or semantic considerations in the original languages. But beyond this, we were divided as to just how much (let alone in what ways) the Bible could be used as a fruitful source of theory for the social sciences. One group was of the view that none of the biblical references to what we might call psychological, social, economic, or political norms were ever intended to provide theoretical anchors for Christian social scientists. They insisted that the Bible addresses itself only to the subject of God and his salvation activities in metahistory and that any attempt to cull from it social science theory or even a loose set of "control beliefs"[12] was dangerously close to biblicism.

The other group, including myself, wanted to steer a fine line between proof-texting literalism on the one hand and a total spiritualizing of the Bible on the other, which would result in a denial of any biblical themes or norms that might govern disciplinary theory, methodology, and criticism. In theologian Sidney Greidanus's words, "The predicament we face here is how to disallow arbitrary interpretations (such as the motion of the sun, the sphericity of the earth, etc.) while granting that a text may mean more than the author himself realized. . . . For since we are dealing with the entire Bible and its progressive revelation, we can discover the development of certain themes which are not necessarily the specific purpose of any one human author, but may well be the purpose of the divine Author."[13] Greidanus goes on to suggest that such themes include the biblical view of humanity, of justice, of stewardship and ownership, of work and play, and of social institutions like marriage, family, and government. By comparing Scripture with Scripture, author with author, the Christian academic can detect the development of certain themes that can serve to guide scholarship.

Yet although such a hermeneutical compromise seems reasonable, it still invites well-intentioned criticism from each side—from Christians who are convinced that there is either much more or much less that can be drawn from the Bible for application to scholarly disciplines. Moreover, even if Christian scholars could finally come to agreement about what academic issues the Bible speaks to—and how much it speaks to them—there would still be endless disagreement about what the Bible actually *concludes* with regard to those issues. To take a perennial example, theologians and social scientists alike might well agree both that the Bible has something to say about male-female relationships and also that a certain set of texts is germane to the theme. But experience tells us that they would still differ mightily about what normative direction those texts actually give.[14]

In the face of all this disagreement, one is tempted to paint a final portrait of the Christian academic in very light brush-strokes indeed.

We simply have no hard and fast model to work from. Arthur Holmes acknowledged this some fifteen years ago when he wrote that Christian scholarship should be perspectival yet at the same time pluralistic. By perspectival he meant that Christian scholars should draw from biblical revelation a vantage point, a worldview from which scholarship proceeds. Moreover, they are to repudiate any claims of ideological neutrality, not just because of the special status of Christian revelation, but because *all* human thought and living is perspectival; it is all undergirded with values and ideology, whether they are acknowledged or not.

Yet Holmes did not even try to spell out the fine details of a Christian perspective because, as a complex and longstanding worldview, Christianity has taken many forms throughout history. To many questions there can be no single Christian answer. Christian scholarship, then, must remain pluralistic, and Christian thinkers need to learn to tolerate differences among themselves while still affirming the commonly held worldview. It is true that some of these differences are the result of theological diversity, but others are due simply to differences in training, experience, and personal and scholarly interests. In Holmes's words,

> We see through a glass darkly. We know in part. The finiteness, the fallibility, the fragmentariness of human understanding require that we grant others the liberty we desire for ourselves; that we be willing to learn from others, and remain open to correction, to new angles, to invigorating insights. The pluralistic character of Christian thought is a blessing, for it safeguards against premature dogmatism and monolithic structures. It will keep us humble and keep us human . . . working creatively and self-critically in all our endeavors.[15]

This plea for tolerance of pluralism within a broad common perspective is a salutary observation on Holmes's part and in keeping with his reputation for balanced insight on such issues. Christian scholars, he believes, are divided not only by group differences, which I have emphasized in this essay, but also by individual differences. Given the combined effects of ecclesiastical, intellectual, socioeconomic, and personal histories on each scholar, it is perhaps a measure of the unifying power of the Holy Spirit that they continue to work together at all! Over against Donald McKay's suggestion that objective, value-free knowledge is a suitable and obligatory goal for Christian scholars, Holmes is of the opinion that the intellectual finitude of scholars, their tendency to see "through a glass darkly," is not so much something to be repented of as something to be accepted in a spirit of proper modesty and tolerance for ambiguity (although McKay is right that it is no excuse for intellectual laziness).

Yet there is both healthy and unhealthy pluralism in Christian scholarship. There is the kind of pluralism that Holmes envisages—that which arises from a creative ferment within a well-trained, mutually supportive, and basically unified group of scholars. But there is also a kind of pluralism that merely reflects confused fragmentation, low morale, and a failure to agree on certain key issues. This is the unhealthy pluralism that Noll warns about in his article on evangelicals and the study of the Bible. We can use this distinction between healthy and un-healthy to inform some programmatic suggestions for ways of enhancing basic unity among Christian scholars while not, at the same time, jeopardizing the healthy pluralism that Holmes holds up as a standard.

First of all, Christian scholars need to reduce the intellectual gap that separates their disciplinary professionalism from their largely amateur ways of approaching theology and biblical scholarship. It is quite true, as Holmes points out, that not all differences and confusions can be resolved by more perceptive theologizing. But surely *some* of them might be. To accomplish this will require time, motivation, and institutional support. But even these will be insufficient to the task if the evangelical theologians and biblical scholars who are to help edu-cate in this regard cannot get *their* act together, at least broadly speak-ing, on such issues as biblical inerrancy, biblical hermeneutics, and the proper use of higher critical tools.

To create the necessary conditions for this task—at least for the task of delineating an acceptable range of positions—the evangelical com-munity as a whole could well declare a twenty-year moratorium on heresy hunting. The pervasive anti-intellectualism of American evan-gelicals, understandable though it has been at many points in recent his-tory, all too often redefines the honest intellectual struggles of Chris-tian scholars in terms of publicly rebellious apostasy. The main result of such anti-intellectualism is the paralysis of original scholarship and its replacement with denominationally dictated and publisher-solicited busy work—to the eventual detriment of the entire constituency. Let evangelicals give the good will of their theologians and biblical scholars the benefit of the doubt, as Noll suggests, and grant them the time and space to wrestle creatively and prayerfully with those issues that lie at the heart and foundation of all the rest of Christian scholarship. Christian scholarship as a whole cannot advance very far as long as we ourselves limit the progress made on these few issues.

Second, just as evangelicals need to abandon both a docetic and a literalist approach to Scripture without at the same time losing sight of its status as the word of God, so Christian academics need to abandon a naively positivistic approach to scholarship without at the same time losing respect for its status as a source of truth. Considerable tension seems to be developing among Christian scholars on this point, especially in the social sciences. Those who adhere to the objectivist ideal insist that because a sovereign God upholds an orderly universe, and because humans are made in his image, scholars can progressively (even if never completely) uncover the stable laws by which the natural and even the social and artistic worlds operate. Those of a more postpositivistic bent are at pains to point out that all scholarship has an irreducibly religious element to it because human beings themselves, whether Christian or otherwise, are all irreducibly religious: they are all characters searching for an author. Consequently, Christian scholars should be at least as sensitive to the "sociology of knowledge" aspects of scholarship as they are to the supposedly enduring fruits of purportedly neutral inquiry.

Without a serious attempt at dialogue in a context of mutual respect, progressive polarization of these positions is more and more likely. Yet surely, in the words of the philosopher Ernan McMullin, "there may be a reasonable halfway house between [positivistic] totalitarianism and well-intentioned anarchy."[16] In other words, it should be possible to incorporate the insights of Kuhn and his successors without reducing academic work to mere subjectivism. A possible route to compromise may lie in the increasing recognition—thanks in large part to the work of neuroscientists, as well as that of philosophers of science like Michael Polanyi—that the process of arriving at valid insights in any discipline is much more complex, much less completely rule-bound, than scholars have tended to assume. From neuroscience comes the accumulating work on the division of labor between brain hemispheres and the strong suggestion that the verbal, sequential, and digital strengths of the left brain (strengths upon which the Western world has vigorously traded ever since the Enlightenment) can be contrasted with the visual-spatial, synchronous, and analogic workings of the right brain.[17] Polanyi contributes historical documentation that innovative scientific work requires, over and above rigorous training and a sophisticated research setting, the intuitive ability to choose a problem of potential significance even before work has begun on it.[18]

This being the case, it is not surprising that McMullin suggests the need to acknowledge *two* faces of science (and, by implication, two faces of all scholarly endeavors), the first a "logical," and the second an "interpretive" face. The first of these does indeed appeal, quite correctly, to rules that are held to be constant no matter what the situation. At the same time, however, scholars attach meanings to what they study and perceive structures in it on the basis of highly personal intuitions and belief structures. This kind of intellectual activity, although vital to creative advance in both the sciences and the humanities, is much more difficult to define. It is more idiosyncratic and more context dependent than knowledge derived from the application of formal procedures. In a sense, it is like the faith that has "the assurance of things hoped for, the conviction of things not seen" (Heb. 11:1), inasmuch as it has a pre-evidential intuition of what conclusions may emerge even prior to working on a given problem.

It is quite possible that some of the tensions in biblical, social-scientific, and other disciplines simply reflect differences between the cognitive styles suggested by McMullin. Some scholars, by training or inclination, are simply more at home with the linear, rule-based, highly logical aspects of scholarship. Others approach their projects in a more diffuse and circumspect manner, drawing insights from a plethora of different sources and only gradually coming to conclusions that, although also amenable to rule-based understanding, were not arrived at directly in that fashion. Perhaps we need to recognize that both styles are needed for optimal progress in Christian scholarship, in the same way that the church at large, if it is to be healthy, needs a balance between piety and activism, and between the conservatism of confessional statements on the one hand and Spirit-led sensitivity to the changing needs of the times on the other.[19]

A third way that Christian scholars can promote unity amid plurality is by striving to be more sensitive to the image they project, however unintentionally, to the constituencies that underwrite their academic efforts. Some scholars are defensive about their fundamentalist backgrounds and are consequently so eager to prove their worthiness to the academic community at large that they form premature and sometimes regrettable attachments to current academic vogues.[20] Many others have been unconsciously influenced by the Platonic assumptions so much a part of mainstream scholarship: they have come to believe that academics are a special breed of philosopher-kings answerable to no one else and that the academy is the only really valid court of appeal in matters of truth and its application. It is important that all scholars articulate not only the currently valid scope of knowledge in their field but also its limits and uncertainties; it is doubly important that Christian scholars do so. Whatever the real achievements of their respective fields, however flattering and simplistic their coverage by the media, however large and prestigious their research grants, Christian scholars must refrain from participating in the constant rhetoric of "imminent breakthrough" practiced by so much of the academic world. Christian scholars must state their conclusions tentatively, with the appropriate limitations and qualifications, balancing their respect for the working of common grace in the academy with a healthy sense of iconoclasm. For in the world of scholarship, as in everything else, we live in the "time between the times." The things of this world are not yet restored to their creational innocence and goodness, and Christian scholars must not lose sight of the antithesis between common grace and common fallenness. They must not become triumphalistic about their academic endeavors.

NOTES

1. Thomas A. Askew, "The Shaping of Evangelical Higher Education since World War II," in this volume; and Philip Gleason, "Two Centuries of Catholic Higher Education in the United States," paper presented at the conference on "The Task of Evangelical Higher Education," Wheaton College, Wheaton, Illinois, 28 May 1985.

2. See Clyde Kluckhohn and Henry A. Murray, *Personality in Nature, Society, and Culture* (New York: Knopf, 1948), 35, where Murray makes this point.

3. Thomas Kuhn, *The Structure of Scientific Revolutions*, rev. ed. (Chicago: University of Chicago Press, 1971); see also I. Lakatos and A. Musgrave, eds., *Criticism and the Growth of Knowledge* (New York: Cambridge University Press, 1970).

4. A. G. Zwier, "The Crisis in Social Psychology: A Theoretical and Empirical Study" (M.A. thesis, University of Auckland, New Zealand, 1980).

5. For an elaboration of this point see also Mary Stewart Van Leeuwen, *The Person in Psychology: A Contemporary Christian Appraisal* (Grand Rapids: Eerdmans, 1985), esp. chaps. 1, 5, 10.

6. Donald M. McKay, "Objectivity in Christian Perspective," *Journal of the American Scientific Affiliation* 36 (December 1984): 235. See also David G. Myers, *The Human Puzzle: Psychological Research and Christian Belief* (San Francisco: Harper and Row, 1978), esp. chaps. 1, 2.

7. McKay, "Objectivity," 235.

8. Mark A. Noll, "Evangelicals and the Study of the Bible," in *Evangelicalism and Modern America,* ed. George Marsden (Grand Rapids: Eerdmans, 1984), 113.

9. Ibid., 111-12.

10. Ibid., 111.

11. Ibid., 117-18.

12. See Nicholas Wolterstorff, *Reason within the Bounds of Religion,* 2d ed. (Grand Rapids: Eerdmans, 1984).

13. Sidney Greidanus, "The Use of the Bible in Christian Scholarship," *Christian Scholar's Review* 9 (Summer 1982): 140-41, 143.

14. See, for example, Paul K. Jewett, *Man as Male and Female* (Grand Rapids: Eerdmans, 1975); Virginia Mollenkott, *Women, Men, and the Bible* (Nashville: Abingdon, 1977); Letha Scanzoni and Nancy Hardesty, *All We're Meant to Be* (Waco, Tex.: Word, 1974); Stephen B. Clark, *Man and Woman in Light of Scripture and the Social Sciences* (Ann Arbor: Servant, 1980).

15. Arthur F. Holmes, "The Idea of a Christian College," *Christianity Today,* 31 July 1970, 6-8.

16. Ernan McMullin, "Two Faces of Science," *Review of Metaphysics* 27 (June 1974): 655-76.

17. See, for example, Sally P. Springer and Georg Deutsch, *Left Brain, Right Brain* (San Francisco: W. H. Freeman, 1981).

18. Michael Polanyi, *Personal Knowledge: Towards a Post-Critical Philosophy,* rev. ed. (Chicago: University of Chicago Press, 1962).

19. For further discussion of the relationship between cognitive style and ecclesiastical style, see Mary Stewart Van Leeuwen, "Cognitive Style, North American Values, and the Body of Christ," *Journal of Psychology and Theology* 2 (Spring 1974): 77-88.

20. See, for example, the observations of Ronald L. Numbers, "The Dilemma of Evangelical Scientists," in *Evangelicalism and Modern America,* ed. Marsden, esp. 156.

Teaching for Justice

Nicholas Wolterstorff

Over the past decade and a half, scholars in Christian colleges have spoken a good deal about the need to integrate Christian faith with learning. Here and there, now and then, they have gone beyond talk to produce such learning. In thus urging and practicing integration they have moved decisively beyond the nineteenth-century paradigm according to which Christianity was something to be added onto neutral secular learning. Yet integration alone does not meet the goal of Christian higher education. The goal any teacher seeks in education is to bring about some change in students—an increase of knowledge, understanding, sensitivity, imagination, or commitment. Clearly, just trying to integrate Christian faith with learning is not the same as aiming at some such change in persons. Thus to say that Christian scholars must try to integrate faith with learning so as to produce *Christian* learning is not yet to specify a goal for them as teachers. Even so, the dominant topic of recent discussion in Christian colleges has not been educational goals. Now, I think, is the time to change that; educators in Christian colleges must begin to rethink their received views as to the *curricular goals* of Christian collegiate education.

One of the suggestions that I myself have presented on various occasions has been that Christian teaching should include, among other things, teaching for justice. Usually I have gone on to say that if Christian educators are to teach for justice, they must teach their students what the world is like in which justice is to be practiced. To make this point vivid I have sometimes critically remarked that the students of my own college emerge knowing a good deal more about Periclean Athens and thirteenth-century Paris than they do about twentieth-century Jerusalem or Johannesburg. Some hearers of this remark have concluded that, in my judgment, teaching justice is incompatible with teaching about Periclean Athens or thirteenth-century Paris. Surely that is an illicit inference—and far from my own conviction—yet perhaps the misunderstanding is itself understandable. What Christian educators need is a comprehensive consideration of the curricular goals appropriate to the Christian college in our modern world, showing, among other things, how teaching for justice fits with teaching history.

Many of those who work in the Christian colleges operate with what might well be called the *Christian service model*. The idea is that the goal of Christian collegiate education is to train students to enter Christian service, understanding that to be a certain range of "Christian" occupations or so-called kingdom work—evangelism, Christian education, church work, mission- field medicine, Christian communications, and so on. In most Christian colleges there are probably at least some educators who think in terms of this model, and there are probably some colleges in which *most* educators do their thinking in these terms.

The popularity of this model, if nothing else, makes it imperative that it be taken seriously and engaged. Nonetheless, this is not the occasion to discuss it further. For it regularly happens that even in colleges that begin with this as their prominent model, various dynamics eventually set in that cause people to find it too restrictive. As a result, such training colleges regularly transform themselves into liberal arts colleges. Why this shift so often takes place would be interesting to explore, but on this occasion it may be more profitable to look more closely at some of the models to which people tend to move once they have cast off the Christian service model.

Among the most prominent of these alternatives is what we may call the *Christian humanist model*. What does the Christian humanist hold out as the proper goal of Christian collegiate education? One theme that sounds like a sustained pedal tone in the thought of Christian humanists is *freedom:* education is for freedom. Indeed, many of those who hold this view simply identify liberal arts education with the humanist model of education and then play on the etymology of the word "liberal"—liberal education is education that liberates or frees us. But frees us *from* what and *for* what? No more eloquent answer to that question has ever been composed than that of the English political theorist Michael Oakeshott in his long essay "Education: The Engagement and the Frustration."[1] Indeed, I judge this to be the most profound and articulate essay on education published in our century—and I say this in spite of what I regard as serious limitations in its perspective.

As Oakeshott sees it, to be human is, for one thing, to *understand* the world and oneself. It is to *construe* the world and oneself in one way or another. Or, to put the point another way, it is to *invest* the world and oneself with *meaning*. Yet to be human is also much more than merely to understand. It is also to *respond* to the world thus invested with meaning: to respond in the human way, which is different from the animal way of merely "behaving." To be human is to imagine possibilities in response to one's understanding, to desire some of the possibilities imagined, and then in turn to act on some of those desires. This adventure in understanding, imagining, desiring, and enacting that constitutes us as humans is of course not conducted in solitude. On the contrary, being human is "recognizing oneself to be related to others, not as the parts of an organism are related, . . . but in virtue of participation in multiple understood relationships and in the enjoyment of understood historic languages. . . ."[2]

In sum,

> a human being is the inhabitant of a world composed, not of "things" but of meanings; that is, of occurrences in some manner recognized, identified, understood and responded to in terms of this understanding. It is a world of sentiments and beliefs, and it includes also human artifacts (such as books, pictures, musical compositions, tools and utensils) for these, also, are "expressions" which have meanings and which require to be understood in order to be used or enjoyed. To be without this understanding is to be, not a human being, but a stranger to the human condition.[3]

To enter this humanizing heritage of understanding, imagining, desiring, and enacting requires learning; there is no other way. It is by way of learning that "a postulant to a human condition comes to recognize himself as a human being in the only way that is possible; namely, by seeing himself in the mirror of an inheritance of human understandings and activities. . . ."[4] In Oakeshott's view, only by learning that inheritance, only by making one's acquaintance with it and understanding it, does one become human.

Oakeshott recognizes that much of such learning takes place casually, informally, and episodically, but as he sees it education in the full sense occurs only when that transaction among human beings that constitutes learning-by-being-taught takes the form of *schooling*. There are some five characteristics of schooling, or true education, he says, among which is the one at which I have been aiming, the goal in which the theme of liberation is sounded. For the student, the heir to learning, a central mark of a school

> is that of detachment from the immediate, local world of the learner, its current concerns and the directions it gives to his attention. . . . "School" is a place apart in which the heir may encounter his moral and intellectual inheritance not in the terms in which it is being used in the current engagements and occupations of the world outside (where much of it is forgotten, neglected, obscured, vulgarized or abridged, and where it appears only in scraps and as investments in immediate enterprises) but as an estate, entire, unqualified and unencumbered. "School" is an emancipation achieved in a continuous redirection of attention. Here, the learner is animated, not by the inclinations he brings with him, but by intimations of excellences and aspirations he has never yet dreamed of; here he may encounter, not answers to the "loaded" questions of "life," but questions which have never before occurred to him; here he may acquire new "interests" and pursue them uncorrupted by the need for immediate results; here he may learn to seek satisfactions he had never yet imagined or wished for.[5]

In short, education in the full sense, school education, is for freedom. Authentic education is for liberation and emancipation from the closed-in partialities of one's specific historical and social sitution into the wide open possibilities of humanity's understandings and imaginings and desirings as a whole. The minimal accomplishment of education is bringing about the humanity of the students by initiating them into the realm of meanings that they will inhabit. Its wide overarching goal is to deliver them from the particularity of their concrete situations into the universality of the human condition. A truly "educational engagement," according to Oakeshott, is thus at once both "a discipline and a release; and it is the one by virtue of being the other. . . . Its reward is an emancipation from the mere 'fact of living,' from the immediate contingencies of place and time of birth, from the tyranny of the moment and from the servitude of a merely current condition. . . ."[6]

As the Christian humanist sees it, however, the goal of Christian collegiate education is more than just to free students from their particularity by initiating them into a more universal human consciousness. Oakeshott insists that to be human we must understand not only our world but also our heritage of consciousness; that not only do we invest the world with meaning, but we also invest our cultural heritage with meaning. To this the Christian humanist adds that it is impossible to do this in some generally human way. We can only do this as *religious* beings—and then, as beings of *diverse* religions. Christians come to understand the world and their heritage and to invest them with meaning in one particular—not generally human—way; the Muslim does so in another, and so does any other religious believer.

This particular element of the Christian humanist vision has never been developed more profoundly than by the esteemed Christian philosopher William Harry Jellema.[7] When Jellema surveyed that vast cultural inheritance into which he, along with Oakeshott, ardently believed the student should be initiated, he did not see just an episodic ebb and flow of understandings, imaginings, desirings, and enactings but instead a grand sweeping pattern. He saw the rise and fall of "kingdoms" or "cities," as he called them—of "faith communities." In thus interpreting history he saw himself standing in the lineage of Augustine, who viewed human life in time as the interaction between the City of God and the City of the World—*civitas Dei* and *civitas mundi*. Though Jellema did not regard these kingdoms as identical with cultural activity, he nonetheless saw them as coming to expression in such activity. A *civitas,* he said, "is realized in and by eating and drinking, cobbling and carpentry, work and play, science and education, law and government, love and worship; nothing human but enters into the city."[8]

The structure and course of human history bears the pattern of the struggles among such faith communities. In addition, each such community itself has an internal structure. Determinative of every *civitas* is a worldview, or a "mind," as Jellema was fond of calling it. Thus we speak of the Christian mind, the Greek mind, the mind of pagan antiquity, and the mind of modernity. To go one level deeper, we see that the objective mind or worldview of a *civitas* also has its own internal structure. It too is not just an assemblage; it too has a determinative center.

Every human being, according to Jellema, is forced to give some answer to the question of who God is. Some answer in such a way that they misidentify or misdescribe God; others may be so far mistaken that they even identify something other than God *as* God. Nonetheless, everyone must give an answer, mistaken or not. The answer one gives reveals the mind with which one thinks, and this mind in turn determines one's particular way of being-in-the-world. Or, to state the point better, since that is to put it too individualistically, the mind of a *civitas* reveals its answer to the question of who God is. An individual adopts the mind of a *civitas* and thereby becomes its member by accepting its idea of God. Thus Jellema remarks that "the essence of all choices, the essence of moral choice, is religious decision. The *civitas* chosen is the continuous living expression of a man's religious faith; it is his answer, writ in large letters, to the question who God is."[9]

Education for Jellema was ultimately both a manifestation of the life of some religious kingdom and initation into that life. "Formal education in the schools," he wrote, "articulates the meaning and structure of a chosen *civitas,* also when it professes neutrality; and inseparably in the same process forms, molds, and educates the citizen in the meaning and structure of (whichever) *civitas* [is chosen]. . . . Education is by a kingdom and for citizenship in that kingdom."[10]

The goal of Christian education for Jellema was then to initiate the student into the Christian mind. He was fond of saying that the important thing is not so much *what* one thinks as the mind *with which* one thinks. Students must be freed from the bondage of thinking with the mind of modernity and led to think with the Christian mind. To accomplish this, the educator must lead students to converse with those across the ages who have thought with the Christian mind. It is important to realize, however, that those who have thought with the Christian mind have not had a monopoly on truth. Accordingly, students in Christian colleges must also be engaged in conversation with historical representatives of alternative minds, from which they can learn, but against which they must also struggle.

The curricular model of the Christian humanist has usually been held with far less profundity that it was given by Jellema. Nonetheless, it has proved to be one of the perennially attractive models for Christian educators when they move beyond the Christian service model, especially for those educators working in the humanities.

While there are other models at work in Christian education, we will have to be satisfied with only brief descriptions of them. We might call one of these the *Christian academic-discipline model.* The goal of education in this model is to introduce students to the academic disciplines and thereby to put them in touch with reality to the extent that theory can do that. While those who favor the Christian humanist model characteristically defend their choice by stressing the importance of developing in the student a Christian mind able to engage in discourse with other minds, those who favor the Christian academic-discipline model tend to defend their preference by appealing to the cultural mandate given to humanity at creation.

Oakeshott briefly mentions the academic-discipline model of education and treats it as beginning roughly with Francis Bacon. "In the doctrine of Bacon . . . 'education' stands not for a transaction between the generations of human beings . . . but for a release from all this in which he [the student] acquires 'objective' knowledge of the workings of a 'natural' world. . . ."[11] Elsewhere Oakeshott explains that "knowledge, so the doctrine ran, derives solely from the experience of observation of 'things'; and it represents 'the empire of man over things'."[12]

Oakeshott's depiction of the origins of the academic-discipline model is incomplete and misleading. The idea that the goal of the university is to introduce students to the sciences—the *scientiae,* or the *Wissenschaften*—is in fact much older than Bacon. It was the dominant model already in the medieval European universities and as such is the most venerable postantiquity model of education that we have in the West, more venerable than the humanist model. (We must immediately add, of course, that our understanding of science or *scientia* has changed over the years since the time of the medieval university.)

Deeply embedded in the Western understanding of how *scientia* ought to be practiced has been the lure of certitude and consensus. Never have these lures been so relentlessly pursued as they were by René Descartes. Impressed though he was by the enormous diversity of human opinion, he was nonetheless convinced that it was possible to erect, within this diversity, a tower of *scientia* and to do so on consensus foundations. The method, he thought, was for all theorists to commit themselves resolutely to nothing but that of which they were certain.[13]

Though this Cartesian picture of a science based on consensus and grounded in certitude has had an enormous impact on scholars in the West, it has almost entirely collapsed by now. The rise of our postmodern understandings of the nature of scholarship represent, above all, the repudiation of this, our Cartesian foundationalist inheritance. Christian colleges along with others have participated in this repudiation. Indeed, the recent flourishing of the idea that Christian scholars must integrate their faith with their theorizing can in large part be attributed to the rise of the postmodern understanding of science. Christian scholars can now commit themselves to the project of *Christian* learning.

Descartes would have been horrified at such a development, of course. To allow one's faith a governing role in one's practice of science is to lay at the foundation that very diversity and uncertainty that he was so passionately committed to eliminating. But we in our day have seen that science is unavoidably pluralistic, and some of us have seen that part of its pluralism is rooted in the diversity of humanity's religions. In the practice of science one need not—indeed, cannot—set one's religion off to the side; one's practice of science is (in part) an *expression* of one's religion. Thus those who hold to the academic-discipline model of education do not see the goal of Christian collegiate education as that of introducing the student to neutral academic disciplines. The goal, rather, is to introduce the student to *Christian* learning—to the disciplines as developed and conducted in fidelity to the Christian gospel.

There is yet another model of the proper goal for the Christian college, appropriately called the *Christian socialization model.* Here the goal is to train students for whatever roles, especially occupational or professional, they will be entering, and to teach them to conduct themselves as Christians within those roles. Christian humanists, we have seen, ground their model in the importance of initiating students into the Christian mind, thereby freeing them to participate as Christians in the broad cultural conversation of humanity. And proponents of the Christian academic-discipline model ground their model in the importance of introducing students to the academic disciplines, thereby enabling them to share in the results of the scholar's way of implementing the cultural mandate. In contrast to each of these, the proponents of the Christian socialization model ground their proposal in the importance of training students for engaging in their occupations as Christians, so as thereby to carry out their calling. Christian mind, cultural mandate, Christian calling—those are the basic themes in these three models.

One will notice, of course, that the first model mentioned in this essay, the Christian service model, is really a species of the socialization model. In the Christian service model the college confines itself to training for that narrow range of occupations that constitutes so-called kingdom work. This is clearly just a variety or a narrowing of the Christian socialization model more generally, according to which the college trains for Christian life and action in a wide range of occupational callings.

These, I suggest, are the dominant curricular models to be found in evangelical Christian colleges today, each with its own appeal. No doubt the Christian humanist model appeals especially to those teaching in the humanities; the academic-discipline model especially to those teaching in the natural and social sciences; and the socialization model to those engaged in professional and preprofessional education. But it is evident that each model also has an appeal well beyond its home base. Nonetheless, each of these models seems to me deficient; the goals they propose for Christian collegiate education are not satisfactory. I must forego a detailed discussion of what is lacking in each of them separately, so let me concentrate instead on what is especially deficient in all of them together.

None of these models responds adequately to the *wounds* of humanity; none gives adequate answer to our cries and tears. The academic discipline model reminds us that the cultural mandate requires us to develop the potentials of creation by bringing forth science and art. But what about our liberation mandate to free the captive? The Christian humanist model stresses that we must be freed from our cultural particularities to participate as Christians in the great cultural conversation of humanity. But what about those people who lack the strength to converse because in their stomachs there is no food? The Christian socialization model emphasizes that we must train our students to work as Christians within their occupational callings. But what about all those people who after searching long and hard find no occupation? Our traditional models speak scarcely at all of injustice in the world, scarcely at all of our calling to mercy and justice.

I very much like one of the fundamental themes in John Calvin, that to be human is to be one of those points in the cosmos where God's goodness is meant to find its answer in gratitude. But to this we must add something. To be human, authentically human, is also to be one of those points in the cosmos where humanity's wounds are meant to find an answer in mourning. On those who mourn humanity's wounds and, energized by this mourning, struggle for healing, Jesus pronounces blessing. They shall be comforted, he says. Their cause will be vindicated, their grief turned to joy. The curriculum of the Christian college must open itself up to humanity's wounds.

It should be clear that this is not a proposal to abolish the teaching of the humanities, nor of the sciences, nor of professional education. This is not a call for a curricular model constricted in yet a different direction from those we have canvassed. It is a call instead for a more comprehensive model, a more holistic model—a model that incorporates the arts and the sciences and the professions and, yes, the worship and the piety of humanity along with the wounds of humanity and brings them together into one coherent whole rather than setting them at loggerheads with each other. What might such a model be? What should be the curricular goal of Christian collegiate education?

There is in the Bible a vision of what it is that God wants for his human creatures—a vision of what constitutes human flourishing, a vision of the appointed destiny of authentic human existence. The vision is not that of disembodied individual contemplation of God; thus it is not the vision of heaven, if that is what one takes heaven to be. Rather, it is the vision of *shalom*—a vision first articulated in the poetic and prophetic literature of the Old Testament but prominent in the New Testament as well under the rubric of *eirene,* peace.

Shalom is intertwined with justice, and the shalom community is the *just* community. There can be no shalom without justice. In shalom, each person enjoys justice, enjoys his or her rights. If individuals are not granted what is due them, if their rightful claim on others is not acknowledged by those others, if others do not carry out their obligations to them, then shalom is wounded.

But the demands of justice do not exhaust our responsibilities to our fellow human beings. And beyond that, the right relationships that lie at the basis of shalom involve more than right relationships to other human beings. They involve right relationships to God, to nature, and to oneself as well. Hence while the shalom community is the just community, it is also more than that. It is the *responsible* community in which God's laws for our multifaceted existence are obeyed.

But the shalom community is more even than the just and responsible community. We may all have acted justly and responsibly and yet shalom may be wounded, for the community may be lacking the *delight* of its people. A nation may be living in justice and peace with all its neighbors and yet its members may still be miserable in their poverty. Shalom is the antithesis of this; it is at its highest delight in one's relationships. To dwell in shalom is to delight in living before God, to delight in one's physical surroundings, to delight in life with one's fellows, to delight even in life with oneself.

What then is our relation to this appointed human destiny of shalom? What is our relationship to the vision of the just and responsible community of delight? The biblical witness is clear. The vision of shalom comes to us as a two-part command to bring shalom to the world, a command that incorporates both a liberation mandate and a cultural mandate. Thus as we pray and struggle for the incursion of shalom into our world, we are to work both for the release of the captives and for the release of the enriching potentials of God's creation. Yet more than prayer and struggle for the incursion of shalom into our world is asked of us. The vision of shalom is not only a mandate but also an invitation to celebration and mourning. We are to celebrate the flickerings of shalom that appear among us, and we are to mourn when our world falls short of true shalom.[14]

And now for the last link: Can the Christian college do anything else than guide its endeavors by this vision of shalom? If God's call to all humanity is to be liberators and developers and celebrators and mourners, and if to that call of God the church of Jesus Christ has replied with a resonant yes, then will not the Christian college also have to find its place within this great commission? Of course. Yet as it does so it must keep in mind the uniqueness of its place. The college is not a political action organization, not an architectural firm, not a mission board. It is a school. And it is as a school that the lure of shalom will direct and energize it. In short, the curricular model I propose for Christian collegiate education is the *shalom model*. The goal for which Christian educators are to teach is that their students be agents and celebrators of shalom, petitioners and mourners.

Will a curriculum aimed at shalom teach the sciences? That depends on whether the knowledge of reality achieved by the sciences contributes to that mode of flourishing that the Bible calls shalom. No doubt it does. We are created to find fulfillment in knowledge of God and of his world.

Will a curriculum aimed at shalom teach the arts? That depends on whether knowledge and practice of the arts contributes to the mode of human flourishing that is shalom. Assuredly it does. Without art, life limps.

Will a curriculum aimed at shalom teach history? Will it teach about Periclean Athens and thirteenth-century Paris? That depends on whether historical knowledge contributes to the mode of human flourishing that is shalom. One cannot escape the conviction that it does. Where our knowledge of what it was to be human in other times and other places is diminished, there our own humanity is diminished.

Will a curriculum aimed at shalom cultivate piety and teach liturgy? That too depends on whether such cultivation and such learning contribute to the mode of human flourishing that is shalom. Without a doubt, shalom is never complete without participation in the disciplines of piety and the liturgy of the church.

And last, will a curriculum aimed at shalom teach for justice? Will it present to its students the injustice and deprivation of the world? Will it teach them to recognize those for themselves? Will it ask what if anything can be done about those wounds? Will it ask what *should* be done about them? Will it teach for liberation? One cannot escape the conviction that it will.

If Christian collegiate education is to adopt the shalom model, Christian academics will have to engage in serious reflection on many issues. Suffice it to mention just two. For one thing, they will have to reflect seriously on how their education can acquire an energizing impact on the students' commitment to justice. Thus their reflections on curriculum will require, as counterpart, reflections on pedagogy. When professors teach poetry, they do not just set poetry in front of their students and let them do with it what they will. They try to nourish in them a love for good poetry. When teaching chemistry or history or economics in the curriculum, instructors do not just set the discipline in front of the students and let them do with it what they will. They try to cultivate in them a love for learning. When faculty members conduct college chapel services, they do not just speak in cool and objective tones about God and his kingdom; they try to develop in their students a love for them. Can educators do otherwise when it comes to justice? Can they do anything less than strive to cultivate in their students a love and a passion for justice?

How do they do that though? Sad to say, there is not a scrap of evidence that setting the abstract disciplines in front of students does any good whatsoever by way of energizing them for the cause of justice, nor is there a scrap of evidence that initiating them into the cultural conversation of humanity does any such good. It is true, of course, that academic disciplines are not *irrelevant* to the practice of justice and the doing of mercy. The point is, however, that by themselves they do not *energize* anyone for that.

What does? Three things are worth mentioning. First, giving students *reasons* for acting as the teacher thinks they should act can help promote the cause of justice and mercy. In other words, casuistry helps. But of course, giving reasons presupposes that the teachers themselves have thought seriously about such issues, starting from their shared commitment to the Bible. There's one of the "rubs"!

Second, it helps to give to the great issues of our day a human face and a human voice—which presupposes, of course, that the ivy-covered brick walls that separate the academy from the world must have a good many holes knocked in them so that the world can get in and the academy can get out. Once you have heard Christian Palestinians speak about the anguish of their people you will not be the same—nor will you be the same once you have heard Jewish persons speak about the anguish of *their* people. Unless, that is, your fear of what would happen if you responded to their cries is so deep that sympathy is overwhelmed. Fear is the mortal enemy of sympathy.

Third, modeling helps. There is no better way for teachers to cultivate a passion for justice in their students than by themselves exhibiting that very passion. Education is in good measure teachers replicating themselves. That can be a painful truth for teachers to acknowledge. Admittedly it is pleasant for teachers to think that their love for good music has a modeling effect on their students, and it is pleasant to think that their love for history has a similar modeling effect. But we teachers would all strongly prefer that it not be the case that our indifference to the wounds of the world has a modeling effect on our students.

I should add that it is not only the comportment of teachers but the comportment of entire institutions that has a modeling impact on students. If a Christian college preaches love and justice while practicing stinginess and surliness and sexism, we know what sort of students it will tend to produce: students preaching love and justice while practicing stinginess and surliness and sexism.

To acknowledge these points about modeling is to begin to have one's thinking about school education turned upside down. Customarily faculty think that teaching takes place in classrooms and that everything else is support for that. The truth is that the total institution in its entire comportment functions educatively; what transpires by way of talk in the classroom is only one component in this vast process. "Is there nowhere to hide?" we ask desperately. The answer is, "No, there is not." But lest we despair, let us remember that our honest confession of failure can also be a model to our students. And let those of us who are Christian remember as well to point our students to another model, to him who is *our* model: Jesus Christ.

I have made the point that energizing students for the doing of justice is vitally important. But this can never be separated from the academic tasks of the Christian college: practice and scholarship must go hand in hand. Thus another topic that calls for Christian reflection is the need for praxis-oriented scholarship—that is, scholarship that analyzes social structures with an eye to the call for justice. Christian scholars must begin to ask how they can supplement pure theory with praxis-oriented theory.

The suggestion that education in the Christian college should aim at shalom encounters worries and objections from all sides. In closing, let me mention just two. Some professors will say, "Are you asking that we give up all the esteem and accomplishment we have attained in the scholarly community from years of hard work, and that we go into this new and vague thing that you call 'praxis-oriented theorizing'?" I can only answer that it is unclear whether we must give up esteem and accomplishment. But it is clear that some educators must spend at least some of their time in scholarship aimed at helping to lift the burdens of humanity.

Members of the evangelical colleges must be brutally honest with themselves here. It is more likely that prominent scholars in major universities will undertake this kind of scholarship than it is that scholars in evangelical colleges will do so. When viewed from a distance, Christian colleges appear to be in an enviable position for making creative innovative contributions to American education, including contributions of the sort called for here. But when one actually associates with the faculty members of such colleges, one soon discerns that many of them have deep feelings of insecurity about their place in the world of scholarship. Those feelings prompt some to drop out of scholarship entirely while they prompt others to try to equal the scholars at major universities at the game of pure scholarship. We will have to address these feelings head-on if they are not endlessly to inhibit scholarship in the service of justice.

A second objection the shalom model encounters is the feeling that the pursuit of praxis-oriented scholarship would politicize the college, thereby alienating its community and introducing strife into its faculty. I myself have pointedly been asked whether I think we should try to turn all our students into advocates of the right of the Palestinians to their own state. The thinly veiled point of the question, of course, is that anyone can foresee the calamitous consequences of doing that!

Notice how curious this anxious question appears when seen in the context of what Christian educators do generally. Nobody thinks that something illicit occurs in teaching philosophy if a professor communicates to students the conviction that Thomas Reid's philosophy is better than David Hume's. Nobody thinks one is doing something illicit in teaching music if one communicates to students one's conviction that

Beethoven's music is better than Boccherini's. But if someone defends the rights of the Palestinians in some course, then suddenly a plaintive plea for objectivity breaks out.

In response to such cries of foul, we must readily admit that school policy is to be distinguished from the policy and practice of individual faculty members. No college should adopt as an institutional policy the requirement that Beethoven be taught as being a better composer than Boccherini, nor Reid a better philosopher than Hume. But we cannot leave the matter at this point of distinguishing college policy from individual practice, comfortable as that would be. For though the Bible does not present God as preferring Beethoven to Boccherini, it does say that the cries of the poor, of the oppressed, and of the vicitimized touch his heart, and it does indicate that the groans of his now polluted earth bring tears to his eyes. Thus we are touching here not on issues of taste but on issues of right teaching, or orthodoxy. We are touching on our understanding of the nature of God. If a college is to commit itself to serving the God of the Bible, it must commit itself, as an academic institution, to serving the cause of justice and peace in the world. If it does not so commit itself, it is serving another God. Around this conclusion there is no detour. The God who asks Christians to go into all the world to preach the gospel of Jesus Christ is the same God who loves mercy and justice.

So Christian teachers can and should discuss among themselves effective and sensitive ways of teaching for justice. They can and should discuss effective ways of opening up their students to the wounds of the world. They can and should discuss effective and sensitive ways of handling the controversies that will arise when they teach for justice. But the God whom believers acknowledge in their lives and celebrate in worship is asking that they do indeed teach for justice-in-shalom. For that God is the God revealed in Jesus Christ, the Prince of Shalom. The graduate who prays and struggles for the incursion of shalom into our glorious but fallen world, celebrating its presence and mourning its absence—that is the graduate the Christian college must seek to produce.

NOTES

1. Michael Oakeshott, "Education: The Engagement and the Frustration," in *Education and the Development of Reason,* ed. R. F. Dearden, P. H. Hirst, and R. S. Peters (London and Boston: Routledge and Kegan Paul, 1972), 19-49.

2. Ibid., 20-21.

3. Ibid., 21.

4. Ibid., 22.

5. Ibid., 24-25.

6. Ibid., 47-48.

7. The best of Jellema's works on this subject are "Calvinism and Higher Education," in *God-Centered Living: Calvinism in Action: A Symposium,* ed. H. Henry Meeter (Grand Rapids: Baker, 1951); and his pamphlet "The Curriculum in a Liberal Arts College" (Grand Rapids: Calvin College, 1958).

8. Jellema, "Calvinism and Higher Education," 120.

9. Ibid., 121.

10. Ibid., 122.

11. Oakeshott, "Education," 31.

12. Ibid., 30.

13. In his later work, Descartes conceded that this method would not do for the natural sciences; see, for example, *The Principles of Philosophy,* trans. Reese P. Miller and Valentine R. Miller (Hingham, Mass.: Kluwer Academic, 1983).

14. I discuss these matters more thoroughly in my book *Until Justice and Peace Embrace* (Grand Rapids: Eerdmans, 1983), esp. "Interlude I."

Knowing and Doing: The Christian College in Contemporary Society

Richard J. Mouw

In the opening pages of *An Enquiry Concerning Human Understanding* David Hume observes that "moral philosophy, or the science of human nature, may be treated after two different manners." One approach views the human person "chiefly as born for action." Employing "the most amiable colors" as they display their vision of the good life, defenders of this approach "make us *feel* the difference between vice and virtue" as they attempt to "bend our hearts to the love of probity and true honor."[1]

The second way of treating the science of human nature, according to Hume, views the human person as "a reasonable rather than an active being." Defenders of this view are not so much concerned to "engage the affections" of a person or to get someone to *feel* the difference between right and wrong; rather they treat "human nature as a subject of speculation" and attempt to find out what is at work when a human being's affections *are* engaged by one or another pattern of vice or virtue. They are not so much interested in exciting a person's sentiments as in understanding what is happening when someone else is doing the exciting. These kinds of thinkers, Hume notes, do not even try to make their speculations intelligible to "common readers"; instead, they "aim at the approbation of the learned and the wise; and they think themselves sufficiently compensated for the labor of their whole lives, if they can discover some hidden truths, which may contribute to the instruction of posterity."[2]

Hume's distinction, while formulated in eighteenth-century Scotland, has a familiar ring in twentieth-century North America. These two different manners of treating the science of human nature have certainly made their presence known in discussions of the proper aims of higher education. Some insist, for example, that the college or university campus must be a place whose intellectual design should promote the engaging of "the affections" in the service of various programs of societal reform. They want educational institutions to make a direct attempt at altering or reforming certain moral commitments on the part of students. University-level education should make students "*feel* the difference between vice and virtue," bending their "hearts to the love of probity and true honor." Others resist these calls to praxis-oriented scholarship by defending the ancient vision of a community of scholars committed to the disinterested pursuit of learning. It is not the task of persons involved in higher education to traffic in sentiments and affections, such folks argue. Rather, they must ask the speculative questions which will lead to a detached understanding both of the operations of human sentiment and affection and of the environment in which various programs of virtue and vice are formulated and pursued.

Hume's distinction, then, as applied to discussions of the aims of higher education pits the defenders of detached learning against those who insist that the educational process must have as its immediate goal the cultivation in students of virtuous affections and commitments. And Hume is correct in thinking that the proponents of "knowledge for its own sake" have often had to engage in battle against the lovers of virtue. But they have also had to fight in somewhat different wars against different opponents.

That this is the case is evident from the line of argument found in John Henry Newman's *The Idea of a University.* When Newman wrote this classic treatise on university education he was very much concerned with opposing a strong trend in his day in favor of professional training in a university context. The professionalists scorned the notion of "disinterested" learning, not because they were especially enthusiastic about educational endeavors which would promote patterns of moral virtue, but because they were convinced that the university should aim directly at cultivating those skills necessary for professional engagement.

Newman was very disturbed by this emphasis on "Useful Education," and he set out to expose "the fallacy . . . that no education is useful which does not teach some temporal calling, or some mechanical art, or some physical secret."[3] Newman himself, in his account of proper university education, treats a "cultivated intellect" as "a good in itself"; but the possession of such an intellect, he argues, also enables its possessor "to be more useful, and to a greater number." In the long run, as Newman views the situation, the promotion of disinterested learning could better achieve the goals sought by the advocates of professional education than even their own professionally focused methods could.[4] A rigorous liberal education can thus promote the general goals of the professions because, as Newman insists, "that training of the intellect, which is best for the individual himself, best enables him to discharge his duties to society. . . . It prepares him to fill any post with credit, and to master any subject with facility."[5]

The defenders of "the cultivation of the intellect" in North American evangelical environs have often had to contend with a form of opposition slightly different from those mentioned thus far. In his recent historical study of Christian colleges, William Ringenberg provides us with abundant evidence that the founders and supporters of Bible colleges in the United States and Canada were often driven by a strong emphasis on "practical Christian training" in opposition to such disinterested learning.[6] For the early supporters of such schools, "practical training" meant preparation for the tasks of evangelism, foreign missions, and congregational ministries, and Christian higher education was viewed as a means for providing the requisite skills for such tasks. While there were occasional suggestions made that the cultivation of the intellect was a thing to be valued, the overwhelming emphasis in the Bible school movement was on imparting the "know-how" for "Christian work." As F. W. Farr of the Nyack Missionary Training Institute put it in 1887, "It is best to know and to do, but it is better to do without knowing than to know without doing."[7]

It is this kind of "practical" focus—the focus on proclaiming the gospel in a lost and dying world—with which evangelical defenders of the liberal arts have often had to contend. Thus when Arthur Holmes insists, in his *Idea of a Christian College,* that the main question we must ask about higher education is not "What can I do with it?" but "What can it do to me?"[8] he is pointing to a tension which in the evangelical world is often understood as a choice between "doing the Lord's work" on the one hand and "worldly learning" on the other. When Holmes argues for the importance of being exposed to a liberal arts education in which rational inquiry, historical awareness, and a sensitivity to the foundations of value judgments are encouraged, he is cutting against the grain of some deeply entrenched evangelical patterns.

The ways in which people have defended the notion of disinterested learning, against a variety of more "practical" orientations, have an important bearing on the question of how Christian colleges are to deal with societal issues. How should Christian colleges address, if at all, questions of pressing societal concern? What should they be doing by way of preparing Christian students to wrestle with practical questions of political and economic import? These various arguments—about the relationship of "the cultivation of the intellect" to the promotion of virtue or educating for the professions or training for evangelism—have an important bearing on discussions of the Christian college's role in contemporary society. Evangelicals need to be both a knowing and a doing people. Critical reflection is a vital component of intelligent Christian activism, but because of the history and current cross pressures facing evangelicals, they must struggle to sustain responsible integration of learning and commitment.

When I first became engaged in the study of evangelical political thought and action in the late 1960s, I became convinced—and I still maintain my conviction—that the development of a proper evangelical social ethic necessitates the repair of some significant defects in the thought patterns of twentieth-century evangelicalism. Indeed, three specific defects merit special attention: tendencies toward otherworldliness, anti-intellectualism, and a spirit of ecclesiastical separatism.[9]

The prevalence of these three tendencies in evangelicalism since the movement's origins is ably documented by F. Ernest Stoeffler in an essay on the legacy of seventeenth-century Pietism. Stoeffler, who has done much to combat widespread caricatures of early Pietism, argues that while the movement has contributed many good things to the modern world, it has also "contributed . . . to some of those features of American Protestantism which are . . . less admirable." He singles out in particular the same kinds of characteristics or tendencies which have troubled many observers of twentieth-century evangelicalism. He suggests, first, that Pietism has contributed to a tendency among some Protestants to be "escapist in their theology, putting the emphasis on blessedness in the hereafter rather than justice for all here and now." Second, he believes Pietism has encouraged "a certain anti-intellectual atmosphere" among Christians. And third, he also attributes to the Pietist influence an American Protestant "tendency toward sectarian fragmentation."[10]

It is especially the first two of these tendencies which concern us here. North American evangelicalism has exhibited—perhaps, as Stoeffler's analysis suggests, because of the influence of a degenerate, or degenerating, form of Pietism—strong tendencies toward otherworldliness and anti-intellectualism. In recent decades there have been significant efforts among evangelicals to correct these defective tendencies, not only in the neoevangelical movement which emerged after

World War II, but also more recently in the neofundamentalist movement associated with the activities of the Reverend Jerry Falwell, who
has promoted both a new brand of thisworldly Christian activism and
a new respect for Christian scholarship among fundamentalist Christians.

It is by no means an easy task, however, to coordinate the efforts to
correct the defects of otherworldliness and anti-intellectualism. It is
possible, for example, to react strongly against the otherworldly tendencies of evangelical pietism without at the same time thinking it
necessary to provide remedies for evangelical anti-intellectualism. Indeed, there are patterns of present-day Christian activism which sit very
well with anti-intellectual proclivities. It is not impossible to find, for
example, evangelicals who at one time in their lives disparaged intellectual pursuits on the grounds that such things divert our attention from
the all-important task of winning souls for Jesus Christ and who now
disparage intellectual pursuits on the grounds that such things divert our
attention from the all-important task of confronting the corporate evils
associated with capitalism and militarism.

When we consider the relationship between higher education and
efforts for social change, then, we must be very careful about sorting
out the various strains and tensions which are at work among evangelicals. To raise the question of how Christian colleges ought to deal with
matters of societal concern is to touch sensitive nerves in an evangelical community which still struggles with tendencies toward otherworldliness and anti-intellectualism. Here too it is necessary to be sensitive to the phenomenon of "contextualization."

It is important to recognize that some evangelical scholars who insist that evangelical scholarship and teaching should be protected from
a focus on practical concerns and commitments do so because of hard-
fought battles that they have waged, and continue to wage, against anti-
intellectualism within the evangelical community. In a speech that he
gave to a convention of Christian school principals in 1950, Henry
Zylstra defended the perspective of the educational traditionalist who
wants foreign languages as an integral part of education. "He wants
them not for reasons of trade and holiday. He wants them not solely for
their utility in research. He wants them mainly because he thinks that
an adequately philosophical mind is not possible unless it is disciplined
by the rationality or logic of the literature of our civilized West."[11]

For many evangelical scholars this kind of defense of "unuseful"
learning continues to have a strong attraction. It is especially strong for

those who are familiar with those varieties of evangelicalism which desperately need the discipline of critical reflection, even (perhaps especially) the kind of critical reflection which does not have immediate importance for praxis. Remembering Arthur Holmes's distinction, we can say that these evangelical scholars have come to see the importance of asking, with reference to the collected wisdom of Western civilization, "What can it do to me?" without having to ask immediately "What can I do with it?" If we acknowledge, then, that the old strains of anti-intellectualism continue to make their presence known in the evangelical community and need to be countered, we can understand and perhaps sympathize with some evangelical scholars who resist calls for praxis-oriented higher education.

It is also important to try to understand those Christian educators who are supporters of a strong praxis focus. Some of them are mainly interested in the kind of "Useful Education" which Newman associated with views of "Locke and his disciples." In setting forth their views they will sometimes criticize in very explicit terms educational schemes which place a high value on "disinterested learning" or "pure theory." In so doing they may seem to be echoing the "better to do without knowing than to know without doing" manifesto of Nyack's F. W. Farr, or to be espousing the kind of missionary activism that led A. B. Simpson to describe Christian education as training "the foot soldiers of God's army."[12]

It would be wrong to dismiss these present-day educators as merely the old "practical training" people parading in new disguises, just as it would be wrong to think of proponents of "education for radical Christian witness" in those terms. In many cases these parties are consciously attempting to correct the other defect which we have mentioned, the otherworldliness of evangelical pietism. The "practical training" of the professionalists and the political activists is very much a thisworldly evangelical praxis orientation. As such it is far removed from the otherworldly pragmatism of previous generations of Christian educators, whose praxis was defined exclusively in terms of foreign missions and domestic evangelism.

How should the evangelical colleges attempt to correct the defects of anti-intellectualism and otherworldliness? They should understand, first of all, that one does not properly correct these defects by embracing their opposites. The proper antidote to anti-intellectualism is not hyperintellectualism, nor is a myopic thisworldliness the right remedy for otherworldliness.

A better remedy is to make of the Christian educational community a setting in which men and women can integrate intellectual pursuits into a larger pattern of Christian service. These integrative efforts can foster the kind of self-understanding which presupposes what Arthur Holmes describes as a "unified conception of personality such that the person as a whole thinks and chooses and feels and acts: thinking can proceed neither without choosing goals and assumptions nor without emotion."[13] Holmes rightly warns us against confusing the Christian understanding of intellectual pursuits with "the Enlightenment conception of reason as unimpassioned and uncommitted, detached and neutral on matters of faith and value." Rather we need an understanding of rationality that helps us to see things in a larger perspective and to think systematically toward the goal of developing "a unified understanding."[14]

This integrating perspective will, in turn, establish the framework in which thisworldly and otherworldly concerns and relationships may be woven into a consistent pattern of Christian discipleship. The Marxist insistence that Christianity is a "pie-in-the-sky" religion contains a legitimate observation about the nature of Christian belief. As evangelical Protestants, Roman Catholics, Eastern Orthodox believers, and other adherents to some branch of classical Christianity are quick to acknowledge, Christian faith requires that we nurture a view of reality in which both the things that are seen and the things that are unseen have their rightful place. A thoroughly *Christian* activism must be grounded in a hope that is directed toward that which is beyond this present world. Evangelical pietism has seldom been a very "passive" business, however. For North American evangelicals, otherworldliness has not meant a withdrawal from action; instead, it has functioned as a kind of stimulus to action, albeit an action that fits into a view of life in which preparation for the world-to-come is a central motif.

Evangelical otherworldly activism has also been supplemented by spiritual disciplines which facilitate temporary withdrawal from activist pursuits. These disciplines—prayer, contemplation, the devotional study of the Scriptures, fasting—seem to be essential elements of the evangelical style as such, and they are very worthy of being retained and nurtured, even in a pattern of evangelical discipleship which has been purged of various defects. Similar disciplines are encouraged by many Roman Catholic liberation theologians, in spite of popular stereotypes which might convey a different impression. Gustavo Gutiérrez, for example, who functions for many as an example par excellence of a thisworldly activist, nonetheless insists in *A Theology of Liberation* that there will necessarily be a "useless" element in proper spirituality: "Prayer is an experience of gratuitousness. This 'leisure' action, this 'wasted' time, reminds us that the Lord is beyond the categories of useful and useless. God is not of this world."[15] Evangelicals have always recognized the need for this kind of "wasted" time in the presence of God. It is the "useless" cultivation of the spiritual disciplines that helps us to keep things in perspective, to view our lives and activities in the light of eternity's values.

A similar case can be made for the importance of the "wasted" time of critical scholarly reflection in the Christian community. When Christian scholars set aside practical questions and issues of immediate importance and step back from "useful" activity, they may well gain new and important perspectives on reality—the kind of "unified understanding" Holmes talks about. For the Christian scholar this kind of "leisure" action takes place before the face of the Lord; it too is a kind of spiritual activity. The reality of this spiritual-intellectual discipline makes up the core of truth in both the attacks on merely "useful" education and in the corresponding defenses of detached or disinterested learning. This core of truth must be honored in our own attempts to understand the proper patterns of the Christian college's address to matters of societal concern.

The Christian college can and should be an important integrating center of efforts to remedy both anti-intellectualism and otherworldliness. Thus Christian colleges ought to promote critical reflection on matters pertaining to Christian social obligations, insisting both that critical thought must address questions of pressing societal concern and that the patterns of Christian activism must be subjected to the discipline of careful scholarly reflection. Integrating critical reflection and a concern for social obligations can provide evangelicals with a significant means of self-correction as well as a way of honoring the God who is, in Gutiérrez's words, "beyond the categories of useful and useless."

How *should* such patterns be encouraged at Christian colleges? In what ways may a college, as college, legitimately deal with pressing social issues? Surprisingly little has been written on this subject. But analogous questions have been much discussed with reference to the institutional church. In those discussions a false choice has sometimes been posed. Many people have assumed either that the church will take "official" stands on matters of public policy—by means of "political sermons" or pastoral letters or synodical declarations or the like—or that, in the absence of official stands, such matters will be left to the discretion of the individual Christian in the role of private citizen. But these are not exclusive options. One alternative is for the institutional church to encourage and sponsor communal dialogue regarding pressing societal issues without giving official endorsement to a specific policy—but also, thereby, without giving the impression that wrestling with such policy questions is a purely individual matter.

A similar option is also available to the Christian college. Christian institutions of higher education do not need to make "official" commitments on matters of public policy in order to deal with those matters. Nor should they give the impression that wrestling with social specifics is beyond the scope of the educational mission, a matter for private consciences to deal with. Colleges do not have to formally accept a specific assessment of U.S. strategy in Central America, for example, or support specific schemes to better the lot of the urban poor, or take a position on Canadian trade relations with Poland. But they can "officially" declare, at least implicitly by their allocations of resources, that these matters—along with many others which bear on our Christian obligations to promote both justice for the poor and righteousness among the nations—are important for Christian discussion in the academic setting.

I doubt that it is necessary to argue this case too strenuously. Christian colleges are already doing this kind of thing in many ways. Nicholas Wolterstorff argues that Christian colleges ought to pursue, self-consciously and aggressively, the task of showing students how the gap between theory and practical efforts at social reform ought to be bridged.[16] If I understand him correctly he is in effect asking for an intensification and expansion of activities which are already taking place on Christian campuses: courses dealing with specific societal issues, internships, seminars focusing on practical applications, campus-wide assemblies and forums, guest lecturers, panel discussions, and so on.

None of this really requires that faculty members and administrators of Christian colleges be identified with specific policy endorsements with regard to pressing societal issues. But is there also a place, are there times when there *must* be a place, for more official commitments in this area of concern? Are there occasions, for example, where a college has a right to require its employees to take official stands on such matters? The answers to these questions are clearly affirmative. This is not to say that we should expect Christian academic institutions to require many such stands, or to do so often. But there do seem to be situations in which commitments of this sort may legitimately be required.

Again it is helpful to draw parallels to the institutional church. Even those Christians who have argued against the church's right or authority to pronounce on specific matters of public policy have usually allowed for at least the possibility of rare situations in which the church must speak in clear terms about such questions. The situation in Nazi Germany is often singled out as a case in point. It is difficult to see how we can avoid applying the same considerations to a Christian college. A general principle of this sort seems to hold for both churches and colleges: a Christian institution, as an institution, is required to take an official stand on a matter of public policy when not doing so would constitute disobedience to the gospel of Jesus Christ.

There can be legitimate arguments, of course, about whether such a condition is in fact ever in force. Some might argue, for example, that an actual situation in which institutions of higher learning would be required by the demands of the gospel to take a specific stand on a societal issue is impossible, or extremely difficult, to imagine. Others might hold that while one can think of a situation in which this kind of institutional commitment might seem legitimate, the precedents that would be set are so dangerous that it is better for a college to proceed as if such situations will never arise. Others will argue that one cannot simply rule out the possibility of such situations and that therefore a college must be open to considering the demands posed by specific cases as they arise. This last viewpoint has much to commend it. It is possible to conceive of situations in which *any* Christian college would be required by the claims of the gospel to take official stands on matters of social, political, or economic policy. Nazi Germany and present-day South Africa provide us with clear examples of such cases.

It also seems reasonable to expect some degree of pluralism among Christian institutions in dealing with a variety of issues—the same kind of pluralism that shows up on a purely theological level. All evangelical colleges require, for example, some kind of doctrinal or theological commitments from their faculty members; but the nature and extent of these commitments vary significantly from institution to institution. These variations are well founded, for evangelical colleges differ greatly in the nature of their sponsorship. Mark Noll has recently written some very helpful comments on this pluralistic situation, noting that "the relationship between [evangelical] colleges and the constituencies which they serve can be very different in spite of the fact that they advertise nearly identical educational goals." Noll points specifically to some key differences: "Some evangelical colleges are the lengthened shadow of one person or family. Others rest securely within a particular denomination, and still others serve complex interdenominational networks."[17]

It is necessary that we take these differences into account in assessing the social responsibilities of specific institutions. The exploration of the implications of the biblical call to justice, righteousness, and peace ought to take place on all Christian campuses. But we can rightly expect, or so it seems to me, at least, that a Mennonite college will require or encourage its academic employees to operate within a certain range of viewpoints on matters of the use of lethal violence—a requirement which might not be so understandable in another kind of evangelical college. Similarly, a Dutch Reformed college may have especially good reasons for wanting to know what its faculty members think about South African apartheid. In these particular cases, of course, the social issues in question have a confessional kind of status in the communities mentioned. A commitment to peace making is fundamental to the historic Anabaptist vision, and Calvinist communities have special reasons for exploring the doctrinal deviations which often shape racist practices. Thus there seem to be social issues which certain kinds of Christian educational communities must address by virtue of their unique confessional and theological identities.

Even on such matters, however, it is important that Christian institutions not preclude too quickly—by administrative or ecclesiastical fiat—critical reflection on questions which are deserving of scholarly attention. There are certain ways of shutting off the discussion of important issues before the discussion has run its course; in most cases, such actions are simply unworthy of an *academic* institution. Given past evangelical patterns of stifling debate and prematurely closing off critical inquiry, we might do well to nurture a bias in favor of keeping these kinds of discussions going. As Mark Noll has put it, "The challenge to evangelical higher education is to open doors wide to any political or social position which claims to rest on Christian foundations, but then to go on to rigorous scrutiny of the position and its supposed Christian base, never allowing the gospel to be equated with any changeable form of human conviction."[18] This is good advice, especially if we are also wary of the comparable danger of allowing a clear requirement of the gospel to be passed off as nothing more than a changeable form of human conviction.

I conclude with a brief look at a case in point. The Winter 1985 issue of *Christian Activist*—a newspaper published by Schaeffer V Productions—devoted considerable attention to attitudes about abortion on evangelical campuses and singled out Wheaton College for special consideration. Under the heading "Why Wheaton College Should Be Put Out of Its Misery," statements by a variety of students, professors, and campus guests were made to support the writer's contention that both indifference to the abortion issue and even pro-abortion attitudes were a prominent presence at Wheaton. *Christian Activist* concluded with a plea that Christians supporting Wheaton College withdraw their support in favor of "clearly committed Christian institutions who will train students, not confuse them, and whose ultimate value is truth, not fashionability."

This attack on Wheaton is shoddy stuff. For example, there is a significant gap between *Christian Activist*'s claims about the views of people who teach at Wheaton and the evidence offered in support of these claims. Indeed, the worst offense committed by Wheaton faculty members, according to the evidence *Christian Activist* presents, seems to be that they have suggested that there might be exceptional circumstances in which a decision to abort a fetus might be justified— such as a case in which the life of the mother is seriously threatened. The people who write for this periodical seem to think, not so much that it is impossible that such a situation might occur, but rather that it complicates the issue and thus weakens the pro-life movement's polemical power.

This is not the place to argue the pros and cons of the abortion issue. Suffice it to say that one can be strongly opposed to the present-day slaughter of the unborn and yet still think that there are important aspects of abortion policy which ought to be discussed freely and openly on Christian college campuses. It might be legitimate for Christian colleges to require, as some already have, that their employees oppose abortion on demand. But such a requirement ought not preclude dialogue about how best to work for the creation of a social and legal climate in which the rights of the unborn are respected and protected, nor should it stifle discussion about how to relate these matters to even larger questions concerning the promotion of justice and peace in the world.

F. W. Farr was probably correct when he insisted that "it is better to do without knowing than to know without doing." But he was surely correct when he prefaced this with the observation that "it is best to know and to do." For the North American evangelical community this is an important reminder. Evangelicals must work at being more responsible people, in both their knowings and their doings. Indeed, it is precisely the question of how to integrate the two—how to be intelligently active people—that seems to be an item of crucial importance for present-day evangelicalism. *Christian Activist's* treatment of the abortion issue provides us with clear evidence that the goal of intelligent Christian activism is not an easy one for evangelicals to attain. Yet it is an important goal to promote if inflamed rhetoric and the bearing of false witness are to give way to a dialogue in which nuances of formulation and differences in strategy can be discussed in mutually edifying ways.

To desire that kind of dialogue is not necessarily to love confusion or to lust after fashionability, as the *Christian Activist* alleges. Of course it *can* be, and Christian scholars must constantly be on guard against the temptation to evade responsibility in the name of "free inquiry." But the promotion of an atmosphere in which mutually challenging dialogue takes place can be a significant step toward responding positively to the apostolic appeal that we not be conformed to this world, but that we seek instead the transformation of our *minds,* so that we can exercise the sober judgment that is given to us according to the measure of our faith (Rom. 12:2-3). To bring that kind of sober judgment to bear on issues of great import in a world broken by the injustice and unrighteousness that human rebellion has established, so that God's people may be equipped for the discerning performance of every good work—this is "detached" learning at its best.

NOTES

1. David Hume, *An Enquiry Concerning Human Understanding* (Chicago: Henry Regnery, 1956), 1-2.

2. Ibid., 2.

3. John Henry Newman, *The Idea of a University* (New York: Rinehart, 1960), 126.

4. Ibid.

5. Ibid., 134-35.

6. William C. Ringenberg, *The Christian College: A History of Protestant Higher Education in America* (Grand Rapids: Eerdmans, Christian University Press, 1984), 157-73.

7. F. W. Farr, quoted in ibid., 165.

8. Arthur F. Holmes, *The Idea of a Christian College*, rev. ed. (1975; Grand Rapids: Eerdmans, 1987), 29.

9. See, for example, my "New Alignments: Hartford and the Future of Evangelicalism," in *Against the World for the World: The Hartford Appeal and the Future of American Religion*, ed. Peter Berger and Richard Neuhaus (New York: Seabury, 1976).

10. F. Ernest Stoeffler, "Epilogue," in *Continental Pietism and Early American Christianity*, ed. F. Ernest Stoeffler (Grand Rapids: Eerdmans, 1976), 270-71.

11. Henry Zylstra, *Testament of Vision* (Grand Rapids: Eerdmans, 1958), 136.

12. A. B. Simpson, quoted in Ringenberg, *The Christian College*, 161.

13. Holmes, *The Idea of a Christian College*, 37.

14. Ibid., 37, 38.

15. Gustavo Gutiérrez, *A Theology of Liberation: History, Politics and Salvation*, trans. and ed. Sister Caridad Inda and John Eagleson (Maryknoll, N.Y.: Orbis, 1973), 206.

16. See Nicholas Wolterstorff, "The Mission of the Christian College at the End of the Twentieth Century," *Reformed Journal* 33 (June 1983): 16-18; see also his essay in this volume, "Teaching for Justice."

17. See Mark A. Noll's introduction, "Christian Colleges, Christian Worldviews, and an Invitation to Research," in Ringenberg, *The Christian College*, 33.

18. Ibid., 36.

III
Advancing the Mission

The Tasks of Evangelical Christian Colleges

Warren Bryan Martin

Many people in the kennel of college experts, especially the old dogs, remember David Riesman's book *Constraint and Variety in American Education.*[1] They likely recall that Riesman categorized colleges and universities into what he called a snake-like procession. He noted that the head of this snake-like procession, composed of the so-called avant garde institutions, often twisted and turned back on itself, while the middle part tried to catch up with where the head had been. The consequence, he said, was that the middle part often seemed to be moving in two directions at once—forward to where the head had been and also back to where it was at the present time. The institutions that would today occupy this undifferentiated middle are those that the Carnegie Classification categorized as Doctorate-granting Universities I and II and Comprehensive Universities and Colleges I and II. There is no doubt that as these institutions in the bulging middle chase the head of the procession they are going in several directions at once. While Riesman was too kind to dwell on the fact that the snake-like procession of academe had a tail, we do not hesitate to spell out what he only implied: the tail is made up of those colleges consigned to a category called Liberal Arts Colleges II—the last of the six main categories, the end of the line.

As we did not hesitate to infer what Riesman did not spell out, so we do not hesitate to raise a question he did not ask: Should colleges in the category called Liberal Arts II be pushing these days to get up into Liberal Arts I, pushing like a third monkey on the gangplank of Noah's ark? No indeed. Most colleges in Liberal Arts II should not be imitative, repetitive, and ultimately redundant. They should, instead, strive to take possession of their assigned category and make it distinctive. They should redefine the terms of engagement, set appropriate criteria for success, and, in effect, force that organization called the Carnegie

Foundation—the one with the hubris to classify other organizations—to make a special and honored place for them. That place would no longer be at the dead end of the old snake-like procession.

Then, when the inevitable question comes, "Why are so few small liberal arts colleges, particularly church-related colleges, in Liberal Arts I?" the honest rejoinder could be that they are not there for reasons of conscience and choice. These colleges do not accept the educational philosophy of Liberal Arts I colleges, a "philosophy" that features pluralism and relativism. They do not accept the criteria for faculty success that emphasize research over teaching, publications over service, the Ph.D. as the sole badge of competence, loyalty to professional guilds above loyalty to the college. Evangelical colleges especially do not accept education narrowly defined: that is, the idea that one's education is for cognitive rationality, for job training, for the training of the mind alone, or even for head and hands together.[2]

These last colleges, the colleges of evangelical Christianity, believe that an appropriate educational philosophy not only is realistic and humane but also makes a place for transcendence. Theirs is a philosophy that features education not only for intellectual growth but also for imagination and insight. Their concern is to be attentive not only to the voices of human leaders but to the voice of the Spirit. These colleges know that to make research and scholarship—professional papers and publications—the main criteria for advancement in the profession of academics is not only to threaten the needed emphasis on teaching and service, but also to make all faculty members live by a standard that is appropriate for not more than 20 percent of them. For the majority of faculty to steer their wagons by that star is to doom themselves to a professional life of frustration, guilt, and defeat—stargazing in the most detached and debilitating sense.

To make the doctorate degree not only the guild card of certification for college teaching but also the measure of faculty competence and institutional quality is to engage in perhaps unintentional but still-damaging deceit. There is simply no proof that a typical, narrow-bore Ph.D. program of study prepares one for effective college teaching; yet at the same time there is proof that such a program is likely to *limit* effectiveness—particularly for work in the general education program and in a college's essential emphasis on the interconnectedness of ideas and fields of study.

I repeat: for reasons of conscience and quality, evangelical colleges should march to a different drummer. For reasons of educational effectiveness as well as institutional integrity, these colleges ought not accept the conventional criteria of excellence, at least not in an unqualified way. The independent college, and the evangelical Protestant college even more, should be a countervailing force to the status quo. This is a way to make that category called Liberal Arts II, which has been at the tail of the snake, into a source of creativity and audacity. Independent colleges should become centers of innovation and change, centers of institutional vitality and distinctiveness so that, as with the rattlesnake, people will pay more attention to the tail than the head because the action there reveals that which is to come.

Such leadership is not beyond the realm of possibility. There have been individuals and institutions known to be innovators rather than imitators, leaders rather than followers. This was the case with Alexander Meikeljohn at Amherst and Wisconsin, with Robert Hutchins at Yale and Chicago, with Royce Pitkin at Goddard, and Arthur E. Morgan at Antioch. Perhaps you remember that in the 1930s and again in the 1950s Antioch, Reed, Bennington, Berea, and a few other colleges were respected leaders in higher education—places known for responsible forms of innovation.[3] There is revived interest in innovation now, solid innovation—timely means to enduring ends. After a decade of educational delinquency when controlled innovation gave way to uncontrolled experimentation, when principle succumbed to opportunism, there is again heightened concern to find better ways to do the job right.[4]

But practically speaking, what should be done? What *can* be done? What would be realistic as well as right? Let me suggest just a few areas of innovation where work needs to be done, the sort of work that independent colleges could do.

Humane and Effective Management

First, there is work to be done in the area of institutional management. For a decade or more liberal arts colleges have been trying to catch up with the management techniques of the rest of higher education. They have been trying to master so-called scientific management—cost curves, econometric models, market profiles, and sales strategies. All of this is important. If college administrators and faculty fail to run their enterprise efficiently—if they allow, for example, an escalation of costs well above inflation—they will soon face what doctors and hospitals are facing now: not only empty beds and undersubscribed rosters but also a powerful challenge from outside commercial firms. If the Humana Corporation can make their hospitals pay, and also work, corporations like it may turn their methods and expertise to the management of colleges and universities in order to make them "pay" and "work" as well.

Thomas Peters and Nancy Austin recently published *A Passion for Excellence,* a new book with powerful advice appropriate for the colleges under discussion here. First, they say, take exceptional care of your customers; and second, never stop innovating. That's it.[5] *A Passion for Excellence* challenges certain management principles that have been axiomatic for forty years. Peters and Austin argue that the idea that the bigger the facility the cheaper it can make the product requires reassessment and modification. Some efficiencies can in fact lead to other inefficiencies: real-world experience shows that small plants often outperform larger ones. In large plants, as in the military, managers and workers feel less accountable; they lose productivity, efficiency, and quality control. This is why Hewlett-Packard and Minnesota Mining and Manufacturing (3M) have made it a rule of thumb that the ideal plant should have somewhere between two and three hundred employees. Small is indeed beautiful. Moreover, major innovations often come from small groups of people. A case in point is the skunk works at the Lockheed Corporation, a small creative unit within the larger corporation crucial to the development of the stealth attack bomber.

That tag—skunk works—leads to another point. Innovation is a messy process. There's an irreducable sloppiness about it. Minnesota Mining and Manufacturing has accepted that reality; can we? Independent colleges, including evangelical Christian colleges, have an opportunity to make a necessity into a virtue. They already are small units; and they could work from that to become places that make possible collaboration and the integration of functions—without giving up specialization at the same time. They should be, as corporate consultants put it, "tight-loose": tight about basic principles, loose about the actual working out of the means to achieve the goals. Rosabeth Kanter talks about "quiet entrepreneurship" at the level of middle managers, and Robert Reich talks about "flexible workers" as the key to the new dynamism.[6] You could do the same in higher education.

Could small independent colleges do a better job of management than their larger and more prestigious counterparts by combining technical skills and human sensibilities? For example, can we find within our tradition resources for the future, even as other colleges seem to be trying to escape the old traditions? Consider one matter: American life is too much driven by materialism and acquisitiveness, by "cruel capitalism," the worst aspects of the competitive market system. In this day when materialism is rampant, when the accepted lifestyle says "if you've got it, flaunt it," when selfishness and ostentation, pretention and affectation are not only visible but even desirable modes of behavior, then the evangelical Christian college is or should be a countervailing force. Even in oil-rich America, the Christian college should avoid the "new money crude" style. The Christian college community ought to be characterized by simplicity, modesty, self-restraint, and the spirit of service; by rectitude, courtesy, and compassion; by acts of cooperation more than competition; by the life of generosity and the attitude of magnanimity.

Independent colleges should be out-of-step with the lock-step imposed by conventional leaders in higher education, the head of the snake, for reasons of principle as well as pragmatism. Consider this statement: Policy in American higher education is influenced more by economic than by educational considerations. If that assertion is true, and Alexander Astin among many other observers believes it is, then we must address and attempt to reverse that condition. In his new book *Achieving Educational Excellence,* Astin states:

> Even though the research evidence clearly indicates that student involvement and development are enhanced by living on campus, attending a four-year rather than a two-year institution, and attending a small rather than a large institution, the major trends in American higher education since World War II have all been in the opposite direction. That is, the proportion of commuter students has increased, two-year colleges have proliferated, and institutions have grown steadily larger. The impetus behind such trends is economic rather than educational. Commuter colleges obviate the need to construct expensive residential facilities, two-year colleges are cheaper to operate than four-year colleges, and large institutions presumably offer certain economies of scale.
>
> It might be argued that academia, like its students, simply reflects the values of the larger society. But the real question, it seems to me, is whether higher education ought to be no more than a mirror. Perhaps we should introduce some alternative values to undergraduates.[7]

The management style of the independent college ought to reflect Christian values or principles clearly. But can it be done? Indeed it can.

Something similar is already being done by some business leaders who make no claim to being religiously motivated but who show that they know what it means to be humane. A recent book about corporate leadership, *CEO: Corporate Leadership in Action* by Henry Levinson and Stuart Rosenthal, looks at the behavior of six corporate leaders— not names on *Fortune* magazine's "Ten Toughest Bosses" list but still leaders of six corporate success stories. These executives, including Tom Watson of IBM, have shown in their business lives certain values that Christian educators could do well to emulate. Each disdained the self-aggrandizing accoutrements of power and the luxurious materialism of so many of their peers. Levinson and Rosenthal note about them that "out of a consistent internal value system, there is a common unity to what they think, what they believe, what they do, and how they practice management."[8]

There is some significance in all of this for management practices in Christian colleges. We have not paid enough attention to making sure that current management systems, their styles and strategies, are consistent with the principles of simplicity and service that must characterize first-rate evangelical colleges. Let us begin to do so.

The case against the management of our colleges goes still further. But be warned that the burden gets heavier as we go. Consider the problem of the cost of attending college. Currently, private colleges, like private universities, cost some two to five times as much as public institutions. In the last ten years, college tuitions and related costs have more than doubled: during the 1970s they rose with inflation, but since the 1980-81 school year they have risen progressively faster than inflation. Now they are rising at double the rate of inflation.[9] We are now caught in a vicious cycle—raising tuition to cover costs even while one of the fastest growing costs is financial aid to students to offset the rising cost of tuition. No industry in the nation is currently able to raise its prices more than the inflation rate without a more than commensurate decline in sales and revenues. Is there any reason to suppose that in this respect colleges are different from industry—that they can continue to raise their prices faster than the rate of inflation without serious consequences? Consider another question as a possible response: Could independent colleges—especially evangelical colleges—stop imitating other institutions in their cost structure as well as in their social environment and academic purposes? Is this a way we can break the vicious cycle?

Education for Commitment

Having suggested areas for innovation in management, let us now turn to possibilities for innovation in mission. Independent colleges and universities, like other institutions of higher education, emphasize that it is their mission to help students develop basic skills and job competencies. Indeed, most of the emphasis in education is now placed on technique—as technique relates to professional careers, interpersonal relationships, and personal development. Independent colleges and universities, again like the others, come to this mission of providing job competency, social skills, and individual development with an orientation and a set of attitudes that run through their educational programs rather like certain themes run through a musical composition. But the independent college, particularly the evangelical Christian college, should be more critically aware of that orientation and the resulting attitudes than other colleges and universities are.

Frances FitzGerald, in her book *America Revised,* reminds us that at all levels of education so much of what students retain from classroom encounters is an orientation, a mood, a set of impressions rather than specific textbook content. She cites from her own experience a conversation about a book a friend had read.

> "Wonderful book. I'll never forget the scene of Lincoln after the Battle of Gettysburg looking over the graves in the cemetery and a voice crying out to him, 'Calhooon! Calhooon!'" The memory of my friend was not, as it turned out, perfectly accurate, for in David Saville Muzzey's *American History* William Lloyd Garrison is speaking at a banquet in Charleston after the war, and about him Muzzey asks rhetorically, "Did the echoes of his voice reach a grave over which stood a marble stone engraved with the single word 'Calhoun'?" Still, my friend had remembered the dramatic irony, and that was surely the essence of this particular passage.
>
> In some general sense, this may be the truth of the matter: What sticks to the memory from those textbooks is not any particular series of facts but an atmosphere, an impression, a tone.[10]

An atmosphere, impression, attitude—these endure whether one is thinking about American history in the schools or about general and liberal education in the colleges. What educators give students, ultimately, is an orientation toward learning and a set of attitudes caught in the phrase "a feel for history," or a sense of things important and not important.

The modern university's unacknowledged and too-often unexamined assumptions that together constitute an orientation include pluralism, relativism, materialism, individualism (and perhaps also positivism and reductionism). The dominant attitudes in the university include skepticism sliding off into cynicism, self-centeredness deteriorating into subjectivism, acquisitiveness escalating toward raw greed, and freedom of choice blurring toward the recognition of no limits at all.

The church-related college, the evangelical college, will also have an orientation toward the great issues—from human nature to the meaning of history. To pursue this latter point, as an example, the evangelical college takes the Bible and church history far too seriously to permit cavalier attitudes toward the meaning of any other sort of history. It cannot and will not entertain the idea that history is "bunk," or merely the tricks the living play on the dead, or a fable agreed upon, or "sound and fury, signifying nothing." Furthermore, the evangelical college will emphasize attitudes that are consistent with the Christian ethic or ethos, attitudes appropriate for a person or institution that dares to identify with the name of Christ.

Consider the problem of creating in church-related colleges an appropriate orientation and cluster of attitudes toward an array of the most fundamental, bedrock issues—issues that always show complexity and require commitment. For most of us today complexities seem to be in the process of overwhelming commitment. We feel as though we should take a stand, that we should make a commitment not only about the importance of history but about the nature of humanity and human nature. But just as we prepare to decide and to act, we are often immobilized by complexities revealed in our own lives. While there are those who profess to find simplicity on the other side of complexity, many of us find there only complexity compounded.

And what we know about our personal lives, we also see in the public life of society—especially in the centers of influence. George Steiner, author and critic, described the city of New York recently to an audience at the royal Society of Arts in London by saying, "It is not the Federal City, not the National City, but the Empire City, which imperiously lays claim to being the capital not of its country but of our current climate of modernity." New York, he continued, is a place of total challenge to the constraints of psychological and physical activity. "Gone are not only the practical divisions of day and night—the chili dog sales peak after midnight, and ice cream sales at the stand outside the Plaza Hotel peaked during last winter's blizzard—but also gone are those old notions of privacy and discretion, swept aside in a kind of intimacy of shared revelation that has become almost the style, the new rhetoric of experience."[11] New York is a city where "that fabled pursuit of happiness"—or at least the pursuit of marketable angst, which is another form of happiness—is the hallmark of the age. There's complexity for you—and commitment too. For that crazy, depraved city is also the place where people dream, where art, dance, humor, architecture, and music flourish. Where everything goes, the creative imagination leaps ahead. So it is in New York, the capital city of the twentieth century.

Should Christian scholars join in? Should they try to carry the values of the city of the empire to our stations in the hinterland? Many of the born-again seem to go along—preppies and yuppies and guppies all grooving to gospel-rock while driving their BMWs to the Crystal Cathedral. But there are other voices from other rooms, radical Christians, sojourners on this earth who hear the divine mandate to turn the world upside down. Complexities neither seduce them nor freeze them in indecision. Complexities make their task more difficult, but they do not reduce their commitment to translating the Bible's call for justice and peace into demands for worldly justice and help for the people God favors—the poor and afflicted. These evangelicals say in Washington what Pope John Paul II said in the hostile Netherlands: Christianity is hard. They echo the words of Kierkegaard: "Let others make life easy. I must make life hard."

Just as one's actions will be influenced by the orientations and attitudes that prevail in one's city and country, so one's actions in a college will be influenced by the orientations and attitudes of the institution and one's colleagues—particularly their attitudes toward the issues on which so much of modern life turns. These include:

Individualism and communitarianism—the need to acknowledge the importance of individuality while at the same time asserting that there is now special reason to move toward community.

Change and tradition, emphasizing the authority of tradition in the context of the American fascination with change.

The scope of reason and the depth of passion, including the necessity for *interdiction and remission*—when to say "No more" and when to say "even so."

Global understanding and national identity, with both driven by the presence of complexity and the demand for commitment.

Do you believe that Jewish history and Christian history speak to these issues? Both to the complexities and to the commitments? If the answer is yes, the evangelical college should have the stuff with which to design innovations in management and mission that will push the institution from conformity and imitation to clarity and distinctiveness and transform it from the dead-end tail of the snake-like procession of higher education to the rattle that catches everybody's attention.

We may get a better perspective on the privileges and responsibilities of evangelical colleges by thinking about higher education not as a snake but as a big river, the Mississippi for example. On the surface the current flows rapidly and it carries a lot of traffic along, from boats and barges to water bugs and garbage. Below the surface, however, there is a deep current, moving more slowly and yet more powerfully, cutting the channel and determining the course of the river. Evangelical colleges are moved only superficially by the rapidly changing surface current of higher education. It is the deeper, more powerful current of God's word that provides the resources and special guidance to the evangelical colleges. If a school catches that current, its life on the surface is affected even as the deep channel of its course is being cut. It is time for all of us and for all the leaders of evangelical colleges to go down deeper and stay down longer, even if it means coming up muddier. The mud, after all, will wash off. But the experience with the deep current will never leave us; and the colleges we represent will be better than before.

NOTES

1. David Riesman, *Constraint and Variety in American Education* (Garden City, N.Y.: Doubleday, 1958).

2. Telling comparisons of these educational philosophies are made by Douglas Sloan, *Insight/Imagination* (Westport, Conn.: Greenwood, 1983); and Huston Smith, *The Purposes of Higher Education* (New York: Harper and Sons, 1955).

3. See Frederick Rudolph, *The American College: A History* (New York: Vintage, 1962).

4. Warren Bryan Martin, "The Legacy of the Sixties: Bloodied but Unbowed," *Change* 14 (March 1982): 35-38.

5. Thomas Peters and Nancy Austin, *A Passion for Excellence* (New York: Harper and Row, 1985); see also Thomas Peters and Robert Waterman, *In Search of Excellence* (New York: Harper and Row, 1982).

6. Rosabeth Kanter, *The Change Masters: Innovation for Productivity in the American Corporation* (New York: Simon and Schuster, 1985); Robert Reich, *The Next American Frontier* (New York: Penguin, 1983). See also Frank Newman, *Higher Education and the American Resurgence* (Princeton: Princeton University Press, 1985).

7. Alexander Astin, *Achieving Educational Excellence* (San Francisco: Jossey-Bass, 1985), 224.

8. Levinson and Rosenthal, quoted in "Keeping Tradition in the Face of Change," *New York Times,* 13 January 1985, sec. 4, p. 15; see also *CEO: Corporate Leadership in Action* (New York: Basic, 1984).

9. Roy E. Moor, "Business Prospects for Midwest Liberal Arts Colleges," 12-13, a paper given at the symposium "The Liberal Arts College: The Next 25 Years," held on 22-23 June 1984 under the sponsorship of the Great Lakes Colleges Association and the Associated Colleges of the Midwest.

10. Frances FitzGerald, *America Revised* (Boston: Atlantic-Little Brown, 1979), 18.

11. George Steiner, "Warning Sounded on New York City," *New York Times,* 27 May 1985, 11.

Rendering unto Caesar:
The Dilemma of
College-Government Relations

David K. Winter

While American evangelical Christians have gained new influence and acceptance in recent decades, their colleges have encountered some highly threatening situations in matters of government policy. Some evangelical colleges have been challenged in the courts and by government agencies because they insist on exercising religious preference in hiring and promotion, others because they maintain their right to receive government aid for students and academic programs. While such pressures sometimes put the future of these colleges in a double bind, evangelical educators continue their longstanding disagreements over how broad their involvement with the government should be. Some stress the need to protect their internal religious freedom and are often willing, in exchange, to give up public support for Judeo-Christian values and symbols, including government funds for religiously infused education. Others argue that the government has a responsibility to preserve the democratic pluralism of American higher education by offering support to a wide range of colleges and universities, including those with thoroughgoing religious commitments.

These issues have ceased to be the grist for detached debates. In the past thirty years, evangelical colleges have participated very actively in the educational establishment, and many of them have become dependent on government funds, especially in the form of grants and loans to students. Threats to college-government relations, then, are threats both to their continued active participation in the mainstream of American higher education and to their very survival. In the near future, these colleges may be forced to choose between expressing their Christian beliefs throughout their campus life on the one hand and receiving any form of government support on the other. This choice would have a devastating effect on evangelical higher education, and Christian college leaders can no longer pretend that these issues can never affect their schools. To provide just a framework for discussion, let me first trace the course that has led toward this dilemma, then explain the issues presently under debate, and finally suggest that evangelical leaders think about how their movement's traditional ideal of being in the world but not of it can produce a satisfying strategy for college-government relations.

Over the past forty years, as Thomas Askew has clearly shown, evangelical colleges have grown in number, resources, and degree of participation in the larger world of higher education.[1] The presidents, deans, and faculty members of these hundred or so schools have entered vigorously into the affairs of state and national educational associations. Evangelicals hold influential positions in the Council of Independent Colleges, the National Association of Independent Colleges and Universities, the regional accrediting associations, and the state organizations of independent higher education. Evangelical colleges have been recipients of the many federal and state funding programs which have had a phenomenal growth in the past twenty years.[2] In addition, there have been numerous opportunities for evangelical colleges to benefit from governmental support for faculty research projects, the acquisition of scientific and technical equipment, campus construction, faculty development programs, and experimentation with new teaching techniques.

These opportunities developed at the same time that Christian colleges were becoming increasingly comfortable within the higher educational system of our country. They were happy to be accepted as regular members of the establishment and to conform in most ways to the practices and values of their secular colleagues. For this reason, few evangelicals noticed, or at least seemed to notice, their growing dependence upon the government for financial support. For the most part, those who did notice did not seem at all alarmed by this trend, for there was no indication that the government was interested in controlling college programs or activities. There were a few colleges known for their conservative posture who not only consistently refused direct government support but also warned that this support would bring with it government control and interference.[3] The majority of evangelical colleges, however, were swept along by the growing acceptance and respect they enjoyed and were pleased to have greater visibility and opportunity for leadership within American higher education. The benefits were attractive, and the dangers seemed small.

This relationship to the rest of the higher educational establishment and to the government reflected an important change in the attitude of evangelicals generally toward government and society. They had moved from a radically antisecular position to the belief that the church must work not only for individual conversion but for the betterment of society as a whole. This approach encouraged cooperative working relations between evangelical colleges and the various agencies of government.

As the cost of higher education has escalated, tuition and fees at independent colleges have become increasingly unaffordable for students and their families. In the last ten years students have been able to pay their tuition costs at independent colleges only by heavy dependence upon grant and loan money from federal and state governments. It is not unusual for student revenues to pay for 60 to 80 percent of the total operating budget of an independent college; and federal and state grants and loans may in turn account for roughly 25 to 30 percent of the revenues received from students. Therefore anywhere from 15 to 25 percent of the operating budget of a typical college may be received indirectly from various federal and state grant and loan programs.[4] Students in evangelical colleges have participated in such programs along with students of all higher educational institutions, but because such a high percentage of evangelical students come from middle- or even low-income families, it is probable that they are more dependent upon this source of assistance than college and university students generally.[5]

Although very few of the evangelical colleges are opposed to direct federal aid in the form of faculty research grants, institutional development programs, and even subsidies for construction costs, this remains a small part of their total income. It would be possible for them to forego this source of revenue entirely, but most of these colleges would lose several million dollars per year if they refused to accept students who use government support to pay part of their tuition costs. It is very hard to imagine how the vast majority of evangelical colleges would survive under those conditions.

Is there much danger that college students will no longer receive this financial aid? That risk appears not only possible, but to many people it is very likely. At the time this paper was being written the U.S. Senate and House of Representatives were seriously considering a number of proposals which, if enacted, would virtually destroy the existing federal aid programs. Particularly hard hit would be students from middle-income families, who comprise the vast majority of students at evangelical colleges. The new proposals would exclude most of these families on the basis of their income from any federal support under these programs.[6] Furthermore, those still eligible would be restricted to a maximum award which would not come close to tuition costs. Thus middle-income students would be ineligible for aid, and lower-income students would be eligible for only one-half or two-thirds of the actual cost, with no other means at their disposal for paying or borrowing the remaining amount. Even Secretary of Education William Bennett has admitted that the administration's proposals would probably produce a substantial shift of students from independent colleges to public higher educational institutions.[7]

It is reasonable to ask how this approach could reduce the overall cost of government when the education of these students at public institutions would be much more costly in tax support than the modest financial aid which enables them to attend independent colleges. The answer to this question is clear. The policy would not reduce the overall cost of education to government, but it would shift that cost from the federal government to state governments. If the federal government reduces student financial aid, of which it has been the primary source, many students presently attending independent colleges will move to public institutions, most of which are state universities. Thus the individual states would find it necessary to enlarge their institutions and seek additional funds from their citizens through property and income taxes. The amount of federal tax revenues devoted to higher education would go down, but state taxes would consequently have to go up.

The effect upon independent colleges would be far more severe than upon higher education generally. In most cases the amount of financial aid students receive from the federal government is much greater than what they receive from the state. There is little indication that state governments would choose to, or even be able to, increase student financial aid. Thus there would likely be a dramatic reduction in total financial aid to students attending independent colleges. Moreover, because a larger number of students would attend state institutions the states would need to spend much more for public higher education, decreasing even further their ability to support students attending independent colleges.[8]

The ramifications of such a change in federal student aid policy would be exacerbated by stipulations in many state constitutions, particularly of western states, which explicitly prevent state money from being used to support nonpublic education. In fact, even if Congress does not change student aid programs, such state stipulations in concert with other federal rulings will likely change the face of nonpublic higher education. In a recent decision, the U.S. Supreme Court ruled that aid to students is in fact aid to the institutions they attend.[9] If this ruling were applied at the state level today, many independent colleges would be in very serious trouble as students now eligible for modest assistance would be ruled ineligible. This Supreme Court ruling may be recognized ultimately as a disaster in the history of Christian higher education. Nor is it entirely logical: as others have pointed out, that same logic would regard food stamps as government support for particular grocery stores. This approach is being used to justify an extension of government interference and control in the affairs of higher educational institutions, simply because most students bring with them some form of federal financial aid, such as government guaranteed loans they have received from private financial institutions.

A more serious problem confronts the colleges that are not only independent but evangelical as well. Some of the language in the state constitutions and in the policies of these states restricts any public money from being sent in support of institutions which are "pervasively sectarian." In a strict and technical sense it can be argued that Christian colleges are not sectarian. But it seems very likely that when this is tested, government officials will conclude that certainly these institutions *are* pervasively sectarian. Some of the specific features government officials may find most significant include the homogeneity of the student body in terms of religious orientation, restrictions on the faculty to espouse a wide variety of positions and values, a requirement to attend chapel, required academic courses in doctrine or theology, the designation of certain buildings or facilities for religious purposes, and the existence of statements in the catalog regarding a central religious purpose or mission.[10]

Should Christian colleges in these states be tested by these criteria in any publicly charged situation, they would face serious problems. At Westmont, for example, the college motto is "In all things Christ preeminent," taken from Colossians 1:18. The College generally presents itself in that light, indicating that every campus program expresses its commitment to Jesus Christ. Westmont claims this makes a significant difference, that faith in Christ influences athletic programs, student activities, and the way in which academic courses are taught. Yet when the officials from the state or federal government visit

Westmont's campus they hear a different emphasis. College officials, in order to dispel any charges of being narrowly or harmfully sectarian, speak of the genuine academic freedom that exists, the diversity—within limits—that is represented among students and faculty, the lack of discrimination in race and sex, and the generous spirit Westmont seeks to foster in its students toward people of different convictions.

In spite of their good intentions, evangelical educators can easily be seen as speaking out of both sides of their mouths. They very much desire that all faculty and perhaps all employees be personally committed to the evangelical Christian faith. Many educators would like to continue requiring that all students have a Christian commitment, that they abide by behavioral standards they believe are thoroughly Christian, and that they enroll in a series of courses in which they can develop their understanding of Scripture and the Christian faith. Yet it seems likely that given the trend of greater public scrutiny of government expenditures to private organizations such as religious schools, there will be increasing questions regarding the eligibility of evangelical colleges for public funds. These schools will be under pressure to relax or discontinue some of their religious activities if they are to remain eligible for direct or indirect government support. How extensive and far-reaching this pressure may be will vary from state to state. There is at least the potential that evangelical educators will give in on one issue after another until all significant remnants of their Christian mission have been eliminated.

Be that as it may, at the very time in history when evangelical colleges are being pressured to reduce their religiosity and perhaps even their Christian commitment, there is another force that is beginning to bring pressure in the opposite direction. Civil rights laws, which specifically exclude churches and church-related institutions from compliance with broad-ranging antidiscrimination legislation, encourage evangelical colleges to emphasize their religiousness. Because they are Christian institutions, they have not been required to employ or even accept as students those without a Christian commitment.

In the past few years, however, this privilege has been threatened and is currently in jeopardy. The Internal Revenue Service is now deciding whether particular institutional policies are true expressions of religious beliefs. Christianity, for example, is considered a legitimate religion in this country and is granted certain exemptions under the tax code. But if a college's particular brand of Christianity leads it to prohibit interracial dating, then that college may no longer be eligible for tax exemption. The implications down the road of this particular decision against Bob Jones University[11] are disturbingly clear. The civil rights movement has become such a powerful force within this society that under its mandate the religious rights of people are protected only when they do not seem to conflict with current values regarding ethnic, sex, race, age, or handicap discrimination.

Recently, one evangelical college was in litigation with its state government over whether it is sufficiently religious to qualify for an exemption from the general prohibition of religious discrimination in the hiring of employees. In this particular case, which was eventually settled in favor of the college, the school's advocates presented all evidence possible to indicate the comprehensive and pervasive nature of its evangelical Christian commitment.[12] It appears that in the near future all Christian colleges will have to demonstrate more clearly their fundamentally religious nature if they are to maintain their freedom to hire employees on the basis of religious preference. Even churches may be in danger of losing this freedom.

So evangelical colleges find themselves in a strange position. In order to maintain their students' eligibility for government financial assistance they may be forced to minimize the extent of their Christian activities. Yet in order to maintain the right to exercise religious preference in hiring they need to appear as religious as possible. In the opinion of some, evangelical colleges are being drawn into a trap. There may be no way they can continue receiving government support—even the indirect support they receive from students who bring federal or state financial aid—and at the same time maintain their freedom to use religious preference in the hiring of employees.

Note that government officials are quick to declare themselves innocent of any desire to limit the operation of evangelical colleges. In fact, they frequently pay these schools tribute for the diversity they represent within higher education. But then they go on to warn evangelical educators that if Christian colleges are so religious that they must exclude people who do not share the evangelical persuasion then, of course, the government cannot possibly support them with public funds.[13]

Behind these political matters are some very fundamental philosophical issues related to the role of the Christian church in society. These questions are not new, of course. The history of the Christian church provides examples of earnest Christians who maintained their separation from the world, sometimes to the point of irrelevance, as other Christians assumed leadership in the secular society, on occasion selling their souls in the process. Currently, such diversity among evangelicals as that represented by Jerry Falwell and Jim Wallis reminds us that it is very difficult for evangelicals to reach agreement on the appropriate stance of Christians toward government and society. In all probability Christian colleges will never establish a secure and consistent role within the context of higher education and the government unless the evangelical movement resolves the fundamental issues in its relationship to American public life.

One expression of this dilemma evangelicals face is the question, Should evangelicals consider themselves part of what our government represents, and thus have a legitimate right to share its benefits, or does the government represent the secular component of society from which Christians should separate themselves? More specifically, if in fact government money comes (in part) from taxes paid by evangelical Christian people, shouldn't researchers at evangelical colleges apply for federal grants along with faculty from any other institution? If evangelical colleges are effectively educating a portion of society's young men and women shouldn't the government assist them in that task, which is surely for "the public good"? If cultural and religious pluralism represents the American way of life, why should colleges and universities dominated by secular and humanistic philosophies be heavily subsidized by public funds while tax-paying Christian families receive little or no assistance for the education of their sons and daughters in Christian institutions?

Within the evangelical world there seem to be three distinct attitudes or approaches toward the government. There are some who are so heartened by the success that evangelicals have had in gaining leadership roles in American public life that they seek to increase their influence even further and to assume responsibility for at least the moral direction of American government. Many evangelicals seem to assume that an evangelical of perhaps conservative persuasion should control the affairs of our national life. Those who operate from this point of view find themselves arguing vigorously for the constitutional right to practice their religion at the same time they are arguing for the prohibition of behavior which is inconsistent with their particular religious beliefs.[14]

In contrast to the above, a second group of evangelicals argues with equal passion that Christians should have as little as possible to do with government. They see the government as the foremost expression of "the world" they are to "flee from" and are thus proud of the contrast between themselves and all that the government represents. Adherents of this approach require that they separate themselves from society in general and imply that they should sever all financial dependence upon national, state, and local governments.

A third group of evangelicals believe they should actively work within the governmental process toward the goal of a national pluralism that would allow a fair opportunity for evangelical institutions as an appropriate and legitimate part of our national life. Of course this requires a respect for the rights of those with whom they differ and a willingness to compete fairly in the marketplace of ideas and activities.

Christian colleges each express a particular combination of these three approaches toward society and government. Moreover, this combination for any college is not fixed and unchanging. At times evangelical colleges are eager to join those evangelicals who wish to see government more effectively control and enforce conservative laws which appear compatible with their beliefs. At other times they give the impression that the government is their great enemy and cynically refuse to cooperate or participate in its affairs. Then there are times when they join forces with respected church-related colleges and simply seek a fair share of government support for independent colleges with a religious heritage.

This ambiguity in our posture toward the government and American public life in general may have contributed to the development of an awkward and even dangerous situation for Christian colleges. In the near future they may find themselves vacillating between acceptance of their heavy dependence upon the government for financial support and a growing desire to be independent and even more explicitly Christian in their educational programs and campus activities.

Three basic strategies come to mind for evangelical colleges to consider as a response to this predicament. First of all, some colleges are aggressively challenging in the courts the government's influence and control. Up to this point it appears that this effort has not been successful. In comparison with the situation ten years ago, several factors have changed: the Internal Revenue Service is now playing an active role in determining the tax-exempt status of religious colleges; the Supreme Court has ruled that government assistance to students is evidence of assistance to their institutions; and it appears that in the future the U.S. Congress may legislate that government assistance to any part of an institutional program brings all activities of that institution under federal review and control.[15]

The second approach is expressed when evangelical colleges continue to go about their business with the hope that the government will not investigate their religious activities and hiring policy. This approach appears to be simply unrealistic, for some colleges are being investigated at the present time, and there is no reason to believe there will be less interest in this matter by the government in the future. It is a dangerous approach as well. If colleges do not prepare for a challenge from the government, they may feel compelled, when the challenge does come, as it likely will, to concede either some of their present religiously based control over hiring and admissions or their present levels of governmental financial support.

There is a third approach, however. Colleges could prepare their defense in advance of the challenge. A proper and effective defense will require a new and thorough evaluation of all aspects of present policies to determine whether they are indeed essential to the Christian mission of an institution. If they are not, they could be eliminated. If they are, they could and should be strengthened. There might not be agreement among evangelical colleges and universities, but at least individual colleges could determine where to draw the line between which compromises are possible and which are impossible if they are to maintain their Christian purpose.

Leaders and supporters of Christian higher education have devoted relatively little effort to a tough-minded examination of the various components of their programs and strategies, nor to an evaluation of the effectiveness of these components in performing their Christian educational mission. Evangelical educators must choose their battles carefully, for some policies and programs are more important than others. Some institutions, for example, may choose to give up religious preference in the hiring of certain categories of employees. Some might decide to accept a percentage of students who have not made a Christian commitment if there is clear indication of their personal support for the Christian program of the institution. On the other hand, it is clear that the decision to hire regular faculty or administrators who are not deeply committed to the Christian faith would begin a process leading to the eventual extinction of the Christian character of an institution.

Can evangelical colleges retain their distinctive and essential Christian characteristics and programs and, at the same time, be considered sufficiently nonsectarian to receive direct or even indirect assistance from the federal and state governments? How evangelicals answer this question must be consistent with biblical principles and represent a realistic appraisal of their relationship to American public life. Their answer must not be based upon expedience, or simply on pressures from government, but upon a strong and thoughtful concept of the evangelical role and responsibility within American higher education. They may be called upon to provide the answer sooner than they think.

For Further Reading

Balz, Frank J. *Federal Student Assistance and Categorical Programs.* Washington, D.C.: National Institute of Independent Colleges and Universities (NIICU), 1981.

Fiske, Edward B. "Higher Education's New Economics." *New York Times Magazine,* 1 May 1983.

Hodgkinson, Virginia Ann. *Perspectives and Projections: Student Aid Planning and Educational Policy.* Washington, D.C.: NIICU, 1982.

Lewis, Karen J. *Grove City College v. Bell and Its Aftermath.* Washington, D.C.: Congressional Research Service, Library of Congress, 1985.

Making the Case for Independents. Washington, D.C.: National Association of Independent Colleges and Universities, NIICU, 1983.

Vande Graaf, Paul J. "The Program-Specific Reach of Title IX." *Columbia Law Review* 83 (June 1983): 1210-44.

Wilson, Charles H., Jr. *Tilton v. Richardson.* Washington, D.C.: Association of American Colleges, 1971. *Tilton v. Richardson* was the first test of the legality of making federal grants to church-related colleges.

NOTES

1. See Thomas A. Askew's essay, "Evangelical Higher Education Since World War II," in this volume.

2. The major growth in federal aid stems from the Higher Education Act of 1965 and the Educational Amendments of 1972 and 1976. This legislation authorized the Pell Grant (formerly the Basic Educational Opportunity Grant, or BEOG), the Supplemental Educational Opportunity Grant (SEOG), the State Student Incentive Grant (SSIG), the College Work Study Program (CWS), the National Direct Student Loan program (NDSL), and the Guaranteed Student Loan program (GSL). In the four years following the 1976 amendments the total distributed for all six programs increased from $4,296,120,784 in 1976 to $6,645,304,054 in 1979—a 54.7 percent increase. These and other figures are found in Frank J. Balz, *Federal Student Assistance and Categorical Programs* (Washington, D.C.: National Institute of Independent Colleges and Universities, 1981).

3. Of the colleges that refused direct federal support, Grove City in Pennsylvania is the best known because of the Supreme Court ruling in *Grove City College v. Bell*, 104 S. Ct. 1211 (1984), which concluded that aid to students constitutes federal assistance to the college as well. While Grove City received no federal money directly, some 5 percent of its students received BEOGs and 15 percent were aided by GSLs. Direct federal aid has been refused by other evangelical colleges including Bethel College (Minn.) and Wheaton College (Ill.), and by Christian-oriented colleges such as Hillsdale College (Mich.).

4. At Westmont, state and federal government student aid in 1984-85 totaled about $2,750,500, or 20 percent of the total operating revenues. This percentage has decreased since 1981 as federal aid has been cut.

5. A 1982 study of 59 Christian College Coalition schools revealed that all of the colleges participated in some federal student financial aid program and that together they received over $96,900,000 in federal aid, which amounted to an average of $1,076 per participating student in each federal program. Many students participated in more than one program.

6. The newsletter of the American Council on Education, *Higher Education and National Affairs* (11 February 1985), reported that under President Reagan's budget proposals, including capping eligibility for GSLs at an adjusted gross family income of $32,500, almost one million middle-income borrowers would be ineligible for the GSL program. In addition, 808,000 middle-income students would be dropped from eligibility for Pell Grants.

7. Keith B. Richberg, "Bennett Backs College Aid Cuts," *Washington Post*, 12 February 1985.

8. In California, the 1983 expenditure for public colleges and universities was $3,758,126,000, and the amount spent for state scholarships in private colleges was $45,268,000. If six to eight thousand students moved from private to public colleges, the required increase in state expenditures for public college scholarships and facilities would be considerably more than $45 million. See the California Postsecondary Education Commission's *Director's Report*, January, February, 1982.

9. *Grove City College v. Bell*, 104 S. Ct. 1211 (1984).

10. Charles H. Wilson, Jr., *Tilton v. Richardson* (Washington, D.C.: Association of American Colleges, 1971), 15, 32, 42-52.

11. "Bob Jones University v. United States," *Higher Education and National Affairs*, 8 October 1982, 1-4.

12. *Seattle Pacific University v. State of Washington.* See also "Court Rules with Seattle Pacific in Employment Practices Dispute," *Christian College News* 11 (April 1986): 1.

13. *Tilton v. Richardson* was the first test of the legality of making federal grants to church-related colleges. What was clearly prohibited then (and not rescinded since) was "exclusion of students and faculty members on strictly religious grounds." Wilson, *Tilton v. Richardson,* 48.

14. Many court cases illustrate this religious fervor; note, for example, *Wallace v. Joffree,* 104 S. Ct. 1704 (1984), concerning prayer in public schools; *Vaughn v. Reed,* 313 F. Supp. 431 (1979), concerning religious instruction on school premises; *Dale v. Board of Education, Lemmon Independent School District,* 316 N.W. 2d 108 (S. Dak. 1982), concerning teaching biblical creationism in public schools. Activities relating to the issue of abortion are another arena of concern.

15. Two bills were introduced in the 99th Congress: S272, the "Civil Rights Amendment Act of 1985," and S431/HR700, the "Civil Rights Restoration Act of 1985." Both bills would expand the meaning of "program" or "activity" to include the total educational institution—that is, rules for the operation of any federally assisted program or activity could be extended to cover the operation of the entire institution if funding for the program is to be continued. S431 has been stalled since 1985 and in the spring of 1987 was in the Senate Labor and Human Resources Committee. Edward Kennedy, Committee Chair, held hearings in April 1987. The American Council on Education supports the measure, while the National Association of Independent Colleges and Universities has represented the problems its passage would cause independent institutions.

Consumerism and the Christian College: A Call to Life in an Age of Death

Douglas Frank

The popular evangelist Billy Sunday, whose charisma dominated American revivalism in the beginning decades of our century, contributed the following social critique during the course of his New York City revival crusade in 1917.

> I believe the most God-forsaken, good-for-nothing, useless woman on earth is an American society woman whose life is frappes and there is nothing, my friends, to her but a frame upon which to hang fashionable clothes, and a digestive apparatus to digest highly seasoned foods. . . . Hags of uncleanness today, they walk our streets, they ride in their limousines, sail in their private yachts, they look from behind French plate glass and hide behind rich tapestries. . . . They quaff their wine from gold and silver tankards and they eat from . . . hand-painted china and society today, my friends, is fast hastening to the judgment that overtook Pompeii . . . when God Almighty made old Mount Vesuvius vomit and puke in a hemorrhage of lava.[1]

Sunday was not a very well educated man, but he had an instinctive feel for the meaning of his times and for the special anxieties of fellow Christians and fellow Americans as they made their passage into the twentieth century. In his indictment of the "American society woman," Billy Sunday showed himself something of a prophet. The evangelist was describing in his own idiom that fruit of modernity which was only beginning to ripen in his time, the consumer culture. It was still too early for him to see that the delights of material display and self-gratification would eventually spread beyond the wealthiest classes, whose excesses bore the brunt of his indictment. That spread was not far off, however. At the very moment he spoke, in fact, advertisers and their agents were consciously shaping their ads to hook the envy of middle-class Americans for the luxurious tastes of the aristocracy, and economic conservatives were commending capitalism for its ability to provide aristocratic comforts to the masses. Sunday's focus on the woman as paradigmatic consumer, on the other hand, while obviously sexist, revealed a solid intuition, since advertisers unabashedly directed their media appeals to what they perceived to be the more easily exploited sex. As one advertiser exclaimed, "the proper study of mankind is MAN, . . . but the proper study of markets is WOMAN."[2]

The growth of advertising and the rise of consumerism in America are receiving increasing scholarly attention of late, and many scholars agree that the period from 1890 to 1920 marked the most rapid acceleration of these trends. Worries about industrial overproduction were rife. Giant industrialists and the new advertising agencies, bolstered by recent findings in psychology, made it their business to replace the old ethic of self-restraint, thrift, and the suppression of impulse or desire with a new ethic of instant self-gratification and the cultivation of infinite desire.[3] Their messages were blatant assaults on the old Protestant morality.[4] Life is for fun, they said; seek luxury, comfort, and ease. Every human desire is healthy, particularly those we can gratify for a small price.

Billy Sunday sensed an assault on Christian morality, but he did not have the distance on his own time or the critical tools to understand it fully. His loyalty to the free enterprise system, the very source of this assault, was unshakeable. He saw no irony in his self-serving public associations with John Wanamaker, for example, even though Wanamaker owned one of the earliest and most successful department stores, those "temples of consumerism," and as one of the leading advertisers of his day was in the front ranks of the prophets of self-gratification.[5] This association was especially ironic in light of Sunday's statements that men and women "are hiding behind and beneath stocks and bonds, dry goods, infidelity, whiskey, beer, love of ease, my friends, Sunday and Sabbath desecration. Genuineness, purity, Christian nobility and integrity are lost in the search for fortune, and in their ambition to gratify their desires to drink at the bubbly spring of pleasure."[6] While he knew the wrongness of it, Sunday could think of no antidote for the decay of morality but personal salvation and heroic moral exertion, which, as today's television religion amply illustrates, the twentieth-century consumer society would have no trouble co-opting.[7]

Christian college students, faculty, and administrators today need to heed Billy Sunday's earlier warnings, for daily and hourly they are utterly encircled and battered by the central, nonnegotiable message of fully matured consumerist society: at all costs, gratify your desires and drink at the bubbly spring of pleasure. It is no longer a secret that something has happened since the 1950s to alter the relationship of the evangelical subculture to the wider American culture.[8] I suggest that this change is the result of evangelicals' encounter with the irresistible power of the media within a context of the infinite proliferation of goods and services.

The single crucial step for evangelicals, I suspect, was the decision to permit television into the Christian home. Television is the single most powerful tool for destroying both sales resistance and any moral prohibitions which would inhibit profligacy. Since Billy Sunday's day, all the advertising media have developed ever more persuasive means to propagate the ethic of immediate self-gratification. Their appeals to deep human yearnings to escape, to possess, to copulate, to win, to be utterly happy and fulfilled are by turns blatant and subliminal. Their promises to fulfill these longings by means of their product are lies, but very seductive lies. Even when we recognize these promises for what they are, we cannot escape the penetration of their images into our spirits, nor can we easily resist joining the media-contrived consensus: life is for the gratification of desires and for drinking at the bubbly spring of pleasure.[9]

Television, movies, magazines, and popular music encircle and possess all modern people to some degree with these messages. But our youth have never breathed any other air than this—indeed, they come to college with TV sets under their arms and rock music plugged into their heads—and they are unaware of how consciously contrived and polluted is the medium they inhabit. Some of their parents and church leaders suspect, though, and have tried to fight the more blatant results with Billy Sunday's rudimentary techniques—that is, by urging self-restraint and high moral standards. This has created dissonance for youth, all the more confusing because parents and churches themselves are under the spell of consumerism and self-gratification. Witness their unthinking purchase of each new gadget that comes on the market, their love affairs with new cars and the latest fashions, their luxury vacations sponsored by reputable Christian organizations and authorities, the material displays prevalent on television's so-called Christian talk shows, and the compulsion Christian congregations feel to compete in building the most ostentatious "state of the art" churches. Evangelical students have had to live with authorities who use God and the Bible to keep them "good" while the ubiquitous consumer propaganda urges them to do whatever feels good. Very early, it appears, the propaganda wins out, both at the level of a grinding inner yearning and more obviously at the level of behavior. But in evangelical youth, this often does not come without a nagging burden of guilt.

A provocative new study of evangelical college students by James Davison Hunter indicates that during four years of college education these students become increasingly more "civil" and tolerant of moral deviation, less vocationally and morally ascetic, and more "secularized" in matters of family and sex roles.[10] Hunter's documentation is far-reaching and productive of rich insights. While he hypothesizes that the educational process is itself responsible for the increased "secularization" of college students, I would argue that the college experience is merely permissive and reinforcing of tendencies that already exist. The students who enter evangelical colleges as freshmen are thoroughly secularized already. They already believe that feeling good is the only thing that counts. They are already civil and tolerant—and thus already prepared for the ethic of "anything goes" on which the consumer culture thrives. Education comes to their rescue by offering them a critique of and a certain freedom from the authorities, like family, church, and Bible, that made them live their secularized lives with an accompanying burden of guilt. Too often, of course, their critique is adolescent and intellectually cheap. Rather than a biblically rooted affirmation of faith in the living God who dissolves human moralities and cultural securities, it is a quick fix for an intolerable dissonance.

At our colleges, in my experience, these students meet and come to trust faculty who have been raised in (and are at odds with) an authoritarian, anti-intellectual, and ideologically inflexible environment. These faculty—especially the younger generation, who more readily attract the interest of college students—are themselves often immature in their rebellion against embarrassing subcultural constraints. They have been secularized, at the deepest of levels, in graduate school and may be hanging onto belief by the slimmest of threads—emotional loyalties, the convenient selective ignoring of key biblical insights, shaky intellectual and spiritual rationalizations, and constant hidden compromises. These faculty members are themselves tossed to and fro by the ethic of immediate self-gratification just as their students are. And they are often embittered because, in a sense, they are not permitted to grow up but must assent to doctrines and abide by moral codes that represent constituency prejudice rather than personal conviction.

As a result of all this, many faculty members tend to hide themselves in their academic disciplines and to talk about God in politically safe, though often insincere, terms, or to depict him as a distant and purely intellectual reality, or even not deal with him at all. Many suffer from an evangelically approved failure of imagination, if not inspiration. They have never caught the vision of an evangelicalism which is boldly prophetic and also humble, critical of its own institutions as well as of society at large, in faithful obedience to Scripture and to the God who stands above both religion and culture. Nor have they seen the possibilities of that kind of moral and intellectual ambiguity that flows from faith and humility rather than from consumerism, secularism, and unbelief. The dissonance and confusion of our professors—often observed by administrators concerned more for public orthodoxy than for real commitment and often hidden behind attractive personalities or articulate lectures—play into the hands of students who are in the market for a quick fix. Those students cannot possibly realize what emotional and spiritual time-bombs lie behind such a grab-bag of subterfuges, compromises, and unresolved personal pathologies.

These things will not change until a bracing blast of truth is admitted to the halls of evangelical academe. It will take an uncommon courage for our faculties to confront the depths of our hidden unbelief and despair as well as the extent of our infection by the many forms of consumerism and secularism. At the same time, however, it will be increasingly difficult to hide our mild distaste for the book that continually calls us to die, when all about us beckons us to live the life of gusto. I pray we will face afresh the word that supports neither moral rigidity nor doctrinaire permissiveness, neither the myths of the patriotic Right nor the idealism and naivete of the Left. And I pray that we may embrace the God whose wrath cannot be read out of the Bible and who judges the follies of humanity in order that he might save humans. If we do not do these things, I am afraid we will only encourage the prolongation of the restless immaturity which is one of the most ineluctable and enduring fruits of the consumer society.

If an evangelical faculty does struggle to speak the truth about the living God—and thus also about its own rampant unbelief, an unfaithful evangelicalism, and an enslaving society—it will more than likely find itself fighting an administration hopelessly stuck in the mire of consumerism. Those of us who have pursued careers within the Christian college setting know how readily our college administrations have adopted modern rationalizing and bureaucratizing procedures to conduct the business of the institution, particularly in matters financial.

They have done so even though the logic of technical efficiency (which requires utter devotion to finding "the one best way," according to Jacques Ellul)[11] is not complete until its reign is total.

The Christian college is thus more and more difficult to distinguish from Revlon or Miller Beer. Increasingly, and particularly in times of economic contraction, its goal is that of any modern corporation, namely, financial stability and institutional longevity.[12] It is too often run for the benefit of the bureaucrats who make the decisions—albeit the "necessary ones"—and not for the benefit of its students. To achieve its goals, it must treat donors as a source of capital, parents and students as its "market," graduates as its "product," and faculty and staff as "labor costs." Its appeals for money or students are ever more technically flawless and reminiscent of television advertising. Its promises of customer satisfaction—whether vocational success, evangelical leadership, spiritual heroism, individuality, or finding a mate—are inflated, generally untested, and, I believe, illusory. Promotional literature is designed with wishful thinking, not the truth, in mind. Its source is the latest scientific information about which images appeal to and manipulate the psyche most effectively. Faculty are often unaware of the promises being made on their behalf, or react with cynicism if they are aware. Parents are generally told whatever they want to hear by administrators who either have no idea what goes on in the classroom and dormitory or cannot speak it aloud if they do.

Parents, meanwhile, often collaborate with administrators in the institutional politics of deception and self-deception. What they seem to want to hear is that their children will remain respectable evangelicals, and will make it in the consumer society. Young adults function as consumable items for these parents, making them look good in the eyes of their peers, as would a nicely tailored suit of clothes or a facelift. In this milieu, the gospel of Jesus Christ itself becomes a kind of commodity, a potion which, if taken in correct doses, promises to help a student be a *better* doctor, *better* businesswoman, *better* engineer—but not, for that reason, less affluent or less enslaved.[13] The Christian college—oddly enough unexamined by the critical, educated eye on which the liberal arts prides itself—joins the biggest game in town, the compulsive but unconscious and unremarked genuflection before the idol of consumerism. It rocks no one's boat, except by accident, and it attracts none of the opprobrium that good religious people heaped upon Jesus when he suggested that the best among them was a slave to sin and a child of the devil, the father of lies.

The seemingly unstoppable secularization of evangelicalism, upon which Hunter and others have remarked[14] and which I have been relating to the demon of consumerism, will not be turned back by college personnel who honor the institution's survival more than speaking the truth. Our bureaucratic conservatism, which sometimes approaches cynicism, will dictate that we continue Billy Sunday's slavish adherence to the myths of America, which are not unlike the myths of Babylon during Habakkuk's day: that we are a superior nation, that we are a truly free people, that our affluence is a reward for godliness, that our morality qualifies us for political leadership, that the free enterprise system is biblical, that technology is a neutral tool that we can use freely for good or evil.[15] No doubt, we will continue to honor the strange contradiction which gives us the best of both worlds—an insistence that America is falling into the hands of infidels and degenerates, but that she is also God's favorite and that we deserve as much of her bounty and security as the sinners next door. This will keep us from admitting that we are a culture utterly enslaved and in extremis. You cannot raise funds with this message. It would not please alumni to list their divorces, abortions, and suicides alongside their marriages, children, and advancements in the alumni magazines. But you can hear this message in the voices of certain old or dying men and women of our day, who cannot keep quiet about the tissue of lies which is modern society; and you can see it in the faces, and the troubled lives, of the young men and women who come to us for a Christian education.

The old and dying (or dead) that I am thinking of are not much listened to by evangelicals. But they are not obscure thinkers: Ernest Becker, Walker Percy, Jacques Ellul, Isaac Bashevis Singer, Flannery O'Connor, William Stringfellow, old Uncle Sammler of Saul Bellow's novel—and there are others. *They* know we are in extremis. Together, they issue a powerful indictment of our times as "an authentic dark age," in Stringfellow's words, "a time in which the power of death is pervasive and militant and in which people exist without hope or else in pursuit of transient, fraudulent, or delusive hopes."[16] On the surface, prosperity reigns—even happiness. "Never has there been a world so rich, . . . so full of avid consumers," admits Jacques Ellul; but never, he persists, "have people reached a comparable degree of moral, spiritual, and psychic decadence. . . ."[17]

It is the old and dying among our social prophets who can see how thoroughly modern humans have given themselves over to the power of death—"not the death people die," in the words of Walker Percy, "but the death people live."[18] A powerful manifestation of death, asserts Stringfellow, is the technologically inspired "articulation of conditioning, marketing, and merchandising techniks capable of utterly overpowering the human faculties of reason or conscience, of neutralizing human critical responses, and of programming more or less everyone to purchase and consume whatever technology produces."[19] And where do the churches stand, as our society commits collective suicide?[20] The churches, Walker Percy laments, "smell of death," and "believers now believe anything and everything and do not love the truth, are in fact in despair of the truth, and that is death."[21] We must suspect, according to one, that God has abandoned us.[22] Ellul captures well the mood of these old men and women: "I am sick over the world I shall leave behind, sick at heart, physically and intellectually sick."[23]

But these are just the old. What of the young? They are not listened to either, I think. So often, as well-manicured consumers, they appear successful, glib, and happy. But their eyes, and their lives, tell of the fragility of their sense of self, their inability to find firm footing in a landscape of lies and false promises. Too often they tell of parents whose own indefinite desires and yearnings for fulfillment eventuated in the bearing of children as commodities for their own pleasure. Their parents loved them on the condition they not complicate a lifestyle of corporate climbing and personal freedom. Their absent fathers and emotionally starved and distant mothers bequeathed to their children the oral cravings, the capacity only for shallow relationships, the longing for quick intimacy, the violent swings of self-esteem and the deep rage that mark both the narcissistic parent and child. Our students speak to us of a trust between the generations that has been broken: by divorce, by cold estrangement, by violence and sexual abuse in the home, by enslavement to fun-seeking alternating with cheap moralism, by day-care desertion and the rest of the symptoms mirroring the disintegration of the contemporary family[24]—the contemporary evangelical family too, as we who fill the pews certainly must know from personal experience.

The symptoms of our college students speak increasingly of a psychological battering at the hands of a society which unrelentingly conspires to sell goods rather than nurture human beings. Those symptoms are familiar to college counseling departments: bulimia and anorexia, boredom and inertia, suicidal urges and depression, obsessions with bodily appearance, profligate and almost panicked but generally unfulfilling sexual activity, anger and helplessness and emptiness—all indications that they have heard the messages whose effect is to deprive them of any sense of self, to encourage anxiety, self-consciousness, unfulfillable yearnings, and the oral hunger of the ideal consumer. The violence our society perpetrates against the human spirit is nowhere more evident, in my opinion, than in the lives of the most sensitive of our Christian college students.

There is a part of me that wishes to say farewell to the evangelical subculture, my subculture, whose gradual demise we seem to be witnessing in our day. Its combination of sterile rationalism, self-inflated heroism, Enlightenment complacency and rigid moralism, defensiveness, and self-congratulation, along with its domestication of God and its too-ready identification of its own ways with God's ways—all this seems a historic tragedy to me. When the times called for a faithful, humble remnant witnessing to the God who says, "I am doing a work in your days which you would not believe if told," we evangelicals built instead a pious Tower of Babel within which to fortify our sense of superiority. It is only now becoming obvious that our tower was poorly built in the first place, and that it is crumbling under the artillery of modernity. In this crumbling, and in our society's surrender to the lusts of its heart, perhaps we see the judgment of a merciful God. But in any crumbling, people get hurt. Our students are foremost among these people. If we do not mourn for a crumbling subculture, we must at least mourn for our students, in the spirit of Jesus in Luke 19:41-44:

> And when he drew near and saw the city he wept over it, saying, "Would that even today you knew the things that make for peace! But now they are hid from your eyes. For the days shall come upon you, when your enemies will cast up a bank about you and surround you, and hem you in on every side, and dash you to the ground, you and your children within you, and they will not leave one stone upon another in you; because you did not know the time of your visitation.

I plead with you for these young people, dying while encircled by plenty and its ceaseless propaganda. Do not enlarge the climate of lies in which they must live, just to keep the dormitories full. Do not embellish the propaganda of consumerism with a tawdry sheen of Christian moralism, just to make our students the upwardly mobile urban and suburban professionals that many of their parents admire. I plead with you not to hide from them the truth about our disintegrating society and world, just to help them achieve the short-term happiness that is the very essence of the consumer mentality. I plead with you not to falsify and bring reproach on the gospel of Jesus Christ by reading the Scriptures exploitively and selectively, either to justify the enslaving status quo of a consumer culture or to offer critiques of an evangelical subculture which arise out of rebellion and unbelief rather than faith in the living God.

Let us begin to forge a biblical alternative to the poles of pharisaism and cynicism, and let us make sure it has some critical bite. I urge you not to turn the good news into a consumer commodity that offers success and happiness instead of sorrow and suffering and the joy that smiles through real tears. I plead with you not to take satisfaction in brave and sterile defenses of inerrancy which turn the Bible into a wooden relic, all the more because it is so generally unread, disbelieved in its most pointed messages, and an object of intense though subdued hatred by many of our students, if the truth be known. If you do not love the word of God more than life itself, more than the institution you work for, more than the salary you make; if you do not crave and are not gripped by its truth; if you do not find in it the word which casts a strangely penetrating—the only really surprising—light on all of human learning; if you do not see in it a wisdom more compelling, though also more foolish, than the latest manuals for fund-raisers or the current drivel of *Megatrends* and *In Search of Excellence;* then, I beg of you, confess these matters openly and humbly to your colleagues and your students, making them a matter of dialogue and prayer, and letting the public relations chips fall where they may. If you cannot do that, then for the sake of our students reexamine your decision to teach or administer in the Christian college.

Christ's call to us in Christian colleges today is the same call he has always given to humans: repent and be saved; weep and lament and be sorrowful, for our sorrow will be turned to joy; believe and proclaim the testimony of Jesus; worship God; know the truth and continue in his word; and finally be set free. These all mean something to education, but we have not begun to ask what. They call us, not to rush into action, not to devise a program for shoring up evangelicalism as the technocrat and the bureaucrat in us might do, but to wait and to pray and to witness to the righteousness and the faithfulness of the God of Jesus Christ. If we wait and pray and witness thus, perhaps God will grace our emptiness with a fresh, disturbing, and unforeseeable breeze from his Spirit, and save our Christian colleges from the triviality, the irrelevance, and the brilliant success of Diet Pepsi. If he does not, our colleges will only continue to add the weight of religion to the oppressive forces which hold humanity, more firmly with each passing day, in their grip of death.

NOTES

1. Sunday, "Why Call Ye Me Lord," sermon, New York, 15 April 1917, typescript, 25-26; box 6, reel 9, collection 61, Papers of William and Helen Sunday, Library of Grace Theological Seminary, Winona Lake, Indiana (microfilm in the Archives of the Billy Graham Center, Wheaton, Illinois). This collection is cited hereinafter as the Sunday Papers.

2. Quoted in Michael Schudson, *Advertising, The Uneasy Persuasion: Its Dubious Impact on American Society* (New York: Basic, 1984), 173.

3. Recent studies of the rise of consumerism include Daniel Boorstin, *The Americans: The Democratic Experience* (New York: Random House, 1974), 89-164; Stuart Ewen, *Captains of Consciousness: Advertising and the Social Roots of the Consumer Culture* (New York: McGraw-Hill, 1976); Stuart Ewen and Elizabeth Ewen, *Channels of Desire: Mass Images and the Shaping of American Consciousness* (New York: McGraw-Hill, 1982); Richard Wightman Fox and T. J. Jackson Lears, eds., *The Culture of Consumption: Critical Essays in American History 1880–1980* (New York: Pantheon, 1983); and Neil Harris, "The Drama of Consumer Desire," in *Yankee Enterprise: The Rise of the American System of Manufactures,* ed. Otto Mayr and Robert C. Post (Washington, D.C.: Smithsonian Institution Press, 1981), 189-217.

On the rise of modern advertising, consult Stephen Fox, *The Mirror Makers: A History of American Advertising and Its Creators* (New York: William Morrow, 1984); Daniel Pope, *The Making of Modern Advertising* (New York: Basic, 1983); and Schudson, *Advertising, The Uneasy Persuasion.*

Representative early advertising psychologists include Harry L. Hollingworth, *Advertising and Selling: Principles of Appeal and Response* (New York: D. Appleton, 1913); D. T. Howard, *The Psychology of Advertising* (New York: Dodd, Mead, 1921); and Walter Dill Scott, "The Psychology of Advertising," *Atlantic Monthly* 93 (January 1904): 29-36.

Selected helpful treatments of economic and social developments at the turn of the century include Robert H. Wiebe, *The Search for Order, 1877–1920* (New York: Hill and Wang, 1967); Alan Trachtenberg, *The Incorporation of America: Culture and Society in the Gilded Age* (New York: Hill and Wang, 1982); and Alfred D. Chandler, Jr., *The Visible Hand: The Managerial Revolution in American Business* (Cambridge: Harvard University Press, Belknap Press, 1977). See especially Chandler's accounts of the growth of the tobacco and breakfast cereal industries, 290-94.

4. For a seminal study of the impact of consumerist capitalism on the Protestant ethic, see Daniel Bell, *The Cultural Contradictions of Capitalism* (New York: Basic, 1976).

5. On Sunday's association with Wanamaker, see William G. McLoughlin, Jr., *Billy Sunday Was His Real Name* (Chicago: University of Chicago Press, 1955), esp. 56-58, 147, 253. An excellent study of the symbolism of the department store in the rising culture of consumerism in industrialized societies is Michael B. Miller, *The Bon Marché: Bourgeois Culture and the Department Store, 1860–1920* (Princeton: Princeton University Press, 1981).

6. Sunday, "Hidden Among the Stuff," sermon, New York City, 27 May 1917, typescript, 9; box 8, reel 9, Sunday Papers.

7. Sunday's prescriptions for social and moral decay are summarized in McLoughlin, *Billy Sunday,* 122-37.

8. A wide variety of Christian thinkers have commented on or implied such changes, including Donald G. Bloesch, *The Future of Evangelical Christianity: A Call*

for Unity Amid Diversity (Garden City, N.Y.: Doubleday, 1983), 65-66; Jerry Falwell, *Listen America!* (Garden City, N.Y.: Doubleday, 1980); James Davison Hunter, *American Evangelicalism: Conservative Religion and the Quandary of Modernity* (New Brunswick, N.J.: Rutgers University Press, 1983), esp. chap. 6, "Accommodation: The Domestication of Belief"; James Davison Hunter, *Evangelicalism: The Coming Generation* (Chicago: University of Chicago Press, 1987), 161; Virginia Stem Owens, *The Total Image; or, Selling Jesus in the Modern Age* (Grand Rapids: Eerdmans, 1980); Richard Quebedeaux, *The Worldly Evangelicals* (San Francisco: Harper and Row, 1978), 10ff.; Herbert Schlossberg, *Idols for Destruction: Christian Faith and Its Confrontation with American Society* (Nashville: Thomas Nelson, 1983); Gary Scott Smith, *The Seeds of Secularization: Calvinism, Culture, and Pluralism in America, 1870–1915* (Grand Rapids: Eerdmans, 1985); and J. A. Walter, *Sacred Cows: Exploring Contemporary Idolatry* (Grand Rapids: Zondervan, 1979), 167-68.

9. For an incisive and prophetic treatment of propaganda in general, see Jacques Ellul, *Propaganda: The Formation of Men's Attitudes* (1965; New York: Vintage, 1973). Neil Postman, *Amusing Ourselves to Death: Public Discourse in the Age of Show Business* (New York: Viking, Penguin, 1985), may well provide the best study of television to date. For additional insights, consult the following: Ewen and Ewen, *Channels of Desire;* Gregor T. Goethals, *The TV Ritual: Worship at the Video Altar* (Boston: Beacon, 1981); Jerry Mander, *Four Arguments for the Elimination of Television* (New York: William Morrow, 1978), esp. chap. 7, "The Centralization of Control"; Frank Mankiewicz and Joel Swerdlow, *Remote Control: Television and the Manipulation of American Life* (New York: Ballantine, 1978); Horace Newcomb, ed., *Television: The Critical View*, 3d ed. (New York: Oxford University Press, 1982), esp. the essays by Paul M. Hirsch, Michael Novak, Roger Rosenblatt, and Todd Gitlin; Owens, *The Total Image,* 36-38; and Tony Schwartz, *Media: The Second God* (Garden City, N.Y.: Doubleday, Anchor, 1983), esp. the section "How Commercials Work."

10. Hunter, *Evangelicalism: The Coming Generation,* 157-86.

11. Ellul, *The Technological Society* (New York: Vintage, 1964), 21.

12. In *The Technological Society,* Ellul eloquently argues, and amply documents, the modern domination of ends by means. Efficiency has become an end in itself—with hardly anybody noticing or questioning its domination, so convincing are its ideological and spiritual rationalizations.

13. My thanks to Sam Alvord for this insight and phraseology.

14. See, for example, Peter L. Berger, *The Sacred Canopy: Elements of a Sociological Theory of Religion* (Garden City, N.Y.: Doubleday, Anchor, 1969); Os Guiness, *The Gravedigger File: Papers on the Subversion of the Modern Church* (Downers Grove, Ill.: InterVarsity, 1983); and Michael Harrington, *The Politics at God's Funeral: The Spiritual Crisis of Western Civilization* (New York: Penguin, 1985).

15. For various versions of these myths, see Jarram Barrs, *Who Are the Peacemakers: The Christian Case for Nuclear Deterrence* (Westchester, Ill.: Crossway, 1983); Jerry Falwell, *Listen America!;* George Gilder, *Wealth and Poverty* (New York: Bantam, 1981); Michael Novak, *The Spirit of Democratic Capitalism* (New York: Simon and Schuster, 1982); and Franky Schaeffer, *Bad News for Modern Man: An Agenda for Christian Activism* (Westchester, Ill.: Crossway, 1984).

Books which challenge these myths, with varying degrees of persuasiveness and biblical fidelity, include Peter L. Berger, *Pyramids of Sacrifice: Political Ethics and Social Change* (Garden City, N.Y.: Doubleday, Anchor, 1976); Jacques Ellul, *Living Faith: Belief and Doubt in a Perilous World* (San Francisco: Harper and Row, 1983); Bob Goudzwaard, *Idols of Our Time* (Downers Grove, Ill.: InterVarsity, 1984); Robert D.

Linder and Richard Pierard, *Twilight of the Saints: Biblical Christianity and Civil Religion in America* (Downers Grove, Ill.: InterVarsity, 1978); Mark A. Noll, Nathan O. Hatch, and George M. Marsden, *The Search for Christian America* (Westchester, Ill.: Crossway, 1983); Philip Slater, *The Pursuit of Loneliness: American Culture at the Breaking Point*, rev. ed. (1970; Boston: Beacon, 1976); William Stringfellow, *An Ethic for Christians and Other Aliens in a Strange Land* (Waco, Tex.: Word, 1976); Stringfellow, *The Politics of Spirituality* (Philadelphia: Westminster, 1984); and Nicholas Wolterstorff, *Until Justice and Peace Embrace* (Grand Rapids: Eerdmans, 1983).

16. Stringfellow, *Politics of Spirituality*, 69.

17. Ellul, *Living Faith*, 211.

18. Percy, *The Second Coming* (New York: Farrar, Straus, Giroux, 1980), 271.

19. Stringfellow, *Politics of Spirituality*, 71-72.

20. Ellul, *Living Faith*, 211.

21. Percy, *The Second Coming*, 272.

22. Stringfellow, *Politics of Spirituality*, 70.

23. Ellul, *Living Faith*, 211.

24. For revealing insights on the contemporary family, see Thomas J. Cottle, *Children's Secrets* (Garden City, N.Y.: Doubleday, Anchor, 1980); David Elkind, *The Hurried Child: Growing Up Too Fast Too Soon* (Reading, Mass.: Addison-Wesley, 1981); Christopher Lasch, *The Culture of Narcissism: American Life in an Age of Diminishing Expectations* (New York: Norton, 1978); Alice Miller, *Prisoners of Childhood: The Drama of the Gifted Child and the Search for the True Self* (New York: Basic, 1981); Michael Novak, "Family Out of Favor," *Harper's*, April 1976, 37-40; and Marie Winn, *Children without Childhood* (New York: Pantheon, 1983).

The Gospel Mandate for an Inclusive Curriculum

Ruth A. Schmidt

The fact that women make up at least half of the human race was never a controlling factor in the development of the liberal arts curriculum which most students—female and male—still study in American colleges and universities. In the last fifteen years, however, scholars and teachers in thousands of classrooms in all types of institutions of higher learning have taken great strides toward the goal of providing a balanced or inclusive view of humankind in the liberal arts curriculum. Although the impetus for this crucial intellectual development did not come from Christian colleges, they of all institutions of higher learning have the most compelling reasons to strive to be in the forefront of the development of inclusive curricula.

The curriculum passed down by the liberal arts tradition through a number of centuries was originally developed for a privileged portion of humanity: Western white males of the privileged class.[1] But now, of course, our colleges and universities do not limit admissions to that small group; enrollments in postsecondary institutions reflect the diversity of humanity to a much higher degree than ever before. There are now more women than men enrolled in colleges and universities in the United States, and evangelical colleges most likely have an even higher-than-average percentage of women in their enrollments.[2] But as yet, the curricula taught at evangelical (and other) colleges lags behind recognizing the presence and prominence of women—and certain other groups—in higher education. A curriculum that would best serve this student population must be inclusive: it must first of all take seriously the fact that women are half the human race; and then it must be attentive to the nature and quality of women's lives and their contributions to society and thus provide a balance to the recognition of the achievements and experiences of men.

Women are not the only ones excluded by present curricula,

however. Wherever teachers have begun to take seriously that women
are half the human race, other questions of exclusion from the curriculum based on race, nationality, and class have also been raised.[3] A
truly inclusive curriculum must respect the needs, concerns, and
achievements of people of other, non-Western, cultures as well. In their
interpretation of the gospel, evangelicals have made John 3:16 their
favorite verse. We now have the opportunity to develop curricula which
will reflect the inclusiveness that lies at the heart of this verse—"For
God so loved the *world*"—and that should lie at the heart of the evangelical vision of the gospel.

The Christian church—in the evangelical world especially, with its
emphasis on worldwide evangelism—has taken seriously at least one
sense in which the gospel is for all people. The missionary enterprise is
one of which Christians can be justly proud in many respects. Yet Christians, while proudly proclaiming that their faith has brought emancipation and benefits to women, have not always been eager to see and carry
out the truth of Galatians 3:28—that "there is neither Jew nor Greek,
there is neither slave nor free, there is neither male nor female; for you
are all one in Christ Jesus." Such biblical beliefs should have made
Christian colleges the leaders in the movement for an inclusive curriculum. Sadly, however, this has not been the case because Christian
educators have been closer followers of their secular training in the
academic disciplines than interpreters of the inclusive message of the
gospel.

Christian scholars are to be concerned with the pursuit of truth.
With their secular colleagues they share an academic interest in pursuing and teaching the truth. But they come to their task from a different
perspective: they believe in God as the source of all truth and in Christ
as the way, and the truth, and the light. Many disciplines have been
shown to be biased in their research and teaching, but any proclaimed
truth about humankind cannot really be the truth unless the perspective
of all humankind is included. By excluding important members of
humanity from their research and teaching, Christian scholars show that
they value these less; they reduce the humanity of—they "dehuman-
ize"—some of those made in God's image.

Christian believers have dwelt on the profound effect of Eden and
the expulsion from Paradise, but they have not borne a thoroughgoing
witness to the way in which Christ's coming heals the brokenness
resulting from original sin. Evangelicals have often understood original
sin as the rupture between God and human beings, but they have some-

how assumed that one result of that fundamental rupture, the antagonism between male and female, is a natural consequence not to be tampered with. Thus while they are very concerned about the healing of the breach between God and humans through Christ's death, they have in some cases been less than willing to heed the fact that the war between the sexes comes to peaceful resolution in the gospel. They see the rift between male and female as something that cannot be alleviated by us in this world. Some have gone so far as to argue, as Daniel McGuire has, that "sexism is the elementary human sin. If the essential human molecule is dyadic, male/female, the perversion of one part of the dyad perverts the other."[4] If evangelicals are to seek wholeness for men and women, however, they need a fundamental healing of the antagonism between the sexes, the sinful domination of women by men, and the waste of God-given talents by females.[5] If Christian colleges are to empower their students for full lives in society and in God's realm, not only must academic materials and methods include all of what the gospel teaches about the value of all God's people, but the discoveries of the research on gender, class, and race in the last fifteen years must be incorporated into the curriculum.

Evangelical scholars have long wrestled with the questions of the proper relationship of faith and knowledge. It is an especially pressing struggle for many because evangelicals have for the most part done their graduate work in institutions where each subject is studied from the perspective of a secular worldview. The differences and conflicts between the secular and the evangelical worldviews first became issues in the science curriculum. In recent years, however, scholars have become more aware of the philosophical biases which underlie the study of the social sciences and the humanities as well; thus evangelicals in those fields have also had to wrestle with the perspectives and underlying assumptions which affect one's theorizing, research, experiment design, and conclusions. Ultimately, scholars had to realize that their presuppositions influenced the curriculum itself of institutions of higher education.

Until the women's movement began to touch scholars in colleges and universities in the late 1960s and early 1970s, and until these scholars (principally female but also including a number of males) began to look at the traditional curriculum with new eyes, there were very few who had realized how narrow the liberal arts curriculum was in its reflection of only one small part of the human race. The women's movement began to sensitize women within the academic community, and they began to apply the tools of scholarship that they had learned at male-centered universities to ask questions about the lack of any sort of balance in the attention devoted to women's lives, women's perspectives, and even to the accomplishments of women.[6]

These scholars, who began to develop teaching materials reflecting women's points of view, soon realized that they had a monumental task ahead of them. First there was the problem of research: collecting and including the accomplishments of women in history, literature, and the arts who *did* make it in a man's world. Another task was more theoretical: trying to answer the question of why there were not more women who accomplished and achieved in a male-dominated world. Some of the early courses that tried to create some balance in literature, for example, dealt with women authors who had been neglected in the anthologies or whose works had dropped out of the accepted canon. Paul Lauter has shown that, in standard texts of American literature, what may seem like an immutable canon is in reality an ever-changing list of authors to be taught. Writers go out of fashion and come into fashion, and the number of women in anthologies has varied surprisingly over the years.[7]

The discoveries of these pioneers in creating a more balanced curriculum have opened up a host of new questions. How would the inclusion of the experiences of women in the record of Western culture affect scholarship in various fields? What were the conditions for judging artistic accomplishment which might cause one to overlook women's talents? What were women doing on the homefront when males went off to war to have their exploits, their triumphs and defeats, which are recorded in political and military history?[8] Does the discipline of psychology really have anything to say about female psychology? Carol Gilligan's work on moral development, for example, has opened all of our eyes to the fact that men's and women's socialization is so different that what may be considered characteristic of maturity for one sex may indeed be almost precluded by definition for the other.[9] One illustration of this insight comes from the Christian influence on American culture. The attributes of the authentic Christian character—the "fruits of the Spirit," as Scripture calls them—include those qualities which have traditionally been enjoined on women by American culture. Thus the messages given to women by culture and by Scripture have been very similar. But the messages our culture gives to men often go counter to the gospel message. The ideal Christian man filled with the fruits of the Spirit is a far cry from the image of the ideal man according to American culture. Failure to see this in the Christian church has of course resulted in putting an extra burden on American males: the eminently Christian virtues are precisely those that are considered feminine in our culture.

It is vitally important for college curricula not just to "add women and stir," as the phrase has it, but rather to acknowledge and accept the direction given in the majority of disciplines by this fundamental questioning. This is especially important in the social sciences. As Elizabeth Kamarck Minnick has stated, "What women's studies lead to is not a few add-on works or courses, but a transformation of how we approach knowledge, the transformation that allows us to stop *saying* that 'Man' includes us all and start making it do so . . . by fundamentally changing the partiality of the base of our whole tradition."[10] Why was it that for years anthropologists talked about "man the hunter" and emphasized this aspect of the provision of food, when in fact among many peoples the primary providers were the women, who gathered food day after day? Valuing what men do and undervaluing what women do leads to just such blindness. In economics, neither the exclusion of women's work in the home from the calculation of goods and services in the gross national product nor the social implications of job discrimination and different pay scales for women and men are peripheral issues.

The current discussion of the problems and pitfalls of pay scales based on comparable work, recognizing, for example, that more training and skill may be necessary for clerical work than for plumbing, is yet another example of the importance of gender as a category of research and as a consideration in public policy.[11] An understanding of the factors that cause men's work to be valued higher than women's work would lead us to a consideration once again of the two spheres which have been assigned to men and women. To men goes the public sphere of political action and the world of business, and to women the private world of the home. While we are quite aware that these lines have frequently been blurred—and will be increasingly blurred in our late twentieth-century world—the underlying beliefs concerning men's and women's work color our lives daily, influence the way our world is organized, and still dominate the liberal arts curriculum in most places.

What are the practical difficulties of trying to develop an inclusive curriculum? Curricular changes since the development of women's studies and research on women have followed two basic modes. The first follows the path of developing wholly new and separate courses in women's studies in a wide variety of disciplines, beginning with such topics as women in literature, women authors, psychology of women, sociology of sex roles, women in classical times, and women in the work force. These courses are then frequently organized in interdisciplinary programs. There are now thousands of courses in women's studies in colleges and universities in the country and hundreds of programs leading to minors, majors, and graduate degrees.[12] The second mode is the transformational mode, in which the new research on women, including material which might very well be used in separate women's studies courses, is used to transform the courses normally taught in the various liberal arts subjects by including women's and men's perspectives together. New questions are generated when we ask, "What would our curriculum look like if we seriously acknowledged that women are half of the human race?"[13]

The former mode is that followed in most large universities while the second mode is more characteristic of smaller institutions. Of course, faculty members who teach specific women's studies courses and in women's studies programs cannot help but transform what they do in any other courses they may teach that are not considered specific to the women's studies curriculum. Thus whenever faculty members are truly committed to an inclusive curriculum, the new research on women will necessarily lead them to transform their courses continually, just as any area of new knowledge may change what and how they teach. In some disciplines, such transformation may be accomplished rather deftly and without any upheaval, while in other disciplines it may be very difficult to add the new materials because they fundamentally question and revise the old perspectives.

In small colleges, the transformational mode is the one which has the best possibility of being assimilated because it does not entail expansion of the curriculum but rather a transformation of the curriculum. Of course it is very difficult to implement a true curricular transformation, and it is very hard to determine to what degree the curriculum has been transformed into an inclusive one—one cannot go to the catalogue and simply count up the number of courses offered in women's studies as an indication of inclusiveness. Furthermore, none of this is likely to happen by chance. It is unlikely that any institution would be able to develop a curriculum sufficiently integrated without first establishing a definite program for the development of faculty expertise and commitment to such a project.[14]

An inclusive curriculum that would not only include women and men on an equal footing but also reduce Western blindness to other cultures is, in many ways, a more difficult problem. Small colleges do not have the expertise and resources to deal with all cultures. Even with a major commitment, it appears, it would likely still be impossible to teach students about Asia, Africa, and Latin America to the same degree that we teach them about the Western European tradition and American life. Even if we lumped together in a very simplified form the vast breadth of geography and the myriad cultures of whole continents, we would still be left with an enormously daunting task.

But though the problem may be insurmountable, there are at least two things we can do if we are truly committed to being more inclusive of all of the human race. One is to make a point of at least referring to other perspectives and other cultures as we teach courses in the traditional or the transformed curriculum. Students should continually be reminded that because of practical considerations these courses can discuss only a small portion of the world and that their point of view is seriously limited. More importantly, educators can insist that students gain at least some exposure to another culture significantly different from their own. Such cross-cultural experience can sensitize students to the particularizing effects of culture and to the limitations of being unicultural, as well as lead them to see their own situation differently. Many of our institutions already do this by making foreign experience or at least a course in cross-cultural issues a mandatory part of the course of study. This can do much to reduce students' isolation and narrowness of vision. Educators could also require as part of the liberal arts curriculum significant, in-depth study of another language and culture—including the   principal languages and cultures of the *whole* world.

What this all suggests is that from a very large spectrum of material which could be taught, there is always selection, there is always choice. We see that even within disciplines choices must be made about what is most important, about what *must* be included and what can be let go. Therefore, when it comes to developing an inclusive curriculum, our attitudes and our criteria of selection are vital. Much can be done by sensitizing faculty and students to the importance of viewing the world from a more inclusive perspective, and then actually trying to do it. The inclusion of formerly excluded groups often leads to a greater understanding of the interconnectedness of all. The study of the role of women in developing nations, for example, brings into focus many issues at once. The role of women and men in food production and subsistence, the political and social arrangements which affect economics, the effect on the family of moves to the city, the arts and literature produced by old and changing societies—all these things are interlocked. A commitment to an inclusive curriculum can provide new models for curricular development and interaction. This has already been demonstrated by the success of the women's studies movement in bringing together scholars from disparate parts of the university and college. Inclusiveness is thus one way of fostering a wholeness which has often been lacking in undergraduate curricula of the last twenty years.

When we read Christ's statement in John 8:32, "The truth will make you free," we understand that freedom comes from the liberating power of Christ. Yet just as the gospel is liberating to all, so an inclusive curriculum which informs all persons about their past, their potential, and their future liberates and empowers all. The Christian college thus has powerful incentives for developing an inclusive curriculum. If we are to follow the gospel proclamation that in Christ there is neither Jew nor Greek, slave nor free, male nor female, let us in the expression of God's truth include all people in the research and teaching of our colleges. Only thus can we be true to the pursuit of truth and to the gospel mandate for all.

NOTES

1. See the following essays: Florence Howe, "Feminist Scholarship—The Extent of the Revolution," 5-21; Elizabeth Kamarck Minnick, "A Feminist Critique of the Liberal Arts," 22-38; and Gerda Lerner, "The Challenges of Women's History," 39-47; all in *Liberal Education and the New Scholarship on Women,* report of the Wingspread Conference, Association of American Colleges, ed. Florence Howe (Washington, D.C.: Association of American Colleges, 1981). This report also contains a series of conference recommendations to institutions, administrators, education associations, and disciplinary groups on the need to transform the liberal arts curriculum.

2. Women make up between 51 and 52 percent of college and university students in the U.S. *A Guide to Christian Colleges* (Grand Rapids: Eerdmans, 1984) reveals that in 68 colleges for which male and female enrollment is given, women outnumber men by a ratio of about 7 to 6 (34,898 to 29,980).

3. The second summer conference on a balanced curriculum, sponsored by Wheaton College (Mass.) in 1985, was devoted to the needs of minority, working-class, and third-world women. The Women's Studies Association and journals such as *Women's Studies Quarterly* have increasingly raised questions of race, ethnicity, and class as necessary corollaries of the focus on gender.

4. McGuire, quoted in Anne E. Carr, "The Search for Wholeness," *Criterion* 23 (Autumn 1984): 5.

5. The Evangelical Women's Caucus, International (1357 Washington Street, West Newton, MA 02165) is an organization of women and men with the goals of presenting "God's teaching on female-male equality to the whole body of Christ's church," and calling "both women and men to mutual submission and active discipleship."

6. This progression can be traced in the early history of women's studies programs in universities and colleges and is evident in the volumes of *Women's Studies Quarterly* (begun in 1972 and until 1981 published under the title *Women's Studies Newsletter*), published by Feminist Press, 311 East 94th Street, New York, NY 10128.

7. Paul Lauter, *Reconstructing American Literature* (Old Westbury, N.Y.: Feminist Press, 1983).

8. For an illuminating overview of many questions raised by the new scholarship on women, see Peggy McIntosh's essay in *The Forum for Liberal Education* 4 (October 1981); and her essay in the April 1984 issue of the same journal. See also my article "Liberal Learning for Both Sexes," *Liberal Education* 67 (Fall 1981): 200-204. For more detailed information on contemporary scholarship, see *Signs: Journal of Women in Culture and Society,* published since 1975 by the University of Chicago Press; and the directory of centers of scholarship on women, a reprint from *Women's Studies Quarterly* 12 (Spring 1984): 17-29, available from Feminist Press.

9. Carol Gilligan, *In a Different Voice: Psychological Theory and Women's Development* (Cambridge: Harvard University Press, 1982).

10. Minnick, "A Feminist Critique of the Liberal Arts," in *Liberal Education and the New Scholarship on Women,* 30.

11. The issue of comparable pay for comparable work will continue to be a lively one in legislative halls and courtrooms as well as in academic circles for some time to come. The fear with which business and government leaders attack the concept indicates the magnitude of the impact expected should this principle of equity become law or the norm in practice.

12. *Women's Studies Quarterly* publishes an annual updating of the women's

studies programs in colleges and universities. The list in the Fall 1984 issue runs to eleven pages.

13. This is essentially the same question posed by McIntosh in her essay in *The Forum for Liberal Education* (October 1981). For those who have not followed the development of women's research and women's studies, the listings under "Resources" in the same issue, 16-18, will be revealing and helpful.

14. For many examples of the transformational mode see "How to Integrate Women's Studies into the Traditional Curriculum," report from the SIROW (Southwest Institute for Research on Women) Conference, held in 1981 at the University of Arizona in Tucson. One of the most comprehensive programs for developing expertise and commitment in faculty is the one I initiated at Wheaton College (Mass.) under the title "Toward a Balanced Curriculum." This project was supported initially (1980–1983) by the Fund for the Improvement of Post-Secondary Education. See *Toward a Balanced Curriculum: A Sourcebook for Initiating Gender Integration Projects,* ed. Bonnie Spanier, Alexander Bloom, and Darlene Boroviak (Cambridge, Mass.: Schenkman, 1984); the bibliographies in this publication will provide ample sources of research on women in academic disciplines as well as material on inclusive curriculum projects.

Minorities in Evangelical Higher Education

Alvaro L. Nieves

Introduction

Minorities in higher education, an issue many thought resolved during the tumultous sixties, is once again of interest to educators, politicians, and the general public. Minority populations in the United States have increased as a proportion of the total population in recent years, and current demographic trends indicate that their continued growth will contribute to changing the cultural climate of American life.[1] American institutions of higher education in particular will face these changes—and have to respond to them. The greatest growth in minority populations has come at a time when American colleges and universities have experienced very definite financial pressures. The costs of higher education have escalated in recent years, in large part because of high rates of inflation through the 1970s;[2] and this increase in costs has combined with recent declines in public funding levels to create increased competition for the educational funds that are still available. Furthermore, recent court decisions and Justice Department policy statements indicate a decreasing resolve to pursue affirmative action.[3] Thus many minority students and leaders are expressing concern about what appears to be a narrowing of opportunities. Indeed, they see recent declines in minority enrollments in colleges and universities as a major symptom of a distressing new rise in discrimination.

The status of minorities in evangelical higher education reflects some of these same trends, as I will show by examining the status of minorities in member colleges of the Christian College Coalition. The need for improvement is great, but so is the potential. Evangelical colleges have the resources and the ability to take some modest but practical steps to attract and effectively serve minorities in ways especially appropriate to their evangelical educational mission.

National Trends

Higher education would face problems in accommodating the aspirations of minority groups even if their populations were growing at the national rate. In fact, they are growing much faster. Immigration, just one source of minority population growth, has increased dramatically in the past half-century, rising from approximately 53,000 per year during the 1930s to around 600,000 per year in the 1980s. These figures do not even take into account undocumented immigration, estimates of which range from a conservative low of 500,000 to a high of 2 million per year. Moreover, the rate of growth among immigrant groups in America is even higher than immigration figures indicate because many of the immigrant populations are among the most rapidly reproducing segments of the population. The reduction in birthrates, which has resulted in declining college enrollments, has been largely a white and middle-class phenomenon. Black and Hispanic birthrates are still high—45 and 53 percent higher, respectively, than the rate for whites. At this rate of growth, blacks and Hispanics will comprise one fourth of the American population by the year 2000.[4]

As most politicians have discovered, minorities have become a powerful, if not dominant, force in urban centers throughout the United States. This is to be expected since the minority segments of the U.S. population constitute a majority in some twenty-five major cities, including Miami, Chicago, and Atlanta. Estimates indicate that by the year 2000 minorities will predominate in more than fifty cities.

While the number of blacks, Asians, and Hispanics increases dramatically, so does the cost of a college education. In the decade between the academic years 1973–74 and 1983–84 the cost of a college education increased 108 percent at public colleges and universities and 138 percent at private schools. The average cost for tuition and room and board at a private college for the 1983–84 academic year was $7,540.[5] This figure is close to that of member schools of the Christian College Coalition, where the cost for the 1983–84 school year ranged from $4,414 to $9,674 and averaged just under $7,000.[6] The increase in costs has come at the same time student aid was dropping—a combination of changes that has had an especially dramatic adverse effect on minority segments of the population. Over the period from 1978 to 1983, the average financial aid sum awarded per black student at private colleges and universities dropped by 1.9 percent and aid per Hispanic student dropped 4.5 percent. Yet during the same period, aid per white

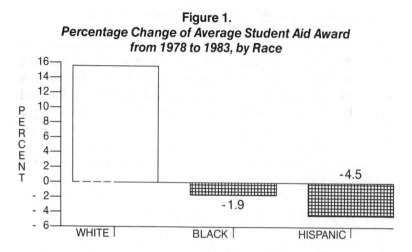

Figure 1.
*Percentage Change of Average Student Aid Award
from 1978 to 1983, by Race*

student in private colleges and universities actually increased 15.6 percent.[7]

The combination of higher costs, reduced aid, and a general political and economic climate unfavorable to many minorities has had a devastating effect on college enrollment rates of blacks and Hispanics in the United States. A recent article in *Education Week* thoroughly documents the declining proportion of these minorities able to participate in higher education.[8] The decline is present in all states and at all levels, from junior colleges to graduate and professional schools.[9] At the same time, according to Leonard Haynes III, vice president of Southern University in Louisiana, the federal government is communicating a false message that is discouraging minority students. The message, he says, is that "somehow or another affirmative action is no longer necessary, that blacks and other minorities have achieved parity and equity and there is now a fair chance for everybody to go where— and as far as—they want to go."[10] Yet according to the report in *Education Week,* the proportion of black high school graduates going to college dropped 11 percent in the six-year period from 1975 to 1981. During the same period, although Hispanic college enrollments grew in absolute numbers, there was an 18 percent decline in the proportion of high school graduates going on to college.[11]

The Status of Minorities in Christian Colleges

From a minority standpoint, the situation in higher education in general is bleak. Does this picture change when one looks at the member schools of the Christian College Coalition? Although current and retrospective statistics are not available to document changes in minority enrollments, a look at the figures for 1983–84 is instructive. *Peterson's Guide to Four Year Colleges: 1985* shows the percentage of blacks, Native Americans, Asians, and Hispanics enrolled in most four-year colleges in the United States in 1983–84, including those of the Christian College Coalition. The average for all minority groups in Coalition colleges was 7.2 percent, representing a mean of fewer than 79 for colleges with an average total enrollment of nearly 1,072. A closer look shows that, on the average, blacks made up 3.7 percent, Hispanics 1.8 percent, Asians 1.1 percent, and Native Americans 0.6 percent of enrollments in Coalition colleges (which leaves white enrollment at 92.8 percent). Comparable 1982 enrollment figures for all four-year private institutions in the nation show rates of 10.4 percent for blacks and 2.15 percent for Hispanics. For four-year public colleges black enrollment averaged 19.5 percent while Hispanic enrollment was just over 2 percent.[12] Obviously, Coalition colleges lag behind the rest of the nation in enrolling minorities.

While students comprise the most obvious component of the higher education profile, the composition of the rest of the academic community—faculty, staff, and administration—is also important. In a recent survey of Coalition schools, an attempt was made to obtain such figures. Unfortunately, because initial data on minority staff composition are incomplete and the follow-up is still under way, a complete analysis is impossible. However, approximately 27 percent of academic deans and vice presidents have returned surveys, and at least their *perceptions* of the situation are revealing. When asked to indicate their degree of satisfaction with the number of full-time minority faculty, over 90 percent of these deans and vice presidents stated they were either *somewhat* or *very dissatisfied* (52.4 percent of them reported being somewhat dissatisfied while 38.1 percent of them were very dissatisfied). By comparison, only 79 percent of the respondents indicated dissatisfaction with the number of part-time faculty. If we can consider the relative degrees of satisfaction as a rough measure of the relative numbers of minority faculty in full-time and part-time positions, we may speculate that probably there is a greater proportion of minority faculty in part-time than in full-time positions. In response to similar questions about the number of minority persons in administrative positions, some 95 percent of the respondents indicated dissatisfaction of greater or lesser degree. Whether the conclusions of this admittedly very sub-jective assessment will hold up depends on the survey's follow-up. I expect to find, however, that the Coalition's record on minority staff hiring in comparison to the record of other private and public institu-tions is highly consistent with the previous comparative results on minority student enrollment. That is, I expect to find that Coalition schools lag behind.

This same survey of member schools of the Christian College Coalition also requested certain information concerning budget and programs that might indicate a climate supportive of minority students enrolled in Coalition schools. Such a climate is considered essential to attracting minority students to private colleges. Programs might include special recruiting efforts as well as support projects to help retain those minority students who have enrolled. Evidence of a climate positive to minorities may also be seen in the number of staff employed full or part time in minority programs. In addition, of course, an institution's com-mitment to recruitment and retention of minorities may be demonstrated by budget items targeted for such purposes.

Preliminary examination of the survey results indicate that, of those Coalition colleges reporting, none had clearly separate budget categories for minority recruitment or retention. Approximately 24 per-cent have established a separate minority counseling service, while 28 percent indicated that they employ one or more full-time staff in minority program positions such as Director of Minority Affairs. In ad-dition, 19 percent of the responding schools indicated that they employ one or two part-time staff in a minority program function.

In addition to minority recruitment and supportive programs, the number of faculty and administrators who are themselves minority-group members—and thus role models for minority students—is often pointed out as an important component of a supportive climate. One might expect from the high degree of dissatisfaction among Coalition deans with the number of minorities in faculty and administrative posi-tions that they would attempt to change things—that they would active-ly recruit minority professionals. And in fact, about one third of the schools responding to the survey indicated that they did systematically recruit minorities, while an additional 7 percent did so occasionally.

If schools do recruit and hire minorities, they still face the problem of retaining them, just as they face the problem of retaining minority students. It is important that faculty be involved in the decisions made about selecting and retaining other faculty members. Without such involvement minority faculty suffer an increased sense of alienation from the institution. It is cause for concern that more than 90 percent of responding schools report that minority faculty are either seldom (66.7 percent) or never (23.8 percent) involved in faculty selection. It is similarly distressing that more than 76 percent indicate that minorities are either seldom (42.9 percent) or never (33.3 percent) involved in promotion or tenure decisions.

Besides the makeup of the student body, besides the composition of the faculty and administration, the presence of minorities on a school's governing board can help reveal its attitudes and policies toward minorities. Indeed, legally speaking, these boards generally *are* the institution. In this context we may justifiably ask, What is the makeup of the boards of trustees of Christian College Coalition schools? We can get some answers from Michael E. Collette of Anderson College, who compared boards of trustees of public, private, and Coalition colleges in a number of different ways. His findings indicate that at Coalition member schools, minority representation on governing boards in 1984 was only 1.7 percent. This figure is much lower than the approximately 6.0 percent minority representation on the boards of all private colleges and universities and the 12.8 percent representation on the boards of public colleges and universities.[13]

The increasing costs of education and declining enrollments have forced both students and institutions to innovate. Students have found it necessary to alter their educational plans in the face of fiscal reality. Some may have decided to attend less costly state institutions instead of private colleges; others may have decided to attend schools nearer to home so as to reduce living and transportation costs. Similarly, many colleges and universities have had to implement innovative programs, marketing techniques, and creative financing in the face of declining

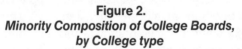

Figure 2.
Minority Composition of College Boards,
by College type

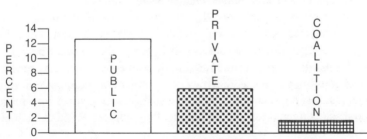

enrollments. Such innovations were for the most part neither thought of nor necessary during periods of high growth in the past, when the problem was one of expansion rather than retrenchment. It is clear, however, that innovations in programs and marketing have become essential to the success, if not the very survival, of many colleges.

Schools have been increasingly concerned with marketing themselves as they compete for a portion of a shrinking applicant pool. Yet many of these schools have ignored the fact that this shrinkage has occurred largely among whites while minority populations have been increasing dramatically. Thus instead of desperately marketing themselves in the shrinking portion of the pool, perhaps schools could better maintain enrollments through a planned and directed expansion into minority groups—the as-yet untapped and ignored portion of the pool.

Is this a possible strategy for schools in the Christian College Coalition to pursue in order to maintain enrollments and to better fulfill the mandate of Christian higher education? Are the minority markets really there for Coalition member schools? In trying to answer this last question it may be instructive to examine the racial and ethnic composition of the Metropolitan Statistical Areas (MSAs) close to Coalition colleges in comparison to the composition of the colleges themselves.

The following statistical table provides a capsule view of the racial and ethnic composition of the nearby metropolitan areas and the minority composition of the schools themselves.

Figure 3.
Ethnic Composition

	Metro Areas*	Coalition College
White	82.5%	92.8%
Black	12.1%	3.7%
Hispanic	5.5%	1.8%
Asian	1.5%	1.1%
Native American	0.8%	0.6%
All Minorities	19.9%	7.2%

*Represents metropolitan statistical areas close to Coalition colleges. The total adds up to more than 100 percent because of rounding and because of some possible double-reporting of Hispanics.

It is striking that while whites constitute, on the average, 82.5 percent of the population of metropolitan areas nearest to Coalition colleges, the colleges themselves experience a white enrollment of 92.8 percent—a full ten percentage points higher. Looking at all minorities taken together (7.2 percent is actually an inflated figure because it includes Asians, while in the admissions process Asians are most often not treated as minorities), the percentage of minorities in Coalition schools is less than half of that represented in the MSAs. If positive steps in the direction of minority recruitment and retention are not undertaken, this gap can only widen.

Nearby metropolitan areas may, admittedly, not be traditional recruiting grounds for the private schools in the Coalition; yet for various reasons including those already mentioned it is expedient to cast a practical eye in their direction. National trends indicating rapid growth of minority populations have serious practical implications for private colleges in general and Christian colleges in particular. In the face of a dwindling white and an increasing minority pool, the potential for substitution is hard to ignore. Self-interest alone ought to be enough to impel colleges to actively recruit minorities; indeed, the very survival of some institutions may be at stake. According to one recent account, "the demographic data are so stark that . . . researchers suggest that in ignoring the growing black and Hispanic populations, higher- education institutions may be ignoring the nation's—and their own—future."[14]

But nobody, especially Christians, should act merely out of self-interest. Even our colleagues in secular schools recognize that there should be more to admissions criteria than predicted academic performance and the ability to pay. Even at very selective universities like Harvard the representation of minorities is a critical concern. As Robert Klitgaard suggests in his recent book *Choosing Elites,* "How we choose elites matters for social efficiency and social justice."[15] He then proceeds to discuss the objectives of selection and explains that they may be "analyzed under the rubric of maximizing the social value added of choosing one set of students rather than another."[16] What he is suggesting is that any set of selection criteria—implicit or explicit—involves certain costs and benefits. Costs and benefits accrue not only to the students rejected or chosen but to the entire institution, to society as a whole, and, most importantly for Christians, to the kingdom.

One benefit the institution derives from the admission of minorities is cultural diversity on campus. This may be especially important to Christian colleges with a stated objective of preparing students for ministry, because opportunities for Christian service in the future will increasingly be urban and cross-cultural. If Christian colleges take positive action, they can be both more just in offering educational opportunities to minorities and also more effective in preparing stu-

dents for a modern ministry. Eliminating racially exclusive environ-
ments and providing increased opportunities for cultural diversity are
important starting points. If problems stemming from historical and
cultural conditioning, the social structure, and psychological factors are
to be overcome, such positive actions are simply required.

Failure to take such steps will result in the continuation of a situation aptly described by David Claerbaut in his book *Urban Ministry.*

> As a child reaches adulthood and plans, perhaps, to go into Christian
> ministry, he attends a Christian college with a largely white faculty,
> staff, and student body, finally to finish in a white middle-class semi-
> nary that tries to prepare him for working with all kinds of people. If by
> then he is not to some extent a purveyor of racism and prejudice, it
> would be rather surprising, for all agree that a person's environment is
> a major influence on his attitudes, values, beliefs, and behaviors.[17]

Increasing cultural diversity by recruiting students and staff from
minority segments of the population and urban areas is not only in the
interest of the survival of evangelical colleges, it is also just and consistent with the colleges' stated objectives of preparing students for
Christian service.

Recommendations

It is certainly not easy to determine how best to accomplish the
goals of increasing minority student enrollment and retention, recruiting and retaining minority faculty, and increasing minority participation and influence in all levels of campus decision making. But perhaps
a few modest proposals will prove helpful. Coalition schools should:

1. Establish working relationships with potential minority constituencies in those metropolitan centers nearest them. These might include churches, high schools, Bible colleges, social and evangelistic
ministries, and public agencies. The relationships should be long-term
with the aim of providing mutual opportunities.

2. Teach extension courses in nearby cities, developing innovative
teaching and internship programs of an interdisciplinary nature. Where
possible such programs should be located in minority neighborhoods
and directed by minority faculty.[18]

3. Initiate discussions with traditionally black colleges of similar
religious persuasion to create a faculty exchange program, since obtaining minority faculty through "normal" recruiting methods is difficult,

at best.[19] This will expose white students in Coalition colleges to minority faculty, provide role models for minority students, and provide white faculty with an opportunity to gain a greater sensitivity to the meaning of minority status. Such an exchange program might function best under the aegis of the Christian College Coalition.

4. Identify promising minority graduate students and sponsor them in graduate school with the goal of adding them to the college faculty. This should involve a contractual obligation on the part of the students to later serve on the faculty of the sponsoring institution. A variant of this could involve minority fellowships granted by the entire Coalition with the commitment on the part of the student to serve in any one of the Coalition colleges. This broader fellowship would serve to broaden the base of possible openings and the range of fields available to prospective minority faculty.

5. Nominate minority-group members to governing boards when the terms of white members expire or their positions become vacant for other reasons. Such a practice would provide greater information and broader perspectives on important policy decisions. Further benefits would include increased contact with minority constituencies and a broadening of the applicant pool.

6. Increase minority faculty participation in college governance. This will serve to decrease any sense of alienation and improve rates of retention.[20]

7. Make other structural improvements to improve the climate for minority faculty and students on campus. While each institution is different and in some ways unique, every school can develop programs to provide a more supportive climate. This may mean working with white faculty and students as well as minorities to improve mutual sensitivity. Remedial programs, recognition of the worth of minority cultures, and assistance to full minority participation in the life of the campus community can all be helpful.[21]

Conclusion

Americans have benefited from the fruits of one of the most productive economic systems in history. But, as John Perkins writes, "we lack the moral will to distribute the fruits of our production in a more equitable way."[22] One of our greatest productive resources has been our system of education, both private and public, which provides one of the mechanisms by which distribution of other benefits is determined. But here too we have failed the demands of equity. For this reason, if for no other, we must take seriously the challenge to provide more equitable access to the Christian college community. And we must do so not just because it "seems" right but because God has already spoken to our unjust distribution of resources: "The Lord maintains the cause of the afflicted, and executes justice for the needy" (Ps. 140:12). And he gives his warning to the oppressors: "Woe to those who . . . keep writing oppression, to turn aside the needy from justice and to rob the poor of my people of their right. . . . What will you do on the day of punishment, in the storm which will come from afar?" (Isaiah 10:1-3).

Too often, essays such as this stop at describing the status quo. They communicate observations that can hardly be contradicted but just as often neglect policy implications. The report is shelved, people are left feeling guilty, and nothing else happens. I hope I have avoided some of those problems by providing specific recommendations as a basis for action. Obviously, these recommendations are not equally appropriate in all situations. A strategy that may be effective for a college located in or near a metropolitan area may not work on a rural campus. Similarly, what can be accomplished is to an extent dictated by financial resources and by the experience and backgrounds of faculty and staff. We cannot accomplish everything all at once. What is important, however, is that each school begin to apply its resources to fulfilling the biblical mandate. God does not, after all, call us to be immediately successful; he does call us to be faithful.[23]

NOTES

1. See, for example, John Naisbit, *Megatrends: Ten New Directions Transforming Our Lives* (New York: Warner, 1982); for indications of demographic characteristics and trends based on the 1980 Census see A. G. Dworkin and R. J. Dworkin, *The Minority Report: An Introduction to Racial, Ethnic and Gender Relations* (New York: Holt, Rinehart and Winston, 1982).

2. Thomas D. Snyder, "Statistic of the Month: Tuition Costs Follow Inflation Trends," *American Education* 19 (November 1983): inside back cover.

3. This appears obvious from recent Justice Department actions seeking to rescind prior federal policy involving minority hiring quotas. Examples include a recent Tennessee case involving a city fire department promotion policy and a Chicago case involving hiring and promotion in that city's police department.

4. Percentages computed from birthrates recorded in 1980 Census: Hispanics, 95.4 births per thousand women; blacks, 90.7 births per thousand women; and whites, 62.4 births per thousand women. M. Sandra Reeves, "Minorities and College, A Time Bomb: Hard-Won Enrollment Gains are Quietly Deteriorating," *Education Week*, 17 April 1985, 1, 12ff.

5. Snyder, "Statistic of the Month."

6. *A Guide To Christian Colleges* (Grand Rapids: Eerdmans, Christian College Coalition, 1984).

7. Between 1978 and 1983, the average award for white students rose from $2032 to $2348 (+15.6%); during the same period the average award for black students dropped from $2844 to $2790 (–1.9%), and for Hispanic students it dropped from $3238 to $3092 (–4.5%). Reeves, "Minorities and College," chart, 13.

8. Ibid., 12-13.

9. Reeves, citing the American Council on Education's Third Annual Status Report, states that "despite their increasing share of the college age population, blacks and hispanics have gained no ground as a proportion of those enrolled in or graduating from colleges." "Minorities and College," 12. Just how bad the situation really is or may become is increasingly difficult to determine since the amount of information gathered by the federal government is declining by direction of the Office of Management and Budget. Presumably, this is an attempt to reduce the public reporting burden.

10. Quoted in Reeves, "Minorities and College," 12.

11. Ibid.

12. Susan G. Broyles, *Fall Enrollment in Colleges and Universities, 1982* (Washington, D.C.: National Center for Education Statistics, 1982), 62-63. For Hispanics this level of enrollment in public colleges represents a large decline from the 1978 high of 3.5 percent back to about the 1970 figure of 2.1 percent. And this is in spite of an absolute increase in the population of Hispanics.

13. Michael E. Collette, "Comparison of Boards of Trustees of Member Institutions of the Christian College Coalition with Other Institutions of Higher Learning" (Ed.D. diss., Indiana University, 1984), 47, 94, 96.

14. Sheppard Ranbom and J. R. Sirkin, quoted in Reeves, "Minorities and College," 12.

15. Robert Klitgaard, *Choosing Elites* (New York: Basic, 1985), 179.

16. Ibid., 180.

17. David Claerbaut, *Urban Ministry* (Grand Rapids: Zondervan, 1983), 130.

18. Extension courses may be offered in cooperation with local church congregations. One good example of such an effort is that offered in Chicago under the aegis of

SCUPE (Seminary Consortium for Urban Pastoral Education), which involves a number of seminaries in the Midwest.

19. A national computerized faculty-exchange program was established through a grant from the Exxon Education Foundation. Scott Heller discusses this program in "New National Program Lets Faculty Members Sample Academic Life on Other Campuses," *Chronicle of Higher Education*, 29 February 1984, 15, 17. The Christian College Coalition should explore the possibility of piggy-backing on this existing service or beginning a new one.

20. A number of recent articles address this issue; two good examples are Robert J. Menges and William H. Exum, "Barriers to the Progress of Women and Minority Faculty," *Journal of Higher Education* 54 (March-April 1983): 123-43; and William H. Exum et al., "Making It at the Top," *American Behavioral Scientist* 27 (January-February 1984): 301-24.

21. See, for support, Robert A. Blanc, Larry E. DeBuhr, and Deanna C. Martin, "Breaking the Attrition Cycle: The Effects of Supplemental Instruction on Undergraduate Performance and Attrition," *Journal of Higher Education* 54 (January-February 1983): 80-91; Rick Turner, "Factors Influencing the Retention of Minority Students in the 1980s: Opinions and Impressions," *Journal of Non-White Concerns in Personnel and Guidance* 9 (July 1980): 204-14; Donald H. Smith, "Admissions and Retention Problems of Black Students at Seven Predominantly White Universities," *Metas* 1 (Spring 1980): 22-46.

22. John Perkins, *With Justice For All* (Ventura, Cal.: Regal, 1982), 148, 152.

23. I wish to express my appreciation to my colleagues in the Department of Sociology and Anthropology at Wheaton College for their discussion and comments on many of the issues in this paper. Thanks also go to Joel Carpenter for the many helpful suggestions he offered, and to Dawn Sopron, my very capable research assistant. Without the cooperation of Karen Longman and the Christian College Coalition this paper would not have been possible. Portions of this essay appeared in an earlier article in *Urban Mission* (November 1985).

Why No Major Evangelical University? The Loss and Recovery of Evangelical Advanced Scholarship

George M. Marsden

One of the oddest anomalies in American religion today is that there is no major evangelical research university. While there are a few clearly evangelical institutions that call themselves universities and have developed some graduate-level professional schools, and while in the South some true universities are more or less evangelical, still no major evangelical school is a distinguished center for distinctly Christian postgraduate research and theorizing.

This state of affairs is especially puzzling if we realize that until about a hundred years ago evangelical Protestants conducted most of American higher education. In the mid-nineteenth century the presidents of most colleges, including the predecessors of many of the great universities like Yale, Princeton, Michigan, and Illinois, were Protestant clergymen. As the universities emerged after the Civil War, most of them still had compulsory chapel. Even Harvard, though no longer evangelical, did not drop compulsory chapel until 1886. During the same era, John D. Rockefeller contributed many of his millions to create a great Baptist university, the University of Chicago. Yale at the time was still a center for the integration of advanced scholarship and evangelical piety, and Princeton University always had clergymen as president until 1902, when the pious academic Woodrow Wilson agreed to try his hand at administration.[1]

Today, evangelical Protestants are one of the largest religious groupings in America. Although they are fragmented, they have the resources for almost any project they put their minds to—not excepting education. Evangelicals have built some fine seminaries whose caliber rivals that of their old-line Protestant counterparts, and they support a lively network of Christian liberal arts colleges staffed by competent faculties growing in quality. Many evangelicals also finance substantial school systems at the primary and secondary levels. But as a group they apparently have little interest in supporting Christian scholarship at the highest academic level. Not only do they not have a first-level research university, they struggle to find money to support even very modest amounts of university-level scholarship, such as that in research institutes.

In maintaining this stance, America's evangelicals are conspicuously repudiating one of the most influential traditions in the Western Christian heritage. Since the Middle Ages, Christian universities have been keys to the task of shaping Western civilization and Western thought. Throughout the history of the church, Christian scholars have turned the course of Western culture. The Reformation itself was born of a university scholar's insight.[2] One cannot argue as an excuse, then, that in the twentieth century it is no longer possible for Christians to maintain universities. To see that Christian university education is still possible today, one need only look at the network of Catholic universities in America. While not all of these Catholic schools are solid centers for Christian scholarship, some certainly are; and as such they demonstrate the continued viability of the Christian research university.[3]

So we are left with the question why American evangelicals have rejected the educational traditions of Western Christianity and of their own Protestant and evangelical heritages. What has happened to make a community of such size and resources so indifferent to education at the highest level? And what can be done now to remedy the situation?

To help answer the first question, we can sketch briefly the historical circumstances that led from the era of evangelical dominance of America's highest education to the almost total evangelical abdication in this area of Christian witness today. The demise of evangelical leadership in higher education is intimately related to three other developments, all of which took place between the 1870s and the 1920s: the rise of the specialized research university, the secularization of American culture, and the fundamentalist controversies.

The new research ideal for universities prompted educational reformers in the latter part of the nineteenth century to take a dim view of evangelical higher education. The old-style evangelical colleges of the mid-century had been havens for intellectual generalists. Clergymen-presidents taught broadly ranging courses in moral philosophy as the capstone of the college curriculum. Teachers were typically overworked, had to teach wide varieties of subjects, and only occasionally set their intellectual standards high.[4] Around the 1870s, however, America's leading educators adopted the German university model for advanced study, a model that stressed the scientific character of graduate education. The doctorate degree, akin to degrees in the natural sciences in that it required original technical research, became the standard. Each discipline was eventually professionalized and isolated as a technical speciality. Generalists were no longer welcomed.

This reform, which indeed raised American academic standards, provided the occasion for dropping many subjects, such as moral philosophy, which had easily and naturally been infused with Christian philosophical perspectives. Moreover, the "scientific" standards of the time were associated with objectivism and efforts to remove bias; thus the new specialized academics often endorsed them simply as a practical methodology. Religious people could leave their religious views aside when engaging in academic inquiry—not because they did not take them seriously but because they regarded them as inappropriate for "scientific" academic study. Their religious angle of vision, though significant, was to be confined to a special realm of "faith." Other academics adopted a scientific approach to their disciplines as part of a larger naturalistic worldview. In either case the result was the same. Professionalization of the disciplines was associated with separating them from explicitly religious considerations.[5]

These developments were important aspects of the larger process of the secularization of American life. All of Western civilization was secularizing at this time, and Americans felt under pressure to keep pace. Moreover, part of the development was inevitable and virtually necessary. Although from the start America had official disestablishment of the churches, it had a de facto establishment of evangelical religion, as the tradition in most colleges and early universities demonstrated. Massive immigration after the Civil War, however, made the nation much more conspicuously pluralist. Elementary equity meant that Americans had to begin considering the rights of Catholics, Jews, and other minorities in public institutions. Though this process was sometimes slow, such concerns combined with those of secularists to increase the pressures for removing evangelicalism as a factor in university curricula.

These developments coincided, moreover, with the modernist-liberal versus fundamentalist-conservative split in American Protestantism. Modernism developed largely among Protestants who had been reared as evangelicals but who were looking for a version of Christianity more congenial to the standards of the modern age. Modernists, or theological liberals, attempted to rescue Christianity from the jaws of the new scientific-secular thought by insisting that the essence of Christianity lay in those areas, such as religious sentiments or ethics, that science could not touch. This "Kantian defense," as it has been called, thus separated the process of knowing into two distinct realms, a realm of faith and a realm of science.[6]

Essential to the modernist defense of Christianity was the conviction that matters of faith could, and should, be separated from the sciences, that is, from the academic disciplines. Accordingly, by the early twentieth century many modernist Protestants and their moderate allies held as an important principle the view that higher education should be secular. Largely for this reason, we can witness in early twentieth-century America the otherwise astounding phenomenon of American Protestants voluntarily abandoning the most powerful bulwark of their cultural influence. Gradually, and yet willingly, they virtually abandoned the network of colleges and universities that they had controlled. In denominational schools they often held on to strictly "religious" practices, such as chapel, well into the twentieth century; but as a matter of principle they dropped Christianity as a normative influence in the general curriculum.[7] So we find that American Protestant thought in the liberal tradition in twentieth-century America is confined almost solely to special "religious" institutions, that is, to theological seminaries. Accordingly, one finds twentieth-century Protestant theologians energetically discussing social issues, but seldom do other Protestant academics reunite their faith and discipline to talk about such subjects as Christian views of sociology, economics, or political science.

Fundamentalists, on the other hand, were left out in the cold as far as university-level education was concerned for somewhat different reasons. In Protestant academic centers, the liberal Protestant solutions to the challenges of the new thought were those that won out and flourished. Conservatives and fundamentalists were unable to compete with the liberal domination of education, especially in the prestigious educational system of the North. In response to their loss of influence, some fundamentalists emphasized the anti-intellectual aspects of their revivalist heritage. They simply condemned higher education and concentrated their energies on building Bible institutes. Other fundamentalists and conservative Protestants were not against higher education in principle, but in practice they were left without the resources to support any more than a few minor colleges. Though there were fundamentalist and conservative scholars scattered here and there, by about the 1940s the situation looked bleak for the survival of fundamentalist intellectual life.[8]

A recovery, however, was beginning. Some fundamentalists worked hard to rebuild the intellectual traditions of their movement. These reformers eventually became known as "neo-evangelicals" and concentrated their efforts most effectively in founding Fuller Theological Seminary in 1947 and establishing *Christianity Today* as a serious evangelical journal in 1956. Friends of Billy Graham, these neo-evangelicals were involved in his split with separatist fundamentalism, which became an irreparable rift in 1957.[9]

In the early 1960s, with the urging especially of Carl F. H. Henry, editor of *Christianity Today,* some neo-evangelicals seriously explored with Graham the possibility of establishing an evangelical university in the New York City area. According to Henry, the money was available, especially from the conservative evangelical oil magnate J. Howard Pew, and enough qualified academics were interested to make the project viable. The project foundered, however, on a lack of consensus among those who would support it. Some believed that if Graham were to raise money for the school then he could be expected to be president or chancellor; but that created opposition from those who felt he should concentrate full-time on evangelism. Pew, moreover, was unsure whether he should back the venture or put his money behind a conservative Presbyterian seminary instead. Another wealthy potential supporter, Maxey Jarman, distrusted conventional academia because he thought that it always drifted toward liberalism. He favored Bible institutes. The principal Christian liberal arts colleges feared that a university would drain away their best faculty and wondered if it would not be best to build graduate programs gradually, at their existing institutions. Others worried about whether traditionally strict evangelical mores would be maintained at a university. And, as the breakup of the original faculty of Fuller Seminary over the question of biblical inerrancy was just then demonstrating, it was not at all clear that evangelicals could agree on a doctrinal basis that would both satisfy the conservative leadership and not alienate some of the best scholars. Confronted with all these issues, the proponents of the university simply let the matter drop.[10]

Though the Christian university never got beyond the talking stage, some other developments were perhaps more important for higher education in the fundamentalist and evangelical communities. Conservative Protestantism in America had, for some time, been fragmented into almost countless small groups, some of which were distinguished by their ethnic identities, others by their somewhat sectarian religious heritage (such as the Holiness and Pentecostal groups), while others in the South had been separated from the Protestant liberal mainstream by regional factors. Most of these communities prospered, especially after World War II, and many of them had their own small colleges or Bible institutes that eventually developed into liberal arts colleges. By the 1960s many conservative evangelicals were receiving doctorates and staffing these colleges, which by the 1980s had together grown into the formidable network of the Christian College Coalition. Moreover, evangelicals with advanced degrees were also spreading their influence beyond the bounds of their own communities as many other conservatives were found on university faculties throughout the country.

Evangelical attitudes toward university education were, however, far from forming a consensus. Some academically accomplished evangelicals, reacting to fundamentalism's often artificial ways of relating faith to learning, argued that Christian perspectives need have little impact in university-level education. Furthermore, despite the growing numbers of evangelical Ph.D.'s and the burgeoning of Christian liberal arts education, evangelical communities demonstrated hardly any more interest in university education than they had at their academic nadir in the 1930s and 1940s. This was due in part to the perennial problem of evangelicalism itself—that it is not one entity but a coalition of fragmented subgroups, each with its own standards and agenda. Those who might support a Christian university recognized that any effort to found one on a broad base would face some exceedingly difficult challenges, even as the earlier neo-evangelical effort had. In the meantime, some of the subgroups, especially those built by evangelists, have established their own "universities." Only time will tell whether the largely professional programs now being developed at institutions such as Oral Roberts University in Tulsa, Pat Robertson's CBN University in Virginia Beach, and Jerry Falwell's Liberty University in Lynchburg, Virginia, will engender Christian scholarship of the highest caliber. As universities, however, most of these are at present embarrassing misnomers. Both in scope and scholarly production they hardly compare to rather modestly scaled secular universities—much less to a Princeton or a Johns Hopkins. They do demonstrate, though, that even some very conservative evangelical constituencies are willing to support at least the idea of a university.

What should be striking about this story is that the lack of a major evangelical Christian research university in America is the product of an unusual set of circumstances, not the result of either a lack of resources or any principle inherent in evangelicalism. As to the resources, not only are there many highly qualified evangelical Ph.D.'s, but evangelicals can mobilize vast amounts of money for all sorts of programs that catch their imagination. Moreover, one would suppose from the efforts they already put into seminary and collegiate education that support for Christian academic work at the highest level would be the next logical step.

Evangelicals lament that American culture is dominated by what is popularly called a "secular humanist" ethos. They invest huge amounts of time, energy, and money into political efforts to combat such influences. Yet few of them take seriously enough the idea that education is even more effective than politics as a way of influencing the culture of the nation. As John Van Engen shows in his essay, there was a time in Western Christendom when both state and ecclesiastical authorities looked to scholars for guidance. The state is still heavily dependent on the knowledge generated by universities and research institutes; but, for reasons that Nathan Hatch has skilfully summarized in his essay in this book, most American evangelicals today seem to have lost the sense of the importance of education, except for the most immediate practical purposes, and have forsaken this vital resource for guidance and witness rooted in their Western Christian heritage.

This neglect is especially ironic in light of the structure of modern evangelicalism. Evangelicals have a very low view of the institutional church, and many of their most prominent leaders operate with almost no regard for any ecclesiastical authority whatsoever. While evangelicals typically claim to rely on "the Bible alone" instead of such authority, they in fact rely on certain traditions of biblical interpretation. Yet these traditions often make contradictory claims. Where, in the absence of ecclesiastical authorities, are evangelical Christians to turn in judging among these conflicting claims? They might turn to faithful Christians who are also responsible scholars: to those who have critically examined the various communities' traditions and their biblical interpretations with the intent of bringing them closer to understanding the true meaning of God's revelation. Yet seeking out such authority is precisely what evangelicals have not done. They have not conceded that even though scholars do not always agree, they are potentially far more reliable guides than popularizers are.

We have seen how evangelicals have lost their commitment to scholarship at the highest level, but that leaves open a further question: How can they recover a commitment to Christian scholarship of the highest order?

It is clear that the sad state of the relationship between evangelicalism and higher scholarship cannot be corrected all at once. Evangelicals should take the first step immediately, however, and should make it a high priority. That is, evangelical leaders need to stress the importance of Christian scholarship in a major and sustained effort to raise popular consciousness. Modern culture needs forceful intellectual contributions from Christians which define, assess, and encounter the critical issues of the world today. Though scholars form only one small part of the body of Christ and not the most important part, they should be a vital part. Evangelical spokespersons who lend their influence and endorsements to new ventures in missions, social ministries, political witness, and even professional religious education need to trumpet the cause of advanced Christian scholarship. Devoted Christian attention to the realm of ideas may not have the immediate appeal of, say, Scripture translation, but its strategic importance cannot be denied. As J. Gresham Machen noted in 1912, with an observation that has lost none of its relevance since, "what is today a matter of academic speculation begins tomorrow to move armies and pull down empires."[11]

Christian scholarship of the highest order does not operate on mere good wishes, however. It requires that those who care about Christian learning support their best scholars by providing settings which will free them to think, discuss, and write. They need to be freed from the distracting and enervating demands of full course loads and committee work if they are to devote themselves to their scholarly callings.

A second step in the rejuvenation of evangelical advanced scholarship can and must be implemented very soon: evangelicals should regroup and mobilize their current academic resources. Rather than attempting to surmount the formidable obstacles to the founding of a full-fledged university, they should establish a number of high-quality research institutes, on the order of, say, the Brookings Institution, the American Enterprise Institute, the Institute for Advanced Study at Princeton, or the Humanities Center in North Carolina. These would provide congenial, collegial settings for Christian thought and a network for mutual support and encouragement between communities of Christian intellectuals. Such institutes could be funded for relatively modest amounts, with a variety of them costing only a fraction of even a small university.

One of the great strengths of the research institute model is its versatility. There are so many intellectual tasks to be done for the kingdom of God that a number of these centers could be founded without fear of competition, and with the intention of complementarity and cooperation. Some could reflect the special emphases and doctrinal heritages of various evangelical subgroups, such as Calvin College's Center for Christian Scholarship, which brings together scholars principally from the Reformed tradition. Some research institutes, following the example of the Institute for Christian Studies in Toronto, would focus on theoretical problems in some of the foundational academic disciplines like theology, philosophy, history, psychology, the history and philosophy of science, social and political theory, and aesthetic and literary interpretation. Others would be issues-and-problems oriented, with a ministry to such spheres as business, foreign affairs, or domestic policy. And still others, like the Institute for the Study of American Evangelicals at the Billy Graham Center, would encourage scholarship in a particular discipline or interdisciplinary field of study with a strategic bearing on contemporary Christian witness.

The structure of life and work at such centers could also vary with their purpose and special mission. Let me suggest, however, a generic pattern that could be adjusted in a variety of ways. Study centers would be built around a director (who would function as both a resident scholar and administrator) and a core group of senior research scholars on long-term appointment. In addition, visiting scholars would be invited to reside at the institute for one to three semesters, either to pursue their own projects or to join in team research efforts. Junior "fellows," who might be doctoral candidates at secular universities or recent Ph.D.'s already engaged in teaching, would be invited to participate in occasional seminars or projects.

These study centers would be the hubs of evangelical scholarly work, especially in disciplines not studied in theological seminaries. They would host academic and public conferences, lecture series, and occasional seminars for graduate credit. They would pursue publishing projects to follow through on their sponsored research, featuring monographs, topical symposia of essays, and perhaps journals. They would serve as clearing houses and communication centers for fellowships of Christian scholars and professionals, such as the American Scientific Affiliation or the Christian Legal Society. They would provide expert guidance, testimony, and research reports on matters of intrachurch and larger public concern. In general, these centers would be a resource for the life of the church, the life of the nation, and the concerns of the world in ways that at present are difficult if not impossible for scattered, poorly supported, and underutilized evangelical scholars.

In this way, the real goals of an evangelical research university—penetrating the highest level of the critical thought of culture and offering thoroughly Christian wisdom for public application—could be accomplished, and accomplished soon.

NOTES

1. A valuable summary of these developments and of other literature on the subject is Mark A. Noll, "Christian Thinking and the Rise of the American University," *Christian Scholar's Review* 9 (1979): 3-16. For a secularist view, see Richard Hofstadter, "The Revolution in Higher Education," in *Paths of American Thought*, ed. Arthur M. Schlesinger, Jr., and Morton White (Boston: Houghton-Mifflin, 1970), 269-90. A useful standard work is Laurence R. Veysey, *The Emergence of the American University* (Chicago: University of Chicago Press, 1965). On Yale, see Louise L. Stevenson, *Scholarly Means to Evangelical Ends: The New Haven Scholars and the Transformation of Higher Learning in America, 1830-1890* (Baltimore: Johns Hopkins University Press, 1986).

2. E. Harris Harbison, *The Christian Scholar in the Age of Reformation* (1956; Grand Rapids: Eerdmans, 1983), esp. 103-35 on Luther. See also the essay by John Van Engen in this volume.

3. David J. Hassel, S.J., discusses the problems and possibilities for Christian influence in universities today from a Catholic perspective in his *City of Wisdom* (Chicago: Loyola University Press, 1983).

4. Noll, "Christian Thinking," 4-8. See also the essays on the old Christian college by Noll ("The Revolution, the Enlightenment, and Christian Higher Education in the Early Republic") and William Ringenberg ("The Old-Time College"), both in this volume.

5. One of the finest studies of this phenomenon is Bruce Kuklick, *The Rise of American Philosophy, Cambridge, Massachusetts, 1860-1930* (New Haven: Yale University Press, 1977).

6. William R. Hutchison, *The Modernist Impulse in American Protestantism* (Cambridge: Harvard University Press, 1976), 122-32.

7. John Barnard traces these processes at work in one notable institution in *From Evangelicalism to Progressivism at Oberlin College, 1866-1917* (Columbus: Ohio State University Press, 1969).

8. For a fuller treatment of the fate of conservative evangelical higher education in these years, see Mark Noll's essay "The University Arrives in America," on the response of evangelicals to the academic revolution between 1870 and 1930; and Virginia Brereton's essay "The Bible Schools and Conservative Evangelical Higher Education, 1880-1940" both in this volume.

9. George M. Marsden, *Reforming Fundamentalism: Fuller Seminary and the New Evangelicalism* (Grand Rapids: Eerdmans, 1987).

10. Note Carl F. H. Henry's remarks made while he served as a panelist for a session titled "A Christian Research University?" at the conference "The Task of Evangelical Higher Education," held at the Billy Graham Center, Wheaton, Illinois, 30 May 1985. Audio tape.

11. J. Gresham Machen, "Christianity and Culture," *Princeton Theological Review* 11 (January 1913): 1-15; quote is from p. 7.